Guide to SAS/DB2™

Other McGraw-Hill Books in Mini and Mainframe Computing

ISBN	AUTHOR	TITLE
0-07-056578-3	Sherman	*The CD-ROM Handbook*
0-07-039006-1	Lusardi (hardcover)	*Database Experts' Guide to SQL*
0-07-039002-9	(softcover)	
0-07-016609-6	DeVita (hardcover)	*Database Experts' Guide to FOCUS*
0-07-016604-8	(softcover)	
0-07-036488-5	Larson (hardcover)	*Database Experts' Guide to Database 2*
0-07-023267-9	(softcover)	
0-07-048550-X	Parsons	*Database Experts' Guide to IDEAL*
0-07-008207-3	Brown	*Database Experts' Guide to SAS/DB2*
0-07-065120-5	Tran	*Introduction to DB2 Programming*
0-07-000474-9	Adrian	*The Workstation Data Link*
0-07-057336-0	Simpson, Casey	*Developing Effective User Documentation*
0-07-007248-5	Brathwaite	*Analysis, Design, and Implementation of Data Dictionaries*
0-07-035119-8	Knightson	*Standards for Open Systems Interconnection*
0-07-044938-4	McClain (hardcover)	*VM and Departmental Computing*
0-07-044939-2	(softcover)	
0-07-046302-6	Nemzow	*Keeping the Link*
0-07-038006-6	Lipton	*User Guide to FOCUS™*
0-07-057296-8	Simon	*How to Be a Successful Computer Consultant*
0-07-016188-7	Dayton (Ranade, Ed.)	*Integrating Digital Services*
0-07-002673-4	Azevedo (Ranade Series)	*ISPF: The Strategic Dialog Manager*
0-07-050054-1	Piggott (Ranade Series)	*CICS: A Practical Guide to System Fine Tuning*
0-07-043152-3	Morgan, McGilton	*Introducing UNIX™ System V*
0-07-050686-8	Prasad (Ranade Series)	*IBM Mainframes*
0-07-065087-X	Towner (Ranade Series)	*IDMS/R Cookbook*
0-07-062879-3	Tare (hardcover)	*UNIX™ Utilities*
0-07-062884-X	(softcover)	
0-07-045001-3	McGilton, Morgan	*Introducing the UNIX™ System*
0-07-062295-7	Su	*Database Computers*
0-07-041920-5	Milenkovic	*Operating Systems Concepts and Design*
0-07-010829-3	Ceri/Pelagatti	*Distributed Databases*

Guide to SAS/DB2™

Diane E. Brown

Intertext Publications
McGraw-Hill Book Company

New York St. Louis San Francisco Auckland Bogotá
Hamburg London Madrid Mexico Milan Montreal
New Delhi Panama Paris São Paulo
Singapore Sidney Tokyo Toronto

This text is intended for use with Version 5 of the SAS System.

Library of Congress Catalog Card Number 89-83766

10 9 8 7 6 5 4 3 2 1

ISBN 0-07-008207-3

Intertext Publications/Multiscience Press, Inc.
One Lincoln Plaza
New York, NY 10023

McGraw-Hill Book Company
1221 Avenue of the Americas
New York, NY 10020

Composed by Context, Inc.

Contents

Preface

The demand for data to support business decisions is rapidly increasing. This is evident from the constant changes in hardware and software. Relational database management systems and fourth-generation languages are critical components of the technology that will be used to meet these demands. Relational database management systems are just beginning to be implemented in the business world. Although fourth-generation languages have been around for several years, capabilities have been expanded to support a wider variety of applications and enhanced to simplify usage by non-data processing professionals. Also, fourth-generation languages are becoming more widely accepted by data processing professionals as an alternative to third-generation languages for many applications.

IBM'S relational database management system, Database 2, and SAS Institute's fourth generation language, SAS®, are front runners in this technology. Database 2, commonly referred to as DB2, is becoming an integral part of the systems architecture in large IBM installations. SAS, popular for its statistical capabilities, has a complete line of products offering a wide range of capabilities to both programmers and end users. These capabilities include reading and writing virtually any file format, file and data manipulation, many built-in functions and procedures, several types of report writers, data entry, user-friendly system front ends, econometric time series, matrix algebra, quality control, and graphics, just to name a few.

The Database Experts' *Guide to SAS/DB2*™ is a practical user-oriented approach to learning SAS/DB2 and the basics of DB2 itself. Also covered is SQL (Structured Query Language), which is used to communicate with DB2 as well as other relational database management systems. This book is intended for everyone who uses SAS and needs to access data stored in DB2 tables. This includes end users, statisticians, data analysts, programmers, system programmers, database administrators, information center staff, or their management.

I want to thank John McCoy, Ph.D., for reviewing the practicality of the approach taken in this book relative to the SAS system and for correcting many English errors. I much appreciate my husband, Ed Brown, for his support in writing this book and in the many hours he spent proofing it. Also, special thanks go to my parents, Pat and Martha Michael, who provided me with the education it took to get to this point in my career.

Chapter 1

Introduction

Today's computer application systems need not only to support the daily transaction processing of the business at hand, but also to provide management information as a basis for making appropriate business decisions. The technology of relational database management systems and fourth-generation languages is a means of providing management information. With a new emphasis on management information through this new technology comes a need for a new kind of "programmer." The programmer must now understand the business and be able to report and analyze data in support of that business. This new programmer may be more appropriately called a data analyst. However, to obtain the data for this analysis, this person must stay abreast of computer technology, with an emphasis on relational database management systems and fourth-generation languages.

Staying current with the technology is not an easy task. Not only is the technology changing rapidly, but the amount of technology is enormous. Users find themselves reading and searching through volumes of documentation, updates to documentation, magazines, and consulting with other users, trying to gather the technical information required to support their data needs. The documentation and educational processes within the computer arena are just beginning to direct attention toward the needs of the data analyst.

The Database Experts' Guide to SAS/DB2 will provide the SAS user with the knowledge of DB2 and SAS/DB2 required to support data analysis and reporting functions, which are the ultimate objectives. The illustrations and examples included will not only help the user understand this technology, but can be used as a guide to the development of his or her own applications.

Chapter 2, The Relational Model, begins by describing the concepts upon which relational database management systems are based. Chapter 3, IBM'S Database 2, addresses the DB2 environment, describing and documenting subjects most often required by users. Features of DB2 normally addressed by the Database Administrator rather than by users, are lightly touched or not described. Structured Query Language, commonly referred to as SQL, is used to access data stored in DB2 tables. An overview of the SQL language is given in Chapter 4, Structured Query Language. Emphasis is placed on the SQL SELECT statement which is used for data extraction. SQL statements used for creating, loading, and updating DB2 tables are also covered, but the user will have to obtain installation-specific information from the DB2 Database Administrator in his company for many of these statements. Chapter 5, Introduction to SAS/DB2, provides an overview of the SAS/DB2 procedures, their purpose, the flow of execution, and the environments in which they can be executed. SAS/DB2 consists of three procedures, PROC DB2EXT, PROC DB2LOAD, and PROC DB2UTIL. These procedures can be executed interactively in line mode or Display Manager or in batch programs. Chapters 6 and 7, PROC DB2EXT in Display Manager and PROC DB2EXT in Batch, discuss and illustrate the use of PROC DB2EXT to create a SAS data set from data stored in a DB2 table(s). Chapters 8 and 9, PROC DB2LOAD in Display Manager and PROC DB2LOAD in Batch, cover the use of PROC DB2LOAD to create and load a DB2 table from data stored in a SAS data set. Chapters 10 and 11, PROC DB2UTIL in Display Manager and PROC DB2UTIL in Batch, cover the use of PROC DB2UTIL to update data stored in DB2 tables with data stored in SAS data sets. Chapter 12, Advanced Applications, illustrates more complex SAS/DB2 applications, combining the appropriate SAS/DB2 procedures and SQL statements. Chapter 13, THE SAS/FSP Interface, discusses the use of the SAS/FSP product to browse and edit data stored in DB2 tables.

The Database Experts' Guide to SAS/DB2 was designed both as a training manual and a reference for users when writing their own applications. Because it can be used as a reference, the reader will find some repetition of key points. I recommend that everyone cover Chapters 2 through 7. This will take the user through the foundations of DB2 and SQL and provide the information required to use the SAS/DB2 procedure, PROC DB2EXT. PROC DB2EXT is used to create a SAS data set from data stored in DB2 table(s) and is the most frequently used SAS/DB2 procedures. Review questions and answers are provided for Chapters 2 through 7, and exercises are included in Chapters 6 and 7 to give the user practice using the PROC DB2EXT procedure. Many users will never have to create and load a DB2 table or update a DB2 table, which are capabilities provided by the SAS/DB2 procedures, PROC DB2LOAD and PROC DB2UTIL, respectively. Therefore, many users may wish to cover Chapters 8 through 11 only on an as-needed basis. Everyone should review Chapter 12, Advanced Applications, to provide insight into more complex applications and to see how PROC DB2LOAD and PROC DB2UTIL can be used. I also recommend scanning the information on the SAS/FSP interface in Chapter 13 if your company has the SAS/FSP product.

Several examples are provided throughout this book to support the explanations and definitions. Examples used to illustrate the three SAS/DB2 procedures are based on sample DB2 tables shown in Appendix C. Chapters 6 and 7, which cover the use of PROC DB2EXT, also contain exercises which the user may wish to perform. These exercises are also based on the sample tables shown in Appendix C. If you want to execute the SAS/DB2 examples given in Chapters 6 through 12 or complete the exercises in Chapters 6 and 7, these sample tables will need to be loaded on your mainframe. This can be done through data entry using Appendix C. You can also send a $25 check or money order to Technical Education & Consulting, Inc. at the address below to obtain a copy on diskette:

Attn: Diane E. Brown
Technical Education & Consulting, Inc.
8340 Galley Court
Indianapolis, IN 46236

This diskette will contain the sample tables shown in Appendix C and programs, SQL statements, and maps used in examples throughout this book. A program for loading the DB2 sample tables is included. The diskette is a 5 1/4 HD diskette. I would also appreciate any comments you have concerning this book and other needs, particularly relative to SAS.

Chapter

2

The Relational Model

The idea for relational database management systems (DBMS) was derived from the need for a better way to manage data. These data must not only support daily business transactions as in the past, but must also be easily accessible for analysis. Dr. E. F. Codd, a mathematician who worked for IBM, used the theories of relational mathematics to develop guidelines for relational database management systems. These guidelines continue to be expanded as the use of relational database management systems increases. These guidelines constitute what are referred to as the relational model.

Definition

A relational database management system can be thought of as a set of sequential or flat files, called tables. The tables consist of rows and columns, as flat files consist of records and fields, and SAS data sets consist of observations and variables. The following diagram illustrates this.

Often, when data are stored in files or SAS data sets, most data elements (fields/variables) required by the system are stored in a single file. The main concept behind a relational DBMS is that the data elements are stored in a set of tables. Each table is based on an entity. An entity is any object upon which other data elements are

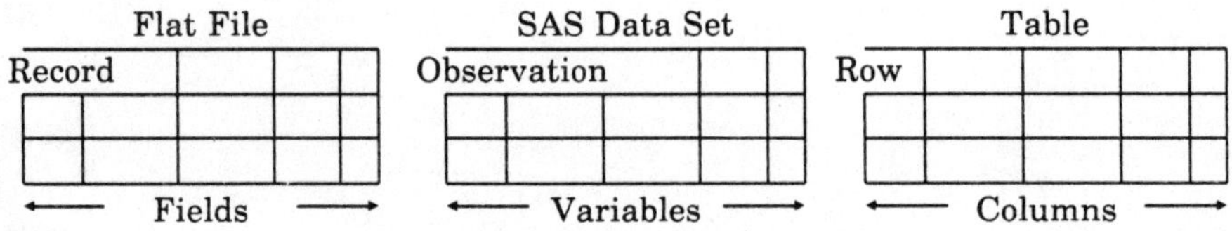

based. Figure 2-1 illustrates a relational database management system containing seven tables, based on the entities:

Table A	Student general information
Table B	Class officers
Table C	Students in clubs
Table D	Student enrollment in courses
Table E	Club information
Table F	Course information
Table G	Teacher general information

The columns in each of these tables relate directly to the corresponding entity. The tables relate to each other through common columns. This provides the ability to join multiple tables in order to extract the information needed for a particular application. There is a lot to be taken into consideration when joining relational tables. This subject will be addressed later in this chapter. These tables are called base tables. There are other types of tables and these will also be discussed later in this chapter. Until that point, all discussion will refer to base tables.

Guidelines

Data independence is one of the guidelines of the relational model. The user should not have to specify information such as data access method, data structure, data location, or data type within a program. The program will specify what data are needed, but not how to retrieve them. Thus, the relational DBMS not only provides easy access for the user, but makes it possible that changes to the tables, such as adding a new column, will not require any changes to application programs.

The relational database management system itself should determine the most efficient access method. This comes into play particularly when data are needed from multiple tables within the system. The relational system knows the attributes of each table such as how

TABLE A

Student	Address	Grade	Phone
Ruth	103 Beech	12	8781234
Alice	67 Teel Rd.	10	2533467
Linda	St. Rd. 3	11	5647831
Martha	R.R.#6	12	5294540
Cheryl	234 5th Ave	9	8452999
. . .			

TABLE B

Class	Pres	Sec-Treas
9	Baker	Apple
10	Miller	Hardwick
11	Adams	Jones
12	Pritt	Dodd

TABLE C

Student	Club
Alice	Choir
Alice	Band
Linda	Chrblk
Cheryl	Pompom

TABLE D

Student	Course
Ruth	History
Ruth	English
Ruth	Math
Alice	Science

TABLE E

Club	Sponsor
Choir	Hutson
Band	Hutson
Chrblk	Keesling
Pompom	Kellum

TABLE F

Subject	Teacher	Room
English	Sanders	211
History	Meyer	215
Math	Hutson	131
Science	Keesling	113

TABLE G

Teacher	Address	Phone	Educ	Salary	Hiredte
Hutson	R.R. 1	5295885	M.S.	31000	083166
Keesling	Rd 103 West	5210100	M.A.	28000	090171
Kellum	123 Park	5647231	B.S.	24000	081578
. . .					

Figure 2-1 Relational database management system tables.

the data are physically stored and the size of the tables. Using this information, the relational software should be able to select the most efficient way to access the required data — in particular, which table to access first.

The relational model should have a universal language that is used to define, extract, update, and control the data. Structured Query Language (SQL) has been developed to support this guideline. SQL is used to access data stored in relational database management systems, no matter in what language the application program is written. This includes third-generation languages such as COBOL and fourth-generation languages such as SAS.

A set of one or more rows can be processed with a single command. This set of rows is referred to as a result table. This is a new concept for programmers, who are used to processing data one record at a time. Commonly used third-generation languages, such as COBOL, PL/1, and FORTRAN, can only process one record at a time. The SAS data step, where user processing occurs, also processes one record at a time. However, groups of observations (SAS data sets) can be passed to subsequent data and procedure steps within a SAS program. This still doesn't qualify as set processing, but is closer than one record at a time processing throughout the entire program.

Relational software should have the ability to perform distributed processing. Tables that exist on different computers should be able to be accessed by a single program by transporting sets of rows across telecommunication lines. This capability may be a while in coming for many relational DBMSs.

Data consistency and integrity should be provided by the relational DBMS. This can be accomplished through the use of primary and foreign keys. A primary key consists of one or more columns, which together uniquely define a row within a table. In the following Table 1, Student is the primary key because its value uniquely defines each row. However, in Table 2 it is the combination of Student and Course which uniquely defines the row and therefore jointly forms the primary key. Every table should have a primary key, and the value of the key cannot be missing (null). A table with no relationship to other tables need not have a primary key.

The domain of a column is the set of values that column can have. In some cases, the values of the domain are restrictive. The column, Score, in Table 1 has a restrictive domain. The value of Score is a numeric from 0 to 100.

Suppose for every value of Course in Table 2, a row exists in the following Table 3. This row is represented by the column, Class, which is the primary key of Table 3. The column, Course, in Table 2 is then called a foreign key of Table 2. When data are needed from more than one table, the foreign keys and primary keys can be used to "join" the corresponding rows. For example, you may wish to pro-

TABLE 1

Student	Grade	Score
Ed	11	96
Wally	12	81
Chuck	10	75
Pat	12	90
Max	9	80

TABLE 2

Student	Course	Score
Ed	Math	97
Ed	Science	82
Wally	English	85
Wally	Math	76
Pat	Math	68
Pat	English	85
Pat	Science	98

TABLE 3

Class	Teacher	Room
English	Campbell	211
Math	Michael	113
Science	Dudley	125

RESULT TABLE

Student	Course	Teacher
Ed	Math	Michael
Ed	Science	Dudley
Wally	English	Campbell
Wally	Math	Michael
Pat	Math	Michael
Pat	English	Campbell
Pat	Science	Dudley

duce a report containing Student, Course, and Teacher. To accomplish this, Table 2 and Table 3 are joined using the foreign key, Course, from Table 2 and the primary key, Class, from Table 3. The result table from this join is shown.

All values (the domain) of foreign keys must exist as primary keys in another table, with the exception of null values for foreign keys. This is termed REFERENTIAL INTEGRITY. Although primary and foreign keys are used to join tables, their main function is to maintain REFERENTIAL INTEGRITY. REFERENTIAL INTEGRITY is supported in DB2 Version 2 and later. For example, if one or more rows were added to Table 2 that contained the value, "History", for Course, then a primary key value of "History" must also exist in Table 3.

When foreign keys exist, not every value in the domain of the primary key will necessarily exist as a foreign key. For example, just because a primary key value of "History" exists in Table 3, does not mean that any foreign key values of "History" exist in Table 2.

Operations

Certain operations can be used to manipulate tables to produce the desired result table. These operations functionally produce the same results that you are familiar with when manipulating SAS data sets. In the explanation of these operations, I will draw comparisons with SAS statements you are familiar with. However, these SAS statements will not be used to perform these operations. SQL must be used to perform operations on relational DBMS tables.

The SELECTION operation provides the capability of selecting only those rows in a table which meet specific criteria. This can be compared to the SAS subsetting IF statement and the DELETE statement.

Often, only some of the columns in a table are desired on the result table. This operation is called PROJECTION. When only specific variables are desired on a SAS data set, a combination of approaches may be taken. First, if you are reading a non-SAS file, you would read only those variables that are desired. Another approach is to use the KEEP or DROP statement to specify what values to store on the SAS data set.

When two or more SAS data sets are concatenated into one SAS data set, the observations in the first SAS data set are written, followed immediately by the observations in the second SAS data set, and so on. Thus, if the first SAS data set had 20 observations, the second SAS data set had 10 observations, and the third and last SAS data set had 30 observations, the concatenated SAS data set would have 60 observations. SAS data sets that are concatenated normally have most or all of the same variables. To perform this operation in SAS, PROC APPEND or a SET statement naming the SAS data sets to be concatenated is used. This operation is called UNION in the relational model.

The foundation of the relational model is the design, a system of tables, and the ability to combine information from more than one table to produce the result table. The combination of tables is called a JOIN. This operation has some similiarities and some differences to the SAS MERGE statement, which is used to combine information from two or more SAS data sets. First, let's review the SAS MERGE and then compare it to the relational JOIN. This is important, because the JOIN operation cannot be used as you are used to using the MERGE statement in SAS.

Figure 2-2A shows two SAS data sets, one with "pre" scores and one with "post" scores. Figure 2-2B shows the SAS code to MERGE these two SAS data sets and the SAS data set resulting from this

MERGE. The variable, Id, specified in the BY statement, controls how the observations are combined. Observations from the two SAS data sets with the same value of Id are combined to form a single observation in the merged SAS data set, Both. Values of Id which exist only in one of the two SAS data sets still become observations in the merged SAS data set, but will have missing values for variables from the opposite SAS data set.

The IN data option can be used for processing and selection based on whether the merge key (Id in this case) was on both incoming SAS data sets or only on one of them. The IN option names a variable whose value is 0 if the incoming SAS data set did not contribute to the output observation and is 1 if the incoming SAS data set did contribute to the output observation. The code to create the IN variables and their respective values on the SAS data set, Both, is shown in Figure 2-2C. Note that the values of the IN variable are shown for illustration only; they are not actually saved on the SAS data set, Both. When the IN variables are used in the merge of two SAS data sets, three combinations of the IN variable values exist. When both Bef and Aft are equal to 1, this indicates that both incoming SAS data sets contributed to the new merged SAS observation. When Bef is 0 and Aft is 1, then the SAS data set, Pre, did not contribute and the SAS data set, Post, did contribute. When Bef is 1 and Aft is 0, then the SAS data set, Pre, did contribute and the SAS data set, Post, did not contribute.

Figure 2-2D shows how the IN variables can be used to create a SAS data set, Match, containing only those Ids that were on both incoming SAS data sets. This is accomplished by a subsetting IF statement, selecting only those observations with both IN variables, Bef and Aft, equal to 1. When testing for a value of 1 for the IN variable, the 1 does not have to be specified in the IF statement. When testing for a value of 0, the NOT sign (Γ) can be used prior to the IN variable name.

Figure 2-2E shows how the IN variables can be used to create the SAS data set, Onpost, containing all the Ids on the incoming SAS data set, Post, no matter whether they were on the incoming SAS data set, Pre, or not. This is accomplished by a subsetting IF statement, selecting only those observations where the IN variable, Aft, is equal to 1. This is a short way of selecting two of the three merge combinations; those observations where Bef equals 0 and Aft equals 1 and those observations where Bef equals 1 and Aft equals 1.

SAS affords a great deal of flexibility when merging SAS data sets, especially when the IN variables are used. Operationally, SAS reads the observations in the incoming SAS data sets concurrently and se-

SAS Data Set - PRE

Id	Prescore
01	50
02	63
03	95
04	0

SAS Data Set - POST

Id	Pstscore
01	85
02	90
05	71

(A) SAS DATA SETS

```
DATA BOTH;
     MERGE PRE POST;
     BY ID;
```

SAS Data Set - BOTH

Id	Prescore	Pstscore
01	50	85
02	63	90
03	95	.
04	0	.
05	.	71

(B) SAS MERGE

```
DATA BOTH;
     MERGE     PRE(IN=BEF)
               POST(IN=AFT);
     BY ID;
```

SAS Data Set - BOTH

Id	Prescore	Pstscore	Bef	Aft
01	50	85	1	1
02	63	90	1	1
03	95	.	1	0
04	0	.	1	0
05	.	71	0	1

(C) SAS MERGE WITH IN OPTION

```
DATA MATCH;
     MERGE     PRE(IN=BEF)
               POST(IN=AFT);
     BY ID;
     IF BEF & AFT;
```

SAS Data Set - MATCH

Id	Prescore	Pstscore	Bef	Aft
01	50	85	1	1
02	63	90	1	1

(D) SAS MERGE SELECTING MATCHES

```
DATA ONPOST;
     MERGE     PRE(IN=BEF)
               POST(IN=AFT);
     BY ID;
     IF AFT;
```

SAS Data Set - ONPOST

Id	Prescore	Pstscore	Bef	Aft
01	50	85	1	1
02	63	90	1	1
05	.	71	0	1

(E) SAS MERGE SELECTING ALL ON POST

Figure 2-2 SAS MERGE statement.

quentially and determines whether to combine the incoming observations into a single output observation by matching the variable or variables specified in the BY statement.

Now, let's examine the JOIN of relational tables. I will begin by explaining how a JOIN takes place operationally, because this has an effect on the flexibility and capability of the process, and it is not the same as the SAS MERGE statement. When columns are needed from more than one table, the first operation that takes place is the CARTESIAN PRODUCT. This operation creates a preliminary result table which is the combination of every row on the first table with every other row on every other table needed in the JOIN. The number of rows resulting is then equal to the product of the number of rows on each individual table. Figure 2-3A shows two relational tables, containing the same data used in Figure 2-2A as SAS data sets, to produce the CARTESIAN PRODUCT. The CARTESIAN PRODUCT is shown in Figure 2-3B. It is very unlikely that the CARTESIAN PRODUCT in itself would produce results that would be of value in a practical application. The only rows in the CARTESIAN PRODUCT that make sense are those rows where the column, Id, from the Pre table matches the column, Num, from the Post table. When doing a JOIN, you must combine the operations of CARTESIAN PRODUCT and SELECTION. SELECTION is the operation that allows only specific rows to be selected from a table. Select from the CARTESIAN PRODUCT only those rows where Id is equal to Num. The result of this SELECTION is shown in Figure 2-3C. It is also common to use the operation, PROJECTION, following the SELECTION. PROJECTION is the operation that allows only specific columns to be selected from a table. In this example, it is not neccessary to keep both Id and Num since they contain the same value after the SELECTION operation. The result of the PROJECTION is shown in Figure 2-3D. To summarize, the JOIN actually consists of three operations: the CARTESIAN PRODUCT, SELECTION, and PROJECTION.

The final result table shown in Figure 2-3D is equivalent to the SAS MERGE shown in Figure 2-2D, which represented selecting only those observations with the same value of Id. What is missing from the relational JOIN is the ability to select rows that exist on one table and not another, or rows on one table whether they exist on the other table or not. These operations are not possible because the CARTESIAN PRODUCT is used as the methodology for the JOIN. For example, we might want rows on the table, Pre, that are not on the table, Post. There is no way to express this need logically. We could not say that we wanted rows where the column, Id, from

Relational Table - PRE

Id	Prescore
01	50
02	63
03	95
04	0

Relational Table - POST

Num	Pstscore
01	85
02	90
05	71

(A) RELATIONAL TABLES

CARTESIAN PRODUCT of PRE and POST

Id	Num	Prescore	Pstscore
01	01	50	85
01	02	50	90
01	05	50	71
02	01	63	85
02	02	63	90
02	05	63	71
03	01	95	85
03	02	95	90
03	05	95	71
04	01	0	85
04	02	0	90
04	05	0	71

(B) CARTESIAN PRODUCT

SELECTION from the CARTESIAN PRODUCT

Id	Num	Prescore	Pstscore
01	01	50	85
02	02	63	90

(C) SELECTION from the CARTESIAN PRODUCT

PROJECTION from the SELECTION

Id	Prescore	Pstscore
01	50	85
02	63	90

(D) PROJECTION from the SELECTION

Figure 2-3 SQL JOIN Operation.

the table, Pre, was not equal to the column, Num, from the table, Post. This expression would result in the remainder of the CARTESIAN PRODUCT, which does not produce those rows on Pre and not on Post. This capability may be added as a guideline of the relational model as it becomes more refined.

The design of a relational database management system is critical to avoid situations where a JOIN may delete rows which make business sense to keep. One way to resolve the problem in the example shown previously is to include rows in both tables for all Ids and set the columns equal to null when no data are given for a specific Id value.

Whether using the SQL JOIN operation or the SAS MERGE statement, four possible situations exist, based on whether the foreign and primary keys (JOIN) or the BY variables (SAS MERGE) have multiple rows/observations with the same value:

One to One
One to Many
Many to One
Many to Many

Keep in mind that the SQL JOIN, through the CARTESIAN PRODUCT, SELECTION, and PROJECTION, produces a result table containing only those rows from the requested tables that match, whereas the SAS MERGE keeps all observations from the incoming SAS data sets. Aside from this, a one-to-one, one-to-many, or many-to-one SQL JOIN produces the same result as a SAS MERGE. However, the many-to-many SQL JOIN does not produce the same results as a SAS MERGE. Figure 2-4 illustrates this difference using the same data as Table 1 and Table 2 for the SQL JOIN, and as SAS data set 1 and SAS data set 2 for the SAS MERGE. Table 1 contains two rows (observations) with a value of A for Key. Table 2 contains three rows (observations) with a value of A for Key. Since a JOIN begins with the CARTESIAN PRODUCT, this results in 6 rows (2 rows * 3 rows), produced by joining each row in Table 1 with every row in Table 2. The SAS MERGE, reading the two SAS data sets sequentially, joins the first observation in SAS Data Set 1 with the first observation in SAS Data Set 2, and the second observation in SAS Data Set 1 with the second observation in SAS Data Set 2. It then runs out of observations with a value of A for Key from SAS Data Set 1. SAS then uses the last observation with a value of A for Key, which is observation 2. Observation 2 from SAS Data Set

Table 1
SAS Data Set 1

Key	Xvalue
A	X1
A	X2

Table 2
SAS Data Set 2

Key	Yvalue
A	Y1
A	Y2
A	Y3

SQL JOIN Results

Key	Xvalue	Yvalue
A	X1	Y1
A	X1	Y2
A	X1	Y3
A	X2	Y1
A	X2	Y2
A	X2	Y3

SAS MERGE Results

Key	Xvalue	Yvalue
A	X1	Y1
A	X2	Y2
A	X2	Y3

Figure 2-4 Many-to-many SQL JOIN versus SAS MERGE.

1 is matched with observation 3 from SAS Data Set 2. Practically, the result produced by the SQL JOIN is probably more useful. Note that SQL does not produce a note specifying that a many-to-many join was performed. A many-to-many MERGE in SAS is noted in the SAS log.

The results of the JOIN operation are dependent on the presence of REFERENTIAL INTEGRITY. Figures 2-5, 2-6, and 2-7 illustrate three situations that can occur when joining two tables. All three examples show two tables, Enroll and Subject. The rows in these two tables differ for each of the three examples. The primary key of the table, Enroll, is the combination of the columns, Student and Course. The primary key of the table, Subject, is the column, Class. Relating to Class is the foreign key, Course, on the Enroll table.

The relational DBMS shown in Figure 2-5 has REFERENTIAL INTEGRITY because every value of the foreign key (Course from the Enroll table), also exists as a primary key (Class from the Subject table). The reverse is also true; every value of the primary key exists as a foreign key. However, this is not a requirement for REFERENTIAL INTEGRITY.

The relational DBMS shown in Figure 2-6 also has REFERENTIAL INTEGRITY because for every foreign key there is a primary

Relational Table - Enroll

Student	Course	Score
Jack	Math	77
Jack	Science	85
Troy	English	67
Troy	Math	94
Troy	Science	81

Relational Table - Subject

Class	Teacher	Room
English	Campbell	211
Math	Michael	113
Science	Dudley	125

CARTESIAN PRODUCT of Tables Enroll and Subject

Student	Course	Score	Class	Teacher	Room
Jack	Math	77	English	Campbell	211
Jack	Math	77	Math	Michael	113
Jack	Math	77	Science	Dudley	125
Jack	Science	85	English	Campbell	211
Jack	Science	85	Math	Michael	113
Jack	Science	85	Science	Dudley	125
Troy	English	67	English	Campbell	211
Troy	English	67	Math	Michael	113
Troy	English	67	Science	Dudley	125
Troy	Math	94	English	Campbell	211
Troy	Math	94	Math	Michael	113
Troy	Math	94	Science	Dudley	125
Troy	Science	81	English	Campbell	211
Troy	Science	81	Math	Michael	113
Troy	Science	81	Science	Dudley	125

SELECTION and PROJECTION of CARTESIAN PRODUCT

Student	Course	Score	Class	Teacher	Room
Jack	Math	77	Math	Michael	113
Jack	Science	85	Science	Dudley	125
Troy	English	67	English	Campbell	211
Troy	Math	94	Math	Michael	113
Troy	Science	81	Science	Dudley	125

Figure 2-5 REFERENTIAL INTEGRITY. (A primary key exists for every foreign key; a foreign key exists for every primary key).

key. The reverse is not true in this example because Class has a value of 'History', which is not a value of the foreign key, Course.

Relational Table - Enroll

Student	Course	Score
Jack	Math	77
Jack	Science	85
Troy	English	67
Troy	Math	94
Troy	Science	81

Relational Table - Subject

Class	Teacher	Room
English	Campbell	211
Math	Michael	113
Science	Dudley	125
History	Adams	323

CARTESIAN PRODUCT of Tables Enroll and Subject

Student	Course	Score	Class	Teacher	Room
Jack	Math	77	English	Campbell	211
Jack	Math	77	Math	Michael	113
Jack	Math	77	Science	Dudley	125
Jack	Math	77	History	Adams	323
Jack	Science	85	English	Campbell	211
Jack	Science	85	Math	Michael	113
Jack	Science	85	Science	Dudley	125
Jack	Science	85	History	Adams	323
Troy	English	67	English	Campbell	211
Troy	English	67	Math	Michael	113
Troy	English	67	Science	Dudley	125
Troy	English	67	History	Adams	323
Troy	Math	94	English	Campbell	211
Troy	Math	94	Math	Michael	113
Troy	Math	94	Science	Dudley	125
Troy	Math	94	History	Adams	323
Troy	Science	81	English	Campbell	211
Troy	Science	81	Math	Michael	113
Troy	Science	81	Science	Dudley	125
Troy	Science	81	History	Adams	323

SELECTION and PROJECTION of CARTESIAN PRODUCT

Student	Course	Score	Class	Teacher	Room
Jack	Math	77	Math	Michael	113
Jack	Science	85	Science	Dudley	125
Troy	English	67	English	Campbell	211
Troy	Math	94	Math	Michael	113
Troy	Science	81	Science	Dudley	125

Figure 2-6 REFERENTIAL INTEGRITY. (A primary key exists for every foreign key; a foreign key does not exist for every primary key.)

Relational Table - Enroll

Student	Course	Score
Jack	Math	77
Jack	Science	85
Troy	English	67
Troy	Math	94
Troy	Science	81
Bertie	History	79

Relational Table - Subject

Class	Teacher	Room
English	Campbell	211
Math	Michael	113
Science	Dudley	125

CARTESIAN PRODUCT of Tables Enroll and Subject

Student	Course	Score	Class	Teacher	Room
Jack	Math	77	English	Campbell	211
Jack	Math	77	Math	Michael	113
Jack	Math	77	Science	Dudley	125
Jack	Science	85	English	Campbell	211
Jack	Science	85	Math	Michael	113
Jack	Science	85	Science	Dudley	125
Troy	English	67	English	Campbell	211
Troy	English	67	Math	Michael	113
Troy	English	67	Science	Dudley	125
Troy	Math	94	English	Campbell	211
Troy	Math	94	Math	Michael	113
Troy	Math	94	Science	Dudley	125
Troy	Science	81	English	Campbell	211
Troy	Science	81	Math	Michael	113
Troy	Science	81	Science	Dudley	125
Bertie	History	79	English	Campbell	211
Bertie	History	79	Math	Michael	113
Bertie	History	79	Science	Dudley	125

SELECTION and PROJECTION of CARTESIAN PRODUCT

Student	Course	Score	Class	Teacher	Room
Jack	Math	77	Math	Michael	113
Jack	Science	85	Science	Dudley	125
Troy	English	67	English	Campbell	211
Troy	Math	94	Math	Michael	113
Troy	Science	81	Science	Dudley	125

Figure 2-7 NO REFERENTIAL INTEGRITY. (A primary key does not exist for every foreign key; a foreign key exists for every primary key.)

The final result table does not contain a row with History as a value. It is not selected because it does not have a match against the values of Course. Practically, this is probably satisfactory.

The relational DBMS shown in Figure 2-7 does not have REFERENTIAL INTEGRITY. The value, History, of the foreign key, Course, does not exist as a value of the primary key, Class. The reverse is true; every value of the primary key also exists as a foreign key. The lack of REFERENTIAL INTEGRITY causes a problem on the final result table because the row from the Student table with the History Course was eliminated during SELECTION.

REFERENTIAL INTEGRITY is a critical component of the relational model. Even if the DBMS has REFERENTIAL INTEGRITY, the JOIN process does not give you the capability that you have with the SAS MERGE statement of using the IN option to distinguish between matches and mismatches. If the application needs this capability, you can always use SQL to extract data from each table separately, and then use the SAS MERGE statement to combine the information into one SAS data set.

Types of Tables

The tables discussed thus far in this chapter are called Base Tables. Data are stored in Base Tables. Another type of table frequently used is called a View Table. A View Table is not a physical table, but rather a logical one encompassing one or more Base Tables. A view could be a subset of a single Base Table, consisting of only specific rows and/or columns. This type of view is often established for security reasons, but is also a good idea when certain users need to see only specific rows or columns in a Base Table. A view can also be a combination of rows and columns from more than one Base Table. This type of view is basically the result table of a JOIN. For tables that are commonly joined, this type of view can be a convenience. Another type of table is a query table. A query table is merely a user's result table after performing a series of operations. Since it is a table, it can be used in subsequent requests (called queries) just like Base Tables and View Tables. With SAS/DB2 the result table is transformed into a SAS data set which will be used in subsequent requests rather than query tables. View Tables and Query Tables have names just as the Base Tables do, so it is transparent to the user what type of table he is accessing.

Conclusion

There are several relational database management systems on the market, running on personal computers, minicomputers, and large mainframes, and some that run on multiple platforms. Some of these relational DBMSs adhere to more of the guidelines of the relational model than others. And the relational model is still being refined, so relational software is going through changes to support these guidelines. There have also been software changes made to increase performance, which has been a problem for large relational database management systems. You will also find a great deal of add-on software on the market to provide capabilities which the relational software itself does not.

Review

Questions

1. Data processing generally has used the term file to refer to a collection of data. SAS files that contain a collection of data are called SAS data sets. What corresponds to these terms in a relational database management system?
2. A file consists of records and fields and a SAS data set consists of observations and variables. What corresponds to these terms in a relational table?
3. What is the logical basis upon which a table is developed?
4. What language is used to access a relational DBMS?
5. What uniquely defines a row, in a relational table, and what does it consist of?
6. What is a foreign key?
7. What is REFERENTIAL INTEGRITY?
8. What three operations are used when tables are joined? Define these operations.
9. How does a JOIN differ from a SAS MERGE?

Answers

1. The term table corresponds to a file or a SAS data set.

2. A row in a table corresponds to a record in a file or an observation in a SAS data set. A column in a table corresponds to a field in a file or a variable in a SAS data set.
3. The columns in a relational table are based on an entity.
4. SQL (Structured Query Language) is the universal language to access relational database management systems.
5. A primary key uniquely defines a row and it consists of one or more columns in the table.
6. The values of a foreign key are used to match against the primary values in another table when an application requires data from more than one table.
7. A relational DBMS is said to have REFERENTIAL INTEGRITY when a primary key exists for every foreign key. A foreign key does not necessarily have to exist for every primary key.
8. A JOIN is performed through the operations, CARTESIAN PRODUCT, SELECTION, and PROJECTION. The CARTESIAN PRODUCT is the combination of every row of a table with every row of every other table. SELECTION is the process of selecting a subset of the rows in a table, in this case a subset of the CARTESIAN PRODUCT. PROJECTION is the process of selecting a subset of the columns in a table.
9. A JOIN and a SAS MERGE differ in two aspects.

   - A JOIN produces a result table consisting of those rows that matched from the tables being joined. A SAS MERGE produces a SAS data set consisting of all observations from the SAS data sets being merged.
   - A many-to-many JOIN produces the combination of every row with a given value on the first table with every row with that value on the second table. For example, if the first table had two rows with a given value and the second table had three rows with that same value, the result table would contain six rows with that value. A many-to-many MERGE in SAS produces a SAS data set containing the same number of observations with a given value as the SAS data set with the most observations with that same value. Using the same example, the resulting SAS data set would have three observations.

Chapter

3

IBM'S Database 2

IBM's Database 2, commonly called DB2, is IBM's relational database management system, running on the MVS operating system on large mainframe computers. Version 1 came out in 1985 and was primarily used for small personal applications. It was difficult to manage and performance was a problem.

Release 1.2 was available in the spring of 1986. It offered increased performance; but as DB2 applications grew, performance once again became a problem, although not as severe. Also in Release 1.2, the Optimizer was added, which determines the best data access path, which is one of the guidelines of the relational model. However, the Optimizer did not always select the best access path and this adversely impacted performance. Support for QMF (Query Management Facility) was added with Release 1.2. QMF is an end-user reporting tool using SQL to access data stored in DB2 tables. It is fine for simple reporting, but lacks the data manipulation, data analysis, and complex reporting capabilities which SAS provides.

In spring 1987, Release 1.3 of DB2 became available. It again offered improved performance. Also available were data types for dates and times, providing capabilities similar to the date and time handling capabilities available with SAS.

Version 2 became available in the fall of 1988. Version 2 provides better security features, a resource governor to restrict the amount of computer use per program, much improved performance, support for the C programming language, and probably the best of all, REFERENTIAL INTEGRITY.

The DB2 Environment

DB2 runs in the MVS/XA operating environment (Multiple Virtual Storage/Extended Architecture) or the MVS/370 environment. DB2 can be accessed concurrently by the following:

- TSO (Time Sharing Option): TSO foreground is where SAS Display Manager runs. DB2 can be accessed through Display Manager.
- Batch: This is sometimes referred to as TSO background. DB2 can be accessed by SAS batch programs.
- CICS (Customer Inquiry Control System): CICS is a transaction-driven inquiry/update system. SAS does not run under CICS, so this environment will not be discussed in this book.
- IMS/VS: Typically IMS databases (DB) are used in the IMS/VS environment. DB2 can also be used as a database system in the IMS/VS environment. Again, SAS does not run in this environment, so it will not be discussed.

Figure 3-1 illustrates the DB2 operating environment as it interacts with these other products.

The DB2 Subsystem

The DB2 software is divided into three components, the Resource Lock Manager, Database Services, and System Services.

DB2 tables may be in the process of being updated by an application at the same time a user is trying to access those data. The Resource Lock Manager (IRLM — IMS/VS Resource Lock Manager) protects the integrity of the data. Users will be temporarily "locked out" while data are being updated. The application makes a determination whether to write the update to the DB2 table. If the update is made, it is said to be "committed." If for some reason the application decides the update should not be made, perhaps because the update data are incomplete, the DB2 table is "rolled back." A rollback restores the data to the values held when the last commit was performed. Whether the application commits or rolls back, the data are then "released" so that other applications or users can have access.

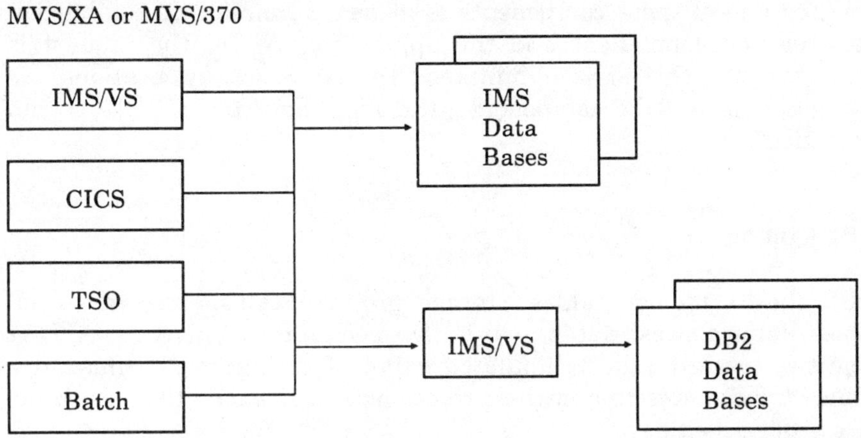

Figure 3-1 The DB2 operating environment.

DB2 saves all commits to Log Files. With the use of these Log Files, tables can be restored to their form prior to commits.

DB2 Base Tables and indexes are stored in 4K logical pages. A lock can be placed on a page or subpage at the lowest level and on a tablespace at the highest level. Locking cannot be set at the row level. This inability has received a lot of criticism and, hopefully, will be addressed in future releases of DB2. If the IRLM is not tuned properly, it is possible for a lock to occur after a user has begun to access those same data. This will result in the data being taken away from the user. A SAS data set will be created containing those rows the program had already extracted when the lock occurred. A SQL error will appear on the SAS log (error -911), but the program will end with a condition code 0. Be sure to review the SAS log. If you encounter this type of problem contact your DB2 Database Administrator.

The Database Services component of DB2 is responsible for managing the creation and access to DB2 objects such as tables, tablespaces, and indexes. It also keeps the DB2 system catalog current. DB2 objects are covered in the next two sections of this chapter.

The System Services component of DB2 manages the DB2 system as it interacts with other products such as TSO, Batch, IMS/VS, and CICS.

When one of these components is in use, a "thread" is established between the component and the application. When the request is complete, the thread is eliminated. To see which applications are using any of the DB2 components, the TSO command, THREAD, can be issued.

DB2 Objects

DB2 objects include tables, storage groups, tablespaces, views, indexes, indexspaces, databases, buffer pools, and synonyms. A DB2 object is created and manipulated using SQL. Figure 3-2 illustrates some of these objects and their relationships to each other. Each object is described here.

Table

As discussed in Chapter 1, The Relational Model, a relational DBMS is a set of tables. Each table consists of rows and columns. The rows correspond to records in files or observations in SAS data sets. The columns correspond to fields in files or variables in SAS data sets. All columns within a table provide data relating to the same subject, called an entity. Table names have two parts, separated by a period. For user-created tables, the first level is the user's TSO ID. For production tables, created by the database administrator, the first level is often PROD, but can be some other naming convention used in your company. The second level of the table name is typically descriptive of the contents of the table. This naming convention is similar to that used for SAS data sets, where the first level refers to a DD in the JCL (including the WORK DD) and the second level is a descriptive name.

Storage Group

A storage group is a group of DASD volumes assigned to DB2. DB2 automatically allocates space for tables on an as-needed basis from these DASD volumes. The same DASD volume can be included in more than one storage group. Often, more than one storage group exists for a relational DMBS, where different storage groups may represent different components of your business. An alternative to

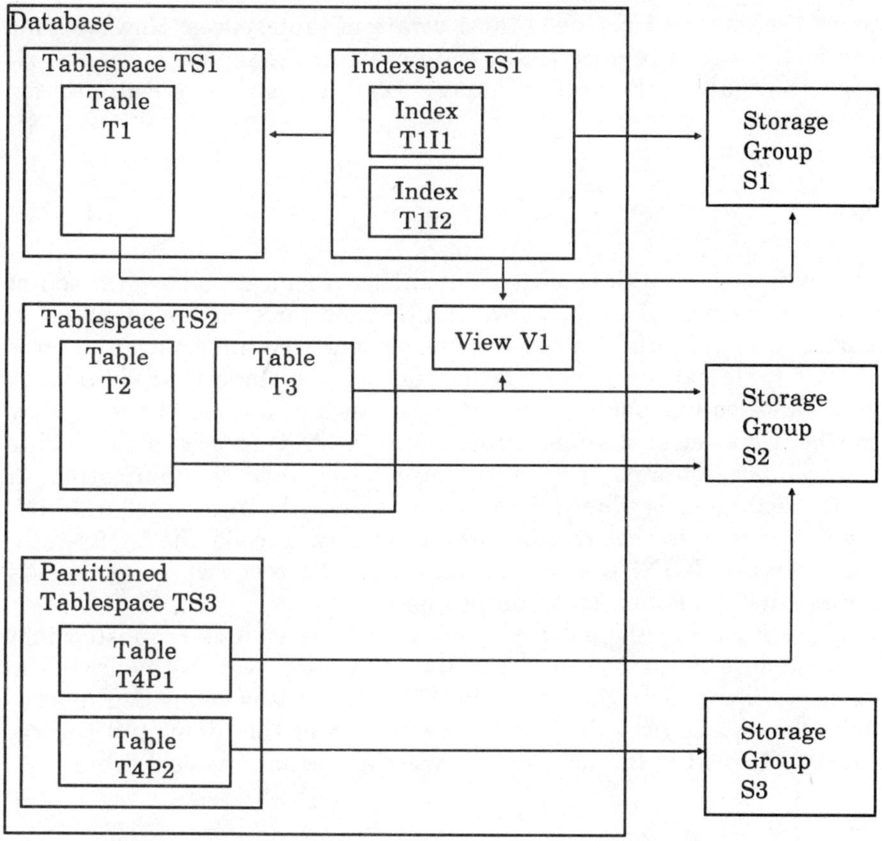

Figure 3-2 DB2 Objects.

using storage groups is to use VSAM data sets. The user will not need to know anything about storage groups.

Tablespace

Tablespaces are the physical spaces where tables are stored. A tablespace can contain more than one table. A tablespace can be divided into partitions and a single table may be stored in more than one partition on the basis of a range of data values. Tablespaces or partitions within tablespaces are important operationally because they are reorganized or recovered independently. For most applications, the user will not need to be aware of tablespaces. However, for applications that require the user to create DB2 tables, more knowledge is required. Refer to Chapter 12, Advanced Applications, for illustrations.

View

A view is not a physical entity, but rather a logical one, comprised of one or more Base Tables. Views can be used for security purposes. If a particular column in a table contains sensitive information, a view of that table can be created which does not include that column. A view can also limit access to particular rows in a table. Thus, a view can be a subset of a single table through limiting access to specific rows and/or columns. Views can also be used for simplification. A perfect example is where a view represents the results of a JOIN. Users can access this result without having to code the SQL statement for the JOIN. Another situation is where the view represents the results of a summarization process.

Views have names just like table names. A view is requested just as a table is requested, and the user may not even be aware he is using a view rather than a table. When a view is requested, operations take place according to the definition of the view, and the result is returned to the user as if it were an actual physical table.

Index

Indexes in tables are similar to indexes in books. An index in a book is used to find the page number where the subject you are interested in is located. An index in DB2 is created based on one or more columns in a table. The index is used to find the rows in the table that contain the required values of the index. Without an index, those rows would have to be located by sequentially examining each row. This is referred to as a tablespace scan. Tablespace scans can use enormous amounts of computer resources, depending on the size of the table. Conversely, the use of indexes can greatly increase the performance of DB2. More than one index can be created for a single table, but care should be taken not to create too many. Too many indexes can increase the maintenance requirements of the table.

Two special kinds of indexes exist. The first is a unique index. A unique index forces the primary key of a table to be unique. If an application tries to update the table so that the primary key has more than one row with the same value, the update will fail. The second kind of index is the cluster index. A cluster index dictates the physical order of the rows in a DB2 table. In other words, a cluster index defines how the rows are physically sorted.

The database administrator is typically the only one who creates indexes. The user needs to be aware of indexes because their use affects the performance of his programs. However, the user cannot control whether his program will use the indexes. Recall that one of the guidelines of the relational model was that the user should not have to determine the access method, only describe the data he needs. The DB2 Optimizer determines the access method and this includes whether the indexes will be used. Unfortunately, the Optimizer does not always select the most efficient access method. Sometimes, the user can get the Optimizer to use an index merely by altering the way the SQL statement is coded. If you use an index in your selection criteria, most likely DB2 will use the index. For example, if student name is the index and you want to select information on a specific student, the use of student name in the selection criteria will probably cause the Optimizer to use the index. The Optimizer will be discussed in more detail later in this chapter.

Indexspace

Indexes are stored in indexspaces just as tables are stored in tablespaces. However, DB2 controls the creation of indexspaces, whereas the database administrator or user creates tablespaces. The user does not need to know anything about indexspaces.

Database

A DB2 database is not a physical entity, but rather a name which refers to group of tablespaces, which in turn includes tables and indexes. The database is provided as an operational tool to be used by database administrators to control its availability to the user community. The user will not need to know anything about databases.

Buffer Pool

Buffer pools are temporary storage areas used to hold data in the process of being manipulated. A buffer pool is used during sorts or joins of DB2 tables, as well as during the updating process associated with tables, tablespaces, indexes, and indexspaces. The user does not need to know anything about buffer pools.

Synonym

Synonyms are typically created by the user to assign a short easy name to a table or view that has a long complicated name.

The DB2 objects covered here must be created in a top down order. The database must be created first, followed by the tablespace, the tables, and the indexes.

The System Catalog

The DB2 System Catalog is a collection of DB2 tables that contain information about DB2 tables. Much of this information is about DB2 objects: databases, tables, views, columns, storage groups, and indexes. The System Catalog also contains information about security relative to DB2 objects. Since these system data are stored in DB2 tables, SQL can be used to read and report these data. However, SQL cannot be used to update the System Catalog. DB2 itself maintains the System Catalog. Version 2 of DB2 will allow some updating of tables in the System Catalog by authorized users.

Users may have an occasional need to inquire into the System Tables. For example, you are probably used to using the TSO command, DSAT, to obtain a list of data sets, when you forget the full name or need some of the data set attributes. In the SAS environment, if you had a SAS data library and could not remember the names of the SAS files in the library, you would use PROC DATASETS or PROC CONTENTS to produce a list of the SAS files. In the DB2 environment, you may need to know the names of all tables with a specific value of the first level of the table name. The following example shows the SQL code and the report containing this information:

```
SELECT NAME, REMARKS                      NAME      REMARKS
  FROM SYSIBM.SYSTABLES                   EMPL      MASTER FILE
  WHERE CREATOR = 'TSID123';              SALARY    1989
                                          TAX       1988
```

How many times have you created a permanent SAS data set, only to forget the names of the variables? In the SAS environment you would use PROC DATASETS or PROC CONTENTS to produce a list of SAS variable names. To obtain a list of the columns in a DB2 table, use the following SQL code:

```
SELECT NAME, COLTYPE, LENGTH        NAME       COLTYPE   LENGTH
FROM SYSIBM.SYSCOLUMNS              SSN        CHAR        9
WHERE CREATOR = 'PROD'              LNAME      CHAR       15
AND TBNAME = 'EMPL';                FNAME      CHAR       10
                                    ADDRESS    CHAR       30
                                    PHONE      CHAR       10
```

Refer to the next chapter for information on coding SQL statements. The first level of the table name for System Catalog Tables is SYSIBM. The second level name along with the column names for the tables most often needed by users is shown in Appendix A. Also note that your DB2 Database Administrator may have the security set so that you cannot read the DB2 System Tables. Instead, your site may provide you with a hard copy of the information they feel you need. You will need the table names, names of the columns in each table, data type, data length, primary keys, foreign keys, which keys to use to join tables, and the indexes. This will still not cover information on tables which you may create, although you should not have to do this very often, if at all.

Data Access

Accessing data stored in DB2 tables using SAS is straightforward by comparison with third-generation languages such as COBOL. With third-generation languages, you must precompile, compile, and bind the program before it can be submitted for execution. The bind process includes checking the SQL statement for errors, checking user authorization, and selecting the access path (the Optimizer). When using SAS, the bind process is performed automatically, as is the compile process. Thus, submitting a SAS/DB2 program is operationally no different from submitting any other SAS program.

The Optimizer determines the data access path on the basis of the access paths available, the composition of the SQL statement, and statistics stored in the DB2 System Catalog. The catalog provides

DB2 with information such as indexes, primary keys, and foreign keys. The choices for access paths include accessing only an index, accessing an index plus using it to access columns from its corresponding table, and a tablespace scan. A tablespace scan is a sequential read of a DB2 table and should be avoided for large tables. If the SQL statement involves joining tables, a variety of these approaches may be used. The processing can be quite complex with some joins and may involve sorting and the creation of intermediate result tables. Although this is transparent to the user, the consumption of computer resources can be quite large.

The Optimizer does not always select the most efficient access path. For complex SQL statements, particularly those involving large tables, the user should verify that the access path is efficient prior to submitting the program. Examination of the PLAN TABLE will give the user this ability. A PLAN TABLE is a DB2 table containing information about the access path such as use of an index versus a tablespace scan, names of indexes used, sort requirements, and table access sequence in cases of a join. The PLAN TABLE is created by the SQL EXPLAIN statement. An EXPLAIN statement can be executed outside the SAS environment using JCL tailored to your company or can be executed inside the SAS environment using the SAS/DB2 procedures, PROC DB2LOAD or PROC DB2UTIL. The two forms of the EXPLAIN statement are:

```
EXPLAIN PLAN SET QUERYNO=number sql statement;
EXPLAIN PLAN FOR sql statement;
```

The SQL statement will be a SELECT statement in most user applications. The SQL SELECT statement extracts data stored in DB2 tables. Every time an EXPLAIN is executed, a plan is added to your PLAN TABLE. You will probably want either to delete the old EXPLAIN each time, or use SET QUERYNO equal to a number of your choice so you can distinguish between plans when viewing the PLAN TABLE. Queryno is a column of the PLAN TABLE.

Because the PLAN TABLE is a DB2 table, the SAS/DB2 procedure, PROC DB2EXT, can read this table and PROC PRINT can produce a report of its contents. Once the PLAN TABLE has been reviewed and found to be satisfactory, the SQL SELECT statement can be used to perform the data extraction. If the PLAN TABLE shows that the access path is not efficient (for example, a tablespace scan of a large table), try recoding the SQL SELECT statement. Usually there is more than one way to code a SELECT statement to produce the same results. Use indexes where possible as the basis for row selection. Other than that, you just have to play with the SELECT statement. A future release of DB2 may include the ability to alter the access method selected by the DB2 Optimizer.

Appendix B lists the columns in a PLAN TABLE with a brief description. The main columns to examine are Tname, Planno, and Accesstype. Planno is a number which indicates the order that tables in a join are accessed. The name of the table is in the column, Tname. Hopefully, the Optimizer will access smaller tables and/or the use of indexes first. Accesstype indicates whether the index was used (I) or not (R).

Your database administrator may have to give you authority to create a PLAN TABLE. The SQL code used to create your own PLAN TABLE is also included in Appendix B. This code is based on the SQL CREATE statement, which is covered in the next chapter, Structured Query Language. This code should be executed using JCL tailored to your company, also provided by your DB2 Database Administrator.

If user-created tables are being joined with production tables, the System Catalog must be updated so that it includes information about the user tables. The DB2 Database Administrator will keep the System Catalog current for production tables. If the System Catalog does not contain any information on a table, the plan will use that table last (Planno), which may not be the most efficient access method. To update the System Catalog after creation of a new table or an update of an existing table, a utility called RUNSTATS must be executed. This is done outside the SAS environment with JCL specific to your company. Chapter 12, Advanced Applications, illustrates the use of a RUNSTATS and a PLAN TABLE, to cause a SAS program to abend when the tables are not accessed in the most efficient order.

Most of you use the OBS option of the INFILE statement or the OBS system option to read only a few records when testing a SAS program. In the DB2 environment this is not possible. Therefore, many companies have created test tables for this purpose. Test tables are just like production tables, except they contain a smaller number of rows. If test tables are not available, you can test your program with a small amount of data by coding selection criteria based on the index.

Security

DB2 has its own security system, which independently protects all DB2 objects (databases, tablespaces, tables, views, indexes) and the type of authority over each object (create, read, update). Although this makes the security flexible, it can also make the administration of security complex. Most companies have a security plan, where certain types of users are given specific capabilities.

When DB2 is installed, a single user ID is established which has total authority. This user is called the System Administrator. The system administrator has the authority to grant and revoke authority to other users through the SQL GRANT and REVOKE statements. The following diagram shows the typical configuration of the levels of DB2 security within an organization:

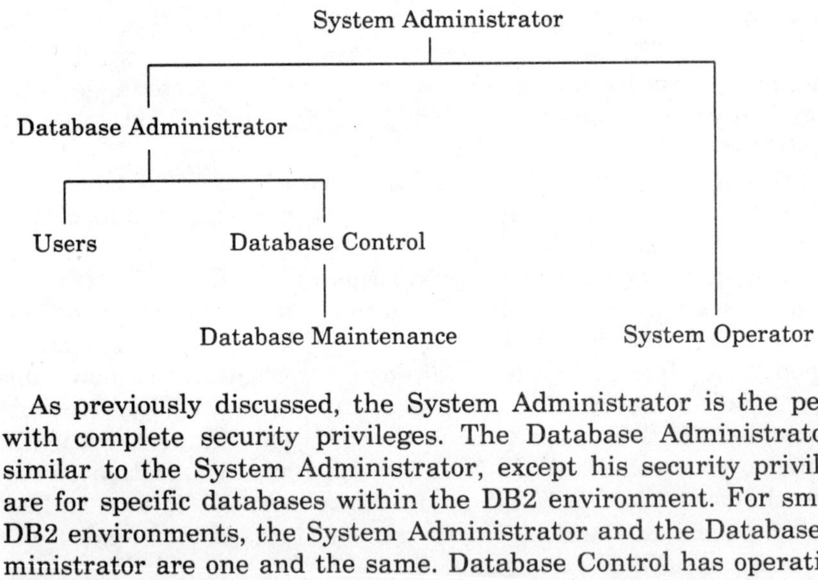

As previously discussed, the System Administrator is the person with complete security privileges. The Database Administrator is similar to the System Administrator, except his security privileges are for specific databases within the DB2 environment. For smaller DB2 environments, the System Administrator and the Database Administrator are one and the same. Database Control has operational authority over specific databases, but does not have the authority to actually access the data. Database Maintenance authority includes the running of certain utility functions. System Operator authority includes privileges to issue specific DB2 commands. These authorization levels may be combined in some organizations.

Typically, it is the Database Administrator who grants authority to users. He can even set up users who themselves can grant and revoke authority to other users. However, if the Database Administrator revokes the authority of one of his users, anyone to whom that user had given authority would also be revoked. Capabilities granted to users vary from company to company. When using SAS/DB2, you will need all or some of the following capabilities:

1. Read specific tables or views.
2. Execute the application plan, PROC DB2EXT.
3. Create and update your own PLAN TABLE.
4. Read specific System Catalog tables.
5. Create your own DB2 tables/tablespace; given this authority, you will also be able to update those tables, create indexes, create views.
6. Execute the application plans, PROC DB2LOAD and PROC DB2UTIL.

At a minimum, you will need points 1 and 2. Point 1 is the ability to read data stored in DB2 tables. Point 2 is authorization to use the SAS procedure, PROC DB2EXT, to read that data. I would recommend number 3, creation of your own PLAN TABLE, so that you can insure the Optimizer is selecting the most efficient access path when reading large tables. Point 4, the ability to read relevant tables in the System Catalog, is for the purpose of obtaining data dictionary information including table names, column names, data types, data lengths, indexes, primary keys, and foreign keys. Your company may supply this information on paper or through the use of a data dictionary product. But make sure you have everything you need, including indexes and information stating what foreign keys match what primary keys. You may also need the ability to create your own DB2 tables for more complex programs. To do this, you will need authority for points 5 and 6. Point 5 gives you the DB2 authorization to create your own tables and tablespaces. Point 6 is the authorization to use the SAS procedures, PROC DB2LOAD and PROC DB2UTIL, respectively to load and update DB2 tables. See Chapter 12, Advanced Applications, for illustrations of this type of program.

If your company has both a test DB2 environment and a production DB2 environment, authority is granted separately for all points shown above. The test and production DB2 environments are separate. You cannot access both environments simultaneously. Thus, you could not join a DB2 table in the test environment with one in the production environment.

In the previous section, Data Access, the term "bind" was used. A bind is the process of checking SQL code, checking user authorization, and selecting an access path. When using third-generation languages such as COBOL, the program must be bound before it can executed. Some companies do not like to give authority for binding to users. This creates a situation where the COBOL user must have the Database Administrator do the bind before the program can be tested. The SAS/DB2 procedures, PROC DB2EXT, PROC DB2LOAD, and PROC DB2UTIL, are themselves bound, so each SAS/DB2 program does not have to be bound separately. The user merely needs the authority to use these SAS procedures.

Views are also used as a security mechanism. Recall that a view is a logical entity, comprised of one or more Base Tables. If a Base Table contains a column with sensitive information such as a person's salary, a view can be created which does not include this column. If a Base Table contains rows with information for different departments, a view can be set up for each department. Users can then be given access to the view that represents their department. Thus, a view can be a subset of a Base Table through limiting access to specific rows or specific columns. When a view represents the result table of a join, access to specific columns and rows can also be limited.

DB2 can also be controlled at a higher level by other security software on the market.

Data Types

The SAS/DB2 procedure, PROC DB2EXT, is used to extract data stored in a DB2 table(s) using the SQL SELECT statement and place it in a SAS data set. Rows in a DB2 table become SAS observations and columns in a DB2 table become SAS variables. SAS and DB2 store data differently. SAS data types are either character or numeric. DB2 has several data types. SAS/DB2 automatically converts the DB2 data types into the standard SAS data types, character or numeric. The user needs to know whether the resulting SAS variable is character or numeric so that it can be processed accordingly (quotes for character data selection, use of appropriate functions, etc.). In addition, the user needs to know the format of DB2 dates.

The only time the user needs to know more about DB2 data types is when an application requires the user to create his own DB2 tables. DB2 tables can be loaded using the SAS/DB2 procedure, PROC DB2LOAD. DB2LOAD loads a DB2 table from data stored in a SAS data set. SAS observations become DB2 table rows and SAS variables become DB2 table columns. Although SAS/DB2 will convert SAS data types to DB2 data types automatically, often the conversion is not appropriate because there are multiple DB2 types for both SAS character and numeric data.

Missing values in DB2 tables are called null values. When a DB2 table is created, each column has a definition relative to null values. There are three ways nulls can be handled:

• NULL	Data value is not required.
• NOT NULL	Data value is required.
• NOT NULL With Default	If data are not assigned a value, a default value will be assigned. The default for numeric data is 0 and the default for character data is blank.

The following presents a short description of each of the DB2 data types:

1. Character (EBCDIC representation)

   - CHAR(N): Fixed-length character data with a length of 254 or fewer positions or bytes. Defined as NOT NULL, the length is N; defined as NULL, the length is N+1.
   - VARCHAR(N): Variable-length character data with a maximum length of 254 or fewer positions or bytes. Defined as NOT NULL, the length is N+2; defined as NULL, the length is N+3.
   - LONG VARCHAR: Variable-length character data with a length greater than 254 positions or bytes.

2. Graphic Character

   - GRAPHIC(N): Fixed-length double-byte character data with a length of 254 or fewer positions and stored in 127 or fewer bytes. Defined as NOT NULL, the length in bytes is 2N; defined as NULL, the length in bytes is 2N+1.
   - VARGRAPHIC(N): Variable-length double-byte character data with a maximum length of 254 or fewer positions and stored in 127 or fewer bytes. Defined as NOT NULL, the length in bytes is 2N+2; defined as NULL, the length in bytes is 2N+3.
   - LONG VARGRAPHIC: Variable-length double-byte character data, where the length is greater than 254 positions stored in 127 bytes.

3. Numeric

   - SMALLINIT: Small integers ranging from -32,768 to 32,767 stored in 2 bytes if defined as NOT NULL and 3 bytes if defined as NULL.
   - INTEGER: Large integers ranging from -2,147,483,648 to 2,147,483,647 stored in 4 bytes if defined as NOT NULL and 5 bytes if defined as NULL.
   - DECIMAL(W,D): Decimal numbers are stored as packed decimal with an implicit decimal point. Decimal values can range from -999,999,999,999,999 to 999,999,999,999,999. W is the total number of positions and D is the number of places to the right of the decimal point.
   - FLOAT: Floating-point number with a range from -5.4E -79 to 7.2E +75.

4. Date/Time — Date/time data types were added in Release 1.3 of DB2.

   - DATE Dates are three parts:

YEAR	YYYY, ranging from 0001 to 9999
MONTH	MM, ranging from 1 to 12
DAY	DD, ranging from 1 to 28/29/30/31, depending on the month

   - TIME Times are three parts:

HOUR	HH, ranging from 0 to 24
MINUTE	MM, ranging from 0 to 59
SECOND	SS, ranging from 0 to 59

   - TIMESTAMP: The combination of date and time as described above, plus an additional 6 positions for fractional seconds.

When date/time values are extracted from a DB2 table, they are presented as a character string. The format of that character string is set by the System Administrator when DB2 is installed. There are four formats; ISO (International Standards Organization), USA, EUR (European), and JIS (Japanese). The most commonly used format is ISO. The ISO and USA formats are:

	ISO	USA
DATE	YYYY-MM-DD	MM/DD/YYYY
TIME	HH.MM.SS	HH:MM AM/PM

SAS/DB2 assumes that DB2 dates and times have been stored in the ISO format. If your company has selected a different format, a zap must be applied to the SAS/DB2 software in order to use these dates/times. If you extract date/time columns from a DB2 table and all the values are missing, chances are your company has installed DB2 with a format other than ISO. Contact the SAS Consultant at your company to have the zap applied.

DB2 dates and times can be used in arithmetic expressions and several date/time functions are available. These will be covered in the next chapter, Structured Query Language. The capabilities are very similiar to those available for SAS dates. As in SAS, these capabilities are based on the way date/time values are stored internally. A SAS date is the number of days since 1/1/60 and a DB2 date is stored as the number of days since 12/31/00. This internal representation is used when an expression calls for arithmetic to be performed. However, when the user codes SQL statements using DB2 date/time values, the character representation will be used. Refer to the next chapter, Structured Query Language, for examples.

Prior to Release 1.3, dates and times were stored as numerics. Dates were normally stored in the form YYYYMMDD so that sorting could be performed. Other date processing such as finding a duration could not be performed within DB2 without extensive routines. Using SAS/DB2 with dates prior to Release 1.3 is not a problem because the user can convert the DB2 dates to SAS dates prior to performing any date logic.

Even though these new date/time data types now exist, DB2 systems that were developed prior to Release 1.3 may still store dates and times in a numeric data type. The user should be aware of this and handle processing of dates and times appropriately.

Review

Questions

1. Users can access DB2 through what products? SAS/DB2 can access DB2 through what products?
2. Explain the Resource Lock Manager using the terms lock, commit, and roll back.
3. Describe the naming convention for DB2 tables.
4. What is the name of the physical space where DB2 tables are stored?
5. What is a view?
6. What is the advantage of indexes?
7. Where can users get information on DB2 column names, data types, data lengths, indexes, and keys?
8. How can you tell if the DB2 Optimizer has choosen the best access path to obtain the data you need?
9. What two kinds of authority does a SAS/DB2 user need at a minimum?
10. How do data types compare between SAS and DB2? When extracting data from DB2 tables to create a SAS data set, how does SAS/DB2 handle those data types?

Answers

1. TSO, Batch, CICS, and IMS/VS can be used to access data stored in DB2 tables. SAS/DB2 can access DB2 through TSO or Batch.
2. When an application that updates a DB2 table is running, users are temporarily locked out. The application finishes and releases the data after performing a commit or a roll back. A commit updates data stored in DB2 tables. A roll back returns the data to their form when the prior commit was performed.
3. DB2 tables have a two-level name. For user created tables, the first level is the user TSO id. For production tables, often the first level is PROD, but could be a naming convention a company adheres to. The second level of the table name is a descriptive name based on the contents of the table.
4. DB2 tables are stored in tablespaces.
5. A view is a logical representation of one or more Base Tables. It could be a subset of a table, based on a portion of the rows

and/or columns. This type of view is often created for security purposes. For convenience, a view is often defined for joins of several DB2 tables.

6. An index allows rows to be accessed directly without sequentially reading every row (tablespace scan) in order to determine if it meets the user's criteria. The index is used when the users selection criteria are based on specific values of the index. The use of the index requires far less computer resources than a tablespace scan.
7. The DB2 System Catalog contains DB2 tables which themselves contain information on DB2 tables.
8. The PLAN TABLE contains information on the access path that the DB2 Optimizer has chosen. The column, Planno, indicates which DB2 table will be accessed first for joins. The column, Tname, is the table name and is used in conjunction with Planno. The column, Accesstype, indicates whether the index or a tablespace scan will be used. The PLAN TABLE is generated with the SQL EXPLAIN statement.
9. At a minimum a SAS/DB2 user will want to read data stored in DB2 tables with PROC DB2EXT. This requires two things; read authority on the desired DB2 tables, and authority to access the application plan, DB2EXT.
10. SAS has only two data types, character and numeric. DB2 has several data types. When extracting data from DB2 tables and placing it in a SAS data set, PROC DB2EXT automatically converts the DB2 data types into the appropriate SAS data type.

Chapter

4

Structured Query Language

SQL, Structured Query Language, is a comprehensive language used to define, manipulate, and control DB2 relational database management systems and many other relational DBMS. SQL is the standard language for relational DBMS and is backed by ANSI (American National Standards Institute) and ISO (International Standards Organization).

SQL statements can be executed through:

- Third-generation languages such as PL/1 or COBOL
- QMF (Query Management Facility), IBM's report writer
- SPUFI (SQL Processor Using File Input), an IBM product for testing SQL statements. SPUFI is a subset of an IBM product called DB2I. DB2I can also be used to execute DB2 utilities and prepare third-generation language programs with embedded SQL for execution.
- SAS/DB2, along with some other fourth-generation languages
- Batch programs using JCL tailored to your company

This book will discuss execution of SQL statements through SAS/DB2 and through JCL tailored to your company.

SQL Components

Structured Query Language consists of several statements used to define, manipulate, and control all aspects of the DB2 environment. These statements are grouped into six categories according to the function they perform. The primary SQL statement used by SAS users is the SELECT statement. This statement is used to extract data from DB2 tables and place them in a SAS data set. Other SQL statements are used to perform such functions as updating a DB2 table, creating a DB2 table or other DB2 objects, controlling the update process, and security; all of which are more often performed by the DB2 Database Administrator than the SAS user.

The three SAS/DB2 procedures, PROC DB2EXT, PROC DB2LOAD, and PROC DB2UTIL, can automatically generate some of these SQL statements and can execute any of them. SQL statements which can be automatically generated by a SAS/DB2 procedure will be noted in the following discussion.

There are six components of the SQL language:

- Data Definition Language (DDL)
  This component controls the creation and maintenance of DB2 objects such as storage groups, tables, tablespaces, indexes, views, synonyms, and databases. This control is handled through the use of three statements: CREATE, ALTER, and DROP. The CREATE statement is used to create a DB2 object. It is used by the SAS/DB2 procedure, PROC DB2LOAD to create a DB2 table. The ALTER statement is used to make changes to specific DB2 objects. It is used by the SAS/DB2 procedure, PROC DB2UTIL, to add a new column to a DB2 table. The DROP statement is used to DROP a DB2 object. It can be executed by PROC DB2LOAD or PROC DB2UTIL, but it cannot be automatically generated by either procedure.
- Data Manipulation Language (DML)
  The data manipulation language is the primary component of SQL required by users. It is comprised of four statements, SELECT, UPDATE, INSERT, and DELETE. The SELECT statement will be covered in detail, as it is used by SAS/DB2 procedure, PROC DB2EXT, to extract data stored in DB2 tables, the capability users will need the most often. The UPDATE, INSERT, and DELETE statements are used for maintenance of DB2 tables. The UPDATE statement is used to change values of columns in a DB2 table. The INSERT statement is used to add new rows to a DB2 table. The DELETE statement is used to delete existing rows from a DB2

table. The UPDATE, INSERT, and DELETE statements are used by the SAS/DB2 procedure, PROC DB2UTIL.

- Data Control
  The data control component controls the operational aspects of the updating process. Included here are the statements, COMMIT, LOCK, and ROLLBACK. An overview of these functions was covered in the previous chapter in the section, The DB2 Subsystem. The COMMIT statement is used by the SAS/DB2 procedures, PROC DB2LOAD and PROC DB2UTIL, to commit work completed by these procedures. The COMMIT, LOCK, and ROLLBACK functions were discussed in the previous chapter in the section, The DB2 Subsystem.
- Security
  The security component controls the type of authorization (read, create, update) to DB2 objects such as tables, tablespaces, storage groups, databases, and indexes. This is done through the GRANT and REVOKE statements. An overview of these functions was covered in the previous chapter in the section, Security. No further details will be covered here.
- Third-Generation Language Access
  The statements in this component (OPEN, CLOSE, DECLARE, FETCH, INCLUDE, DESCRIBE, WHENEVER, PREPARE, and EXECUTE) are used only when SQL code is embedded in programs written in a third-generation languages such as PL/1, FORTRAN, or COBOL. These will not be covered here.
- Other
  There are a few single-purpose SQL statements, only one of which is valuable to the user and that is the EXPLAIN statement. The EXPLAIN statement was discussed in the previous chapter in the section, Data Access. This statement is illustrated in Chapter 12, Advanced Applications.

The CREATE Statement

The CREATE statement can be used to create databases, storage groups, tablespaces, tables, indexes, views, and synonyms. We will cover the creation of tablespaces, tables, indexes, and synonyms, as these are normally the only DB2 objects created by users. Even then, you will need to have your DB2 Database Administrator provide you with some installation-specific information. The DB2 Database Administrator must also give you the authority to create any of these DB2 objects.

The CREATE statement can be automatically generated by PROC DB2LOAD to create a DB2 table which in turn will be loaded using data stored in a SAS data set. To create other DB2 objects, the CREATE statement must be coded and executed using the SAS/DB2 procedures, PROC DB2LOAD or PROC DB2UTIL, or using JCL tailored to your company.

Tablespace

The creation of a tablespace is covered here because it is required in order to create a DB2 table. Ultimately, the creation of the DB2 table is what users may need for more complex applications.

When a tablespace is created, a data set is created in one of the storage groups. A tablespace can be created by the SAS/DB2 procedures, PROC DB2LOAD or PROC DB2UTIL, or by JCL tailored to your company. The general form of the CREATE statement for tablespaces follows:

```
CREATE TABLESPACE tablespace IN database/authorization id
  USING
    STOGROUP storage group
    PRIQTY primary quantity
    SECQTY secondary quantity
    ERASE yes/no
  FREEPAGE free page
  PCTFREE pctfree
  BUFFERPOOL bufferpool
  LOCKSIZE lock size
  CLOSE yes/no
  DSETPASS password;
```

The capital letters shown in this format represent SQL code and the small letters are values that must be set. Tablespace is the name you will give to your tablespace. The tablespace name is alphanumeric up to eight positions in length. Database or authorization id is the first level of the DB2 table name and will probably be your TSO user ID. The database name is alphanumeric up to eight positions in length. Some of the other portions of the CREATE statement are optional. Definitions for the remainder of the CREATE statement will not be given here, as your DB2 Database Administrator will need to supply their values.

Tables

The SAS/DB2 procedure, PROC DB2LOAD, can automatically generate a CREATE statement to create a DB2 table, but PROC DB2LOAD also generates the SQL INSERT statements neccessary to load the DB2 table at the same time. PROC DB2LOAD is the most common approach for SAS users to create a DB2 table. However, a CREATE statement can also be coded by the user to create a DB2 table without also loading the table. This CREATE statement can be executed by the SAS/DB2 procedures, PROC DB2LOAD or PROC DB2UTIL, or executed using JCL tailored to your company. One or more tables can be stored in a single tablespace. However, you may want to create only one table per tablespace because utilities such as copying and recovery (recover status prior to a commit) function on the basis of a tablespace rather than a table. If your DB2 tables are for a specific application, they will probably be temporary. In this case, it really won't matter if you create multiple tables in a single tablespace. The following is the general form of the CREATE statement for tables:

```
CREATE TABLE table
   (column1 datatype1 null/not null/not null with default,
    column2 datatype2 null/not null/not null with default,
    column3 datatype3 null/not null/not null with default,
    ....
    columnN datatypeN null/not null/not null with default)
   IN database.tablespace;
```

The capital letters shown in this format represent SQL code and the small letters are values that must be set. Table is a table name of your choice. Column1 through ColumnN are the DB2 column names of your choice. Table names and column names are alphanumeric up to eighteen positions in length. Datatype1 through datatypeN is the DB2 data type, as defined in the previous chapter, IBM'S Database 2, in the section, Data Types. Also in that section is a definition of NULL, NOT NULL, and NOT NULL WITH DEFAULT. If one of these is not specified in the CREATE statement, the default is NULL, which means missing values are valid. The database parameter will probably be your TSO user ID. The tablespace is the name of a tablespace you have previously created. The tablespace must be created prior to creating a table in that tablespace.

The following is an example of the CREATE statement for a DB2 table, Pers, in the tablespace, Emp89, by the TSO user, TSID123:

```
CREATE TABLE TSID123.Pers
   (Ssn     CHAR(9)          NOT NULL,
    Name    VARCHAR(30)      NOT NULL,
    Dept    VARCHAR(15)              ,
    Mgr     VARCHAR(15)              ,
    Phone   CHAR(7)                  ,
    Salary  DECIMAL(7,2)             )
   IN Tsid123.Emp89;
```

The columns, Ssn and Name, cannot contain null values. All others can contain null values.

Indexes

When an application requires that a user create a table, an index may also be required in order for the DB2 Optimizer to generate the most efficient access path. Indexes are also created to maintain unique rows and to store rows in a specific order. When an index is created, an indexspace is automatically created to hold the index.

The general form of the CREATE statement for indexes is:

```
CREATE UNIQUE/CLUSTERED INDEX database.column
    ON database.table
       (column ASC/DESC)
   USING
     STOGROUP storage group
     PRIQTY primary quantity
     SECQTY secondary quantity
     ERASE yes/no
   FREEPAGE free page
   PCTFREE pctfree
   BUFFERPOOL bufferpool
   SUBPAGES sub pages
   CLOSE yes/no
   DSETPASS password
   ERASE erase parm;
```

The capital letters shown in this format represent SQL code and the small letters are values that must be set. UNIQUE and CLUSTERED are optional and can be specified as needed. Database will probably be your TSO user ID. Column is the name of the column that will become an index. Table is the name of the table containing the index column. Some of the other portions of the CREATE statement are optional. Definitions for the remainder of the CREATE statement will not be given here, as your DB2 Database Administrator will need to supply their values.

Synonyms

Synonyms allow the user to create a short name that corresponds to the actual table name or view name. This is just for convenience. Synonyms can be created with the CREATE statement using JCL tailored to your company or one of the SAS/DB2 procedures, PROC DB2LOAD or PROC DB2UTIL. The following is the general form of the CREATE statement for synonyms:

```
CREATE SYNONYM Synonym FOR Database.Table/Database.View;
```

The capital letters above represent SQL code and the small letters are values that must be set. Synonym is a synonym name of your choice. Database is the first level of the DB2 table or view name. The second level of this name is either the name of a Base Table or a view.

The following example illustrates a synonym:

```
CREATE SYNONYM Clm FOR Prod.medical_insurance_claims;
```

The user can now use the synonym, Clm, rather than code the entire prod table name.

The DROP Statement

The DROP statement can be used to drop databases, storage groups, tablespaces, tables, indexes, views, and synonyms. When one of these objects is dropped, all objects that are dependent on that object are dropped as well. For example, if a tablespace is dropped, all tables in that tablespace are dropped, along with any indexes, views, or synonyms. To drop any of these objects, you must either be the creator of the object or have specific authority to do so.

The DROP statement can be coded and executed using the SAS/DB2 procedures, PROC DB2LOAD or PROC DB2UTIL, or using JCL tailored to your company.

The general form of the DROP statement is:

```
DROP db2object name;
```

Db2object is either DATABASE, STOGROUP, TABLESPACE, TABLE, INDEX, VIEW, or SYNONYM. Name is the name of the DB2 object.

To drop the table, Pers, use the following DROP statement:

```
DROP TABLE Tsid123.Pers;
```

To drop the tablespace, Emp89, use the following DROP statement:

```
DROP TABLESPACE Tsid123.Emp89;
```

When the DROP statement is used to drop a tablespace, the COMMIT statement must also be used or the tablespace name cannot be reused at a later time:

```
DROP TABLESPACE Tsid123.Emp89;
COMMIT;
```

The ALTER Statement

The ALTER statement can be used to alter a storage group, tablespace, table, or index. Only altering a table will be discussed here. A DB2 table is altered to add new columns. New columns must be NULL; null values are allowed. Columns cannot be deleted from a DB2 table; the table has to be dropped and recreated. The form of the ALTER statement for tables is:

```
ALTER TABLE table name
    ADD  new column 1   data type
         new column 2   data type
         ...
         ;
```

The table name is the DB2 table to be altered. The new columns are the names of the new columns to be added. The data type is the desired data type for that column. Refer to the previous chapter, IBM'S Database 2, in the section, Data Types, for more information on DB2 data types. One or more new columns can be added in a single ALTER statement.

The ALTER statement can be automatically generated by the SAS/DB2 procedure, PROC DB2UTIL, to alter a DB2 table. Also generated by PROC DB2UTIL at the same time is the SQL UPDATE statement which is used to load values into the new column(s). To alter other DB2 objects, the ALTER statement must be coded and executed using one of the SAS/DB2 procedures, PROC DB2LOAD or PROC DB2UTIL, or using JCL tailored to your company.

The SELECT Statement

The SELECT statement is used to extract data stored in DB2 Base Tables or views created from these Base Tables. The results of a SELECT statement are then used for reporting and data analysis. Selection criteria allow for the selection of a subset of the rows and/or columns, rows can be sorted, and the results can be summarized based on particular column(s). The SELECT statement is the primary SQL statement used by the user community.

The SAS/DB2 procedure, PROC DB2EXT, uses the SQL SELECT statement to extract data from DB2 table(s) and place the result in a SAS data set. Once this SAS data set is created, any of the capabilities of the SAS system can be used to manipulate, report, and analyze the data. In some situations, PROC DB2EXT will be able to generate the required SELECT statement. When more complex capabilities of the SELECT statement are required, the user will have to edit the generated SELECT statement or code it entirely.

The SELECT statement is comprised of clauses, each beginning with a reserved word. These clauses are shown below, along with a brief description and whether the clause is required.

Clause Keyword	*Purpose*	*Use*
SELECT	DB2 columns desired	required
SELECT	New variables created	optional
FROM	DB2 table/view name(s)	required
WHERE	Row selection criteria	optional
GROUP BY	Summarize by DB2 column(s)	optional
HAVING	Row selection for GROUP BY	optional
ORDER BY	Row sort order	optional

These clauses must be specified in the order listed above. The coding of the clauses is freeform. They can be coded on a single line or on multiple lines. If multiple lines are required, the statement can be split within a clause if needed. The coding can begin in any column. To add structure to the code, I recommend beginning a new line for each clause. The SELECT statement (not each clause) must end with a semicolon.

The minimum required of a SELECT statement is the SELECT clause itself and the FROM clause. In the SELECT clause, you specify what DB2 columns are desired by coding the column names, separated by commas. This is similar to a SAS data set where you refer to the variables by their name. Column locations and data types are not required in order to read the data from DB2 tables or SAS data sets. If all the columns in the DB2 table are needed, an asterisk (*) can be coded rather than specifying every column name.

The FROM clause is used to name the DB2 table(s) or view(s) that contain the columns named in the SELECT clause. If columns from more than one table are needed, the FROM clause will contain the names of each table, separated by commas. This is the way JOINS are coded. The following examples illustrate the SELECT statement with only the FROM clause:

PROD.STUDENT_GENERAL_INFO

Student	Address	Class	Final
JENNY	R.R.#6	12	98
JOE	113 HOLLY	12	87
KELLY	88 CONNER CT	11	88

(1)
```
SELECT Student, Class
FROM Prod.student_general_info;
```

This SELECT statement selects only the columns named, Student and Class, from the DB2 table, Prod.student_general_info, as follows:

Student	Class
JENNY	12
JOE	12
KELLY	11

(2) `SELECT * FROM Prod.student_general_info;`

The result of this SELECT statement is the entire DB2 table. The asterisk indicates all columns are desired.

The DISTINCT Keyword

The DISTINCT keyword is used to produce a result table with rows that have a unique value of a specific column. The DISTINCT keyword is coded in the SELECT clause prior to the column whose values are to be unique.

The DISTINCT keyword is illustrated as follows:

PROD.DEPT_GENERAL_INFO

First	Dept	Floor	Salary	Mgr
MILTON	120	1	55000	Y
MARTHA	130	1	60000	N
MARY LEA	130	1	50000	N
MARLIN	140	2	60000	Y
MIRON	140	2	50000	N
MARVIN	140	2	40000	N

(1) The DISTINCT keyword is used to produce a list of department numbers from a table that has several occurrences of the same department number.

```
SELECT DISTINCT Dept
FROM Prod.dept_general_info;
```

The following result table is produced:

120
130
140

(2) When the DISTINCT keyword is used, other columns that are selected should have only one value for each distinct column. For the column, Floor, this is true. All rows with the same value of Dept are also on the same Floor. However, the column,

First, would have been a bad choice because there are multiple values of this column for the same value of Dept.

```
SELECT DISTINCT Dept, Floor
FROM Prod.dept_general_info;
```

The following result table is produced:

120	1
130	1
140	2

The WHERE Clause

The WHERE clause is used for row selection. If the result of the WHERE clause is true, the row will be selected. If the result is false, the row will not be selected. WHERE performs the same function as a subsetting IF statement or a DELETE statement in SAS. The following examples illustrate the SELECT statement with the WHERE clause:

PROD.STUDENT_GENERAL_INFO

Student	Address	Class	Final
JENNY	R.R.#6	12	98
JOE	113 HOLLY	12	87
KELLY	88 CONNER CT	11	88

(1) This SELECT statement selects only the columns named, Student and Address, and only those rows where Class is 12. The column, Class, happens to be a character data type. Because it is character, the value, 12, must be placed in quotes. If Class were numeric, quotes would not be used. This should be easy to remember because the SAS syntax is the same. Also notice that even though the column, Class, was used as the selection criterion, it does not have to be specified in the SELECT column list.

```
SELECT Student, Address
  FROM Prod.student_general_info
  WHERE Class = '12';
```

The result of this SELECT statement is:

Student	Address
JENNY	R.R.#6
JOE	113 HOLLY

(2) This SELECT statement selects the columns, Student and Final, where the Final is equal to 98. In this case, quotes are not used around the value, 98, because it is numeric.

```
SELECT Student, Final
  FROM Prod.student_general_info
  WHERE Final = 98;
```

The result of this SELECT statement is:

Student	Address	Class	Final
JENNY	R.R.#6	12	98

The selection capabilities of the WHERE clause are greatly enhanced with the use of comparison operators, arithmetic operators, Boolean operators, and special functions. Many of these operators and functions are the same as those available in Base SAS. IBM documentation uses the term, predicate, when referring to these operators and functions. The selection criteria in the WHERE clause can be quite complex and lengthy. The WHERE clause is limited to 32,000 characters. Although it is unlikely that you would reach this limit, if you do, an application can be split into multiple applications in some cases. If indexes are being used, separating the program into multiple programs will not use any more computer resources than submitting a single program. If the WHERE clause cannot be separated or if the application performs a tablespace scan, another alternative is to place your selections in a DB2 table. This DB2 table can then be joined with the Base Table(s) or view(s) to produce the desired result. This strategy will be discussed in greater detail in Chapter 12, Advanced Applications.

Comparison Operators

The following comparison operators can be used in a SQL statement:

Operator(s)		Meaning
=		Equal
¬=	<>	Not equal
<		Less than
<=	¬>	Less than or equal to (not greater than)
>		Greater than
>=	¬<	Greater than or equal to (not less than)

Three of these operations can be expressed in two ways. The first way is far more common than the second one shown. DB2 uses only the symbolic representation of these operators, where SAS also uses abbreviations such as EQ, GT, LE, etc.

When comparisons are made against NULL values, the result is always false.

The following SELECT statement selects those rows with a final value of 90 or more:

```
SELECT Student, Final
  FROM Prod.student_general_info
  WHERE Final >= 90 ;
```

Logical Operators: AND, OR, NOT

Row selection is often based on more than one condition. The AND operator can be used when more than one condition must be true for the row to be selected. The OR operator can be used when at least one condition must be true out of multiple conditions in order for the row to be selected. When NOT is used, a condition is true when the row does not meet the criteria specified in the condition.

When you are dealing with three or more conditions, the AND, OR, and NOT operators may be combined in the selection criteria. In this case, NOT is evaluated first, AND second, and OR last. The user can control the order of evaluation by using parentheses around the condition(s) that should be evaluated first. This is Boolean algebra and is the basis for most programming languages, including SAS, so dealing with logical operators is not anything new.

The following examples illustrate logical operators:

PROD.STUDENT_GENERAL_INFO

Student	Address	Class	Final
JENNY	R.R.#6	12	98
JOE	113 HOLLY	12	87
KELLY	88 CONNER CT	11	88

(1) Final must be greater than or equal to 90 and Class must be 12:

```
SELECT Student, Final
  FROM Prod.student_general_info
  WHERE Final >= 90 AND Class = '12';
```

(2) Class must be 11 or 12:

```
SELECT Student, Final
  FROM Prod.student_general_info
  WHERE Class = '11' OR Class = '12';
```

(3) Final must be greater than or equal to 90 and Class must be 11 or 12. Parentheses must be used around the OR conditions, otherwise the result would be Final greater than or equal to 90 for Class 11, and all Class 12 regardless of the value of Final.

```
SELECT Student, Final
  FROM Prod.student_general_info
  WHERE Final >= 90 AND (Class = '11' OR Class = '12');
```

(4) Class must not be 12:

```
SELECT Student, Final
  FROM Prod.student_general_info
  WHERE NOT Class = '12';
```

The NOT operator is not very straightforward in this example. The same result can be obtained more easily using comparison operators.

```
SELECT Student, Final
  FROM Prod.student_general_info
  WHERE Class Γ= '12';
```

The NOT operator will be used in more practical examples later in this chapter.

The BETWEEN Predicate

Often, selection is needed between two values. Although logical and comparison operators can be used to perform this selection, a special predicate, BETWEEN, can also be used. BETWEEN is not only easier for the user to code, but also is more computer-efficient than using logical and comparison operators. The BETWEEN predicate is inclusive; the values specified are included as a true condition. This is often wrongly viewed as exclusive because the word between, in an English sentence, is exclusive. The BETWEEN predicate can be used on both numeric and character data types.

(1) The following SELECT statements produce the same result, one with comparison operators, one with the BETWEEN predicate:

```
SELECT Student, Final
  FROM Prod.student_general_info
  WHERE Final >= 80 AND Final <= 90;

SELECT Student, Final
  FROM Prod.student_general_info
  WHERE Final BETWEEN 80 AND 90;
```

(2) The NOT operator is used with BETWEEN to select rows where Final is less than 80 or greater than 90; in other words, exclude the range from 80 to 90 inclusive:

```
SELECT Student, Final
  FROM Prod.student_general_info
  WHERE Final NOT BETWEEN 80 AND 90;
```

The IN Predicate

The IN predicate is used to select rows based on the value of a column being equal to one of several values. Although this can also be accomplished using a series of equal conditions connected by the logical operator, OR, the IN predicate is easier to code and more computer-efficient.

(1) The IN predicate is used in the following example to select all rows where Class is 10, 11, or 12. Since Class is character, quotes must be used around the values.

```
SELECT Student, Final
  FROM Prod.student_general_info
  WHERE Class IN ('10', '11', '12');
```

The same result can be obtained using the logical operator, OR. The use of OR can become quite tedious to code when the list of values increases.

```
SELECT Student, Final
  FROM Prod.student_general_info
  WHERE Class = '10' OR Class = '11' OR Class = '12';
```

(2) The IN predicate is used with the NOT operator to select all rows except those where Class is 11 or 12.

```
SELECT Student, Final
  FROM Prod.student_general_info
  WHERE Class NOT IN('11', '12');
```

The LIKE Predicate

The LIKE predicate can be used to select rows based on a column having a value composed of specific characters. The LIKE predicate is used only with character data. Two symbols are used with the LIKE predicate:

%	any number of character positions
_	any one-character position

The LIKE predicate is best understood through examples, which follow.

PROD.STUDENT_GENERAL_INFO

Student	Address	Class	Final
JENNY	R.R.#6	12	98
JOE	113 HOLLY	12	87
KELLY	88 CONNER CT	11	88

(1) The LIKE predicate is used to select rows where the Student name begins with a J. The % is used to indicate that the J can be followed by any number of characters that have any value. The rows with Student values, JENNY and JOE, would be selected.

```
SELECT Student, Final
  FROM Prod.student_general_info
  WHERE Student LIKE 'J%';
```

(2) The LIKE predicate is used to select rows where the second position of the Student name is an E. The _ (underscore) is used to indicate that the E must be the second position. If the % had been used, any student names containing an E anywhere in the name would have resulted in a true condition. The Student names, JENNY and KELLY, have an E in the second position.

```
SELECT Student, Final
  FROM Prod.student_general_info
  WHERE Student LIKE '_E';
```

(3) This example shows the use of two percents (%) to select rows where the Student name begins with a J and contains an E. The names, JENNY and JOE, would be selected. The first % indicates that there could be any number of characters between the J and the E, but there need not be. The value, JENNY, has no characters between the J and the E. The second % indicates that the E could be followed by character positions, but it does not have to be. The value, JOE, does not have any character positions after the E.

```
SELECT Student, Final
  FROM Prod.student_general_info
  WHERE Student LIKE 'J%E%';
```

Arithmetic Operators

Arithmetic operators can be used in the SELECT statement. These operators include:

+	Addition
-	Subtraction
*	Multiplication
/	Division

Arithmetic operators can be used with numeric data. They cannot be used with character data. If arithmetic operators are used on NULL values, the result is always NULL. Addition and subtraction can be used with date/time data. Date/time data will be discussed later in this chapter.

The order of evaluation of these arithmetic operators is multiplication and division first, and addition and subtraction second. Parentheses can be used to perform a specific operation first. Like the logical operators, this is the same way the SAS language and most other languages evaluate arithmetic expressions.

Arithmetic expressions can be used in the WHERE clause to select rows on the basis of the result of an arithmetic expression. Arithmetic expressions can be used in the SELECT clause to create a new column in the result table based on a calcuation. The following examples illustrate these two uses of arithmetic expressions.

PROD.EMP_GENERAL_INFO

First	Last	Ext	Salary	Hiredate
ERIC	BUELL	3425	40000	19891010
GREG	OWENS	3456	60000	19830306
JEREMY	OWENS	3477	50000	19850714

(1) This SELECT statement selects those rows where the Salary is greater than 45000 after a 10% increase and 500 in commissions. ERIC does not qualify, as this calculation produces a value of 44,500. GREG and JEREMY satisfy this condition.

```
SELECT First, Last, Salary
  FROM Prod.emp_general_info
  WHERE Salary * 1.10 + 500 > 45000;
```

(2) A new column is created on the result table which represents the monthly Salary of each individual.

```
SELECT First, Last, Salary/12
  FROM Prod.emp_general_info;
```

The Concatenation Operator

The concatenation operator (||) in the SQL language is the same as it is in the SAS language. The concatenation operator is used to combine one or more columns and/or character strings to create a new column on the result table. The concatenation operator is illustrated as follows:

PROD.EMP_GENERAL_INFO

First	Last	Ext	Salary	Hiredate
ERIC	BUELL	3425	40000	19891010
GREG	OWENS	3456	60000	19830306
JEREMY	OWENS	3477	50000	19850714

Suppose the length of the column, Last, is 15 and the length of the column, First, is 10. A new column is created on the result table which represents a combination of the columns, FIRST and LAST, and a character string.

```
SELECT Last||', '||First, Ext
  FROM Prod.emp_general_info;
```

The following result table is produced:

BUELL , ERIC	3425
OWENS , GREG	3456
OWENS , JEREMY	3477

The full length of the column is used in the concatenation, including blanks when the value is less than the defined column length. When the concatenation operator is used in Base SAS, the TRIM function is often used to eliminate trailing blanks from the result of the concatenation. SQL does not have a function for this purpose.

The SUBSTR Function

The SUBSTR function in the SQL language is similar to the SUBSTR function in Base SAS. The SUBSTR function is used to extract specific positions from an existing character column. This function is usually used to create a new column on the result table. It can also be used with the WHERE clause as a basis for row selection, but the LIKE predicate is usually used for this purpose. The syntax of the SUBSTR function is the same as the SUBSTR function in SAS:

```
SUBSTR(column name,start,length)
```

Column name is the name of an existing column, start is the location of the beginning of the desired value, and length is the number of positions desired.

The SUBSTR function is illustrated as follows:

PROD.EMP_GENERAL_INFO

First	Last	Ext	Salary	Hiredate
ERIC	BUELL	3425	40000	19891010
GREG	OWENS	3456	60000	19830306
JEREMY	OWENS	3477	50000	19850714

Suppose the length of the column, Last, is 15 and the length of the column, First, is 10. A new column is created on the result table which represents a combination of the first letter of the first name, a character string, and the last name.

```
SELECT SUBSTR(First,1,1)||'. '||Last
  FROM Prod.emp_general_info;
```

The following result table is produced:

E. BUELL	3425
G. OWENS	3456
J. OWENS	3477

There are two differences between the SUBSTR function in SQL and the SUBSTR function in Base SAS. First, in SQL the SUBSTR function cannot be performed on numeric columns. If it is, an SQL error will occur and the SELECT statement will not be executed. If the SUBSTR function is used on a numeric variable in SAS, it is converted to character and the SUBSTR is executed. Second, the length of a new column created by the SUBSTR function in SQL is the length specified in the SUBSTR function. In this example, that length is 1. The length of a new variable created by the SUBSTR function in SAS is the same as the length of the variable being substringed. In this example, that length is 10. The LENGTH statement can be used in SAS to set the length prior to executing the SUBSTR function.

Column Functions

Column functions calculate statistics based on the values of a single column and multiple rows. They are not used to calculate statistics based on the values of more than one column, as most SAS functions are. They can be compared to statistics SAS generates through the use of PROC SUMMARY. PROC SUMMARY calculates statistics based on values of a single variable and multiple observations.

When these functions are used, the result table contains only one row unless the GROUP BY clause is used. When the GROUP BY clause is used, the result table will contain one row for every value of the GROUP BY column(s). The GROUP BY clause will be covered later in this chapter and these functions will be illustrated with that clause.

When a column statistic is used on a column that contains NULL values, the NULL values are ignored. For example, if a column had five values, one of which was NULL, only four values would be used in the calculation of the statistics.

The following statistics are available in SQL:

SUM	Addition
MIN	Minimum
MAX	Maximum
AVG	Average
COUNT(*)	Counts the number of rows selected
COUNT(DISTINCT column)	Counts the number of unique values of the column specified (null not counted)

As you can see, the list is not extensive. It is very likely that you will have to use PROC DB2EXT to create a SAS data set from the DB2 table and then use Base SAS to calculate the desired statistics.

The column functions are illustrated using the following table:

PROD.DEPT_GENERAL_INFO

First	Dept	Floor	Salary	Mgr
MILTON	120	1	55000	Y
MARTHA	130	1	60000	N
MARY LEA	130	1	50000	N
MARLIN	140	2	60000	Y
MIRON	140	2	50000	N
MARVIN	140	2	40000	N

(1) The sum, minimum, maximum, and average Salary are calculated for Dept 130.

```
SELECT SUM(Salary), MIN(Salary), MAX(Salary), AVG(Salary)
  FROM Prod.dept_general_info
  WHERE Dept = '140';
```

The result of this SELECT statement shows these statistics in the order they are requested:

150000	40000	60000	50000

(2) The number of people earning over 50000 is counted using COUNT(*). Of those people, the average Salary is calculated after a 10% increase is applied.

```
SELECT COUNT(*), AVG(Salary * 1.10)
  FROM Prod.dept_general_info
  WHERE Salary > 50000;
```

The result of this SELECT statement shows these statistics in the order they are requested:

3	64166.67

(3) The number of unique values of Dept having people who earn more than 50000 is counted using the COUNT(DISTINCT column) function. The maximum Salary of those people earning more than 50000 is also found.

```
SELECT COUNT(DISTINCT Dept), MAX(Salary)
  FROM Prod.dept_general_info
  WHERE Salary > 50000 ;
```

The result of this SELECT statement shows these statistics in the order they are requested:

3	60000

Dates and Times

The date and time functions covered in this section are for dates and times in the Release 1.3 format. Systems developed prior to the installation of Release 1.3 may contain dates and times stored as numeric data. Even though your company may be running under a release after 1.3, it is very likely that dates and times on systems developed prior to that installation were not converted to the new date/time formats. The user should be aware of this and handle processing of dates and times appropriately.

Prior to Release 1.3, dates and times were stored as numerics. Dates were normally stored in the form YYYYMMDD so that sorting could be performed. Other date processing, such as finding a duration, could not be performed within DB2 without extensive routines. Using SAS/DB2 with dates not in Release 1.3 format is not a problem because the user can convert the DB2 dates to SAS dates prior to performing any date logic. This will be illustrated in succeeding chapters.

When date/time values are extracted from a DB2 table, they are presented as a character string. The format of that character string is set by the System Administrator when DB2 is installed. There are four formats; ISO (International Standards Organization), USA, EUR (European), and JIS (Japanese). The most commonly used format is ISO. The ISO and USA formats are:

	ISO	USA
DATE	YYYY-MM-DD	MM/DD/YYYY
TIME	HH.MM.SS	HH:MM AM/PM

SAS/DB2 assumes that DB2 dates and times have been stored in the ISO format. If your company has selected a different format, a zap must be applied to the SAS/DB2 software in order to use these dates/times. If you extract date/time columns from a DB2 table and all the values are missing, chances are your company has installed DB2 with a format other than ISO. Contact the SAS Consultant at your company to have the zap applied.

The following SELECT statement illustrates the selection of a specific date in the WHERE clause:

```
SELECT First, Last
  FROM Prod.dept_general_info
  WHERE Hiredate = '1985-06-17';
```

DB2 can reference the system clock to obtain today's date and time through the keywords, CURRENT DATE, CURRENT TIME, and CURRENT TIMESTAMP.

The following date and time functions are available in DB2. The capabilities are very similar to those available for SAS dates. As in SAS, this capability is based on the way date/time values are stored internally. For example, a DB2 date is stored as the number of days since 12/31/00, whereas SAS dates are represented as the number of days since 1/1/60. This representation enables the user to perform arithmetic calculations on date/time values.

DATE	Converts a timestamp, a character string, or a positive number to a character date.	
	Examples:	DATE('1989-12-22-11.23.31') = 1989-12-22
		DATE('1937033') = 1937-02-02
		DATE(15) = 0001-01-15
		(15 days after 12/31/00)
DAY		The day of the month
MONTH		The month of the year
YEAR		The four position year
DAYS		The number of days since 12/31/00
HOUR		The hour

MINUTE	The minute of the hour
SECOND	The second of the minute
MICROSECOND	The microseconds of the seconds
TIME	Converts a timestamp or a character string to time.
TIMESTAMP	Converts a character string to timestamp format.

(1) The following SELECT statement illustrates the YEAR function to select only those employees who were hired in 1979 or later:

```
SELECT First, Last, Dept
  FROM Prod.dept_general_info
  WHERE YEAR(Hiredate) >= 1979;
```

For dates stored in a numeric format (YYYYMMDD) prior to Release 1.3, the same results could be performed with the following SELECT statement:

```
SELECT First, Last, Dept
  FROM Prod.dept_general_info
  WHERE Hiredate >= 19790101;
```

(2) The DAYS function converts dates to the number of days since 12/31/00 and can be used to find the number of days between two dates. Although not too practical, the following example shows the number of days between 01/01/89 and the Hiredate:

```
SELECT First, Last, DAYS('1989-01-01') - DAYS(Hiredate) FROM
  Prod.dept_general_info
  WHERE YEAR(Hiredate) >= 1979;
```

(3) The following SELECT statement illustrates using the CURRENT DATE and the YEAR function to calculate the length of service in years.

```
SELECT First, Last, YEAR(CURRENT DATE - Hiredate)
  FROM Prod.dept_general_info;
```

The ORDER BY Clause

The ORDER BY clause is used to name one or more columns by which the result table will be sorted. The ORDER BY clause must be coded as the last clause in the SELECT statement.

The ORDER BY clause performs the same function as PROC SORT in Base SAS. By default, the ORDER BY clause sorts in ascending order. To sort in descending order the DESC option is coded after the column to which it applies. When using PROC SORT by contrast, the DESCENDING option is coded prior to the variable to which it applies.

The following examples illustrate the ORDER BY clause:

PROD.DEPT_GENERAL_INFO

First	Dept	Floor	Salary	Mgr
MILTON	120	1	55000	Y
MARTHA	130	1	60000	N
MARY LEA	130	1	50000	N
MARLIN	140	2	60000	Y
MIRON	140	2	50000	N
MARVIN	140	2	40000	N

(1) The following SELECT statement uses the ORDER BY clause to sort the result table by Salary and the WHERE clause to select only non-management staff:

```
SELECT First, Salary, Mgr
  FROM Prod.dept_general_info
  WHERE Mgr = 'N'
  ORDER BY salary;
```

This SELECT statement produces the following result table:

MARVIN	40000	N
MARY LEA	50000	N
MIRON	50000	N
MARTHA	60000	N

(2) The following SELECT statement uses the ORDER BY clause to sort the result table first by Mgr and then by descending Salary:

```
SELECT First, Salary, Mgr
  FROM Prod.dept_general_info
  ORDER BY Mgr, Salary DESC;
```

This SELECT statement produces the following result table:

MARTHA	60000	N
MARY LEA	50000	N
MIRON	50000	N
MARVIN	40000	N
MARLIN	60000	Y
MILTON	55000	Y

(3) The following SELECT statement uses the ORDER BY clause to sort the result table by salary * 1.10. This column does not exist on the DB2 table, so it cannot be referenced by name. Instead, it is referenced in the ORDER BY clause based on its location in the SELECT clause. It is the second variable named, so a 2 is used in the ORDER BY clause. Location numbers can also be used in the ORDER BY clause for DB2 columns rather than coding the full column name.

```
SELECT First, Salary * 1.10
  FROM Prod.dept_general_info
  ORDER BY 2;
```

This SELECT statement produces the following result table:

MARVIN	40000
MARY LEA	50000
MIRON	50000
MILTON	55000
MARTHA	60000
MARLIN	60000

The GROUP BY Clause

The GROUP BY clause is used to name one or more existing DB2 columns which will be used to group multiple rows on a DB2 table to produce a single row on the result table. The result table will contain a row for every unique value of the column(s) named in the GROUP BY clause. Columns defined as LONG VARCHAR cannot be used in the GROUP BY clause.

The columns named in the GROUP BY clause can be compared to the variables named in the CLASS statement when using the Base SAS procedure, PROC SUMMARY. The GROUP BY does not produce different types of summaries such as summaries by two columns, summaries by the first column and not the second, summaries by the second and not the first, and grand summaries like PROC SUMMARY does. The GROUP BY can be compared to PROC SUMMARY with the NWAY option, which produces only those summaries by all variables named in the CLASS statement.

When the GROUP BY clause is used, the result table represents a summary of the DB2 table being processed. Columns named in the GROUP BY clause must also be named in the SELECT clause in order to be passed to the result table. Columns requested in the SELECT clause, other than those also named in the GROUP BY clause, must represent a calculated value. The functions, SUM, MIN, MAX, and AVG must be used to combine values on the incoming DB2 table to produce a single value on the result table. This is similar to PROC SUMMARY, where statistics are named in the OUTPUT OUT statement.

When a column named in the GROUP BY clause contains NULL values, the result table contains a single row with a NULL value. NULL becomes a group. With PROC SUMMARY, the MISSING option must be used for a missing value of the CLASS statement to appear on the output SAS data set.

The following examples illustrate the GROUP BY clause:

PROD.DEPT_GENERAL_INFO

First	Dept	Floor	Salary	Mgr
MILTON	120	1	55000	Y
MARTHA	130	1	60000	N
MARY LEA	130	1	50000	N
MARLIN	140	2	60000	Y
MIRON	140	2	50000	N
MARVIN	140	2	40000	N

(1) The following SELECT statement illustrates a GROUP BY clause to produce a result table which contains the SUM and the AVG Salary per Dept:

```
SELECT Dept, SUM(Salary), AVG(Salary)
  FROM Prod.dept_general_info
  GROUP BY Dept;
```

This SELECT statement produces the following result table, showing the columns in the order they are specified in the SELECT clause:

120	55000	55000
130	115000	55000
140	150000	50000

If the DB2 table, Prod.dept_general_info, were a SAS data set named General, the following PROC SUMMARY would produce the same results:

```
PROC SUMMARY DATA=General NWAY;
  CLASS Dept;
```

```
VAR Salary;
OUTPUT OUT = Gensum
 SUM(Salary) = Sumsal
 MEAN(Salary) = Meansal;
```

(2) The following SELECT uses the GROUP BY clause to produce a result table which contains the MAX and the AVG Salary for each combination of Dept and Mgr for values of Dept other than 120. Note that the WHERE clause must be coded prior to the GROUP BY clause.

```
SELECT Dept, Mgr, MAX(Salary), AVG(Salary)
  FROM Prod.dept_general_info
  WHERE Dept ¬= '120'
  GROUP BY Dept, Mgr;
```

This SELECT statement produces the following result table, showing the columns in the order they are specified in the SELECT clause:

130	N	60000	55000
140	Y	60000	60000
140	N	50000	45000

If the DB2 table were a SAS data set named General, a subsetting statement or DELETE statement would be used to delete Dept 120. Then the following PROC SUMMARY would produce the same results:

```
PROC SUMMARY DATA=General NWAY;
  CLASS Dept Mgr;
  VAR Salary;
  OUTPUT OUT = Gensum
   MAX(Salary) = Maxsal
   MEAN(Salary) = Meansal ;
```

The HAVING Clause

The HAVING clause can be used with the GROUP BY clause to specify criteria which must be met by the group in order for that group to be included on the result table. When a WHERE clause is used with a GROUP BY clause, it is used to specify criteria which must be met by a single row in order to be considered eligible for group processing. In some applications, the WHERE and HAVING clauses produce the same results.

The HAVING clause must be coded immediately after the GROUP BY clause. Like the WHERE clause, comparison operators, logical operators, arithmetic operators, and functions can be used to specify the selection criteria.

The following examples illustrate the HAVING clause:

PROD.DEPT_GENERAL_INFO

First	Dept	Floor	Salary	Mgr
MILTON	120	1	55000	Y
MARTHA	130	1	60000	N
MARY LEA	130	1	50000	N
MARLIN	140	2	60000	Y
MIRON	140	2	50000	N
MARVIN	140	2	40000	N

(1) The following SELECT statement uses the GROUP BY clause to produce a summary result table by Dept and the HAVING clause to select only those values of Dept with an average Salary greater than 50000. This example is like example 1 in the previous section on the GROUP BY clause. The use of the HAVING clause deletes Dept 140, which had an average Salary of exactly 50000.

```
SELECT Dept, SUM(Salary), AVG(Salary)
  FROM Prod.dept_general_info
  GROUP BY Dept
  HAVING AVG(Salary) > 50000;
```

This SELECT statement produces the following result table:

120	55000	55000
130	115000	55000

(2) The following SELECT statement is like the previous example except that a WHERE clause is also used to select only those staff members who are non-management.

```
SELECT Dept, SUM(Salary), AVG(Salary)
  FROM Prod.dept_general_info
  WHERE Mgr = 'N'
  GROUP BY Dept
  HAVING AVG(Salary) > 50000;
```

Prior to the HAVING selection the following rows exist:

130	110000	55000
140	90000	45000

After the HAVING selection, the final result table is:

130	110000	55000

The UNION Keyword

The UNION keyword is used to combine the result tables from more than one SELECT statement into a single result table. UNION can be used to combine result tables based on different DB2 tables or on the same DB2 table. The UNION can operationally use a lot of computer resources. Before executing a UNION, verify (by using the EXPLAIN statement) that indexes are being used, and that if a tablespace scan is used, it is used only on small tables.

The UNION in SQL is similar to the Base SAS procedure, PROC APPEND. PROC APPEND combines two SAS data sets into a single SAS data set. PROC APPEND can be executed multiple times to combine more than two SAS data sets.

When the final results table is created, any duplicate rows are eliminated by default. If duplicates are to be saved, use UNION ALL rather than UNION.

The SELECT list of columns in each of the SELECT statements combined by the UNION should be identical and the columns should have the same data type and length. Some data conversions can be made, but you are best to avoid this due to computer resource utilization.

If the final result table needs to be sorted, code the ORDER BY clause only in the last SELECT statement. Also, ORDER BY must specify the number representing the position of the column in the

SELECT list. The column name cannot be used in the ORDER BY clause with a UNION.

A single semicolon (;) should be coded at the end of the last SELECT statement.

The following examples illustrate the UNION keyword:

PROD.DEPT_GENERAL_INFO

First	Dept	Floor	Salary	Mgr
MILTON	120	1	55000	Y
MARTHA	130	1	60000	N
MARY LEA	130	1	50000	N
MARLIN	140	2	60000	Y
MIRON	140	2	50000	N
MARVIN	140	2	40000	N

The first SELECT statement selects Dept 120 and the second SELECT statement selects employees with a Salary greater than 50000. The first row, MILTON, meets both these criteria, but duplicates are eliminated by the UNION.

```
SELECT First, Salary
  FROM Prod.dept_general_info
  WHERE Dept = '120'
UNION
SELECT First, Salary
  FROM Prod.dept_general_info
  WHERE Salary > 50000;
```

This SELECT statement produces the following result table:

MILTON	55000
MARTHA	60000
MARLIN	60000

Joining Tables

The JOIN operation of relational database management systems was covered in Chapter 2, The Relational Model. The information covered there should be clear in your mind before continuing in this section. A brief summary of the key points is given here.

Tables are joined through the use of primary and foreign keys. A primary key consists of one or more columns which uniquely define a row. A foreign key consists of the same data as the primary key, but is stored on a different table. By matching the values of primary and foreign keys, DB2 tables can be joined.

Operationally, the join operation consists of three parts: the CARTESIAN PRODUCT, SELECTION, and PROJECTION. The CARTESIAN PRODUCT is the combination of every row on one table with every other row on every other table. For example, the CARTESIAN PRODUCT of two DB2 tables, one with 5 rows and the other with 10 rows, is 5 * 10 or 50 rows. SELECTION is the process of selecting those rows within the CARTESIAN PRODUCT whose primary and foreign keys match. The SELECTION process does not happen automatically. The user must code this selection in the SQL WHERE clause. PROJECTION is the process of selecting the desired columns for the result table. This is done by coding the column list in the SELECT clause.

When joining two DB2 tables there are four possible combinations of matching primary and foreign keys: one to one, one to many, many to one, and many to many. One to one means there is only one occurrence on both DB2 tables of the primary and foreign keys, so the match takes place one to one. Many to one or one to many results in the one occurrence being matched to all the many occurrences. The result of a many-to-many join is the CARTESIAN PRODUCT. For example, if one DB2 table had three occurrences and the other had two occurrences, the result table would have six occurrences. This is different from the SAS MERGE which would result in three occurrences, the first two matched one to one and the third matched repeatedly with the second.

When DB2 tables are joined, the word JOIN does not actually appear in the SQL code. The DB2 tables to be joined are all specified in the FROM clause, separated by commas. The desired columns for each are listed together in the SELECT list in any order. If columns from more than one table have the same column name, then the column specification must include the table name or a qualifier assigned to the table name. This will be illustrated in examples which follow. The SELECT statement must also include a WHERE clause that specifies which column or columns on the tables should match. Without the WHERE clause the result table will be the CARTESIAN PRODUCT.

The following examples illustrate the JOIN operation:

PROD.DEPT_GENERAL_INFO

First	Dept	Floor	Salary	Mgr
MILTON	120	1	55000	Y
MARTHA	130	1	60000	N
MARY LEA	130	1	50000	N
MARLIN	140	2	60000	Y
MIRON	140	2	50000	N
MARVIN	140	2	40000	N

PROD.DEPT_NAMES

Deptnum	Deptname
120	FINANCE
130	PERSONNEL
140	MARKETING

(1) The following SELECT statement joins two DB2 tables by matching the primary key, Deptnum from Prod.dept_names, to the foreign key, Dept from Prod.dept_general_info. Since none of the DB2 columns selected from the two tables have the same name, DB2 knows where to access the data. The WHERE clause selects only those rows where Dept is equal to Deptnum from the CARTESIAN PRODUCT (6*3=18 rows).

```
SELECT First, Floor, Dept, Deptname
  FROM Prod.dept_general_info, Prod.dept_names
  WHERE Dept = Deptnum ;
```

This SELECT statement produces the following result table:

MILTON	1	120	FINANCE
MARTHA	1	130	PERSONNEL
MARY LEA	1	130	PERSONNEL
MARLIN	2	140	MARKETING
MIRON	2	140	MARKETING
MARVIN	2	140	MARKETING

(2) Suppose Deptnum from the DB2 table, Prod.dept_names, was named Dept as it is in the other table. To produce the same result as the above example, the table name is specified prior to the column name and separated by a period, as follows:

```
SELECT First, Floor, Prod.dept_general_info.Dept, Deptname
FROM Prod.dept_general_info, Prod.dept_names
WHERE Prod.dept_general_info.Dept = Prod.dept_names.Deptnum ;
```

However, it is probably easier to use qualifiers. Qualifiers are short names that are assigned to the DB2 table names in the FROM clause. The qualifiers can then be used in other SELECT statement clauses to save coding. The following FROM clause assigns a G to the DB2 table, Prod.dept_general_info, and a N to the DB2 table, Prod.dept_names. The G is then used with Dept in the SELECT list and the WHERE clause. The N is used with Deptnum in the WHERE clause.

```
SELECT First, Floor, G.Dept, Deptname
  FROM Prod.dept_general_info G, Prod.dept_names N
  WHERE G.Dept = N.Deptnum ;
```

Specifying column names including either their table name or a qualifier assigned to the table name is good program documentation. Even though they are not needed when column names are unique per table, you should get in the habit of always using them. Your program will be much easier for someone else to read and for you yourself at a later date. The complete use of qualifiers follows:

```
SELECT G.First, G.Floor, G.Dept, N.Deptname
  FROM Prod.dept_general_info G, Prod.dept_names N
  WHERE G.Dept = N.Deptnum ;
```

(3) The following SELECT statement also joins the two DB2 tables, but illustrates that you can include additional selection criteria in the WHERE clause besides the join criteria.

```
SELECT G.First, G.Floor, G.Dept, N.Deptname
  FROM Prod.dept_general_info G, Prod.dept_names N
  WHERE G.Dept = N.Deptnum AND
        (G.Dept = '120' OR G.Dept = '130');
```

This SELECT statement produces the following result table:

MILTON	1	120	FINANCE
MARTHA	1	130	PERSONNEL
MARY LEA	1	130	PERSONNEL

Subselects

Subselects are SELECT statements nested inside other SELECT statements. The nested SELECT statements usually appear in WHERE clauses, but can also appear in HAVING clauses. The nested SELECT statements are enclosed in parentheses and must not contain the UNION keyword or the ORDER BY clause.

Subselects can be very confusing and often use a lot of computer resources because a table will be read multiple times. The user should be aware of the access path prior to running a subselect by using the SQL EXPLAIN statement.

The following table will be used for the examples:

PROD.DEPT_GENERAL_INFO

First	Dept	Floor	Salary	Mgr
MILTON	120	1	55000	Y
MARTHA	130	1	60000	N
MARY LEA	130	1	50000	N
MARLIN	140	2	60000	Y
MIRON	140	2	50000	N
MARVIN	140	2	40000	N

(1) The nested SELECT statement produces a single value, the average Salary of everyone in the table. This value is 52500. The outer SELECT selects employees whose Salary is greater than 52500.

```
SELECT First, Salary
  FROM Prod.dept_general_info
  WHERE Salary > (SELECT AVG(Salary)
                   FROM Prod.dept_general_info);
```

This SELECT statement produces the following result table:

MILTON	55000
MARTHA	60000
MARLIN	60000

(2) The nested SELECT statement produces a table containing a row for every value of Dept, along with the average Salary for that value of Dept. This result is shown. The outer SELECT selects employees whose Salary is greater than ALL of these averages. The keyword, ALL, is then another way of saying, select employees whose Salary is greater than the largest of these Dept averages, which is 55000.

```
SELECT First, Salary
  FROM Prod.dept_general_info
  WHERE Salary > ALL (SELECT AVG(Salary)
                         FROM Prod.dept_general_info
                         GROUP BY Dept);
```

The following is the result of the inside SELECT statement:

55000
55000
50000

The following is the final result table:

MARTHA	60000
MARLIN	60000

(3) The following example is the same as the previous except that the keyword, ANY, is used rather than ALL. The outside SELECT selects those employees whose Salary is greater than ANY of these averages. The keyword, ANY, is then another way of saying, select employees whose Salary is greater than the smallest of these Dept averages, which is 50000.

```
SELECT First, Salary
  FROM Prod.dept_general_info
```

```
WHERE Salary > ANY (SELECT AVG(Salary)
                    FROM Prod.dept_general_info
                    GROUP BY Dept);
```

The following is the final result table:

MILTON	55000
MARTHA	60000
MARLIN	60000

Processing NULL Values

When DB2 columns are defined, they can be defined three ways relative to NULL values:

• NULL	Data value is not required.
• NOT NULL	Data value is required.
• NOT NULL with default	If data are not assigned a value, a default value will be assigned.

This section will describe the processing of DB2 columns that contain NULL values. A NULL value is unknown. It is not 0 or blank. The value may not have been known at the time the row was added to the table.

The following describes the result when NULL values are encountered in operators, functions, and clauses in the SQL SELECT statement:

Comparison Operators	Always results in false condition
Arithmetic Operators	Results in a NULL value
Functions	Not used; ignored
SELECT DISTINCT	Counts one NULL
COUNT(DISTINCT)	Does not count NULLS
COUNT(*)	Counts NULLS; counts all rows
GROUP BY	NULL is a separate group
ORDER BY	Sorts last when ascending

The following examples illustrate the processing of NULL values:

PROD.STUDENT_GENERAL_INFO2

STUDENT	ADDRESS	CLASS	FINAL
JENNY	R.R.#6		98
JOE	113 HOLLY	12	
KELLY	88 CONNER CT	11	88

(1) The following SELECT statement selects rows where Class is not equal to 12. You would think that NULL for JENNY would not be equal to 12 and would therefore be selected. But it is not; NULLS always result in a false condition when used with comparison operators.

```
SELECT Student, Address
  FROM Prod.student_general_info2
  WHERE Class Γ= '12';
```

The following result table is produced:

KELLY	88 CONNER CT

The only way to extract a NULL value is to specify NULL:

```
SELECT student, address
  FROM proc.student_general_info2
  WHERE class IS NULL;
```

The following result table is produced:

JENNY	R.R #6

(2) The following SELECT statement shows that when an arithmetic expression is used on a NULL value, a NULL value results. JOE did not have a value for Final and adding 10 to it still resulted in a NULL.

```
SELECT Student, Final + 10
  FROM Prod.student_general_info2;
```

The following result table is produced:

JENNY	108
JOE	
KELLY	98

(3) The following SELECT statement shows that when a function is used on a NULL value, the NULL value is not used. The average of Final is the average of 98 and 88 only.

```
SELECT AVG(Final)
  FROM Prod.student_general_info2;
```

The following result table is produced:

93

Performance Considerations

The computer resources used by the SELECT statement can be minimized by adhering to a few guidelines. These guidelines include:

- When comparing the value of two columns or comparing the value of one column to a constant, compare like data types.
- When comparing the value of a character column with a character string, make the character string the same length as the column.
- Avoid the use of subselects when possible.
- Avoid the use of arithmetic within a predicate.

The INSERT Statement

The INSERT statement is used to add new rows to a DB2 table or view. The discussion of the INSERT statement here will include only inserting rows in a DB2 table. The INSERT statement can be used to insert rows in a table which is empty, but has been created, or into an existing table. An INSERT statement typically exists for every row to be added to the table and contains the column values for that row. A SELECT statement can also be used in conjunction with the INSERT statement to insert rows in a DB2 table based on rows stored in other DB2 tables. This method will not be addressed in this book, as SAS/DB2 uses data stored in a SAS data set to insert rows in a DB2 table.

The INSERT statement can be generated automatically by PROC DB2LOAD to load observations from a SAS data set into rows in a new DB2 table. The INSERT statement can be generated automatically by PROC DB2UTIL to insert observations from a SAS data set into rows in an existing DB2 table. INSERT statements can also be executed using JCL tailored to your company.

The general form of the INSERT statement for tables is:

```
INSERT INTO table name
  (column 1, column 2, ... column n)
  VALUES (value 1, value 2, ... value n)
```

The table name is the DB2 table to which rows will be added. In parentheses following the table name are the names of the columns in the DB2 table. The values to be inserted in these columns are specified in parentheses following the VALUES clause. The values must be specified in the same order the columns are listed. If more than one row is to be inserted, only the first INSERT statement must specify the DB2 columns. For example, the following three INSERT statements could be used to insert three rows in the DB2 table, Tsid123.projinfo. Notice that character values are padded with blanks to the full length of the column. This is done to increase computer performance.

```
INSERT INTO TSID123.PROJINFO
  (LAST_NAME, FIRST_NAME, BEGIN_DATE, PLAN_END_DATE,
   ACTUAL_END_DATE, PROJECT)
  VALUES('APPLE           ', 'RICHARD   ', 881001., 881201.,
         881201., 'COMPENSATION PLAN   ')
;
INSERT INTO TSID123.PROJINFO
  VALUES('APPLE           ', 'RICHARD   ', 890115., 890301.,
         890301., 'FINANCIAL STATEMENT ')
;
INSERT INTO TSID123.PROJINFO
  VALUES('BAKER           ', 'MARTHA    ', 890715., 890915.,
         890915., 'BROKERS             ')
;
```

The DELETE Statement

The DELETE statement is used to delete rows from a DB2 table. The entire row is deleted, but specific columns within a row cannot be deleted. A WHERE clause is typically used with the DELETE statement to specify criteria to be used for deleting rows. If a WHERE clause is not used, the DELETE statement will delete all rows in the DB2 table. The WHERE clause used in the DELETE statement is the same as the WHERE clause used in the SELECT statement. Refer to the description of the SELECT statement for the proper syntax of the WHERE clause.

The DELETE statement can be generated automatically by the SAS/DB2 procedure, PROC DB2UTIL. The criteria for deletion can be based on column values in the DB2 table or on values stored in a SAS data set. DELETE statements can also be executed using JCL tailored to your company.

The general form of the DELETE statement is:

```
DELETE FROM table name
  WHERE condition;
```

The table name is the DB2 table from which rows will be deleted. The condition describes which rows are to be deleted.

The following example shows a DELETE statement that deletes rows from the DB2 table, Tsid123.projinfo, when the value of the column, Project, is equal to "Brokers." For performance reasons, the value, "Brokers" is padded with blanks to the full length of the column.

```
DELETE FROM TSID123.PROJINFO
  WHERE PROJECT = 'BROKERS    ';
```

The UPDATE Statement

The UPDATE statement is used to change values of columns in a DB2 table. The values of one or more columns can be changed in a single UPDATE statement. A WHERE clause is typically used with the UPDATE statement to specify criteria to be used for selecting the rows to be updated. The WHERE clause used in the UPDATE statement is the same as the WHERE clause used in the SELECT statement. Refer to the description of the SELECT statement for the proper syntax of the WHERE clause.

The UPDATE statement can be generated automatically by the SAS/DB2 procedure, PROC DB2UTIL. The criteria for updating can be based on column values in the DB2 table or on values stored in a SAS data set. UPDATE statements can also be executed using JCL tailored to your company.

The general form of the UPDATE statment is:

```
UPDATE table name
  SET column 1 = value/expression
      column 2 = value/expression
      ...
      column n = value/expression
  WHERE condition;
```

The table name is the DB2 table to be updated. The SET clause names the columns to be updated, followed by an equal sign and the new value or an expression which results in a new value. The WHERE condition describes which rows are to be updated.

The following example shows an UPDATE statement that updates a row on the DB2 table, Tsid123.persinfo. The SET clause updates the column, Vacation_used, by setting it equal to a new value and updates the column, Salary_december, by multiplying the existing value by 1.10. These updates take place for the row satisfied by the WHERE clause. Notice that for performance reasons the values in the WHERE clause are padded with blanks to the full length of the column.

```
UPDATE TSID123.PERSINFO
  SET VACATION_USED = 160
      SALARY_DECEMBER = SALARY_DECEMBER * 1.10
  WHERE LAST_NAME = 'HUTSON ' AND
        FIRST_NAME = 'EVERETT   ';
```

The COMMIT Statement

The COMMIT statement is used to commit changes made by an application to the DB2 table. These changes include creating DB2 objects, dropping DB2 objects, and altering, inserting, deleting, or updating DB2 objects. The COMMIT statement also frees any locks that have been set by the application by the Resource Lock Manager. Refer to the previous chapter in the section, The DB2 Subsystem, for more information about this process.

The COMMIT statement can be generated automatically by PROC DB2LOAD after a specified number of INSERT statements are executed to load a DB2 table with data stored in a SAS data set. The COMMIT statement can be generated automatically by PROC DB2UTIL after a specified number of rows are changed by the INSERT, DELETE, or UPDATE statements used to update a DB2 table using on data stored in a SAS data set.

If COMMIT statements are not used in an application that performs updates, inserts, or deletes, changes will be saved only if the program ends normally. If the program abends or the system goes down while the application is running, no changes will be applied. It is a good practice to use COMMIT statements not only to save changes, but to release locks so that other applications can access objects that were locked by your application.

The form of the COMMIT statement is:

```
COMMIT; or COMMIT WORK;
```

Review

Questions

1. In what ways can SQL statements be executed?
2. If an application required you to create a DB2 table, what must exist prior to creating the table?
3. If a tablespace is dropped, what else is dropped?
4. What SQL statement is most frequently needed by users?
5. What clauses of the SELECT statement are required and what are they used for?
6. What clause is used for row selection?
7. Name the predicates (operators/functions) which can be used in the WHERE clause.
8. How can the result table be sorted by a new value created in the SELECT list?
9. What is the purpose of the GROUP BY clause? What Base SAS procedure produces a similiar result?
10. What clause is used to select the desired groups produced by the GROUP BY clause?
11. How is the SELECT statement coded in order to perform a JOIN?

12. What is the function of the SQL statements, ALTER, INSERT, DELETE, and UPDATE? What SAS/DB2 procedure generates these statements?
13. What value does the COMMIT statement serve?

Answers

1. SQL statements can be executed by third-generation languages such as COBOL and PL/1, by QMF, by SPUFI, SAS/DB2 (and some other fourth generation languages), and through a batch program using JCL tailored to your company. This book will concentrate on execution through SAS/DB2, but will address execution through a batch program as needed.
2. A tablespace must either exist or one must be created to hold the DB2 table.
3. When a tablespace is dropped, all tables in the tablespace are also dropped, along with any indexes, views, or synonyms based on those tables.
4. The SELECT statement is the SQL statement most often used by the user community.
5. The SELECT and the FROM clauses are required in a SELECT statement. The SELECT clause is used to name the desired DB2 columns. The FROM clause is used to name the DB2 table(s) or view(s) containing those columns.
6. The WHERE clause is used to select the desired rows from a DB2 table.
7. Selection criteria used in the WHERE clause can include comparison operators (=, Γ=, <, <=, >, >=), logical operators (AND, OR, NOT), BETWEEN (selecting range of values), IN (selecting list of values), LIKE (selecting a pattern of character values), arithmetic operators (+, -, *, /), the concatenation operator (| | for combining columns and character strings), the SUBSTR function (extracting a portion of a character string), and column functions (MIN, MAX, AVG, SUM).
8. The ORDER BY clause can specify a number representing the location in the SELECT clause. The value in this location will be used for sorting.
9. The GROUP BY clause is used to produce a result table with one row for every value of the column(s) named in the GROUP BY clause. Rows with like values of this column(s) on the Base Table or view are combined into a single value on the result

table. The result table is a summary file, similar to that produced by the Base SAS procedure, PROC SUMMARY.

10. The HAVING clause is used to select the desired groups produced by the GROUP BY clause.
11. The desired columns are coded in the SELECT list. If columns from more than one table have the same name, the table name or a qualifier must be used to designate which table the column is from. The DB2 tables containing the desired columns are listed in the FROM clause, separated by commas. The WHERE clause must be coded to select from the CARTESIAN PRODUCT, those rows where the primary key is equal to the foreign key.
12. The SQL statements, ALTER, INSERT, DELETE, and UPDATE, are all used to make changes to a DB2 table, among other DB2 objects. The ALTER and UPDATE statements are used to add new columns to a DB2 table. The INSERT statement is used to add new rows to a DB2 table. The DELETE statement is used to delete rows from a DB2 table. The UPDATE statement is used to change column values in a DB2 table. The SAS/DB2 procedure, PROC DB2UTIL, generates these statements.
13. The COMMIT statement saves changes to a DB2 table made by an application. It also frees any locks the application has made, making information available to other applications.

Chapter

5

Introduction to SAS/DB2

Most file structures can be accessed directly by Base SAS in a DATA step. A relational DBMS, however, cannot be accessed directly by Base SAS. SAS/DB2 is an interface between the SAS System and the DB2 environment. SAS/DB2 consists of three procedures which can be executed interactively in Display Manager or in line mode, and in batch programs.

With the availability of Display Manager, the interactive line mode is not commonly used and will not be covered in this book. Interactive line mode is driven by statements, as is batch, so refer to chapters covering batch applications of SAS/DB2 if you are interested in interactive line mode. Display Manager offers a much better interactive environment in itself, plus SAS/DB2 in Display Manager is driven by a series of windows that enhance the ease of use. The user has to code only a few statements; everything else is handled through "fill-in-the-blanks" and commands.

The three SAS/DB2 procedures include PROC DB2EXT, PROC DB2LOAD, and PROC DB2UTIL. PROC DB2EXT extracts data stored in DB2 tables and places them in a SAS data set. PROC DB2LOAD creates and loads DB2 tables with data stored in a SAS data set. PROC DB2UTIL is used to add rows to a DB2 table, delete rows from a DB2 table, update column values in a DB2 table, or add new columns to a DB2 table. Also, PROC DB2LOAD and PROC DB2UTIL can be used to execute any SQL statement.

PROC DB2EXT is the most commonly used procedure for SAS users, while PROC DB2LOAD and PROC DB2UTIL perform functions more commonly handled by a DB2 Database Administrator. However, more complex DB2 applications may require you to use PROC DB2LOAD and/or PROC DB2UTIL.

Two chapters will be devoted to each of the SAS/DB2 procedures, one for the Display Manager environment and one for the batch environment. Chapter 12, Advanced Applications, will illustrate more complex applications using a combination of the three SAS/DB2 procedures.

PROC DB2EXT

PROC DB2EXT converts rows and columns from DB2 tables into observations and variables in SAS data sets. Using a procedure rather than a DATA step to create a SAS data set from an external file is an unfamiliar approach. There are pros and cons to using a procedure rather than the DATA step. Procedure steps are easier to code than DATA steps but do not allow as much flexibility in data manipulation. A typical batch-style SAS program that accesses data stored in DB2 tables would have PROC DB2EXT read the DB2 table rather than a DATA step. The remainder of the SAS program is like any other SAS program. Once PROC DB2EXT creates a SAS data set, all the capabilities of the SAS system are at your disposal. Often this SAS data set will be read in a succeeding DATA step for additional processing. It can also be merged with other SAS data sets created from other file structures. This capability is not possible with products such as QMF, which performs strictly on DB2 tables. Other products in the SAS system such as SAS/GRAPH®, SAS/FSP®, and SAS/AF®, among others, can be used in conjunction with SAS/DB2 once a SAS data set is created by PROC DB2EXT.

The process of creating a SAS data set from data stored in a DB2 table includes two intermediate steps. PROC DB2EXT first builds a map which "maps" DB2 columns to SAS variables. The map includes default SAS variable names consisting of the first eight positions of the eighteen position DB2 column name. The map also assigns standard character and standard numeric formats to the SAS variables. These default variable names and formats can be changed by the user as needed. The map then constructs the appropriate SQL SELECT statement. The SELECT statement extracts the required data from the DB2 table(s). The following diagram illustrates this process:

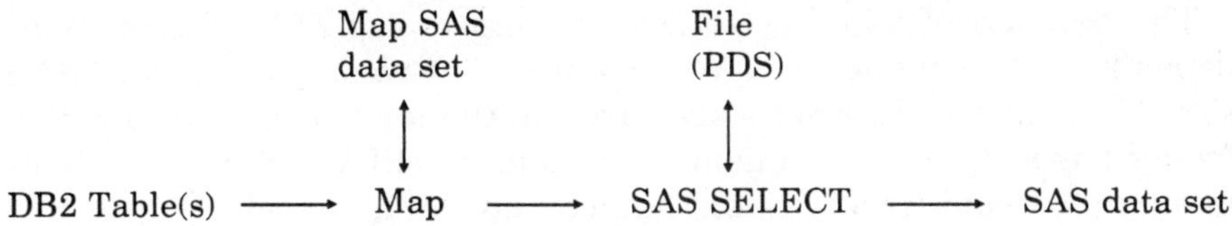

The creation of the map and the SELECT statement can happen behind the scenes, with the user seeing only the end result, the SAS data set created from a single execution of PROC DB2EXT. However, depending on the options used, a single execution of PROC DB2EXT can also be used to produce only the map or only the SELECT statement generated by the map. This map or SELECT statement can then be used as input in subsequent executions of PROC DB2EXT to complete the process, the creation of a SAS data set. The diagram above shows that not only are the map and the SELECT statement created by PROC DB2EXT, but they can also be input to PROC DB2EXT.

When PROC DB2EXT is used to create and save a map, the map is stored as a SAS data set. The mapping SAS data set is usually a permanent SAS data set so that it is available for use in subsequent programs. It is stored in a SAS data library with MEMTYPE=DATA, along with other types of SAS files.

When PROC DB2EXT is used to create and save a SELECT statement, the SELECT statement is generated by a map and/or user coding. A map does not have the capability to generate a SELECT statement that includes all of the clauses, functions, and operators covered in the previous chapter, Structured Query Language. When additional capabilities are needed, the user has the option of coding the entire SELECT statement or editing the one generated by the map. The SELECT statement is stored in an external file, usually as a member of a partitioned data set.

Creating a SAS data set uses more computer resources than creating and saving maps and SELECT statements, particularly when the input DB2 table(s) is large and/or has to be read sequentially (tablespace scan). Maps and SELECT statements can be created and saved in Display Manager, but there may not be enough computer resources in Display Manager to create the SAS data set. To take advantage of the ease of use of PROC DB2EXT in Display Manager, maps and SELECT statements can be created and saved in Display Manager and then used as input to PROC DB2EXT in a batch program.

The decision of whether to save a map or a SELECT statement depends on the application. When a map is saved, user-defined SAS variable names and formats are saved in the map. The map can then be used as input in subsequent executions of PROC DB2EXT without having to assign SAS variable names and formats each time. A SELECT statement cannot produce user-defined SAS variable names and formats. A SELECT statement generated by a map can be edited by the user to take advantage of the enhanced features of the SELECT statement. A SELECT statement can also be coded entirely by the user. Once this has been done, the SELECT statement can be saved and used in subsequent executions of PROC DB2EXT without having to recreate the same SELECT statement each time. A map cannot produce a SELECT statement using the enhanced features of the SELECT statement.

Both a map and a SELECT statement can be used as input to PROC DB2EXT in batch (not in Display Manager), but care must be taken to insure they are consistent. Both must request the same DB2 columns and contain the same WHERE clause, if a WHERE clause is used. More often, when user-defined SAS variable names and formats are needed in addition to the enhanced features of the SELECT statement, a SELECT statement is saved and used as input to PROC DB2EXT along with other PROC DB2EXT statements used to rename and format SAS variables. For that reason, the use of both a map and a SELECT statement as input to PROC DB2EXT will not be covered.

PROC DB2LOAD

PROC DB2LOAD is used to create and load a DB2 table using data stored in a SAS data set. PROC DB2LOAD can also be used to execute utility-type SQL statements such as creating an index or dropping a DB2 table.

The process of creating and loading a DB2 table with data stored in a SAS data set includes two intermediate steps, as does PROC DB2EXT. PROC DB2LOAD first builds a map which "maps" SAS variables to DB2 columns. The map includes default DB2 column names and data types. The default column names are the SAS variable names. The default DB2 data types are CHAR for SAS character variables and FLOAT for numeric variables. These default DB2 column names and data types can be changed by the user as needed.

The map then constructs the appropriate SQL statements which include the CREATE, INSERT, and COMMIT statements. The CRE-

ATE statement creates the DB2 table; a DB2 table already created, but empty, cannot be loaded using PROC DB2LOAD. The INSERT statement loads observations stored in a SAS data set into rows in a DB2 table. An INSERT statement is generated for every observation in the SAS data set and contains the values of the SAS variables. The COMMIT statement, by default, is executed for every three rows loaded into the DB2 table; that is, for every three INSERT statements. This saves the rows on the DB2 table and releases them for access by other applications. The user has the capability to set the number of INSERT statements executed before a COMMIT statement is executed.

The following diagram illustrates the process of executing PROC DB2LOAD:

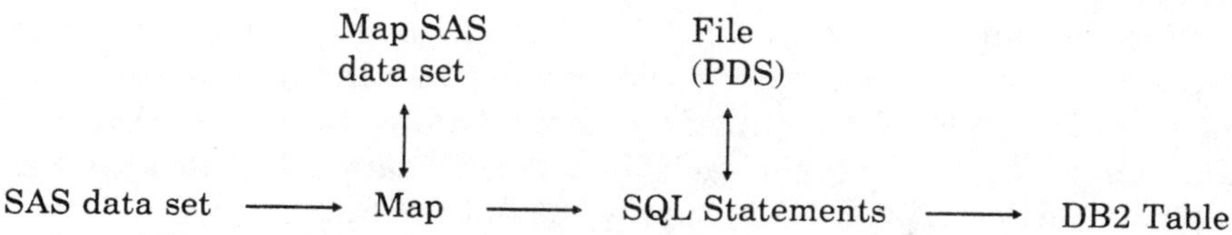

The creation of the map and SQL statements can happen behind the scenes with the user seeing only the end result, the DB2 table created from a single execution of PROC DB2LOAD. However, depending on the options used, a single execution of PROC DB2LOAD can also be used to produce only the map or only the SQL statements generated by the map. This map or these SQL statements can then be used as input to subsequent executions of PROC DB2LOAD to complete the process of creating and loading the DB2 table. The diagram above shows that not only are the map and the SQL statements created by PROC DB2LOAD, but they can also be input to PROC DB2LOAD.

When PROC DB2LOAD is used to create and save a map, the map is stored as a SAS data set. The mapping SAS data set is usually a permanent SAS data set so that it is available for use in subsequent programs. It is stored in a SAS data library with MEMTYPE=DATA, along with other types of SAS files.

When PROC DB2LOAD is used to create and save SQL statements, the SQL statements, CREATE, INSERT, and COMMIT are generated and saved to an external file. This external file is usually a partitioned data set. Because an INSERT statement exists for every SAS observation and because they contain variable values, the size of the external file used to store the saved SQL statements can be quite large.

PROC DB2LOAD can also be used to execute any SQL statement. These are usually utility-type SQL statements such as creating an index or dropping a table. These SQL statements can also be executed by PROC DB2UTIL or by using JCL tailored to your company or by PROC DB2UTIL.

Creating and loading a DB2 table with data stored in a SAS data set consumes more computer resources than saving maps and SQL statements, particularly when the input SAS data set is large. Maps and SQL statements can be created and saved in Display Manager, but there may not be enough computer resources in Display Manager to create and load the DB2 table. To take advantage of the ease of use of PROC DB2LOAD in Display Manager, maps and SQL statements can be created and saved in Display Manager and then used as input to PROC DB2LOAD in a batch program.

When a map is saved, user-defined DB2 column names and data types are saved. The map can then be used as input in subsequent executions of PROC DB2LOAD without having to assign DB2 column names and data types each time. A SAS data set is also used as input to PROC DB2LOAD to supply the data to be loaded.

When SQL statements are saved, they are typically saved to provide the user with the ability to view them prior to execution and to have as a source for problem solving after execution. They are then input to PROC DB2LOAD in a batch program and deleted. SQL statements used to create and load a DB2 table are typically not used more than once because the INSERT statements contain data values which are subject to change. A SAS data set is not used as input to PROC DB2LOAD in addition to the SQL statements because the SQL statements already contain the data values from the SAS data set.

Both a map and SQL statements cannot be used as input to PROC DB2LOAD.

PROC DB2UTIL

PROC DB2UTIL can be used to insert rows in a DB2 table, delete rows from a DB2 table, update column values in a DB2 table, or add new columns to a DB2 table. These functions are typically performed based on data stored in a SAS data set. In addition, PROC DB2UTIL can be used to execute utility-type SQL statements such as creating an index or dropping a DB2 table.

A single execution of PROC DB2UTIL can perform only one of these functions. If rows are to be inserted in a DB2 table, the SQL INSERT statement is used. If rows are to be deleted from a DB2 table, the SQL DELETE statement is used. If column values are to be changed, the SQL UPDATE statement is used. If new columns are to be added, the SQL ALTER and UPDATE statements are used. The COMMIT statement is also used with each of these statements to save changes to the DB2 table and make them available to other applications.

The process of inserting, deleting, or updating a DB2 table or adding new columns to a DB2 table with data stored in a SAS data set includes two intermediate steps, as does DB2EXT and DB2LOAD. PROC DB2UTIL first builds a map which "maps" SAS variables to DB2 columns so that the updates are applied to the appropriate columns. A WHERE clause is usually used when deleting or updating so that the SAS observations are matched with the proper DB2 rows. The map then constructs the appropriate SQL statements, which include the INSERT, DELETE, UPDATE, or ALTER and UPDATE statements, along with COMMIT statements. The following diagram illustrates this process:

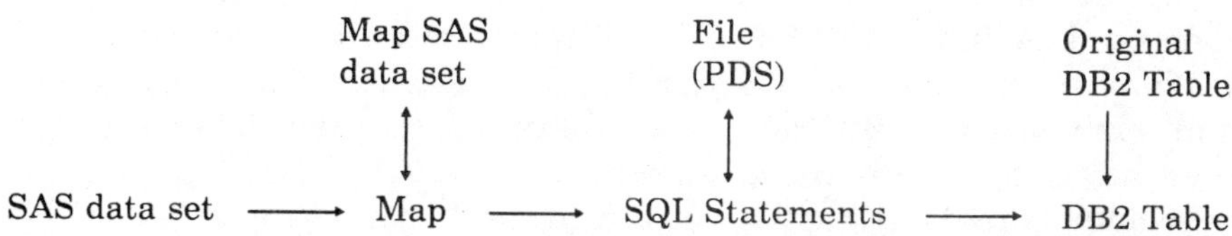

The creation of the map and SQL statements can happen behind the scenes with the user seeing only the end result, the DB2 table updated from a single execution of PROC DB2UTIL. However, depending on the options used, a single execution of PROC DB2UTIL can also be used to produce only the map or only the SQL statements generated by the map. This map or these SQL statements can then be used as input to subsequent executions of PROC DB2UTIL to complete the process, applying changes to the DB2 table. The diagram above shows that not only are the map and the SQL statements created by PROC DB2UTIL, but they can also be input to PROC DB2UTIL.

When PROC DB2UTIL is used to create and save a map, the map is stored as a SAS data set. The mapping SAS data set is usually a permanent SAS data set so that it is available for use in subsequent programs. It is stored in a SAS data library as a MEMTYPE DATA, along with other types of SAS files.

When PROC DB2UTIL is used to create and save SQL statements, the SQL statements, INSERT, DELETE, UPDATE, or ALTER and UPDATE are generated and saved to an external file. This external file is usually a partitioned data set. If several updates are needed, the size of the external file used to store the SQL statements can be quite large.

PROC DB2UTIL can also be used to execute any SQL statement. These are usually utility-type SQL statements such as creating an index or dropping a table. These SQL statements can also be executed by PROC DB2LOAD or by using JCL tailored to your company or by PROC DB2LOAD.

Updating a DB2 table with data stored in a SAS data set consumes more computer resources than saving maps and SQL statements, particularly when several updates need to be made. Maps and SQL statements can be created and saved in Display Manager, but there may not be enough computer resources in Display Manager to actually apply the updates to the DB2 table. To take advantage of the ease of use of PROC DB2UTIL in Display Manager, maps and SQL statements can be created and saved in Display Manager and then used as input to PROC DB2UTIL in a batch program.

When a map is saved, instructions for matching SAS observations and variables to DB2 rows and columns are saved. The map can then be used in subsequent executions of PROC DB2UTIL without developing these instructions again. A SAS data set is usually also used as input to PROC DB2UTIL to provide new data values.

When SQL statements are saved, instructions for matching SAS observations and variables to DB2 rows and columns are converted to SQL statements and SAS variable values are placed in these SQL statements. When SQL statements are saved, they are typically saved to provide the user with the ability to view them prior to execution and to have as a source for problem solving after execution. They are then input to PROC DB2UTIL in a batch program and deleted. SQL statements used to update a DB2 table are typically not used more than once because once the changes have been applied, they will not be applied again. A SAS data set is not used as input to PROC DB2UTIL in addition to the SQL statements because the SQL statements already contain the data values from the SAS data set.

Both a map and SQL statements cannot be used as input to PROC DB2UTIL.

Interface to SAS/FSP

The SAS/FSP (Full Screen Product) procedures, PROC FSEDIT and PROC FSBROWSE, are used to edit and browse, respectively, data stored in SAS data sets. The procedures are interactive and are executed through a TSO CLIST, in line mode, or, through Display Manager. One observation at a time is displayed on the screen, showing the SAS variable names and their values.

If your company has the SAS/FSP product, you can edit and browse DB2 tables directly using PROC FSEDIT and PROC FSBROWSE, respectively. The coding of these procedures is very straightforward and they operate almost identically to their use with SAS data sets. These procedures will be illustrated with a DB2 table in Chapter 13, The SAS/FSP Interface.

Operational Considerations

When using SAS/DB2, as with any other software, you should be aware of the operational aspects, such as computer resource requirements and error handling. This section will discuss these aspects.

SELECT With PROC DB2EXT Versus Base SAS

Many of the capabilities of the SELECT statement can also be performed using Base SAS against the SAS data set created by PROC DB2EXT. The following chart lists the function of each of the clauses in the SELECT statement along with the equivalent SAS procedure or statement:

SELECT Clause	*DB2 Function*	*SAS Equivalent*
SELECT	Select DB2 columns	None; use SELECT
SELECT	Create new columns	Assignment Statement
FROM	Name DB2 table(s)	None; use SELECT
WHERE	Select rows Subsetting	IF/DELETE Statement
GROUP BY	Summarize	PROC SUMMARY/FIRST. & LAST. Variables
HAVING	Select summarized rows	Subsetting IF/DELETE Statement
ORDER BY	Sort	PROC SORT

When computer resource utilization is taken into consideration, a rule of thumb is to use the SELECT statement when possible and use Base SAS when the SELECT statement cannot accomplish the desired result.

The following lists some operations that should be performed using the SELECT statement and why:

- The WHERE and HAVING clauses should be used to select rows meeting certain criteria. This will reduce the size of the SAS data set being created, thus reducing the amount of storage space required. It will also save processing observations which will ultimately be deleted.
- The GROUP BY clause should be used to summarize DB2 table(s). This will reduce the size of the SAS data set being created, and avoid using PROC SUMMARY or some other method of summarizing the data.
- When possible, create new columns through the use of arithmetic operators in the SELECT statement. This may save processing the SAS data set in order to create new variables.
- The ORDER BY should be used for sorting the rows in a DB2 table. However, there may not be much difference in computer utilization compared to PROC SORT.

The following lists some operations that should be performed using Base SAS against the SAS data set created by PROC DB2EXT:

- When conditional processing is required, Base SAS is the answer. Use the Base SAS statements including IF, THEN, ELSE, DO, END, etc. The SELECT statement is really not designed for conditional processing.
- You may have to use PROC SUMMARY or another SAS procedure to generate any statistics that are required. The SELECT statement can only calculate minimum, maximum, average, and sum. However, if the DB2 table(s) are large, you may run into resource problems relative to temporary storage.
- If you see that the SAS data set created by PROC DB2EXT is not exactly what you want, you may be able to use Base SAS to meet your requirements rather than recreating the SAS data set. For example, SAS variable names and formats can be changed in Base SAS. Don't forget to assign a SAS date format. If a SAS date is assigned in PROC DB2EXT, two operations are performed; the value is converted to a SAS date (the number of days since 1/1/60) and the value is formatted. Using Base SAS, the INPUT and PUT

functions can be used to create a SAS date and a FORMAT statement used to assign an output format.

Display Manager

Most companies have either guidelines or constraints set so that the use of interactive resources is kept at some acceptable level. You should be aware of what guidelines you should follow at your company relative to the use of Display Manager.

You should always be able to use Display Manager to create and save maps and SQL statements. However, the creation of SAS data sets using PROC DB2EXT, DB2 tables using PROC DB2LOAD, or updates using PROC DB2UTIL, will probably be limited. Most likely, you will be using Display Manager to create and save maps and SQL statements. These will then be used as input to one of the SAS/DB2 procedures in a batch program.

If your company has test DB2 tables representative of their production counterparts, you will probably want to use these tables for testing your applications. Test tables are usually small enough so that SAS data sets can be created, and DB2 tables can be created or updated in Display Manager.

If you get a DB2 abend while in Display Manager, you may have to exit Display Manager and get back in before you will be able to access DB2 again.

Error Handling

Two kinds of errors can occur when using SAS/DB2 procedures, SQL errors from IBM, and SAS/DB2 errors from SAS.

SQL error numbers are easily recognized because they are negative. Like SAS errors, the error number is displayed along with a brief description of the error. In Display Manager, the error number and description are displayed below the command line. In batch, the error number and description are displayed on the SAS log. When the description is not enough to understand the problem, refer to the IBM publication, IBM DATABASE 2 Messages and Codes (SC26-4113).

When a SQL error occurs, the designated output file (a map, SQL statements, a SAS data set, or a DB2 table) is not created. In a batch program, the program will continue to execute other SAS steps without setting the system option to 0 observations. In other words, if you have DATA steps that are not dependent on the result from the SAS/DB2 procedure, they will execute. An SQL error does not pass a bad condition code, so make sure to review the SAS log.

Each of the SAS/DB2 procedures (DB2EXT, DB2UTIL, and DB2LOAD) have errors specific to that procedure. These errors are not numbered as most SAS errors are. When an error is encountered, the word ERROR appears on the SAS log followed by a description of the error.

Performance Issues

This section will present an overview of performance considerations relative to the SAS/DB2 procedures. It is not intended as a complete discussion of the performances issues associated with DB2, but will provide the user with direction in the use of SAS/DB2.

Knowledge of your DB2 system relative to the tables, their contents, size, column names, and indexes is critical in order to conserve computer resources. When using PROC DB2EXT to extract data stored in DB2 tables, the size of the table is the primary consideration. If the table is large, a tablespace scan (sequential read) should be avoided. Instead, indexes should be used to directly extract the desired rows. The DB2 Optimizer, which determines the access path, will normally use an index if that index is the basis for row selection, as coded in the WHERE clause of the SELECT statement. A SQL EXPLAIN statement can be executed to determine the access path the DB2 Optimizer will use should the SQL SELECT statement be executed. For more information on this topic, refer to Chapter 3, IBM's Database 2, the section, Data Access. Examples of using the SQL EXPLAIN statement are given in Chapter 12, Advanced Applications. The coding of the SELECT statement also impacts the use of computer resources. Refer to Chapter 4, Structured Query Language, the section, The SELECT Statement, for a discussion of these performance considerations.

PROC DB2LOAD uses the SQL statements, CREATE, INSERT, and COMMIT to create and load a DB2 table. PROC DB2UTIL uses the SQL statements, INSERT, DELETE, UPDATE, or ALTER and UPDATE, along with the COMMIT statement, to insert new rows, delete existing rows, update data values, and add new columns, respectively. When these functions are performed by a Database Administrator, DB2 utility functions are used rather than these SQL statements. The DB2 utilities use less computer resources and give the Database Administrator more control over the execution of these functions. I do not recommend the use of PROC DB2LOAD to load large DB2 tables. I do not recommend the use of PROC DB2UTIL to perform extensive updating. These procedures are valuable on a small scale, but large volumes should be performed using DB2 utilities.

The SAS/FSP procedures, PROC FSEDIT and PROC FSBROWSE, can be used to edit and browse DB2 tables, respectively. These procedures should only be used against small DB2 tables. You will experience extremely slow response time when these procedures are used against large DB2 tables. In addition, the use of PROC FSEDIT will cause lockout problems when the DB2 table is accessed by another user.

Review

Questions

1. What are the modes of execution of SAS/DB2?
2. Name the three SAS/DB2 procedures and briefly describe their function.
3. What two intermediate steps are performed by all the SAS/DB2 procedures between the DB2 table and the SAS data set?
4. What takes place when the SAS/DB2 procedures are executed twice in order to produce the final result?
5. What are the advantages of saving maps and SQL statements no matter which SAS/DB2 procedure is used?
6. What SQL statements are automatically constructed by the map for each of the SAS/DB2 procedures?
7. What SAS variable names are automatically created by the map in PROC DB2EXT?
8. If the map in PROC DB2EXT generates the SELECT statement, why should the user have to know how to code SELECT statements?
9. What are the default DB2 column names and data types when PROC DB2LOAD is used to create and load a DB2 table with data stored in a SAS data set?
10. How can utility-type SQL statements be executed?
11. Will the SELECT statement used in PROC DB2EXT satisfy all your reporting and data analysis needs? Why?
12. Can Display Manager be used to execute the SAS/DB2 procedures at all times?

13. Name the two types of errors that can be generated as a result of executing one of the SAS/DB2 procedures.

Answers

1. The SAS/DB2 procedures can be executed in batch, Display Manager, or interactive line mode.
2. PROC DB2EXT is used to extract data stored in DB2 tables and place the result table in a SAS data set. PROC DB2LOAD is used to create and load DB2 tables with data stored in a SAS data set. PROC DB2UTIL inserts rows in a DB2 table, deletes rows from a DB2 table, updates column values in a DB2 table, or adds new columns to a DB2 table. PROC DB2LOAD and PROC DB2UTIL can also execute any SQL statement.
3. A map is created which "maps" rows with observations and columns with variables. The map constructs the appropriate SQL statements, which in turn perform the DB2 function.
4. The SAS/DB2 procedures can be executed so that the final result is produced in a single execution, the final result being a SAS data set for PROC DB2EXT and a DB2 table for PROC DB2LOAD and PROC DB2UTIL. The SAS/DB2 procedures can also be executed twice to produce this final result. The first execution creates and saves either a map or SQL statements. The second execution uses this map or SQL statements as input in order to produce the final result.
5. Creating and saving either maps or SQL statements consumes little computer resources so they can be created in Display Manager. Display Manager is easier to use because little coding is required; panels and "fill-in-the-blanks" are used. The map or the SQL statements can then be used to create either the SAS data set or DB2 table (a SAS data set when using PROC DB2EXT, otherwise a DB2 table) in a batch job. Maps and SQL statements that can be used in more than one subsequent execution of a SAS/DB2 procedure, can be saved and used multiple times without having to develop them for each execution. Saving SQL statements also gives the user a chance to review the statements prior to execution.
6. PROC DB2EXT generates the SELECT statement. PROC DB2LOAD constructs CREATE, INSERT, and COMMIT statements. PROC DB2UTIL produces either the INSERT, DE-

LETE, UPDATE, or ALTER and UPDATE statements, along with the COMMIT statement.

7. SAS variable names consist of the first eight positions of the eighteen position DB2 column name.
8. The SELECT statement generated by the map in PROC DB2EXT cannot utilize many of the capabilities of the SELECT statement. Therefore, the user will often need to edit the SELECT statement generated by the map or code the SELECT statement entirely to take advantage of these additional capabilities.
9. PROC DB2LOAD uses the SAS variable names as DB2 column names. The default DB2 data type for SAS character variables is CHAR and for SAS numeric variables is FLOAT. These can all be changed by the user.
10. SQL utility-type statements such as creating an index, creating a tablespace, or dropping a table, can be executed using PROC DB2LOAD or PROC DB2UTIL in Display Manager or in batch programs. These SQL statements can also be executed using JCL tailored to your company. Using PROC DB2LOAD or PROC DB2UTIL can be convenient if you are already in Display Manager or already executing SAS in a batch program.
11. No. Base SAS has far more capabilities than the SELECT statement. You will be using Base SAS to manipulate the SAS data set created by PROC DB2EXT.
12. Although all the procedures can be executed in Display Manager, computer resource limitations may require some applications to be run as batch programs. This is particularly true when creating a SAS data set using PROC DB2EXT or creating and loading a DB2 table with PROC DB2LOAD.
13. If an error exists in the SELECT statement or other SQL statements, an SQL error is generated from IBM. If an error exists in SAS/DB2 statements other than the SQL statements, a SAS error is generated.

Chapter 6

PROC DB2EXT in Display Manager

PROC DB2EXT is used to create a SAS data set containing data extracted from DB2 table(s). This SAS data set can then be manipulated as needed to produce the desired result.

When a SAS data set is created, one of the following is used as input: a SAS data set, a map, or the SQL SELECT statement. Both a map and a SELECT statement can be used as input as long as they are compatible, but this is typically not done. When only a SAS data set is used as input, a map is generated, and the map generates the appropriate SELECT statement. When a map is used as input, the map generates the appropriate SELECT statement. Whether a SAS data set, a map, or a SELECT statement is used as input, it is ultimately the SQL SELECT statement that extracts the required data from the DB2 table(s).

If a map or SQL statements are used as input to PROC DB2EXT, they were usually created in a previous execution of PROC DB2EXT in Display Manager to take advantage of the ease of use. These maps and SQL statements are typically used as input to PROC DB2EXT in a batch program to create a SAS data set, due to computer resource limitations in Display Manager.

This chapter will present the use of PROC DB2EXT in Display Manager to create a SAS data set containing data extracted from a DB2 table(s) using SELECT statements that can be automatically generated by PROC DB2EXT and using SELECT statements which must be edited or coded by the user. The use of PROC DB2EXT to save a map and use it as input in a subsequent execution of PROC DB2EXT is presented. Also shown is the use of PROC DB2EXT to save a SELECT statement and use it as input in a subsequent execution of PROC DB2EXT. A discussion of when to use a map and when to use SELECT statements is included.

It is assumed that the user is already familiar with the operation of Display Manager and knows how to access it in his company. You will also need to know the value(s) of the DB2 SUBSYSTEM ID. Contact the SAS Consultant at your company for this information. An introduction to PROC DB2EXT was given in Chapter 5, Introduction to SAS/DB2, and this material should be fresh in your mind before beginning this chapter.

Examples given in this section are based on the DB2 tables shown in Appendix C: Sample Tables. Refer to this appendix to familiarize yourself with the sample DB2 tables before proceeding in this chapter. You may choose to follow along in these examples by performing the same operations on the mainframe at your company. These DB2 tables can be entered on your mainframe, or refer to Chapter 1, Introduction, for ordering a copy of these tables.

One of the first operations performed in Display Manager is to allocate any input or output files needed during the Display Manager session. When using PROC DB2EXT, the input files will normally just be DB2 tables. However, the input files could also include a permanent SAS data set containing the map created by PROC DB2EXT in a previous execution or a partitioned data set containing SELECT statements created by either a previous execution of PROC DB2EXT or coded entirely by the user. More often, these previously created maps or SELECT statements are executed in batch to create the SAS data set because of computer resource limitations in an interactive environment such as Display Manager. The output files will be a combination of a permanent SAS data set to store data extracted from DB2 tables, a permanent SAS data set to store the map created by PROC DB2EXT, and a partitioned data set to store SELECT statements generated and/or edited by the user. Again, due to computer resource limitations, the creation of the permanent SAS data set containing data extracted from DB2 tables may have to be executed in batch rather than Display Manager.

TSO allocate statements are used to allocate input and output files needed in a Display Manager session. However, DB2 tables do not have to be allocated. They should be available to your Display Manager session merely by specifying their name. TSO allocate statements should be submitted for permanent SAS data libraries and partitioned data sets. The SAS data libraries will be used to input and output SAS data sets containing data extracted from DB2 tables and/or SAS data sets representing a map. Note that the same SAS data library can contain maps and data SAS data sets. The partitioned data sets will be used for input and output of members containing SQL SELECT statements. One of the forms of a TSO allocate statement is:

```
TSO ALLOC DD(ddname) DSN('data set name') OLD/SHR;
```

Often, X is coded rather than TSO. Ddname is a name of your choice which will be used as a reference to the full file name. The data set name is the name of the SAS data library (excluding SAS data set names in the library) or the name of a partitioned data set (excluding the member names in the data set). The member name can be included in the TSO allocate statement; however, by omitting it, one TSO allocate statement can be used to provide access to all members in the partitioned data set. OLD or SHR is specified as the disposition. OLD gives you exclusive access; no one else can access the data set until you release it from your Display Manager session. OLD must be used with a SAS data library when you intend to output SAS data sets to the library. If SHR is used, other people can read the data set at the same time you are using it. OLD or SHR can be used on partitioned data sets, even when you intend to output to the data set.

After coding the appropriate TSO allocate statements in the PROGRAM window of Display Manager and submitting them, you are ready to access PROC DB2EXT. You are used to coding statements with a SAS procedure, whether the procedure is executed in Display Manager or in batch.

Although PROC DB2EXT can be executed in Display Manager using statements, the real advantage of executing PROC DB2EXT in Display Manager is the availability of a series of panels driven by "fill-in-the-blanks" and commands. PROC DB2EXT statements will be covered in the next chapter, PROC DB2EXT in Batch, and this statement style can also be executed in Display Manager. To access the PROC DB2EXT panels, code and submit the following statements from the PROGRAM window of Display Manager:

```
PROC DB2EXT; RUN:
```

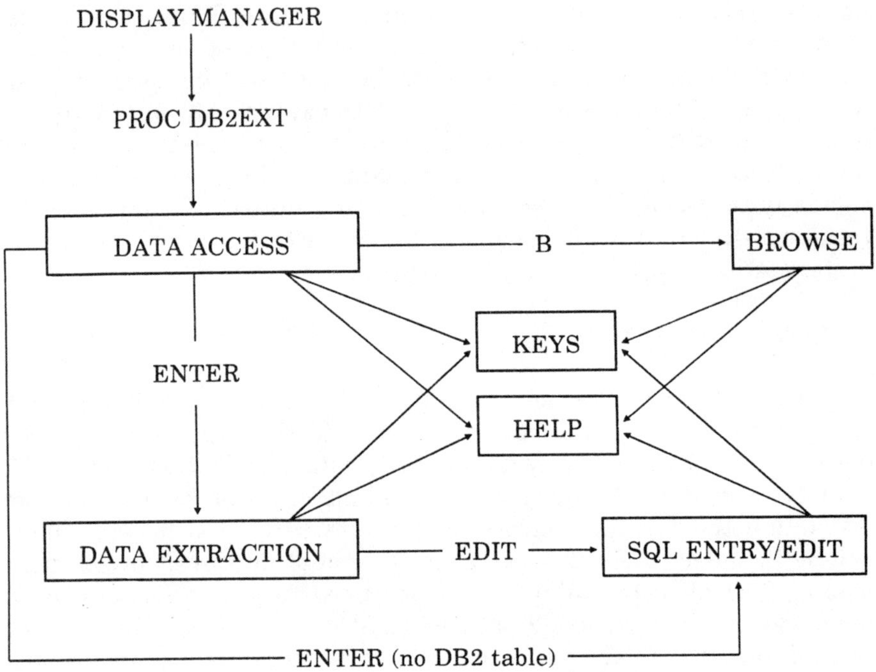

Figure 6-1 Relationship of panels in PROC DB2EXT.

The panels in PROC DB2EXT and their relationship are shown in Figure 6-1. This diagram shows six DB2EXT panels enclosed in boxes: DATA ACCESS, DATA EXTRACTION, SQL ENTRY/EDIT, BROWSE, KEYS, and HELP. The arrows depict the flow going into these panels. The commands or actions to move to these panels are also shown.

The first panel accessed when PROC DB2EXT is executed is the DATA ACCESS panel. Hitting enter takes you from the DATA ACCESS panel to the DATA EXTRACTION panel. If a DB2 table name is not filled in on the DATA ACCESS panel, hitting enter will display the SQL ENTRY/EDIT panel. Hitting enter in itself does not normally perform any action, and the user will have to make sure all the appropriate information has been specified before hitting enter. The EDIT command takes you from the DATA EXTRACTION panel to the SQL ENTRY/EDIT panel. Although not shown, the KEYS command or the HELP command can be specified in any of the four other panels in order to bring up the KEYS or HELP panels.

The panels are exited by the END command and will return you to the previous panel. The only exception is when the SQL ENTRY/EDIT panel is accessed directly from the DATA ACCESS panel. In this case, the END command will bring up the DATA EXTRACTION panel. When you have returned to the DATA ACCESS panel, the B or BROWSE command can be used to browse the SAS data set just created containing either data extracted from a DB2 table(s) or a map. The END command used from the DATA ACCESS panel will return you to Display Manager.

When the END command is issued from the DATA EXTRACTION panel, the SQL ENTRY/EDIT panel, or the KEYS panel execution can occur in addition to displaying the previous panel. When the END command is issued from the DATA EXTRACTION panel, not only is the DATA ACCESS panel displayed, but execution occurs and a SAS data set is created. This SAS data set could contain data extracted from a DB2 table(s) or it could be a map. When the END command is issued from the SQL ENTRY/EDIT, the output SQL file is created if one was requested. If an output SQL file was requested and the SQL ENTRY/EDIT panel is not accessed, the output SQL file is created when the END command is issued from the DATA EXTRACTION panel. When the END command is issued from the KEYS panel, any changes made to the function key definitions are saved.

The DB2EXT panels are described briefly below with detail information on each panel to follow.

- DATA ACCESS: specify input/output files
- DATA EXTRACTION: select DB2 columns, name SAS variables, and specify formats (this is the map)
- BROWSE: browse SAS data set created
- SQL ENTRY/EDIT: generated, coded, or included SQL statements
- HELP: displays help information
- KEYS: display/change commands assigned to function keys

The primary panels of PROC DB2EXT are the DATA ACCESS, DATA EXTRACTION, and the SQL ENTRY/EDIT. The BROWSE, HELP, and KEYS panels serve support functions.

DATA ACCESS Panel

The DATA ACCESS panel is the first panel to be displayed when PROC DB2EXT is executed from Display Manager.

The DATA ACCESS panel is used to specify input and output files. The input files are DB2 tables. The output file is one of either a SAS data set containing data extracted from a DB2 table, a SAS data set containing the map (usually a permanent SAS data set), or a partitioned data set containing a SELECT statement.

If a map created in a previous execution of PROC DB2EXT is to be used as input, the procedure must be coded batch-style and executed strictly in Display Manager. The DATA ACCESS panel does not allow for a map to be used as input. If a SELECT statement created in a previous execution of PROC DB2EXT or a user-coded SELECT statement is to be used as input, leave the DB2 table name blank on the DATA ACCESS panel. This will bring up the SQL ENTRY/EDIT panel, where you can use the Display Manager INCLUDE command to bring in the SELECT statement.

The END command is used to exit the DATA ACCESS panel and returns you to Display Manager. The DATA ACCESS panel is shown in Figure 6-2.

```
                                  DB2 INTERFACE
                                DATA ACCESS PANEL
COMMAND===>
NOTE: FILL IN THE FIELDS BELOW

OUTPUT SQL LIBRARY:                     SAVE SELECTIONS (savesel): N
OUTPUT SAS DATA SET:                    UNIQUE SAS NAMES (unique): N
DB2 SUBSYSTEM ID:

           AUTHORIZATION ID                      TABLE NAME
                  ........                    ..................
                  ........                    ..................
                  ........                    ..................
                  ........                    ..................
                  ........                    ..................
```

Figure 6-2 PROC DB2EXT DATA ACCESS Panel.

The following describes each of the fields on the DATA ACCESS panel. Each description is labeled optional or required to indicate whether a value is required for the field.

OUTPUT SQL LIBRARY (optional): The output SQL library is used when you want to save the SELECT statement generated by the map and optionally edited in the SQL ENTRY/EDIT panel. The data set named here is usually a partitioned data set. The data set must have been allocated using a TSO allocate in Display Manager prior to bringing up the DATA ACCESS panel. If the TSO allocate statement included the member name, then only the ddname needs to be specified. Usually the member name is not specified in the TSO allocate statement, so that all members can be allocated using a single TSO allocate statement. In this case, specify ddname.member, where ddname is the ddname used in the TSO allocate statement and member is a new member to be created. If a member that already exists is specified, that member will be replaced.

OUTPUT SAS DATA SET (required): The output SAS data set is either a SAS data set containing data extracted from DB2 table(s) or a SAS data set containing the map. If the SAVE SELECTIONS field on the DATA ACCESS panel is set to N (no), which is the default, the SAS data set will contain data extracted from DB2 table(s). If the SAVE SELECTIONS field to set to Y (yes), the SAS data set will contain the map.

Usually, the SAS data set is a permanent SAS data set, particularly for maps so that they can be used in subsequent executions of PROC DB2EXT. If the SAS data set is permanent, a two-level name will be specified here. The first level is the ddname specified in the TSO allocate statement and the second level is the SAS data set name. The TSO allocate statement must be submitted in Display Manager prior to executing PROC DB2EXT.

The user does not actually have to specify a value for the OUTPUT SAS DATA SET, even though a value is required. If a value is not given, SAS generates a SAS data set name following the convention, DATA1, DATA2, DATA3, etc., as SAS does when a SAS data set name is not specified in a DATA statement. Therefore, a SAS data set must be created, whether a SAS data set or a map. This is an unfortunate requirement for situations when the objective is to create and save a SELECT statement only. There is a way around this situation and it will be illustrated later in this chapter in the section, Maps and SELECT Statements.

SAVE SELECTIONS (required): The default value, N (no), indicates that the SAS data set named in the OUTPUT SAS DATA SET field is a SAS data set containing data extracted from DB2 table(s). If this value is changed to Y (yes), then the SAS data set named in the OUTPUT SAS DATA SET blank is a map, containing extraction instructions. Refer to the previous definition of the OUTPUT SAS DATA SET for more information.

UNIQUE SAS NAMES (required): By default, SAS variable names are derived from the first eight positions of the eighteen-position DB2 column name. Sometimes the first eight positions of more than one DB2 column name are the same. A SAS data set cannot have more than one variable with the same name. If UNIQUE is set to N (no), as it is by default, an error will occur when more than one DB2 column name has the same first eight positions. The user must then change the name(s) of SAS variables so that they are unique. This is done in the DATA EXTRACTION panel. If UNIQUE is set to Y (yes), unique SAS variable names are created automatically. The first DB2 column with the same first eight positions will retain those as the SAS variable name. A numeric value from 00 to 999 will be appended to the end of the other duplicate variable names and the end of the variable name will be truncated in order to append if needed.

It is a matter of personal preference, but I prefer to leave the UNIQUE option set at N (no) and change the SAS variable names myself. This way a more descriptive name can be assigned. Also if the UNIQUE is Y (yes), you will have to remember in which order the DB2 columns appeared to know which numbered SAS name goes with which value.

DB2 SUBSYSTEM ID (required): This value names the DB2 subsystem you wish to access and is specific to your company. Most companies have at least two subsystems, one for production DB2 and one for test DB2.

When SAS/DB2 is installed, a default value is assigned to the DB2 SUBSYSTEM ID. This value may automatically appear on the DATA ACCESS panel.

With Release 5.18 of SAS/DB2 software, a system option, DB2SSID, can be used to set the value of the SUBSYSTEM ID for the execution of a Display Manager session or a batch job. For example:

```
OPTIONS DB2SSID=DBP;
```

After this system option statement is executed, the value of the DB2 SUBSYSTEM ID is set at DBP and the DB2 SUBSYSTEM ID will not have to be entered. This value will remain in effect until the Display Manager session ends or another OPTIONS statement is executed changing the value.

Contact the SAS Consultant at your company for information on your SUBSYSTEM IDS and how to specify them in Display Manager and in batch programs.

AUTHORIZATION ID and TABLE NAME (optional):

The AUTHORIZATION ID is the first level of the DB2 table name, which is typically the TSO user ID for user-created DB2 tables, and is some standard naming convention specific to a company for production tables. The TABLE NAME is the name of the DB2 table. Up to five DB2 tables can be specified. If two or more tables are specified here, the intended user operation is typically a JOIN, but could be a UNION or subselect.

Specifying an AUTHORIZATION ID/TABLE NAME is optional. If a table is not specified, hitting enter will display the SQL ENTRY/EDIT panel rather than the DATA EXTRACTION panel. In the SQL ENTRY/EDIT panel the user can either code a SELECT statement or bring in a SELECT statement stored as a member of a partitioned data set using the INCLUDE command. More often, a DB2 table(s) will be specified, and hitting enter will bring up the DATA EXTRACTION panel, where the map can be built.

DATA EXTRACTION Panel

When the appropriate information is completed on the DATA ACCESS panel, including the authorization ID(s) and DB2 table(s), hitting enter will bring up the DATA EXTRACTION panel. If the authorization ID and DB2 table are not specified, hitting enter will bring up the SQL ENTRY/EDIT panel.

The user defines the map in the DATA EXTRACTION panel. The definition of the map includes several specifications. First, the user selects the desired DB2 columns. Default SAS variable names and formats are generated for those DB2 columns. The user can specify SAS variable names and formats other than those defaults. In addition, the DATA EXTRACTION panel allows the user to code the WHERE clause of the SELECT statement to specify conditions for row selection.

Labels for the SAS variables are automatically assigned as the DB2 column names. Like any other SAS variable labels, they can be changed through PROC DATASETS or by coding a LABEL statement in a DATA step. They can be changed temporarily for a specific report by coding a LABEL statement in the PROC step which produces that report.

When the DATA EXTRACTION panel is complete, the user will either return to the DATA ACCESS panel using the END command or use the EDIT command to bring up the SQL ENTRY/EDIT panel where the generated SELECT statement can be edited. If the SQL ENTRY/EDIT panel is accessed, the END command will return the user to the DATA EXTRACTION panel. When the END command is issued in the DATA EXTRACTION panel, the user returns to the DATA ACCESS panel and the execution occurs. This execution results in an output file. The output file is either a SAS data set containing data extracted from a DB2 table, a SAS data set containing mapping instructions, or a partitioned data set containing a SELECT statement. The output result depends on how the DATA ACCESS panel was completed. If the END command is issued from a DATA EXTRACTION panel where no DB2 columns were selected, no execution takes place.

The DATA EXTRACTION panel is shown in Figure 6-3, and a description of each field is given. The DB2 table shown in Figure 6-3 is named Persinfo, and DB2 column names and SAS FORMATS are appropriate for this table. These values will be different for other DB2 tables.

TABLE NAME: The TABLE NAME displayed in the upper right-hand corner is the name of the first DB2 table selected on the DATA ACCESS panel. If more than one table was specified on the DATA ACCESS panel, any of these table names could be entered in this field to display the columns in that table. Otherwise, the scroll PF keys, PF7/PF19 (backward) and PF8/PF20 (forward) can be used to view other DB2 columns.

```
             DB2 INTERFACE                        TABLE NAME: PERSINFO
        DATA EXTRACTION PANEL                    SAS DATA SET: WORK.EX1

COMMAND===>
FUNC    COLUMN NAME               SAS NAME        FORMAT
 . *** TABLE- PERSINFO             *** COLUMNS-   30 * SELECTED-   0 *
 .       SOCIAL_SECURITY          ........        $9.
 .       LAST_NAME                ........        $15.
 .       FIRST_NAME               ........        $10.
 .       SEX                      ........        $1.
 .       BIRTH_DATE               ........         7.
 .       ADDRESS                  ........        $20.
 .       CITY                     ........        $15.
 .       STATE                    ........        $2.
 .       ZIP_CODE                 ........        $5.
 .       HOME_PHONE               ........        $7.
 .       HIRE_DATE                ........        7.
 .       OFFICE_EXTENSION         ........        $4.
 .       COST_CENTER              ........        $3.
-------------------- WHERE CLAUSE ----------------------------
```

Figure 6-3 PROC DB2EXT DATA EXTRACTION Panel.

SAS DATA SET: The SAS DATA SET displayed in the upper right-hand corner is the name of the output SAS data set entered on the DATA ACCESS panel.

FUNC: The user can specify four different values on lines under the column heading, FUNC.

- S When S is entered beside a DB2 column name, that column is selected to be extracted from the DB2 table. If S is entered on the first line (the one with ***), all DB2 columns are selected.
- D A D can be entered on any line previously selected by the S function to delete that selection.
- R An R can be entered on the first line (the one with ***) to completely reset all selections previously made with the S function.

A This function is used only when the DISTAB command has previously been entered. The DISTAB command suppresses the portion of the DATA EXTRACTION panel which displays DB2 column information. The A function can be used on the first line (the one with ***) to restore the DB2 columns to the display.

Notice the first line under the FUNC heading. The *** COLUMNS-shows a number which represents the number of columns on the DB2 table whose name is shown after *** TABLE-. The * SELECTED -shows a number which represents the number of DB2 columns selected by the user. This number is zero prior to selection.

If DB2 columns are not selected, issuing the END command from the DATA EXTRACTION panel will display the DATA ACCESS panel and nothing will be executed.

COLUMN NAME: The first line under the COLUMN NAME shows *** TABLE- followed by the name of a DB2 table. The DB2 column names for that table follow. If more than one DB2 table was specified on the DATA ACCESS panel, scrolling forward (PF8/PF20) will display additional *** TABLE- heading followed by the name of another DB2 table. The columns for that DB2 table also follow. The DB2 tables are displayed on the DATA EXTRACTION panel in the same order they were specified on the DATA ACCESS panel. If more than one DB2 table was specified on the DATA ACCESS panel, you can also display the columns associated with that DB2 table by entering the DB2 table name over the value shown after the *** TABLE.

If a DB2 table is not specified on the DATA ACCESS panel, the SQL ENTRY/EDIT panel is displayed. The user can then code a SELECT statement or use the INCLUDE command to bring in a SELECT statement stored as a member of a partitioned data set. Issuing the END command brings up the DATA EXTRACTION panel. In this case, the *** TABLE- heading will display 'FROM SQL' rather than a DB2 table name.

SAS NAME: The SAS NAME is the SAS variable name corresponding to the DB2 column names shown on the same line. If a DB2 column is selected using the S function, hitting enter will display the default SAS variable names. The default SAS variable names consist of the first eight positions of the eighteen-position DB2 column name. The user can change this default SAS variable name merely by typing over it. If the user types SAS variable names in this column, the S function does not have to be used. Entering a SAS variable name in itself selects the corresponding DB2 column.

SAS variable names must be unique whether they are automatically generated or user-defined. Refer to the UNIQUE option of the DATA ACCESS panel described previously to address this situation.

FORMAT: The FORMAT is the SAS FORMAT corresponding the the DB2 column shown on the same line. The default FORMATS generated are standard character for DB2 character data types, standard numeric for DB2 numeric data types, and a SAS date/time format for DB2 date/time data types. These default FORMATS can be changed merely by keying over the values shown. For example, the DOLLARw.d FORMAT could be assigned to numeric data representing money.

SAS date/time formats can be assigned to DB2 date/time values defined as numeric or date/time DB2 data types.

When a SAS date FORMAT is used, two operations occur. First, the DB2 value is converted to a SAS date for storage on the SAS data set. Recall a SAS date is the number of days since 1/1/60. Second, the selected FORMAT will be used when the SAS date is printed. If the date is a DB2 numeric data type, SAS assumes that it is stored in the format, YYMMDD or YYYYMMDD. If it isn't, follow the selected SAS date FORMAT with a slash and the order the DB2 date is stored. For example, DATE7./MMDDYY. A DB2 value of 061752 would be stored as a SAS date value of -2754 and printed as 17JUN52. If the date is a DB2 date data type, the SAS date format, DATE7., is automatically assigned. Other SAS date formats may be assigned by the user. For example, a DB2 date value of 1952-06-17 would be stored as a SAS date value of -2754 and automatically printed as 17JUN52. If the SAS date format, MMDDYY8., was assigned by the user, the date would be printed as 06/17/52.

WHERE CLAUSE: The SQL WHERE clause is used to specify selection criteria which must be met in order for the row to be selected. The WHERE clause was covered in Chapter 4, Structured Query Language. Code the appropriate WHERE clause anywhere below the WHERE clause line shown on the DATA EXTRACTION panel. The SPLIT command (PF2/PF14) can be used to split the DATA EXTRACTION panel at a different location to provide room to code a WHERE clause. Do not code the word WHERE; it is generated by SAS. If a WHERE clause is not used, all rows on the DB2 table(s) will be selected. Note that the WHERE clause should always be used to specify matching criteria when DB2 tables are joined.

SQL ENTRY/EDIT Panel

The SQL ENTRY/EDIT Panel can be accessed in two ways. First, if a DB2 table is not specified as input on the DATA ACCESS panel, hitting enter will display the SQL ENTRY/EDIT panel. The panel will be empty. The user can either code a SELECT statement or use the INCLUDE command to bring in a SELECT statement stored in an external file, usually as a member of a partitioned data set. In order to INCLUDE an external file, a TSO allocate statement must be executed in Display Manager prior to executing PROC DB2EXT.

The second way to access the SQL ENTRY/EDIT panel is to issue the EDIT command from the DATA EXTRACTION panel, after selecting the desired DB2 columns. In this case, the SQL ENTRY/EDIT panel will contain the SELECT statement generated from the map. This SELECT statement can then be edited as desired. In order to use line commands, issue the NUMS ON command to generate line numbers on the left side of the panel.

When the END command is issued from the SQL ENTRY/EDIT panel, the SELECT statement is checked for errors and the DATA EXTRACTION panel is displayed. This is true no matter which way the SQL ENTRY/EDIT panel was accessed. At this time, the user may change SAS variable names and FORMATS. If the DATA EXTRACTION panel was displayed prior to accessing the SQL ENTRY/EDIT panel, SAS variable names and FORMATS changed at that point will not be used.

If SQL errors are present when the END command is issued, an IBM SQL error message will be displayed. The error must be corrected before the END command will display the DATA EXTRACTION panel. The CANCEL command can be issued to exit the SQL ENTRY/EDIT panel without saving any changes made to the SELECT statement.

The SQL ENTRY/EDIT panel is most often used to edit the SELECT statement generated by the map because it does not satisfy the requirements of the application. This will be discussed in more detail later in this chapter in the section, Maps and SELECT Statements.

A SQL ENTRY/EDIT panel containing a SELECT statement generated by a map is shown in Figure 6-4. Notice that a semicolon does not appear at the end of the SELECT statement. SAS automatically generates the semicolon when the SQL ENTRY/EDIT panel is exited. If a semicolon is entered by the user, only one semicolon will be saved.

```
                        SQL ENTRY/EDIT SCREEN

COMMAND===>                                              TEXT EDITOR
 SELECT
  PROD.DEPT_GENERAL_INFO.FIRST, PROD.DEPT_GENERAL_INFO.DEPT,
  PROD.DEPT_GENERAL_INFO.SALARY
  FROM
  PROD.DEPT_GENERAL_INFO
```

Figure 6-4 PROC DB2EXT SQL ENTRY/EDIT Panel.

BROWSE Panel

The BROWSE panel can be accessed from the DATA ACCESS panel using the B or BROWSE command. This command will display the most recently created SAS data set generated by PROC DB2EXT. The SAS data set can be a SAS data set containing data extracted from a DB2 table(s) or a SAS data set containing a map. To display a SAS data set other than the most recently created, use the B or BROWSE command followed by the desired SAS data set name. Use a two-level name when referring to a permanent SAS data set.

The BROWSE panel can be scrolled using PF7/PF19 (backward) and PF8/PF20 (forward). Use the END command or PF3/PF15 to exit the BROWSE panel and return to the DATA ACCESS panel.

Figure 6-5 is an example of the BROWSE panel displaying a SAS data set containing data extracted from a DB2 table.

```
                    SAS Data Set: WORK.EX1          Observations
COMMAND===>                                          First      1
                                                     Last       9
        OBS   LAST_NAM     FIRST_NA     VACATION     EMPLOYEE

        1     ATWOOD       CHUCK             160     H
        2     BROOKS       EDWARD            120     S
        3     DOUGLAS      MILTON            160     S
        4     HUTSON       EVERETT           120     S
        5     KEESLING     GERTRUDE          120     S
        6     MICHAEL      PAT               160     S
        7     MILLER       EMMALYNE          120     S
        8     MORGAN       CHERYL             80     S
        9     PEYTON       JOHN              160     S
```

Figure 6-5 PROC DB2EXT BROWSE Panel.

HELP Panel

HELP can be obtained by issuing the HELP command (PF1/PF13) from the other panels. When the HELP command is issued from the SQL ENTRY/EDIT panel, the HELP information displayed is for the SAS/FSP procedure, PROC FSEDIT. When the HELP command is issued from the BROWSE panel, the HELP information displayed is for the SAS/FSP procedure, PROC FSBROWSE. When the HELP command is issued from the DATA ACCESS or the DATA EXTRACTION panels, help specific to PROC DB2EXT is displayed.

Figure 6-6 shows the HELP panel for PROC DB2EXT. Select the appropriate option and hit enter and information on the topic selected will be displayed. The operation of the HELP panel is explained throughout. To exit the HELP panel, use the END command.

```
                  PROC DB2EXT HELP MENU
 Select Option                                  Press END to return.

This HELP menu lists the categories of command/feature
references for PROC DB2EXT. Enter the option number in the
selection field, and press ENTER. Additional information will be
displayed for the options selected.

     OPTION               DESCRIPTION

       1             PROC DB2EXT Execution Instructions
       2             PROC DB2EXT Screen Descriptions
       3             HELP/PF KEY Command Descriptions
       4             PROC DB2EXT Command Descriptions
       5             PROC DB2EXT WHERE Command Description

 END OF PANEL
```

Figure 6-6 PROC DB2EXT HELP Panel.

KEYS Panel

The KEYS panel is used to display and/or change commands defined to function keys. This panel is displayed by issuing the KEYS command from other PROC DB2EXT panels. The function key definitions shown correspond to the panel the KEYS command was issued from. The KEYS panel can be scrolled using PF7/PF19 (backward) and PF8/PF20 (forward).

Figure 6-7 (A and B) shows the KEYS panel for the DATA ACCESS panel. Scrolling forward displays more definitions as shown in Figure 6-7(B).

```
                          Function Key Definitions
COMMAND===>


Key         Command


  1         HELP
  2         SPLIT
  3         END
  4         EXIT
  5         BROWSE
  6         KEYS
  7         BACKWARD
  8         FORWARD
  9         RESET
 10         DISTAB
 11         EDIT
 12
 13         HELP
 14         SPLIT
 15         END
 16         EXIT
 17         BROWSE
 18         KEYS
 19         BACKWARD
```

Figure 6-7(A) PROC DB2EXT KEYS Panel.

```
                    Function Key Definitions
COMMAND===>

Key      Command

20       FORWARD
21       RESET
22       DISTAB
23       EDIT
24
```

Figure 6-7(B) PROC DB2EXT KEYS Panel.

The following chart summarizes the function key definitions for each of the PROC DB2EXT panels. A definition of these commands is given in the next section, Commands.

FUNCTION KEY DEFINITIONS BY PANEL

Function Key	Data Access	Data Extract	Browse	SQL Entry/Edit	Keys	Help
1,13	HELP	HELP	HELP	HELP		
2,14		SPLIT	HI			
3,15	END	END	END	END	END	END
4,16	EXIT	EXIT	PREVCMD	PREVCMD		
5,17	BROWSE			RFIND		
6,18	KEYS	KEYS		RCHANGE		
7,19		BACKWARD	BACKWARD	BACKWARD	BACK	BACK
8,20		FORWARD	FORWARD	FORWARD	FORW	FORW
9,21		RESET				
10,22		DISTAB	LEFT	LEFT		
11,23		EDIT	RIGHT	RIGHT		
12,24			CURSOR	CURSOR		

The function key definitions for the DATA ACCESS and DATA EXTRACTION panels are the same (as shown on the KEYS panel displayed previously). However, not all commands are valid on both panels. The commands shown for the DATA ACCESS and DATA EXTRACTION panels are commands that are actually valid in these panels.

Function key definitions can be changed by typing in new values on the KEYS panel. The new key definitions are saved permanently in your SAS profile data set, along with function key definitions for Display Manager and all other SAS products that execute interactively.

New function key definitions are saved permanently by issuing the SAVE or END command from the KEYS panel. Changes can be canceled by issuing the CANCEL command prior to issuing a SAVE or END command. If you save changes and want the original values again, your SAS profile can be deleted and reallocated. Contact the SAS consultant at your company for more information on this operation.

Commands

Table 6-1 outlines the commands which are valid in the PROC DB2EXT panels. A definition of each command is given. Some of these commands are defined as function keys. Refer to the previous section, KEYS Panel, for the definition of function keys.

BACKWARD (DATA EXTRACTION, BROWSE, SQL ENTRY/EDIT, HELP, KEYS): BACKWARD moves up in the display of a panel. The function keys, PF7/PF19 are normally used rather than entering the command. With either the command or the key, a number can be specified so that you can go backwards a specified number of lines. MAX can also be used to display the contents of the top of the panel.

BROWSE (DATA ACCESS): The BROWSE command can be issued from the DATA ACCESS panel when the user returns to this panel after completing the appropriate information on other DB2EXT panels. The BROWSE command displays the most recently created SAS data set. The SAS data set can be a

Table 6-1 Valid command by PROC DB2EXT Panel.

	DATA ACCESS	DATA EXTRACT	BROWSE	SQL ENTRY/EDIT	HELP	KEYS
BACKWARD		X	X	X	X	X
BROWSE	X					
CANCEL				X		X
CAPS OFF/ON				X		
CHANGE				X		
DISTAB		X				
EDIT		X				
END	X	X*	X	X*	X	X*
EXIT	X	X				
FIND				X		
FORWARD		X	X	X	X	X
HELP	X	X	X	X		
HI			X			
INCLUDE				X		
KEYS	X	X	X	X		
LEFT				X		
NUMS ON|OFF				X		
PREVCMD			X	X		
RCHANGE				X		
RESET		X				
RFIND				X		
RIGHT				X		
SPLIT		X				

* The END command issued from these panels may cause an action to occur in addition to exiting. Refer to the definition of the END command which follows for more information.

SAS data set containing data extracted from a DB2 table(s) or a SAS data set containing a map. To browse a SAS data set other than the one most recently created, issue the BROWSE command followed by the name of the desired SAS data set.

CANCEL (SQL ENTRY/EDIT, KEYS): This command is used to cancel changes made in the KEYS panel or the SQL ENTRY/EDIT panel. The CANCEL command must be issued prior to using a SAVE or END command in order to cancel the changes.

CAPS OFF/ON (SQL ENTRY/EDIT): When CAPS ON is in effect, all typing done in the SQL ENTRY/EDIT panel will automatically be capitalized after hitting enter. With CAPS OFF, which is the default, the letters will remain small unless the Shift key is used when they are entered.

CHANGE (SQL ENTRY/EDIT): The CHANGE command is used to change the value of a character string. The CHANGE command takes one of the following forms:

```
c string1 string2
c 'string1' 'string2'
```

Quotes must be used when the character string contains blanks or special characters. String1 is changed to string2. The change can be repeated by using the RCHANGE command (PF6/PF18). ALL can be typed after string2 in order to change all occurrences of string1 to string2. Other options that can be used include: NEXT, FIRST, LAST, PREV, WORD, SUFFIX, and PREFIX.

The CHANGE command is often used in conjunction with the FIND command; the FIND command locates string1, giving you a chance to see if you want to change the value before using the RCHANGE command (PF6/PF18).

DISTAB (DATA EXTRACTION): When the DISTAB command (disable table) is issued from the DATA EXTRACTION panel, DB2 column information is suppressed. The heading information for each table is all that is displayed. The following DATA EXTRACTION panel illustrates the results of the DISTAB command:

```
              DB2 INTERFACE                  TABLE NAME: SAMPLE1
         DATA EXTRACTION PANEL           SAS DATA SET: SASOUT.SAMP
COMMAND===>

FUNC    COLUMN NAME          SAS NAME       FORMAT
  . *** TABLE- SAMPLE1         *** COLUMNS-   12 * SELECTED-   8 *
  . *** TABLE- SAMPLE2         *** COLUMNS-   12 * SELECTED-   7 *
  . *** TABLE- SAMPLE3         *** COLUMNS-   12 * SELECTED-   7 *
------------------- WHERE CLAUSE -----------------------------
```

This command can be useful when more than one DB2 table is requested on the DATA ACCESS panel and several DB2 columns exist. It will show a summary of the number of columns that exist and the number that have been selected. The FUNC values R and A can be used to restore the DB2 column information.

EDIT (DATA EXTRACTION): The EDIT command can be issued from the DATA EXTRACTION panel to display the SQL ENTRY/EDIT panel. The panel will show the SELECT statement generated from the map built in the DATA EXTRACTION panel. The SELECT statement can be edited as desired. The END command returns the user to the DATA EXTRACTION panel, where SAS variable names and formats can be altered.

END (DATA ACCESS, DATA EXTRACTION, BROWSE, SQL ENTRY/EDIT, HELP, KEYS): The END command is used to exit the panels listed above. The function keys, PF3/PF15, are usually used rather than entering the END command. The END command will return you to the previous panel. The one exception to this is when the SQL ENTRY/EDIT panel has been displayed from the DATA ACCESS panel by not entering a DB2 table name. In this case, the END command will display the DATA EXTRACTION panel.

When the END command is issued from the DATA EXTRACTION panel, execution occurs and a SAS data set is created. This SAS data set is either a map or contains data extracted from a DB2 table(s), depending on the setting of the SAVESEL field when the DATA ACCESS panel was completed. If an output SQL file is saved and the SQL ENTRY/EDIT panel is displayed, the END command causes the SELECT statement to be written to the output file. Also, when the END command is issued from the DATA EXTRACTION or SQL ENTRY/EDIT panels, they are checked for errors. If an error is present, an error message will be displayed. The error must be corrected before the END command will return the user to the previous panel.

EXIT (DATA ACCESS, DATA EXTRACTION): The EXIT command or the PF4/PF16 function keys used in the DATA ACCESS or DATA EXTRACTION panels, returns the user to Display Manager without executing any of the user input into either of these two panels.

FIND (SQL ENTRY/EDIT): The FIND command is used to find a value. The FIND command takes one of the following forms:

```
f string
f 'string'
```

Quotes must be used when the character string contains blanks or special characters. The find can be repeated by using the RFIND command (PF5/PF17). ALL can be typed after string to produce a message telling how many occurrences of the character string were found. Other options that can be used include: NEXT, FIRST, LAST, PREV, WORD, SUFFIX, and PREFIX.

FORWARD (DATA EXTRACTION, BROWSE, SQL ENTRY/EDIT, HELP, KEYS): FORWARD moves down in the display of a panel. The function keys PF8/PF20 are normally used rather than the command. With either the command or the key, a number can be specified so that you can go forward a specified number of lines. MAX can also be used to display the contents of the bottom of the window.

HELP (DATA ACCESS, DATA EXTRACTION, BROWSE, SQL ENTRY/EDIT): This command is used to bring up the HELP panel. The corresponding function key, PF1/PF13, can be used rather than the HELP command. The HELP information displayed depends on the panel the command was issued from. Help for PROC DB2EXT can be accessed by issuing the HELP command from the DATA ACCESS or DATA EXTRACTION panels.

HI (BROWSE): The HI command or the PF2/PF14 function keys can be used to highlight a specific line on the BROWSE panel. Place the cursor on the line to be highlighted and issue the HI command to highlight that line. To remove the highlight, place the cursor on the line and use the HI command followed by the original color of the line; for example, HI BLUE. To turn off all highlighted lines, use the HI OFF command. To turn all highlighted lines back on, use the HI ON command.

INCLUDE ddname or INCLUDE ddname(member) (SQL ENTRY/EDIT): This command is used to bring in SQL code stored in a partitioned data set. The ddname is the ddname you specified in a TSO allocate statement. If the TSO allocate statement included the member name, only the ddname is specified in the INCLUDE command. If the member name is not specified in the TSO allocate statement, it is specified in the INCLUDE command. The TSO allocate statement must be executed before entering the PROC DB2EXT menu system.

KEYS (DATA ACCESS, DATA EXTRACTION, BROWSE, SQL ENTRY/EDIT): The KEYS command can be issued to display the KEYS panel. This panel shows function key definitions for the panel from which the command was issued. Function key definitions can be changed from the KEYS panel. Refer to the previous section, KEYS Panel, for more information.

LEFT (SQL ENTRY/EDIT): LEFT displays the contents to the left of a panel. The function keys PF10/PF22 are normally used rather than the command. With either the command or the key, a number can be specified so that you can go left a specified number of columns. MAX can also be used to display the contents of the leftmost portion of the window.

NUMS ON | OFF (SQL ENTRY/EDIT): When the SQL ENTRY/EDIT panel is displayed, line numbers do not appear on the left of the screen. The default is NUMS OFF. When the NUMS ON command is issued, line numbers appear on the left of the screen, enabling the user to use TSO line commands to edit the SQL statements.

PREVCMD (BROWSE, SQL ENTRY/EDIT): The PREVCMD recalls the command previously executed to the command line. The command can then be edited and/or resubmitted. The

PREVCMD is usually issued by using the PF4/PF16 function keys.

RCHANGE (SQL ENTRY/EDIT): When a CHANGE command is entered in the command input in the form C 'string1' 'string2' the first occurrence of string1, starting with the first line displayed on the screen, is changed to string2. To change more occurrences of this character string the RCHANGE command or the PF6/PF18 function keys can be used instead of reentering the CHANGE command.

RESET (DATA EXTRACTION): The RESET command clears all selections which have been made on the DATA EXTRACTION panel. PF9/PF21 function keys can be used to issue this command. The result of this command is the same function as the R FUNC.

RFIND (SQL ENTRY/EDIT): When a FIND command is entered in the command input in the form F 'string', the first occurrence of that character string, starting with the first line displayed on the screen, is found. To find more occurrences of this character string the RFIND command or the PF5/PF17 function keys can be used instead of reentering the FIND command.

RIGHT (SQL ENTRY/EDIT): RIGHT displays the contents to the right of a panel. The function keys, PF11/PF23 are normally used rather than the command. With either the command or the key, a number can be specified so that you can go right a specified number of columns. MAX can also be used to display the contents of the rightmost portion of the window.

SPLIT (DATA EXTRACTION): The SPLIT command is used to change where the DATA EXTRACTION panel is split between the display of DB2 columns and the WHERE clause. To change the split location, place the cursor at the location where you wish the DATA EXTRACTION panel to be split and enter the SPLIT command or use the PF2/PF14 function keys.

Creating a SAS Data Set

This section illustrates the use of PROC DB2EXT in Display Manager to create a SAS data set containing data extracted from a DB2 table(s). Figure 6-8 shows the panels used for this purpose.

PROC DB2EXT is executed in Display Manager to bring up the DATA ACCESS panel. After the DATA ACCESS panel is completed,

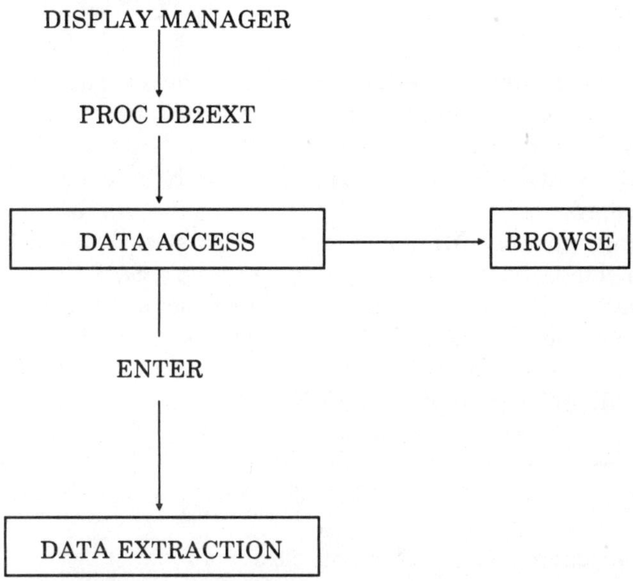

Figure 6-8 PROC DB2EXT Panels for creating a SAS Data Set.

hitting enter displays the DATA EXTRACTION panel. The map is built using the DATA EXTRACTION panel. Here the user selects the desired DB2 columns, SAS variable names, SAS variable formats, and optionally codes an SQL WHERE clause to select specific rows from the DB2 table(s). When the DATA EXTRACTION panel is complete, the END command is used to return to the DATA ACCESS panel and create the SAS data set. The B (BROWSE) command can be used in the DATA ACCESS panel to bring up the BROWSE panel, which is used to view the SAS data set.

If the BROWSE panel shows that the SAS data set is not what you wanted, use the END command (PF3/PF15) to return to the DATA ACCESS panel. The SAS data set will have to be recreated. The DATA ACCESS panel is probably completed appropriately, so just hit enter to bring up the DATA EXTRACTION panel. Unfortunately, the DATA EXTRACTION panel will have to be completed from scratch. Even saving the map, which is created in the DATA EXTRACTION panel, would not save you from having to complete the DATA EXTRACTION panel again. This is because a map cannot be used as an input file on the DATA ACCESS panel.

Example 6-1

This is a basic example used to introduce the execution of PROC DB2EXT in Display Manager. Data are extracted from the DB2 table, Persinfo, and placed in a temporary SAS data set. The flow from the DATA ACCESS, DATA EXTRACTION, and BROWSE panels is illustrated.

Getting into Display Manager is the first step. This varies from company to company, so contact your company's SAS Consultant for this information. Display Manager will look something like the following. Enter the PROC DB2EXT statement along with the RUN statement in the PROGRAM window and submit the statements using the SUBMIT command (PF3/PF15).

```
------------------------------------------------------------------
COMMAND ===>                                     SAS(r) Log   HH:MM

NOTE: COPYRIGHT(C) 1984, 1988 SAS INSTITUTE INC., CARY, NC 27512
USA
NOTE: SAS RELEASE 5.18 AT COMPANY ABC (00000000).
NOTE: CPUID   VERSION = 00   SERIAL = 000000   MODEL = 0000 .
NOTE: SAS OPTIONS SPECIFIED ARE:
      DMS NONEWS FSP FS NODATE
------------------------------------------------------------------
COMMAND ===>                                        Program Editor

00001 proc db2ext;
00002   run;
00003
00004
00005
```

The execution of PROC DB2EXT brings up the DATA ACCESS panel shown below. Enter the name of the OUTPUT SAS DATA SET, Ex1, and the DB2 AUTHORIZATION ID/TABLE NAME, Tsid123.Persinfo. The DB2 SUBSYSTEM ID appears with a value of DBT, which was the value assigned when SAS/DB2 was installed in this particular company. The SAVESEL field defaults to N (no), which means that the SAS data set to be created will contain data extracted from the DB2 table rather than a map.

```
                              DB2 INTERFACE
                            DATA ACCESS PANEL

COMMAND===>
NOTE: FILL IN THE FIELDS BELOW

OUTPUT SQL LIBRARY:                  SAVE SELECTIONS (savesel): N

OUTPUT SAS DATA SET: ex1             UNIQUE SAS NAMES (unique): N

DB2 SUBSYSTEM ID:     DBT

          AUTHORIZATION ID                TABLE NAME
                  tsid123.                persinfo..........
                  ........                ..................
                  ........                ..................
                  ........                ..................
                  ........                ..................
```

Hitting the enter key on the DATA ACCESS panel brings up the DATA EXTRACTION panel shown below. The S FUNC is entered beside the desired DB2 columns. Note that if the S FUNC were entered on the first line beside *** TABLE, all the DB2 columns would be selected.

```
               DB2 INTERFACE                 TABLE NAME: PERSINFO
        DATA EXTRACTION PANEL              SAS DATA SET: WORK.EX1


COMMAND===>


FUNC    COLUMN NAME             SAS NAME     FORMAT
 . *** TABLE- PERSINFO           *** COLUMNS-  30 * SELECTED-   0 *
 s       SOCIAL_SECURITY        ........     $9.
 s       LAST_NAME              ........     $15.
 s       FIRST_NAME             ........     $10.
 .       SEX                    ........     $1.
 .       BIRTH_DATE             ........     7.
 .       ADDRESS                ........     $20.
 .       CITY                   ........     $15.
 .       STATE                  ........     $2.
 .       ZIP_CODE               ........     $5.
 .       HOME_PHONE             ........     $7.
 s       HIRE_DATE              ........      7.
 .       OFFICE_EXTENSION       ........     $4.
 .       COST_CENTER            ........     $3.
------------------- WHERE CLAUSE ----------------------------
```

Although it is not required to hit enter on the DATA EXTRACTION panel after selecting the desired rows, doing so displays the generated SAS variable names. SAS variable names are created as the first eight positions of the eighteen-position DB2 column name. Also displayed after hitting enter is the number of DB2 columns selected, which is 4. Shown below is the DATA EXTRACTION panel after hitting the enter key.

```
            DB2 INTERFACE                         TABLE NAME: PERSINFO
      DATA EXTRACTION PANEL                     SAS DATA SET: WORK.EX1

COMMAND===>

FUNC   COLUMN NAME          SAS NAME      FORMAT
 . *** TABLE- PERSINFO       *** COLUMNS-  30 * SELECTED-  4 *
 .       SOCIAL_SECURITY    SOCIAL_S      $9.
 .       LAST_NAME          LAST_NAM      $15.
 .       FIRST_NAME         FIRST_NA      $10.
 .       SEX                ........      $1.
 .       BIRTH_DATE         ........      7.
 .       ADDRESS            ........      $20.
 .       CITY               ........      $15.
 .       STATE              ........      $2.
 .       ZIP_CODE           ........      $5.
 .       HOME_PHONE         ........      $7.
 .       HIRE_DATE          HIRE_DAT      7.
 .       OFFICE_EXTENSION   ........      $4.
 .       COST_CENTER        ........      $3.
------------------ WHERE CLAUSE ---------------------------
```

Scrolling down (PF8/PF20) displays additional DB2 columns on the table, Persinfo. The next two DATA EXTRACTION panels show scrolling, selecting additional DB2 columns, and hitting enter to display the generated SAS variable name.

```
             DB2 INTERFACE                   TABLE NAME: PERSINFO
        DATA EXTRACTION PANEL              SAS DATA SET: WORK.EX1

COMMAND===>

FUNC    COLUMN NAME          SAS NAME     FORMAT
  .     VACATION_AVAILABLE   VACATION     4.
  .     VACATION_USED        ........     4.
  .     SICK_USED            ........     4.
  .     SALARY_JANUARY       ........     6.
  .     SALARY_FEBRUARY      ........     6.
  .     SALARY_MARCH         ........     6.
  .     SALARY_APRIL         ........     6.
  .     SALARY_MAY           ........     6.
  .     SALARY_JUNE          ........     6.
  .     SALARY_JULY          ........     6.
  .     SALARY_AUGUST        ........     6.
  .     SALARY_SEPTEMBER     ........     6.
  .     SALARY_OCTOBER       ........     6.
  .     SALARY_NOVEMBER      ........     6.
------------------ WHERE CLAUSE ----------------------------
```

```
             DB2 INTERFACE                   TABLE NAME: PERSINFO
        DATA EXTRACTION PANEL              SAS DATA SET: WORK.EX1

COMMAND===>

FUNC    COLUMN NAME          SAS NAME     FORMAT
  .      SALARY_DECEMBER     ........     6.
  .      EMPLOYEE_TYPE       EMPLOYEE     $1.
  .      MANAGEMENT          ........     $1.

------------------ WHERE CLAUSE ----------------------------
```

After selecting the desired DB2 columns, you can change your mind as long as you have not used the END command (PF3/PF15) to return to the DATA ACCESS panel. Shown below is the use of the D FUNC, entered beside two DB2 columns that were previously selected. When you hit enter after using the D FUNC, the SAS variable names will disappear from the column, SAS NAME. This view of the DATA EXTRACTION panel is not shown.

A WHERE clause is entered in the bottom half of the DATA EXTRACTION panel to select only those rows where the Cost_center is 140. The word WHERE is not coded; SAS will generate it. The DB2 column name is used in the WHERE clause, not the SAS variable name. The WHERE clause can be entered at any time and you do not have to have the beginning of the DB2 table displayed.

```
             DB2 INTERFACE                    TABLE NAME: PERSINFO
         DATA EXTRACTION PANEL              SAS DATA SET: WORK.EX1

COMMAND===>

FUNC    COLUMN NAME             SAS NAME      FORMAT
 . *** TABLE- PERSINFO           *** COLUMNS-  30 * SELECTED-  6 *
 d       SOCIAL_SECURITY        SOCIAL_S      $9.
 .       LAST_NAME              LAST_NAM      $15.
 .       FIRST_NAME             FIRST_NA      $10.
 .       SEX                    ........      $1.
 .       BIRTH_DATE             ........      7.
 .       ADDRESS                ........      $20.
 .       CITY                   ........      $15.
 .       STATE                  ........      $2.
 .       ZIP_CODE               ........      $5.
 .       HOME_PHONE             ........      $7.
 d       HIRE_DATE              HIRE_DAT      7.
 .       OFFICE_EXTENSION       ........      $4.
 .       COST_CENTER            ........      $3.
------------------- WHERE CLAUSE ----------------------------
 cost_center = '140'
```

The END command (PF3/PF15) is used to return to the DATA ACCESS panel and create the SAS data set. The DATA ACCESS panel shows extract statistics at the bottom of the screen. In this case, the SAS data set Ex1 has 19 observations and 6 variables. The B (BROWSE) command is entered in the command input.

```
                          DB2 INTERFACE
                        DATA ACCESS PANEL

COMMAND===> b

OUTPUT SQL LIBRARY:                 SAVE SELECTIONS (savesel): N

OUTPUT SAS DATA SET: WORK.EX1       UNIQUE SAS NAMES (unique): N

DB2 SUBSYSTEM ID:    DBT

          AUTHORIZATION ID                TABLE NAME
                  TSID123.              PROJINFO..........
                  ........              ..................
                  ........              ..................
                  ........              ..................
                  ........              ..................

EXTRACT STATISTICS: NUMBER OF SAS OBS CREATED  =       19
                    NUMBER OF SAS VARS CREATED =       6
```

Hitting enter after the B command was entered in the DATA ACCESS panel brings up the BROWSE panel displaying the SAS data set just created, Ex1.

```
                         SAS Data Set: WORK.EX1          Observations
COMMAND ===>                                             First       1
                                                         Last        9
        OBS   LAST_NAM     FIRST_NA     VACATION   EMPLOYEE

          1   ATWOOD       CHUCK             160   H
          2   BROOKS       EDWARD            120   S
          3   DOUGLAS      MILTON            160   S
          4   HUTSON       EVERETT           120   S
          5   KEESLING     GERTRUDE          120   S
          6   MICHAEL      PAT               160   S
          7   MILLER       EMMALYNE          120   S
          8   MORGAN       CHERYL             80   S
          9   PEYTON       JOHN              160   S
```

Use the END command (PF3/PF15) to exit the BROWSE panel and return to the DATA ACCESS panel. Use the END command again to return to Display Manager. The SAS data set Ex1, created through the use of the PROC DB2EXT panels, is like any other SAS data set. It can now be used in DATA and PROC steps in your Display Manager session.

Example 6-2

A permanent SAS data set is to be created containing data from the DB2 table, Persinfo. The UNIQUE option is illustrated, along with user-defined SAS variable names and formats.

A SAS data library must exist or be created before getting into Display Manager. A SAS data library is an OS file with a data set organization (DSORG) of DA and a record format (RECFM) of U. It is not the intent of this book to cover the allocation of a SAS data library, as this is a function of Base SAS.

A TSO allocate statement is then entered in the PROGRAM window of Display Manager and executed using the SUBMIT command (PF3/PF15). The TSO allocate statement should have disposition OLD because you will be writing to it. The PROC DB2EXT statement and a RUN statement are entered in the PROGRAM window next and executed.

```
------------------------------------------------------------------
COMMAND ===>                                      SAS(r) Log   HH:MM

NOTE: COPYRIGHT(C) 1984, 1988 SAS INSTITUTE INC., CARY, NC 27512
USA
NOTE: SAS RELEASE 5.18 AT COMPANY ABC (00000000).
NOTE: CPUID   VERSION = 00  SERIAL = 000000   MODEL = 0000 .
NOTE: SAS OPTIONS SPECIFIED ARE:
      DMS NONEWS FSP FS NODATE



  1  tso alloc dd(sasout) dsn('tsid123.sas.sample') old;
------------------------------------------------------------------
COMMAND ===>                                      Program Editor

00001 proc db2ext;
00002   run;
00003
00004
00005
```

The execution of PROC DB2EXT brings up the DATA ACCESS panel shown below. Enter the name of the OUTPUT SAS DATA SET as Sasout.ex2, where Sasout references the ddname specified in the TSO allocate statement and Ex2 is the name of the SAS data set to be created in that SAS data library. The table, Tsid123.Persinfo, is also entered.

```
                          DB2 INTERFACE
                        DATA ACCESS PANEL


COMMAND===>
NOTE: FILL IN THE FIELDS BELOW

OUTPUT SQL LIBRARY:                  SAVE SELECTIONS (savesel): N

OUTPUT SAS DATA SET: sasout.ex2      UNIQUE SAS NAMES (unique): N

DB2 SUBSYSTEM ID:    DBT

          AUTHORIZATION ID                TABLE NAME
                  tsid123.                persinfo..........
                  ........                ..................
                  ........                ..................
                  ........                ..................
                  ........                ..................
```

Hitting the enter key on the DATA ACCESS panel brings up the DATA EXTRACTION panel shown below. The S FUNC is entered beside the desired DB2 columns.

```
              DB2 INTERFACE                        TABLE NAME: PERSINFO
         DATA EXTRACTION PANEL                SAS DATA SET: WORK.EX2


COMMAND ===>


FUNC   COLUMN NAME            SAS NAME      FORMAT
 . *** TABLE- PERSINFO             *** COLUMNS-  30 * SELECTED-   0 *
 .       SOCIAL_SECURITY     ........      $9.
 s       LAST_NAME           ........      $15.
 s       FIRST_NAME          ........      $10.
 .       SEX                 ........      $1.
 .       BIRTH_DATE          ........      7.
 .       ADDRESS             ........      $20.
 .       CITY                ........      $15.
 .       STATE               ........      $2.
 .       ZIP_CODE            ........      $5.
 .       HOME_PHONE          ........      $7.
 s       HIRE_DATE           ........      7.
 .       OFFICE_EXTENSION    ........      $4.
 .       COST_CENTER         ........      $3.
--------------------- WHERE CLAUSE -----------------------------
```

Although you are not required to hit enter on the DATA EXTRACTION panel after selecting the desired rows, doing so displays the generated SAS variable names. Also shown after hitting enter is the number of DB2 columns selected, which is 3.

The MMDDYY8. SAS date format is entered for the DB2 column, Hire_date. Hire_date is a DB2 numeric data type stored in the format, YYMMDD, which is the order expected by SAS/DB2. Entering a SAS date will cause the SAS variable, Hire_dat, to be stored as a SAS date value, which is the number of days since 1/1/60. In addition, the MMDDYY8. format will be used when this SAS variable is printed. Shown below is the DATA EXTRACTION panel after hitting the enter key and entering a SAS date format.

```
             DB2 INTERFACE                        TABLE NAME: PERSINFO
       DATA EXTRACTION PANEL                SAS DATA SET: WORK.EX2

 COMMAND===>

 FUNC   COLUMN NAME          SAS NAME     FORMAT
  . *** TABLE- PERSINFO          *** COLUMNS-   30 * SELECTED-   3 *
  .       SOCIAL_SECURITY    ........     $9.
  .       LAST_NAME          LAST_NAM     $15.
  .       FIRST_NAME         FIRST_NA     $10.
  .       SEX                ........     $1.
  .       BIRTH_DATE         ........     7.
  .       ADDRESS            ........     $20.
  .       CITY               ........     $15.
  .       STATE              ........     $2.
  .       ZIP_CODE           ........     $5.
  .       HOME_PHONE         ........     $7.
  .       HIRE_DATE          HIRE_DAT     MMDDYY8.
  .       OFFICE_EXTENSION   ........     $4.
  .       COST_CENTER        ........     $3.
--------------------- WHERE CLAUSE ------------------------------
```

Scrolling once (PF8/PF20) displays the second screen where additional DB2 columns are selected, and hitting enter displays the generated SAS variable name. The DOLLARw.d format is used on the three columns representing salaries.

```
              DB2 INTERFACE                     TABLE NAME: PERSINFO
         DATA EXTRACTION PANEL                 SAS DATA SET: WORK.EX2


 COMMAND===>


 FUNC   COLUMN NAME             SAS NAME     FORMAT
   .      VACATION_AVAILABLE    VACATION     4.
   .      VACATION_USED         VACATION     4.
   .      SICK_USED             ........     4.
   .      SALARY_JANUARY        ........     6.
   .      SALARY_FEBRUARY       ........     6.
   .      SALARY_MARCH          ........     6.
   .      SALARY_APRIL          ........     6.
   .      SALARY_MAY            ........     6.
   .      SALARY_JUNE           SALARY_J     DOLLAR8.
   .      SALARY_JULY           SALARY_J     DOLLAR8.
   .      SALARY_AUGUST         SALARY_A     DOLLAR8.
   .      SALARY_SEPTEMBER      ........     6.
   .      SALARY_OCTOBER        ........     6.
   .      SALARY_NOVEMBER       ........     6.
--------------------- WHERE CLAUSE -----------------------------
```

The END command (PF3/PF15) is used to return to the DATA ACCESS panel and create the output SAS data set. When the END command is issued, an error message is displayed on the DATA EXTRACTION panel, saying that duplicate SAS names were either entered by the user or generated by the map. In this case, duplicate SAS names were generated by the map. The first eight positions of the DB2 columns, Vacation_available and Vacation_used, are both Vacation. The first eight positions of the DB2 columns, Salary_june and Salary_july, are both Salary_j. These four duplicate SAS variable names will appear in red on the screen to indicate which variables are duplicates. A SAS data set cannot contain more than one variable with the same name. The user must change these duplicate names before exiting the DATA EXTRACTION panel.

```
             DB2 INTERFACE                        TABLE NAME: PERSINFO
        DATA EXTRACTION PANEL                 SAS DATA SET: WORK.EX2

COMMAND===>
ERROR:   DUPLICATE SAS NAMES WERE ENTERED/GENERATED
FUNC    COLUMN NAME           SAS NAME      FORMAT
  .      VACATION_AVAILABLE   VACATION      4.
  .      VACATION_USED        VACATION      4.
  .      SICK_USED            ........      4.
  .      SALARY_JANUARY       ........      6.
  .      SALARY_FEBRUARY      ........      6.
  .      SALARY_MARCH         ........      6.
  .      SALARY_APRIL         ........      6.
  .      SALARY_MAY           ........      6.
  .      SALARY_JUNE          SALARY_J      DOLLAR8.
  .      SALARY_JULY          SALARY_J      DOLLAR8.
  .      SALARY_AUGUST        SALARY_A      DOLLAR8.
  .      SALARY_SEPTEMBER     ........      6.
  .      SALARY_OCTOBER       ........      6.
  .      SALARY_NOVEMBER      ........      6.
--------------------- WHERE CLAUSE -----------------------------
```

The duplicate SAS names are changed by keying over the generated SAS names with user-selected names. The DB2 column, Vacation_available, is assigned the SAS name, Vacavail. The DB2 column, Vacation_used, is assigned the SAS name, Vacused. The three DB2 columns representing salary are changed to add the numeric value of the month in the last two positions. This change creates a more descriptive SAS variable name.

In many cases the user will want to create his own SAS variable names because the first eight positions of the eighteen-position DB2 column name may not be very descriptive. This can be done initially by keying the SAS name under the column, SAS NAME, rather than using the S FUNC. It can also be done, as it was in this example, by keying over the generated SAS variable names.

```
               DB2 INTERFACE                  TABLE NAME: PERSINFO
          DATA EXTRACTION PANEL              SAS DATA SET: WORK.EX2

COMMAND===>
ERROR:  DUPLICATE SAS NAMES WERE ENTERED/GENERATED
FUNC   COLUMN NAME          SAS NAME      FORMAT
 .      VACATION_AVAILABLE  VACAvail      4.
 .      VACATION_USED       VACused       4.
 .      SICK_USED           ........      4.
 .      SALARY_JANUARY      ........      6.
 .      SALARY_FEBRUARY     ........      6.
 .      SALARY_MARCH        ........      6.
 .      SALARY_APRIL        ........      6.
 .      SALARY_MAY          ........      6.
 .      SALARY_JUNE         SALARY06      DOLLAR8.
 .      SALARY_JULY         SALARY07      DOLLAR8.
 .      SALARY_AUGUST       SALARY08      DOLLAR8.
 .      SALARY_SEPTEMBER    ........      6.
 .      SALARY_OCTOBER      ........      6.
 .      SALARY_NOVEMBER     ........      6.
--------------------- WHERE CLAUSE ----------------------------
```

The END command (PF3/PF15) is used to return to the DATA ACCESS panel and create the SAS data set. The DATA ACCESS panel shows extract statistics at the bottom of the panel. In this case, the SAS data set Sasout.ex2 has 60 observations and 8 variables. The B (BROWSE) command is entered in the command input.

```
                            DB2 INTERFACE
                          DATA ACCESS PANEL

COMMAND===> b


OUTPUT SQL LIBRARY:                  SAVE SELECTIONS (savesel): N

OUTPUT SAS DATA SET: SASOUT.EX2      UNIQUE SAS NAMES (unique): N

DB2 SUBSYSTEM ID:     DBT


        AUTHORIZATION ID                  TABLE NAME
              TSID123.                    PROJINFO..........
              ........                    ..................
              ........                    ..................
              ........                    ..................
              ........                    ..................

EXTRACT STATISTICS: NUMBER OF SAS OBS CREATED  =       60
                    NUMBER OF SAS VARS CREATED =       8
```

Hitting enter after the B command was entered in the DATA ACCESS panel, brings up the BROWSE panel displaying the SAS data set just created, Sasout.ex2. Shown below are the first 19 observations out of the 60 observations on this SAS data set. Notice that Hiredte is formatted using the MMDDYY8. format and that Salary06 is formatted using the DOLLAR8. format. PF8/PF20 can be used to scroll down and PF7/PF19 can be used to scroll up through the 60 observations. PF11/Pf23, can be used to scroll to the right to view the other SAS variables, Salary07 and Salary08, which did not fit on this screen. Use PF10/PF22 to scroll to the left.

```
                         SAS Data Set: SASOUT.EX2      Observations
COMMAND===>                                            First       1
                                                       Last       19
OBS   LAST_NAM  FIRST_NA  HIRE_DAT  VACAVAIL  VACUSED  SALARY06


  1   ADAMS     BILL      11/14/55       160       40    $2,000
  2   APPLE     RICHARD   11/23/47       160       80    $3,000
  3   ATKINS    NANCY     09/15/81       120       56    $3,500
  4   ATWOOD    CHUCK     03/24/65       160       72    $2,420
  5   BAKER     MARTHA    04/01/74       120       40    $2,680
  6   BROOKS    EDWARD    08/13/75       120       80    $5,200
  7   BROOKS    JIM       09/01/72       160      120    $1,900
  8   BROWN     WALLY     05/05/72       160       80    $2,570
  9   BUELL     MAX       04/05/83       120       48    $2,890
 10   BURNETT   ERIC      01/01/89        40        8      $400
 11   CAMPBELL  MARGARET  02/03/79       120       40    $2,520
 12   CLARK     ALMA      03/04/88        40       40    $1,580
 13   CONNOR    BRUCE     05/02/79       120       80    $2,100
 14   CONWELL   LINDA     03/11/85        80       40    $2,310
 15   COOPER    MARGIE    06/18/87        80       80    $1,370
 16   DAVIS     SUSAN     03/05/88        40       16    $1,000
 17   DODD      MARLENA   01/01/89        40        0      $850
 18   DOUGLAS   MILTON    11/09/67       160       40    $4,200
 19   DUDLEY    LOUISA    12/04/66       160      104    $2,100
```

If the UNIQUE option had been changed to a Y in the DATA ACCESS panel, the generated SAS variable names would have been unique. Unfortunately, the DATA EXTRACTION panel would still display duplicate SAS names. However, the END command would return the user to the DATA ACCESS panel without receiving the duplicate SAS names message. When the BROWSE panel was accessed, the unique names would be displayed as follows:

```
                         SAS Data Set: SASOUT.EX2      Observations
COMMAND===>                                            First       1
                                                       Last       19
OBS   LAST_NAM  FIRST_NA  HIRE_DAT  VACATION  VACATI00 SALARY_J

  1   ADAMS     BILL      11/14/55       160       40    $2,000
  ...
```

The DB2 column, Vacation_used, is given the SAS name, Vacati00. This name is not very descriptive and you have to look at the values of the variables, Vacation and Vacati00, to be able to tell which one is Vacation_available and which one is Vacation_used. Using the PF11/PF23 keys to scroll right will display a similiar naming convention for the DB2 columns, Salary_june and Salary_july. In this case, if you did not know that Salary_june was first on the DB2 table, you would not be able to distinguish which column represented June salaries and which column represented July salaries. For this reason, I recommend leaving the UNIQUE option set to N.

Use the END command (PF3/PF15) to exit the BROWSE panel and return to the DATA ACCESS panel. Use the END command again to return to Display Manager.

Exercise 1

Test your understanding of the creation of a SAS data set containing data extracted from DB2 table(s) in Display Manager by completing the exercises described here. The BROWSE panels displaying the result of each extraction are shown on the following pages. The DB2 tables used as input are the same tables used in the previous examples and are shown in Appendix C. The data contained in these tables can be loaded into DB2 tables at your site by keying, or refer to Chapter 1, Introduction, for information concerning ordering copies of the tables.

Report 1

Select the required DB2 columns, as shown on the report, from the DB2 table, Persinfo. Let the SAS variable names default to the first eight positions of the DB2 column name.

Report 2

Select the required DB2 columns, as shown on the report, from the DB2 table, Persinfo. Name the SAS variables as shown on the report. Format the DB2 column, BIRTH_DATE. Select only those rows with a Cost_center of 120 or 130.

Report 1

The SAS data set created in this exercise contains 60 observations and 6 variables. The first 19 observations are shown below in the BROWSE panel.

```
                      SAS Data Set: WORK.EXER1     Observations
COMMAND===>                                        First      1
                                                   Last      19
OBS  LAST_NAM   FIRST_NA  HOME_PHO  OFFICE_E  COST_CEN  MANAGEME


  1  ADAMS      BILL      8293232     3939     100        N
  2  APPLE      RICHARD   9829823     9870     120        N
  3  ATKINS     NANCY     9872342     9824     120        Y
  4  ATWOOD     CHUCK     8234233     9832     140        N
  5  BAKER      MARTHA    8712343     9874     130        N
  6  BROOKS     EDWARD    9078123     9876     140        Y
  7  BROOKS     JIM       9078232     8709     110        N
  8  BROWN      WALLY     8708973     9871     100        N
  9  BUELL      MAX       9870133     8022     110        N
 10  BURNETT    ERIC      9781334     9822     110        N
 11  CAMPBELL   MARGARET  2298422     9825     130        N
 12  CLARK      ALMA      2802340     8921     100        N
 13  CONNOR     BRUCE     9023482     3903     110        N
 14  CONWELL    LINDA     9234928     7823     100        N
 15  COOPER     MARGIE    4298713     9073     100        N
 16  DAVIS      SUSAN     2347033     2398     100        N
 17  DODD       MARLENA   5934020     2343     110        N
 18  DOUGLAS    MILTON    2329842     9835     140        Y
 19  DUDLEY     LOUISA    2398234     9823     130        N
```

Report 2

The SAS data set created in this exercise contains 27 observations and 4 variables. The first 19 observations are shown below in the BROWSE panel.

```
                       SAS Data Set: WORK.EXER2     Observations
COMMAND===>                                         First       1
                                                    Last       19
OBS  LNAME        FNAME                 BDATE     CITY          STATE

  1  APPLE        RICHARD     Fri, Mar 14, 24  INDIANAPOLIS     IN
  2  ATKINS       NANCY         Sun,Mar 8, 53  INDIANAPOLIS     IN
  3  BAKER        MARTHA      Sat, Aug 20, 27  NEW CASTLE       IN
  4  CAMPBELL     MARGARET     Sun, Sep 3, 44  MUNCIE           IN
  5  DUDLEY       LOUISA       Fri, Jan 4, 35  NEWCASTLE        IN
  6  GOETZ        JACK         Sun, Mar 5, 44  MT SUMMIT        IN
  7  HANKS        TROY         Sat, Mar 6, 48  LIBERTY          IN
  8  HARDWICK     DONNIE       Wed, Mar 9, 60  SPICELAND        IN
  9  HARRINGTON   MARLIN       Tue, Sep 5, 44  KNIGHTSTOWN      IN
 10  HUFFORD      STEPHEN     Mon, Jul 12, 65  KENNARD          IN
 11  HUGHES       PEGGY       Mon, Jun 23, 58  SULPHER SPRINGS  IN
 12  JAMES        MARVIN       Sun, Oct 9, 38  SHIRLEY          IN
 13  KAWAN        JOE          Sun, Mar 5, 39  MUNCIE           IN
 14  KELLUM       ELLEN JANE  Fri, Jun 23, 44  KENNARD          IN
 15  KISLING      MARY LEA     Wed, Mar 3, 48  MT SUMMIT        IN
 16  LAUREN       KELLY        Sat, Sep 5, 70  CAMBRIDE CITY    IN
 17  MEEKS        EDWARD      Fri, Apr 29, 55  GREENWOOD        IN
 18  MICHAEL      GARTH       Sat, Sep 10, 55  NEW CASTLE       IN
 19  OLIVER       BETTY       Tue, Aug 22, 44  MUNCIE           IN
```

Enhanced SELECT Statements

PROC DB2EXT creates a SAS data set containing data extracted from DB2 table(s) based on two intermediate steps. The first step is to build a map, which "maps" DB2 columns to SAS variables. The map includes SAS variable names and formats, which can either be generated by PROC DB2EXT or defined by the user. The map is built in the DATA EXTRACTION panel using the DB2 columns contained in the table(s) specified on the DATA ACCESS panel. The map then constructs the appropriate SELECT statement. The SELECT statement extracts the data from the DB2 table(s).

A SELECT statement generated by a map cannot use all the features of the SELECT statement covered in Chapter 4, Structured Query Language. A SELECT statement generated by a map contains the following components of the SELECT statement:

- the DB2 table name(s) entered in the DATA ACCESS panel
- the DB2 columns selected in the DATA EXTRACTION panel
- optionally, a WHERE clause which extracts only those rows meeting specific criteria; the WHERE clause is coded in the bottom half of the DATA EXTRACTION panel

A SELECT statement which can be generated by a map will be termed a Basic SELECT statement from this point on in this book. A Basic SELECT statement cannot contain such features as the GROUP BY, HAVING, or ORDER BY clauses, create new values from existing DB2 columns and constants, or use functions (SUM, MIN, MAX, AVG). When these capabilities are needed, the user must either code the SELECT statement from scratch or edit the SELECT statement generated by the map. SELECT statements containing these features will be referred to as Enhanced SELECT statements from this point on in this book.

This section illustrates the use of Enhanced SELECT statements to create a SAS data set from data stored in DB2 table(s). Figure 6-9 shows the panels which will be illustrated in this section.

PROC DB2EXT is executed in Display Manager to bring up the DATA ACCESS panel. After the DATA ACCESS panel is completed, hitting enter displays the DATA EXTRACTION panel. Only two operations should be completed at this point in the DATA EXTRACTION panel. First, select the desired DB2 columns, letting the SAS variable names default to the first eight positions of the DB2 column name. Second, if a WHERE clause is needed, code it in the bottom half of the DATA EXTRACTION panel. When these operations are

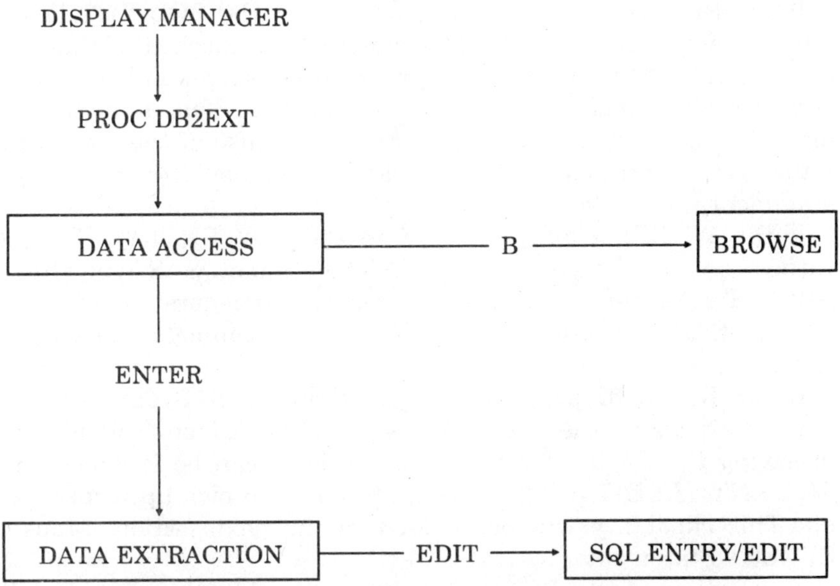

Figure 6-9 PROC DB2EXT Panels for Enhanced SELECT statements.

completed on the DATA EXTRACTION panel, use the EDIT command (PF11/PF23) to bring up the SQL ENTRY/EDIT panel.

The SQL ENTRY/EDIT panel will contain a Basic SELECT statement, generated by the map built in the DATA EXTRACTION panel. At this point, you will probably want to use the NUMS ON command to generate line numbers on the left side of the screen. This will allow you to use line commands such as insert (I), delete (D), copy (C), move (M), copy/move after/before (A/B), and their corresponding block commands, to edit the SELECT statement. When you are satisfied with the SELECT statement, use the END command (PF3/PF15) to exit the SQL ENTRY/EDIT panel.

This will return you to the DATA EXTRACTION panel, where you can now change the SAS variable names and formats. If SAS variable names and formats are changed when the DATA EXTRACTION panel is displayed the first time, these changes will not be saved. When the DATA EXTRACTION panel is complete, the END command is used to return to the DATA ACCESS panel and create the SAS data set based on the Enhanced SELECT statement. The B (BROWSE) command can be used in the DATA ACCESS panel to bring up the BROWSE panel, which will display the SAS data set.

When the END command is issued from the SQL ENTRY/EDIT panel, the syntax of the SELECT statement is checked. If there is an error in the SELECT statement, a negative error number and a description will appear under the command line. This is an IBM SQL error and not a SAS error. Sometimes the cause of the error can be difficult to identify because the location of the error in the SELECT statement is not given.

If the WHERE clause is coded in the SQL ENTRY/EDIT panel rather than in the DATA EXTRACTION panel, SAS will alter the SELECT statement and an SQL error will be generated. This occurs because SAS generates the word WHERE; it cannot be coded by the user.

If the BROWSE panel shows you that the SAS data set is not what you wanted, the entire process must be redone. The advantage of saving the SELECT statement is that it can be included in the SQL ENTRY/EDIT panel, allowing the user to pick up where he left off. This capability will be covered in the next section, Maps and SELECT Statements.

The Enhanced SELECT statements covered in this section will be based on editing the SELECT statement generated by the map. It would be unlikely that the user would want to enter the entire SELECT statement from scratch so this will not be illustrated here. However, if the user does wish to do this, the SELECT statement can be keyed into an empty SQL ENTRY/EDIT panel, which is displayed by not coding a DB2 table name on the DATA ACCESS panel. Using the END command after the SELECT statement is completed will still display the DATA EXTRACTION panel, where SAS variable names and formats can be changed.

Example 6-3

A SAS data set is needed which contains the annualized salary based on the monthly salary for December and the average salary for December. These data are needed by Cost_center and Employee_type rather than for each employee. In addition, the total annualized salary is needed for each Cost_center regardless of the Employee_type. The data should be sorted by Cost_center and Employee_type.

This will require the GROUP BY clause of the SELECT statement, which cannot be generated by a map. The other alternative is to create a SAS data set containing detailed employee statistics and use PROC SUMMARY to create a summary SAS data set by Cost_center and Employee_type. This alternative is feasible only when the DB2 table is small; otherwise, it would require much greater computer resources.

Assume that you are in Display Manager and have executed PROC DB2EXT to bring up the DATA ACCESS panel. On the DATA ACCESS panel, enter the name of the OUTPUT SAS DATA SET, ex3, and the DB2 table, Tsid123.Persinfo.

```
                          DB2 INTERFACE
                        DATA ACCESS PANEL


COMMAND===>
NOTE: FILL IN THE FIELDS BELOW

OUTPUT SQL LIBRARY:               SAVE SELECTIONS (savesel): N

OUTPUT SAS DATA SET: ex3          UNIQUE SAS NAMES (unique): N

DB2 SUBSYSTEM ID:    DBT

         AUTHORIZATION ID              TABLE NAME
                 tsid123.              persinfo..........
                 ........              ..................
                 ........              ..................
                 ........              ..................
                 ........              ..................
```

Hitting the enter key on the DATA ACCESS panel brings up the DATA EXTRACTION panel shown below. The S FUNC is entered beside the desired DB2 column, Cost_center, and hitting the enter key displays the generated SAS name.

```
              DB2 INTERFACE                    TABLE NAME: PERSINFO
        DATA EXTRACTION PANEL                SAS DATA SET: WORK.EX3


COMMAND===>


FUNC    COLUMN NAME               SAS NAME     FORMAT
 . *** TABLE- PERSINFO              *** COLUMNS-   30 * SELECTED-   0 *
 .        SOCIAL_SECURITY         ........     $9.
 .        LAST_NAME               ........     $15.
 .        FIRST_NAME              ........     $10.
 .        SEX                     ........     $1.
 .        BIRTH_DATE              ........     7.
 .        ADDRESS                 ........     $20.
 .        CITY                    ........     $15.
 .        STATE                   ........     $2.
 .        ZIP_CODE                ........     $5.
 .        HOME_PHONE              ........     $7.
 .        HIRE_DATE               ........     7.
 .        OFFICE_EXTENSION        ........     $4.
 .        COST_CENTER             COST_CEN     $3.
--------------------- WHERE CLAUSE ----------------------------
```

Scrolling down twice (PF8/PF20) displays additional DB2 columns that are needed, Salary_December and Employee_type. The S FUNC is used to select these columns and hitting enter displays the generated SAS names. The EDIT command is entered in the command input.

```
             DB2 INTERFACE                     TABLE NAME: PERSINFO
       DATA EXTRACTION PANEL                 SAS DATA SET: WORK.EX3

COMMAND===> edit

FUNC   COLUMN NAME          SAS NAME      FORMAT
 .      SALARY_DECEMBER     SALARY_D      6.
 .      EMPLOYEE_TYPE       EMPLOYEE      $1.
 .      MANAGEMENT          ........      $1.

--------------------- WHERE CLAUSE ----------------------------
```

Using the EDIT command in the DATA EXTRACTION panel brings up the SQL ENTRY/EDIT panel. The SELECT statement generated by the map built in the DATA EXTRACTION panel is displayed. The SELECT statement appears as was discussed in Chapter 4, Structured Query Language. Notice that the DB2 columns are specified using the DB2 table name as a qualifier. SAS generates column names in this format in case more than one DB2 column from separate DB2 tables has the same name. The table name can be edited out of the SELECT statement as long as more than one column from different tables do not have the same name. The NUMS ON command is entered.

```
                        SQL ENTRY/EDIT SCREEN
COMMAND===> nums on                                       TEXT EDITOR

 SELECT
  TSID123.PERSINFO.COST_CENTER, TSID123.PERSINFO.SALARY_DECEMBER,
  TSID123.PERSINFO.EMPLOYEE_TYPE
  FROM
  TSID123.PERSINFO
```

The NUMS ON command generates line numbers on the left of the screen. Line commands can be used to edit the SELECT statement. GROUP BY and ORDER BY clauses are added for summarization and sorting, respectively. The annualized salary based on Salary_december is calculated by multiplying by 12 and using the SUM function to create totals by the columns named in the GROUP BY clause. The AVG function is used to calculate the average of all values of Salary_december for each group formed by the columns named in the GROUP BY clause. When editing is complete, the END command (PF3/PF15) is entered.

```
                         SQL ENTRY/EDIT SCREEN
COMMAND===> end                                          TEXT EDITOR
                                                         Col 001 072
 00001SELECT
 00002  TSID123.PERSINFO.COST_CENTER, sum(SALARY_DECEMBER * 12),
 00003  avg(salary_december),
 00004  TSID123.PERSINFO.EMPLOYEE_TYPE
 00005  FROM
 00006  TSID123.PERSINFO
 00007  group by cost_center, employee_type
 00008  order by cost_center, employee_type
 00009
```

Issuing the END command will return you to the DATA EXTRACTION panel if no SQL errors are found. If errors are found, they must be corrected before you can return to the DATA EXTRACTION panel.

The only DB2 columns displayed on the DATA EXTRACTION panel are those contained in the edited SELECT statement. The two SAS variable names, COMPOUND, represent the two columns that are a result of the SUM and the AVG functions. Any columns created in the SELECT statement based on arithmetic operators, functions, existing columns, and constants are given the SAS name COMPOUND. If more than one column is created, more than one column named COMPOUND is generated. The order the columns were created in the SELECT statement is the order they will be displayed on the DATA EXTRACTION panel. You will need to remember this order to be able to distinguish the columns and name them appropriately. If you can't remember, you can return to the SQL ENTRY/EDIT panel using the EDIT command.

```
            DB2 INTERFACE                        TABLE NAME: PERSINFO
      DATA EXTRACTION PANEL                    SAS DATA SET: WORK.EX3

COMMAND===>

FUNC    COLUMN NAME           SAS NAME     FORMAT
 .*** DB2 TABLE- ** FROM SQL CALL ** ** COLUMNS- 4 SELECTED- 4 *
 .      COST_CENTER           COST_CEN     $3.
 .                            COMPOUND     16.
 .                            COMPOUND     16.10
 .      EMPLOYEE_TYPE         EMPLOYEE     $1.

-------------------- WHERE CLAUSE ---------------------------
```

SAS variable names are changed and the DOLLARw.d format is assigned to the two variables previously named COMPOUND. The variable generated by the AVG function did have 10 decimal places, which are rarely needed.

```
            DB2 INTERFACE                        TABLE NAME: PERSINFO
      DATA EXTRACTION PANEL                    SAS DATA SET: WORK.EX3

COMMAND===>

FUNC   COLUMN NAME            SAS NAME     FORMAT
 .*** DB2 TABLE- ** FROM SQL CALL ** ** COLUMNS- 4 SELECTED- 4 *
 .      COST_CENTER           CCC          $3.
 .                            YRSAL        DOLLAR12.2
 .                            AVGMTHSL     DOLLAR12.2
 .      EMPLOYEE_TYPE         EMPTYPE      $1.

--------------------WHERE CLAUSE ---------------------------
```

The END command (PF3/PF15) is used to return to the DATA ACCESS panel and create the SAS data set. The DATA ACCESS panel shows extract statistics at the bottom of the panel. In this case, the SAS data set ex1 has 13 observations and 4 variables. The B (BROWSE) command is entered in the command input.

```
                              DB2 INTERFACE
                            DATA ACCESS PANEL


COMMAND===> b


OUTPUT SQL LIBRARY:                       SAVE SELECTIONS (savesel): N

OUTPUT SAS DATA SET: EX3                  UNIQUE SAS NAMES (unique): N

DB2 SUBSYSTEM ID:     DBT

            AUTHORIZATION ID                    TABLE NAME
                      TSID123.                  PROJINFO..........
                      ........                  ..................
                      ........                  ..................
                      ........                  ..................
                      ........                  ..................

EXTRACT STATISTICS: NUMBER OF SAS OBS CREATED  =         13
                    NUMBER OF SAS VARS CREATED =         4
```

Hitting enter after the B command was entered in the DATA ACCESS panel, brings up the BROWSE panel displaying the SAS data set just created, Ex3. The data shown here satisfy the reporting requirements except that the total salary by Cost_center regardless of Employee_type is not given. To obtain this total through SQL, another SELECT statement would have to be executed with a GROUP BY of only Cost_center. The result table from each of these two SELECT statements would then be combined using the UNION operation. Although this can be done, it is probably easier for the user and takes less computer resources to use Base SAS to calculate this total.

```
                    SAS Data Set: SASOUT.EX3       Observations
COMMAND===>                                        First       1
                                                   Last       13
       OBS     CCC          YRSAL          AVGMTHSL   EMPTYPE


         1     100    $123,000.00         $1,464.29      H
         2     100     $30,840.00         $2,570.00      S
         3     100     $39,600.00           $660.00      T
         4     110    $128,760.00         $1,788.33      H
         5     110     $80,880.00         $2,246.67      S
         6     110     $15,000.00           $625.00      T
         7     120    $123,720.00         $1,718.33      H
         8     120    $237,720.00         $2,830.00      S
         9     130    $112,200.00         $1,870.00      H
        10     130    $246,600.00         $2,935.71      S
        11     130     $20,400.00           $850.00      T
        12     140     $29,040.00         $2,420.00      H
        13     140    $386,520.00         $4,026.25      S
```

Use the END command (PF3/PF15) to return to Display Manager. A PROC PRINT step is coded in the PROGRAM window and executed to produce the total salary for each Cost_center regardless of Employee_type.

```
--------------------------------------------------------------
COMMAND ===>                                  SAS(r) Log   HH:MM

NOTE: COPYRIGHT(C) 1984, 1988 SAS INSTITUTE INC., CARY, NC 27512
USA
NOTE: SAS RELEASE 5.18 AT COMPANY ABC (00000000).
NOTE: CPUID   VERSION = 00  SERIAL = 000000   MODEL = 0000 .
NOTE: SAS OPTIONS SPECIFIED ARE:
      DMS NONEWS FSP FS NODATE
--------------------------------------------------------------
COMMAND ===>                                      Program Editor

00001 proc print data = ex3 label;
00002   by ccc;
00003   id ccc;
00004   var emptype yrsal avgmthsl;
00005   sum yrsal;
00006   title 'Salary Statistics by Cost Center and Employee Type';
00007 run;
00008
```

PROC PRINT is executed to produce the following report. This example shows that Base SAS must be used to complete some applications. You can not rely totally on SAS/DB2 or on the SQL SELECT statement.

```
   Salary Statistics by Cost Center and Employee Type

COST_CENTER    EMPLOYEE_TYPE          YRSAL        AVGMTHSL
    100              H          $123,000.00       $1,464.29
                     S           $30,840.00       $2,570.00
                     T          $39,600.00         $660.00
-----------                    ------------
    100                         $193,440.00

    110              H          $128,760.00       $1,788.33
                     S           $80,880.00       $2,246.67
                     T           $15,000.00         $625.00
-----------                    ------------
    110                         $224,640.00

    120              H          $123,720.00       $1,718.33
                     S          $237,720.00       $2,830.00
------------                   ------------
    120                         $361,440.00

    130              H          $112,200.00       $1,870.00
                     S          $246,600.00       $2,935.71
                     T           $20,400.00         $850.00
-----------                    ------------
    130                         $379,200.00

    140              H           $29,040.00       $2,420.00
                     S          $386,520.00       $4,026.25
-----------                    ------------
    140                         $415,560.00
                               ============
                                $1574280.00
```

Example 6-4

A SAS data set is needed which contains each employee's full name and annual salary. The name of the department is also needed for each employee. Create a SAS variable that will categorize the staff by salary where $20,000 or more is high, $15,000 to $19,999 is medium, and less than $15,000 is low.

The annual salary is the sum of the 12 monthly salaries; this will require an Enhanced SELECT statement. The department name is found on the DB2 table, Orginfo, so it will have to be joined with the DB2 table, Persinfo.

Assume that you are in Display Manager and PROC DB2EXT has been executed to bring up the DATA ACCESS panel. The OUTPUT SAS DATA SET is called ex4 and two DB2 tables, Persinfo and Orginfo, are requested.

```
                          DB2 INTERFACE
                        DATA ACCESS PANEL

COMMAND===>
NOTE: FILL IN THE FIELDS BELOW

OUTPUT SQL LIBRARY:                  SAVE SELECTIONS (savesel): N

OUTPUT SAS DATA SET: ex4             UNIQUE SAS NAMES (unique): N

DB2 SUBSYSTEM ID:     DBT

          AUTHORIZATION ID                TABLE NAME
                 tsid123.                 persinfo..........
                 tsid123.                 orginfo...........
                 ........                 ..................
                 ........                 ..................
                 ........                 ..................
```

Hitting the enter key on the DATA ACCESS panel brings up the DATA EXTRACTION panel shown below. The S FUNC is entered beside the desired DB2 columns and hitting the enter key displays the generated SAS name.

```
                DB2 INTERFACE                         TABLE NAME: PERSINFO
          DATA EXTRACTION PANEL                     SAS DATA SET: WORK.EX4


COMMAND===>


FUNC    COLUMN NAME              SAS NAME      FORMAT
 . *** TABLE- PERSINFO              *** COLUMNS-  30 * SELECTED-   0 *
 .        SOCIAL_SECURITY        ........      $9.
 .        LAST_NAME              LAST_NAM      $15.
 .        FIRST_NAME             FIRST_NA      $10.
 .        SEX                    ........      $1.
 .        BIRTH_DATE             ........      7.
 .        ADDRESS                ........      $20.
 .        CITY                   ........      $15.
 .        STATE                  ........      $2.
 .        ZIP_CODE               ........      $5.
 .        HOME_PHONE             ........      $7.
 .        HIRE_DATE              ........      7.
 .        OFFICE_EXTENSION       ........      $4.
 .        COST_CENTER            ........      $3.
-------------------- WHERE CLAUSE ---------------------------
```

Scrolling once (PF8/PF20) displays the second screen where additional DB2 columns are selected, and hitting enter displays the generated SAS variable name.

```
              DB2 INTERFACE                    TABLE NAME: PERSINFO
           DATA EXTRACTION PANEL              SAS DATA SET: WORK.EX4

COMMAND===>

FUNC    COLUMN NAME           SAS NAME     FORMAT
 .       VACATION_AVAILABLE   ........      4.
 .       VACATION_USED        ........      4.
 .       SICK_USED            ........      4.
 .       SALARY_JANUARY       SALARY_J      6.
 .       SALARY_FEBRUARY      SALARY_F      6.
 .       SALARY_MARCH         SALARY_M      6.
 .       SALARY_APRIL         SALARY_A      6.
 .       SALARY_MAY           SALARY_M      6.
 .       SALARY_JUNE          SALARY_J      6.
 .       SALARY_JULY          SALARY_J      6.
 .       SALARY_AUGUST        SALARY_A      6.
 .       SALARY_SEPTEMBER     SALARY_S      6.
 .       SALARY_OCTOBER       SALARY_O      6.
 .       SALARY_NOVEMBER      SALARY_N      6.
--------------------- WHERE CLAUSE ----------------------------
```

Scrolling down (PF8/PF20) again displays additional DB2 columns that are needed, Salary_December from Persinfo and Department_name from Orginfo. The S FUNC is used to select these columns and hitting enter displays the generated SAS names. A WHERE clause is coded to select those rows out of the CARTESIAN PRODUCT where Cost_center from Persinfo and Department from Orginfo are equal. The EDIT command is entered in the command input.

```
              DB2 INTERFACE                    TABLE NAME: PERSINFO
         DATA EXTRACTION PANEL               SAS DATA SET: WORK.EX4

COMMAND===> edit

FUNC   COLUMN NAME              SAS NAME     FORMAT
 .      SALARY_DECEMBER         SALARY_D     6.
 .      EMPLOYEE_TYPE           ........     $1.
 .      MANAGEMENT              ........     $1.
 . *** TABLE- ORGINFO              *** COLUMNS-  5 * SELECTED-  1 *
 .      DEPARTMENT              ........     $3.
 .      DEPARTMENT_NAME         DEPARTME     $15.
 .      DIRECTOR                ........     $25.
 .      VICE PRESIDENT          ........     $25.
 .      PRESIDENT               ........     $25.

--------------------- WHERE CLAUSE ---------------------------
cost_center = department
```

Using the EDIT command in the DATA EXTRACTION panel brings up the SQL ENTRY/EDIT panel. The SELECT statement generated by the map built in the DATA EXTRACTION panel is displayed. The NUMS ON command is entered.

```
                      SQL ENTRY/EDIT SCREEN
COMMAND===> nums on                                    TEXT EDITOR

SELECT
 TSID123.PERSINFO.LAST_NAME, TSID123.PERSINFO.FIRST_NAME,
 TSID123.PERSINFO.SALARY_JANUARY,
 TSID123.PERSINFO.SALARY_FEBRUARY,
 TSID123.PERSINFO.SALARY_MARCH, TSID123.PERSINFO.SALARY_APRIL,
 TSID123.PERSINFO.SALARY_MAY, TSID123.PERSINFO.SALARY_JUNE,
 TSID123.PERSINFO.SALARY_JULY, TSID123.PERSINFO.SALARY_AUGUST,
 TSID123.PERSINFO.SALARY_SEPTEMBER,
 TSID123.PERSINFO.SALARY_OCTOBER,
 TSID123.PERSINFO.SALARY_NOVEMBER,
 TSID123.PERSINFO.SALARY_DECEMBER,
 TSID123.ORGINFO.DEPARTMENT_NAME
 FROM
 TSID123.PERSINFO, TSID123.ORGINFO
 WHERE
 cost_center = department
```

The NUMS ON command generates line numbers on the left of the screen. The 12 salary columns are edited so that they are added, resulting in a single value. When editing is complete, the END command (PF3/PF15) is entered.

```
                         SQL ENTRY/EDIT SCREEN
COMMAND===> end                                           TEXT EDITOR
                                                          Col 001 072

00001 SELECT
00002  TSID123.PERSINFO.LAST_NAME, TSID123.PERSINFO.FIRST_NAME,
00003  SALARY_JANUARY + SALARY_FEBRUARY +
00004  SALARY_MARCH + SALARY_APRIL +
00005  SALARY_MAY + SALARY_JUNE +
00006  SALARY_JULY + SALARY_AUGUST +
00007  SALARY_SEPTEMBER + SALARY_OCTOBER +
00008  SALARY_NOVEMBER + SALARY_DECEMBER,
00009  TSID123.ORGINFO.DEPARTMENT_NAME
00010  FROM
00011  TSID123.PERSINFO, TSID123.ORGINFO
00012 WHERE
00013 cost_center = department
00014
```

Issuing the END command will return you to the DATA EXTRACTION panel if no SQL errors are found. If errors are found, they must be corrected before you can return to the DATA EXTRACTION panel.

The only DB2 columns displayed on the DATA EXTRACTION panel are those contained in the edited SELECT statement. The SAS variable, COMPOUND, is the SUM of the 12 salary columns.

```
                DB2 INTERFACE                    TABLE NAME: PERSINFO
          DATA EXTRACTION PANEL                SAS DATA SET: WORK.EX4


COMMAND===>


FUNC    COLUMN NAME              SAS NAME       FORMAT
 .*** DB2 TABLE- ** FROM SQL CALL ** ** COLUMNS- 4 SELECTED- 4 *
 .        LAST_NAME              LAST_NAM       $15.
 .        FIRST_NAME             FIRST_NA       $10.
 .                               COMPOUND       16.
 .        DEPARTMENT_NAME        DEPARTME       $15.

-------------------- WHERE CLAUSE ---------------------------
```

The SAS variable names are changed and the DOLLARw.d format is assigned to the variable representing the SUM of the 12 salaries.

```
                DB2 INTERFACE                    TABLE NAME: PERSINFO
          DATA EXTRACTION PANEL                SAS DATA SET: WORK.EX4


COMMAND===>


FUNC    COLUMN NAME              SAS NAME       FORMAT
 .*** DB2 TABLE- ** FROM SQL CALL ** ** COLUMNS- 4 SELECTED- 4 *
 .        LAST_NAME              LNAME          $15.
 .        FIRST_NAME             FNAME          $10.
 .                               YRSAL          DOLLAR12.0
 .        DEPARTMENT_NAME        DEPT           $15.

-------------------- WHERE CLAUSE ---------------------------
```

The END command (PF3/PF15) is used to return to the DATA ACCESS panel and create the SAS data set. The DATA ACCESS panel shows extract statistics at the bottom of the panel. In this case, the SAS data set, ex1, has 60 observations and 4 variables. If the WHERE clause had not been used, the result would have been the entire CARTESIAN PRODUCT, 300 rows (60 Persinfo * 5 Orginfo). The B (BROWSE) command is entered in the command input.

```
                              DB2 INTERFACE
                            DATA ACCESS PANEL

COMMAND===> b


OUTPUT SQL LIBRARY:                         SAVE SELECTIONS (savesel): N

OUTPUT SAS DATA SET: WORK.EX4               UNIQUE SAS NAMES (unique): N

DB2 SUBSYSTEM ID:    DBT

          AUTHORIZATION ID                       TABLE NAME
                  TSID123.                       PROJINFO..........
                  TSID123.                       ORGINFO...........
                  ........                       ..................
                  ........                       ..................
                  ........                       ..................


EXTRACT STATISTICS: NUMBER OF SAS OBS CREATED  =      60
                    NUMBER OF SAS VARS CREATED =      4
```

Hitting enter after the B command has been entered in the DATA ACCESS panel, brings up the BROWSE panel displaying the SAS data set just created, Ex4.

```
                       SAS Data Set: SASOUT.EX4       Observations
COMMAND ===>                                          First       1
                                                      Last       19
   OBS    LNAME        FNAME          YRSAL      DEPT

     1    BROWN        WALLY        $30,160      PERSONNEL
     2    CLARK        ALMA         $18,800      PERSONNEL
     3    CONWELL      LINDA        $27,500      PERSONNEL
     4    COOPER       MARGIE       $16,090      PERSONNEL
     5    DAVIS        SUSAN        $12,000      PERSONNEL
     6    JOHNSON      HAZEL        $12,200      PERSONNEL
     7    JONES        JOAN          $6,000      PERSONNEL
     8    MARSHALL     MICHAEL       $6,000      PERSONNEL
     9    MEYER        VIVIAN        $5,400      PERSONNEL
    10    MITCHELL     KELLY        $11,250      PERSONNEL
    11    MOORE        RUTH         $10,360      PERSONNEL
    12    SHEPHERD     KANDI        $10,200      PERSONNEL
    13    ADAMS        BILL         $24,200      PERSONNEL
    14    SMITH        SCOTT        $23,400      MARKETING
    15    PHILLIPS     SARAH        $16,940      MARKETING
    16    MARK         MIRON        $18,800      MARKETING
    17    MEISER       MARK         $23,840      MARKETING
    18    HARRIS       JULIE        $21,600      MARKETING
    19    HOLLYWOOD    ALICE        $18,240      MARKETING
```

This SAS data set contains all the requirements except the SAS variable needed to categorize each employee according to his or her annual salary. To create this column in SQL, three SELECT statements would have to be coded, one for each category, which would assign the appropriate character string description. The three result tables would be combined using the UNION operation.

The same result can be produced in a DATA step reading Ex4. It is much easier to code and takes less computer time. The SQL code would require processing the entire DB2 tables three times.

Use the END command (PF3/PF15) to return to Display Manager. A DATA step is coded in the PROGRAM window and executed to produce the SAS variable, Cat, which will categorize each employee according to annual salary. PROC PRINT is then coded to verify the result.

```
-----------------------------------------------------------------
COMMAND ===>                                    SAS(r) Log   HH:MM

NOTE: COPYRIGHT(C) 1984, 1988 SAS INSTITUTE INC., CARY, NC 27512
USA
NOTE: SAS RELEASE 5.18 AT COMPANY ABC (00000000).
NOTE: CPUID   VERSION = 00   SERIAL = 000000   MODEL = 0000 .
-----------------------------------------------------------------
COMMAND ===>                                       Program Editor

data ex4f;
  set ex4;
  length cat $6;
  if yrsal >= 20000 then cat = 'high';
  else if 15000 <= yrsal < 20000 then cat = 'medium';
  else cat = 'low';

proc sort data = ex4f;
 by descending yrsal;

proc print data= ex4f;
  by notsorted cat;
  var lname fname yrsal dept;
  title 'employee annual salaries';
run;
```

PROC FORMAT could be used to assign the labels (low, medium, and high) to the variable, Yrsal, rather than using a DATA step to create the new variable, Cat.

The first page of the results of the DATA step and PROC PRINT is shown below:

```
                    employee annual salaries

 ---------------------- CAT=high ---------------------

 OBS     LNAME          FNAME        YRSAL     DEPT

   1     BROOKS         EDWARD       64200     DEVELOPMENT
   2     PEYTON         JOHN         52100     DEVELOPMENT
   3     DOUGLAS        MILTON       50980     DEVELOPMENT
   4     MICHAEL        PAT          49120     DEVELOPMENT
   5     KAWAN          JOE          48840     SALES
   6     MORGAN         CHERYL       48300     DEVELOPMENT
   7     KEESLING       GERTRUDE     43250     DEVELOPMENT
   8     ATKINS         NANCY        43000     FINANCE
   9     HUTSON         EVERETT      41900     DEVELOPMENT
  10     GOETZ          JACK         38960     SALES
  11     HARRINGTON     MARLIN       37890     FINANCE
  12     APPLE          RICHARD      36420     FINANCE
  13     MEEKS          EDWARD       34400     FINANCE
  14     BUELL          MAX          34110     MARKETING
  15     HARDWICK       DONNIE       34110     SALES
  16     MICHAEL        GARTH        34110     SALES
  17     BAKER          MARTHA       31620     SALES
  18     BROWN          WALLY        30160     PERSONNEL
  19     CAMPBELL       MARGARET     30120     SALES
```

Exercise 2

Test your understanding of the creation of a SAS data set with user-edited SQL SELECT statements by completing the exercises described here. The BROWSE panel displaying the result of each extraction is shown on the following pages. The DB2 tables used as input are the same tables used in the previous examples and are shown in Appendix C. The data contained in these tables can be loaded into DB2 tables at your site by keying, or refer to Chapter 1, Introduction, for information concerning ordering copies of the tables.

Report 1

Create a SAS data set containing only those employees who are salaried (Employee_type = 'S'; use capital S, small s is not the same). The SAS variables required on this data set include Last_name, First_name, Hire_date, Vacation_available, and a new column representing the vacation remaining. Use the MMDDYY8. format on Hire_date.

Report 2

Create a SAS data set summarizing employee information from the DB2 table, Persinfo, by Cost_center and Management for Cost_centers, 130 and 140. The data set should be sorted by Cost_center and Management. The statistics on this SAS data set include the sum of Vacation_available, Vacation_used, and Sick_used. Also include the Department_name from the DB2 table, Orginfo.

Report 1

The SAS data set created in this exercise contains 26 observations and 5 variables. The first 19 observations are shown in the BROWSE panel:

```
                        SAS Data Set: WORK.EXER1      Observations
COMMAND ===>                                          First      1
                                                      Last      19
 OBS    LNAME        FNAME          HIRDTE  VACAVAIL   VACLEFT

   1    APPLE        RICHARD      11/23/47       160        80
   2    ATKINS       NANCY        09/15/81       120        64
   3    BAKER        MARTHA       04/01/74       120        80
   4    BROOKS       EDWARD       08/13/75       120        40
   5    BROWN        WALLY        05/05/72       160        80
   6    BUELL        MAX          04/05/83       120        72
   7    DOUGLAS      MILTON       11/09/67       160       120
   8    GOETZ        JACK         05/23/79       120        40
   9    HARDWICK     DONNIE       04/25/86        80        80
  10    HARRINGTON   MARLIN       04/15/83       120        96
  11    HARRIS       JULIE        03/04/86        80        40
  12    HUFFORD      STEPHEN      03/16/87        80        24
  13    HUGHES       PEGGY        06/22/83       120        40
  14    HUTSON       EVERETT      03/23/74       120        96
  15    KAWAN        JOE          10/30/64       160       120
  16    KEESLING     GERTRUDE     08/08/76       120        96
  17    KELLUM       ELLEN JANE   09/09/69       160        80
  18    KISLING      MARY LEA     05/23/78       120        40
  19    MEEKS        EDWARD       09/03/76       120       120
```

The SELECT statement edited in the SQL ENTRY/EDIT panel is shown below:

```
SELECT
 TSID123.PERSINFO.LAST_NAME, TSID123.PERSINFO.FIRST_NAME,
 TSID123.PERSINFO.HIRE_DATE, TSID123.PERSINFO.VACATION_AVAILABLE,
 vacation_available - vacation_used
 FROM
 TSID123.PERSINFO
WHERE
employee_type = 'S'
```

Report 2

The SAS data set created in this exercise contains 4 observations and 6 variables. They are shown below in the BROWSE panel. You may have to scroll right to view the SAS variable, Deptname.

```
                         SAS Data Set: WORK.EXER2        Observations
COMMAND ===>                                             First      1
                                                         Last       4
OBS   VACAVAIL    VACUSED    SICKUSED    MGT    DEPTNUM   DEPTNAME

  1       1280        680          64     N        130      SALES
  2        160         40          16     Y        130      SALES
  3        400        152           8     N        140      DEVELOPMENT
  4        800        304          72     Y        140      DEVELOPMENT
```

The SELECT statement edited in the SQL ENTRY/EDIT panel is shown below:

```
SELECT
 sum(VACATION_AVAILABLE), sum(VACATION_USED),
 sum(SICK_USED), TSID123.PERSINFO.MANAGEMENT,
 TSID123.ORGINFO.DEPARTMENT, TSID123.ORGINFO.DEPARTMENT_NAME
 FROM
 TSID123.PERSINFO, TSID123.ORGINFO
 WHERE
 cost_center = department and
 (cost_center = '130' or cost_center = '140')
 group by department, department_name, management
 order by department, management
```

Maps and SELECT Statements

This section illustrates the use of PROC DB2EXT in Display Manager to create and save maps and SELECT statments to be used as input in subsequent executions of PROC DB2EXT. These maps and SQL statements can be used as input to PROC DB2EXT in Display Manager, but are more often used in batch programs due to computer resource requirements.

Maps

Although the map has been talked about from a conceptual point of view, it has not really been defined. The map is built in the DATA EXTRACTION panel based on the DB2 table(s) selected on the DATA ACCESS panel. The map contains SAS variable names and formats, either generated automatically or user-defined. Optionally, the map contains a WHERE clause used to select rows which meet specific criteria. The map is a SAS data set and can be saved in a SAS data library, along with other types of SAS files. To create and save a map in PROC DB2EXT, rather than a SAS data set containing data extracted from DB2 tables, you will be using the DB2EXT panels shown in Figure 6-10.

Since the map will probably be used as input in a subsequent execution of PROC DB2EXT in batch, the map needs to be saved permanently in a SAS data library. Therefore, create a SAS data library prior to getting into Display Manager. Once in Display Manager, submit a TSO allocate for a SAS data library. Execute PROC DB2EXT to bring up the DATA ACCESS panel.

In the DATA ACCESS panel, enter the name of the map in the OUTPUT SAS DATA SET blank. The map will have a two-level SAS

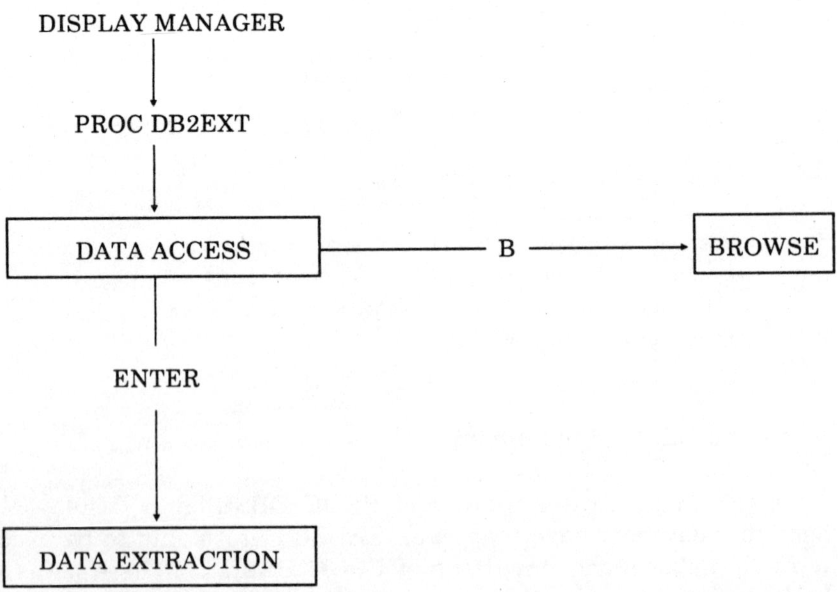

Figure 6-10 PROC DB2EXT Panels used for saving maps.

data set name where the first level is the ddname specified in the TSO allocate statement and the second level is the name of the map. Enter a Y (yes) in the SAVESEL field. If SAVESEL is a Y, the OUTPUT SAS DATA SET will be a map. If SAVESEL is a N, the OUTPUT SAS DATA SET will be a SAS data set containing data extracted from a DB2 table(s).

After completing the DATA ACCESS panel, hit enter to bring up the DATA EXTRACTION panel. On the DATA EXTRACTION panel, select the desired DB2 columns and optionally create your own SAS variable names and formats. If needed, code a WHERE clause to select only those rows meeting specific criteria.

Use the END command (PF3/PF15) to return to the DATA ACCESS panel. You will get the message, SAVE SELECT PROCESS COMPLETED FOR X COLUMNS, where X is the number of DB2 columns selected on the DATA EXTRACTION panel. The BROWSE panel can be used to display the map. The complete WHERE clause may not be displayed on the BROWSE panel due to its length. PROC FSBROWSE or PROC FSEDIT can be used to display the complete WHERE clause.

Thus, the only difference in creating and saving a map rather than a SAS data set is the setting the SAVESEL option to Y. The map will typically be permanent, while a SAS data set containing data is sometimes temporary, in existence only for the Display Manager session. The SQL ENTRY/EDIT panel is not used when creating and saving a map. When a map is later used as input to PROC DB2EXT, the map will generate the SELECT statement, which in turn will be used to create the SAS data set containing DB2 data. Therefore, only a Basic SELECT statement is used for the extraction. If enhanced features of the SELECT statement are needed, the SELECT statement should be saved rather than a map.

A map contains an observation for every DB2 column selected on the DATA EXTRACTION panel. A map contains the following variables:

TABPW: This is the name of the DB2 table. The table name actually appears only on the first observation (representing the first DB2 column) for all observations created from the same DB2 table.

TYPE: This is a numeric representation of the DB2 data type for the column named in the Column variable.

LENGTH: This is the length of the value.

SCALE: This is the number of decimal places.

NULLS: Specifies whether NULLS are allowed. A value of 1 indicates that NULLS are allowed (Yes) and a value of 0 indicates that NULLS are not allowed (No).

COLUMN: This is the name of the DB2 column.

SASNAME: This is the name of the SAS variable, which is either generated as the first eight positions of the DB2 column name or assigned by the user.

FORMAT: This is the format of the SAS variable, which is either generated as standard numeric or standard character or is assigned by the user.

WHEREA:
WHEREB
WHEREC
WHERED
WHEREE
WHEREF
WHEREG
WHEREH

These variables exist only when a WHERE clause is coded and contain the selection criteria coded in the WHERE clause. Each of these WHERE variables (WHEREA-WHEREH) can store selection criteria up to 200 characters because 200 characters is the maximum length of a SAS variable. If your selection criteria is less than 200 characters, only WHEREA will be created. If your criteria is more than 200 characters but not more than 400 characters, WHEREA and WHEREB will be created. Thus, the WHEREA-WHEREH variables are created as needed based on the length of selection criteria coded in the WHERE clause. The maximum length of a WHERE clause that can be stored in a map is 1600 characters. The maximum length of a WHERE clause that can be executed is 32,000 characters. If your selection criteria uses more than WHEREA-WHEREC, and you get an error when the map is used as input to PROC DB2EXT, contact the SAS Consultant at your company. A Zap can be applied to correct the problem.

The variables in the map that are of particular interest to the user are TABPW, SASNAMES, FORMATS, and WHEREA. TABPW is created based on the table(s) specified on the DATA ACCESS panel. SASNAMES and FORMATS are created based on the DB2 columns selected on the DATA EXTRACTION panel. They contain default SAS names and formats unless the user has assigned other SAS names and formats.

When a map is used as input in subsequent executions of PROC DB2EXT, the IN= option of the PROC DB2EXT statement is used no matter whether execution is performed in Display Manager or in batch. The IN= option will be defined in the next chapter, PROC DB2EXT in Batch. Unfortunately, the DATA ACCESS panel is not set up to take a map as input. If you have defined a map and found that it is not what you need, there are alternatives for making corrections. If your company has SAS/FSP, you can use PROC FSEDIT to make changes to a map. Changes can also be made in a DATA step executed in Display Manager or a batch job. If the changes are major, you may want to create the map again.

SELECT Statements

From the previous section, Enhanced SELECT Statements, and from Chapter 4, Structured Query Language, the user is familiar with SELECT statements. I have termed SELECT statements as Basic SELECT statements when they can be generated by a map. A Basic SELECT statement includes the desired DB2 columns, a FROM clause naming the DB2 table(s), and optionally, a WHERE clause to select only those rows meeting specific criteria. SELECT statements containing anything other than this, I have termed Enhanced SELECT statements. Enhanced SELECT statements include such things as other clauses (GROUP BY, HAVING, or ORDER BY), functions (MIN, MAX, AVG, SUM), and the creation of new columns.

Figure 6-11 shows the panels used to create and save SELECT statements.

Since the SELECT statement will probably be used as input in subsequent executions of PROC DB2EXT either in batch or in a later Display Manager session, the SELECT statement needs to be saved permanently. SELECT statements are usually saved as members of partitioned data sets. A partitioned data set needs to be created to store SELECT statements prior to getting into Display Manager. Once in Display Manager, submit a TSO allocate for this partitioned data set. Execute PROC DB2EXT to bring up the DATA ACCESS panel.

In the DATA ACCESS panel, the partitioned data set is specified in the OUTPUT SQL LIBRARY field as a two-level name. The first level is the ddname specified in the TSO allocate statement and the second level is the member name in the partitioned data set. A period (.) separates the two levels rather than parentheses. Parentheses are normally used to denote a member name. If the member specified already exists, it will be replaced.

Unfortunately, PROC DB2EXT requires that a SAS data set be created, whether it is a map or a SAS data set containing DB2 data. If an OUTPUT SAS DATA SET is not entered, a SAS data set name is generated using the naming convention, Data1, Data2, etc. Usu-

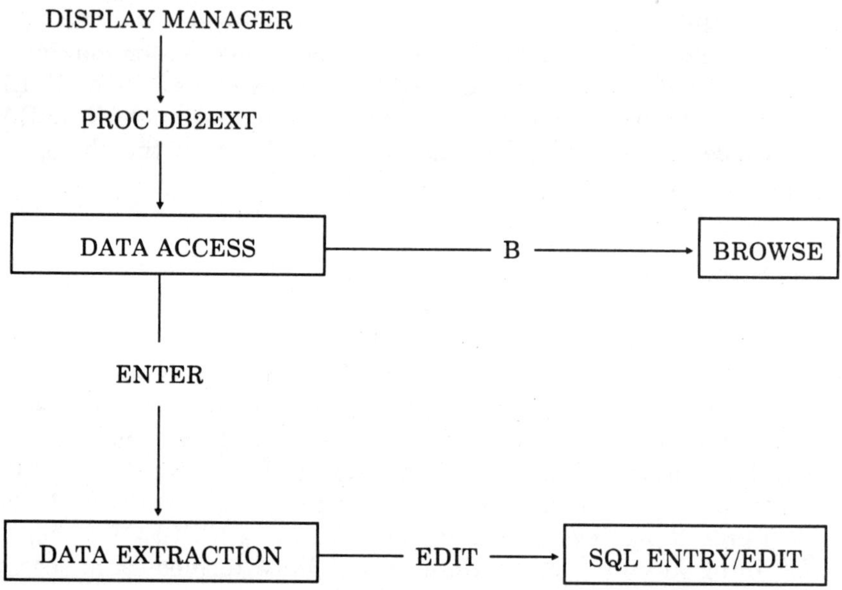

Figure 6-11 PROC DB2EXT Panels used for saving SELECT statements.

ally when you wish to save a SELECT statement, you do not want a SAS data set. Not only that, but creating a SAS data set containing data extracted from DB2 table(s) may require more computer resources than you want to use interactively. What comes to mind is to make the SAS data set a map (SAVESEL set to Y) and avoid using too much computer resources. When both a map and SELECT statement are saved in a single execution, the SELECT statement is saved correctly. The map, which is not needed anyway, is missing the table name in the variable, TABPW. Although this method satisfies the objective, it still seems inappropriate to create a map when it is not needed. Read on for another alternative.

After completing the DATA ACCESS panel, hit enter to bring up the DATA EXTRACTION panel. On the DATA EXTRACTION panel, select the desired DB2 columns, letting the SAS variable names and formats remain at their default value. User-defined variable names and formats cannot be saved in a SELECT statement, only in a map. If needed, code a WHERE clause to select only those rows meeting specific criteria.

Often, when saving a SELECT statement, it will be an Enhanced SELECT statement. An Enhanced SELECT statement is usually created by editing the SELECT statement generated by the map. The EDIT command (PF11/PF23) is used after selections are made on the DATA EXTRACTION panel to bring up the SQL ENTRY/EDIT panel. The SQL ENTRY/EDIT panel displays the Basic SELECT statement created by the map. The user can then edit this SELECT statement as desired. When the SELECT statement is completed, the END command (PF3/PF15) is used to return to the DATA EXTRACTION panel.

It is at this point that the SELECT statement is written to the partitioned data set. Thus, the objective of saving a SELECT statement is complete. If the END command (PF3/PF15) is issued from the DATA EXTRACTION panel, a SAS data set will be created. Since we don't want a SAS data set (a map or SAS data set containing DB2 data), the EXIT command (PF4/PF16) can be issued from the DATA EXTRACTION panel. A SAS data set will not be created and you will return to Display Manager rather than the DATA ACCESS panel.

If a Basic SELECT statement is to be saved, follow the same procedure as the Enhanced SELECT statement. Use the EDIT command to bring up the SQL ENTRY/EDIT panel, even though you do not intend to make any changes to the SELECT statement. Use the END command to return to the DATA EXTRACTION panel and write the SELECT statement to the partitioned data set. Use the EXIT command to skip the DATA ACCESS panel, thus not creating a SAS data set. If the SQL ENTRY/EDIT panel is not brought up, then the SELECT statement is written to the partitioned data set at the same time the SAS data set is created. This occurs when the END command is issued from the DATA EXTRACTION panel to return to the DATA ACCESS panel.

Figure 6-12 illustrates the process of exiting PROC DB2EXT when saving a SELECT statement.

A SELECT statement can be input in subsequent executions of PROC DB2EXT in Display Manager or in batch to create a SAS data set containing data extracted from DB2 table(s). The choice will probably depend on the size of the DB2 table and the amount of computer resources required. The diagram in Figure 6-13 shows the panels required to use a saved SELECT statement. The flow is shown going into and out of these panels.

In order to use a saved SELECT statement in PROC DB2EXT, a TSO allocate statement for the external file containing the SELECT statement must first be submitted in Display Manager. Next, execute PROC DB2EXT to bring up the DATA ACCESS panel.

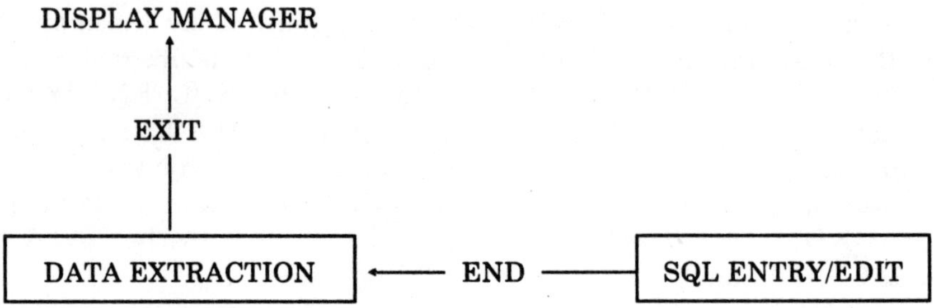

Figure 6-12 Panels used for exiting PROC DB2EXT when saving SELECT statements.

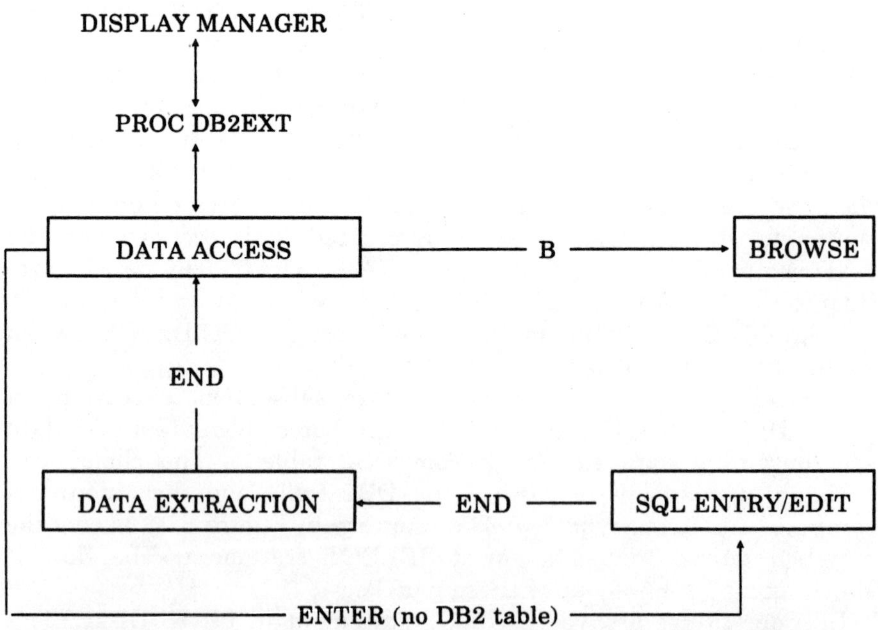

Figure 6-13 Panels used for including a SELECT statement in PROC DB2EXT.

In the DATA ACCESS panel, specify the SAS data set in the OUTPUT SAS DATA SET field. That is the only information filled in on the DATA ACCESS panel. If a DB2 table(s) is specified on the DATA ACCESS panel, hitting enter will bring up the DATA EXTRACTION panel, where a map will be built to generate a SELECT statement. We already have a SELECT statement, so we do not want to bring up the DATA EXTRACTION panel. As shown on the above diagram, hitting enter without specifying a DB2 table will bring up the SQL ENTRY/EDIT panel.

The SQL ENTRY/EDIT panel will be blank. Issue the Display Manager command, INCLUDE, as follows:

```
INCLUDE ddname(membername)
```

The ddname is the ddname given in the TSO allocate statement and the membername is the member containing the SELECT statement you wish to include. The SELECT statement can be edited if desired. When you are satisfied with the SELECT statement, the END command (PF3/PF15) is used to bring up the DATA EXTRACTION panel.

SAS variable names and format can be changed on the DATA EXTRACTION panel if desired. The END command (PF3/PF15) is then issued to return to the DATA ACCESS panel and create an output SAS data set. The B command can be used to bring up the BROWSE panel to display the SAS data set if desired.

Refer to Chapter 7, PROC DB2EXT in Batch, the section, Maps and SELECT Statements, for information concerning the use of SELECT statements in batch.

Maps Versus SELECT Statements

The process of saving and using maps and SELECT statements has been addressed. However, you still may be a little unclear as to which one is appropriate in a given application. Ask yourself some questions about the application. Does it require a Basic or Enhanced SELECT statement? Does it require user-defined SAS variable names and formats, or are the defaults sufficient? The answers to these two questions will guide you in making the decision of whether to save a map or a SELECT statement. The following chart shows four combinations of needs based on the type of SELECT statement and user-defined versus generated SAS variable names and formats.

	Type of Select	*Variable Names & Formats*	*Choice #1*	*Choice #2*
1.	Basic	Default	Map	SELECT
2.	Basic	User Defined	Map	SELECT, RENAME, FMT (Batch) SELECT, DATA EXTRACTION (DM)
3.	Enhanced	Default	SELECT	----
4.	Enhanced	User Defined	Map & SELECT	SELECT, RENAME, FMT (Batch) SELECT, DATA EXTRACTION (DM)

The Basic SELECT statement is defined to contain the DB2 columns selected, the FROM clause containing the names of the DB2 table(s), and optionally, a WHERE clause to select only those rows meeting specific criteria. Enhanced SELECT statements are SELECT statements containing features other than these. Enhanced SELECT statements include such things as other clauses (GROUP BY, HAVING, or ORDER BY), functions (MIN, MAX, AVG, SUM), and the creation of new columns.

Default SAS variable names consist of the first eight positions of the eighteen-position DB2 column name. Default SAS formats are standard character for DB2 character types, standard numeric for DB2 numeric data types, and a SAS date/time format for DB2 date/time data types. Any valid SAS variable name and format can be defined by the user to replace these default values.

Two choices are shown for use of the four combinations of needs. In the first combination it does not matter whether a map or a SELECT statement is used. User-defined SAS variable names and formats stored in maps are not needed. The SELECT statement needed is Basic and can be generated by a map or saved as a SELECT statement.

For the second combination, a map fits because user-defined SAS variable names and formats are required and the map will generate a Basic SELECT statement, which is all that is required. Another choice is the SELECT statement with the RENAME and FMT statements in batch. This will be covered in the next chapter, PROC

DB2EXT in Batch. Another choice for Display Manager is to use the INCLUDE command to bring a saved SELECT statement into the SQL ENTRY/EDIT panel. Using the END command will bring up the DATA EXTRACTION panel, where SAS variable names and formats can be changed as needed.

The third combination requires a SELECT statement to be saved because an Enhanced SELECT statement is required. A map cannot generate this type of SELECT statement.

The fourth combination requires an Enhanced SELECT statement, which means that a SELECT statement should be saved. User-defined SAS variable names and formats are also needed. Although both a map and a SELECT statement can be used as input into a single execution of PROC DB2EXT, this operation is not recommended. In order to use this method, the map and the SELECT statement must be compatible. The observations in the map which represent DB2 columns must also be specified in the SELECT list in the SELECT statement. The second option is the SELECT statement with the RENAME and FMT statements in batch. Again, this will be covered in the next chapter, PROC DB2EXT in Batch. The second option for execution in Display Manager is to use the INCLUDE command to bring a saved SELECT statement into the SQL ENTRY/EDIT panel. Using the END command will bring up the DATA EXTRACTION panel, where SAS variable names and formats can be changed as needed.

When more than one choice exists to satisfy a given application, it is user preference that makes the decision. Some users like maps because little coding is visible when using maps as input in subsequent executions of PROC DB2EXT. Most users seem to prefer SELECT statements because you can see what is being executed when SELECT statements are used as input in subsequent executions of PROC DB2EXT.

Examples

Example 6-5

A SAS data set is needed which contains phone information (Last_name, First_name, Home_phone, and Office_extension), the Department_name and the Director. The SAS variable names should be user-defined. Since this SAS data set will be updated frequently, it is desirable to save the execution instructions in either a map or a

SELECT statement, whichever is appropriate. These instructions will then be used when the SAS data set needs to be updated.

This application requires user-defined SAS variable names and a Basic SELECT statement. In this situation, the map is selected, because user-defined SAS variable names are desired. In order for the map to be available every time the SAS data set needs to be updated, it should be a permanent map stored in a SAS data library.

A TSO allocate statement is then entered in the PROGRAM window of Display Manager and executed using the SUBMIT command (PF3/PF15). The TSO allocate statement should have disposition OLD because you will be writing to it. The PROC DB2EXT statement and a RUN statement are entered in the PROGRAM window next and executed.

```
-----------------------------------------------------------------
COMMAND ===>                                    SAS(r) Log   HH:MM

NOTE: COPYRIGHT(C) 1984, 1988 SAS INSTITUTE INC., CARY, NC 27512
USA
NOTE: SAS RELEASE 5.18 AT COMPANY ABC (00000009).
NOTE: CPUID   VERSION = 00   SERIAL = 000000   MODEL = 0000 .
NOTE: SAS OPTIONS SPECIFIED ARE:
      DMS NONEWS FSP FS NODATE


  1  tso alloc dd(mapout) dsn('tsid123.sas.db2maps') old;
-----------------------------------------------------------------
COMMAND ===>                                       Program Editor

00001 proc db2ext;
00002   run;
00003
00004
00005
```

On the DATA ACCESS panel, enter a Y (yes) in the SAVESEL option and enter the name of the permanent map in the OUTPUT SAS DATA SET field. Two DB2 tables, Persinfo and Orginfo, are needed.

```
                          DB2 INTERFACE
                       DATA ACCESS PANEL

COMMAND===>
NOTE: FILL IN THE FIELDS BELOW

OUTPUT SQL LIBRARY:                 SAVE SELECTIONS (savesel): Y

OUTPUT SAS DATA SET: mapout.mapex5  UNIQUE SAS NAMES (unique): N

DB2 SUBSYSTEM ID:    DBT

         AUTHORIZATION ID               TABLE NAME
                tsid123.                persinfo..........
                tsid123.                orginfo...........
                ........                ..................
                ........                ..................
                ........                ..................
```

Hitting the enter key on the DATA ACCESS panel brings up the DATA EXTRACTION panel shown below. The desired SAS variable names are entered.

```
                   DB2 INTERFACE              TABLE NAME: PERSINFO
             DATA EXTRACTION PANEL          SAS DATA SET: MAPOUT.MAPEX5


COMMAND===>


FUNC    COLUMN NAME                SAS NAME      FORMAT
 . *** TABLE- PERSINFO                *** COLUMNS-  30 * SELECTED-  4 *
 .         SOCIAL_SECURITY         ........       $9.
 .         LAST_NAME               LNAME...       $15.
 .         FIRST_NAME              FNAME...       $10.
 .         SEX                     ........       $1.
 .         BIRTH_DATE              ........       7.
 .         ADDRESS                 ........       $20.
 .         CITY                    ........       $15.
 .         STATE                   ........       $2.
 .         ZIP_CODE                ........       $5.
 .         HOME_PHONE              HOMEPHON       $7.
 .         HIRE_DATE               ........       7.
 .         OFFICE_EXTENSION        OFFEXT..       $4.
 .         COST_CENTER             ........       $3.
 --------------------- WHERE CLAUSE ----------------------------
```

Scrolling down (PF8/PF20) twice displays additional DB2 columns that are needed. The desired SAS variable name is entered for these columns. A WHERE clause is coded to select those rows out of the CARTESIAN PRODUCT where Cost_center from Persinfo and Department from Orginfo are equal.

```
               DB2 INTERFACE              TABLE NAME: PERSINFO
          DATA EXTRACTION PANEL         SAS DATA SET: MAPOUT.MAPEX5

COMMAND===>

FUNC   COLUMN NAME           SAS NAME     FORMAT
 .       SALARY_DECEMBER     ........     6.
 .       EMPLOYEE_TYPE       ........     $1.
 .       MANAGEMENT          ........     $1.
 . *** TABLE- ORGINFO            *** COLUMNS-  5 * SELECTED-  2 *
 .       DEPARTMENT          ........     $3.
 .       DEPARTMENT_NAME     DEPTNAME     $15.
 .       DIRECTOR            DIRECTOR     $25.
 .       VICE PRESIDENT      ........     $25.
 .       PRESIDENT           ........     $25.





--------------------- WHERE CLAUSE ----------------------------
cost_center = department
```

The END command (PF3/PF15) is used to return to the DATA ACCESS panel and create the map. A message to this effect appears below the command line. The message says that 6 columns were selected, which means the map will have 6 observations.

```
                         DB2 INTERFACE
                       DATA ACCESS PANEL

COMMAND===>
NOTE: SAVE SELECT PROCESS COMPLETED FOR 6 COLUMNS

OUTPUT SQL LIBRARY:                  SAVE SELECTIONS (savesel): Y

OUTPUT SAS DATA SET: MAPOUT.MAPEX5   UNIQUE SAS NAMES (unique): N

DB2 SUBSYSTEM ID:    DBT

          AUTHORIZATION ID                TABLE NAME
                  TSID123.                PROJINFO..........
                  TSID123.                ORGINFO...........
                  ........                ..................
                  ........                ..................
                  ........                ..................
```

PROC PRINT is used to display the map, because it provides more room for the WHERE clause than the BROWSE panel. The following is coded in the PROGRAM window of Display Manager and executed:

```
PROC PRINT DATA=MAPOUT.MAPEX5; RUN;
```

The following report is displayed in the OUTPUT window of Display Manager:

```
OBS       TABPW            TYPE  LENGTH SCALE NULLS   COLUMNS

  1  TSID123.PERSINFO      453      15     0     1    LAST_NAME
  2                        453      10     0     1    FIRST_NAME
  3                        453       7     0     1    HOME_PHONE
  4                        453       4     0     1    OFFICE_EXTENSION
  5  TSID123.ORGINFO       453      15     0     1    DEPARTMENT_NAME
  6                        453      25     0     1    DIRECTOR
```

OBS	SASNAME	FORMAT	WHEREA
1	LNAME	$15.	cost_center = department
2	FNAME	$10.	cost_center = department
3	HOMEPHON	$7.	cost_center = department
4	OFFEXT	$4.	cost_center = department
5	DEPTNAME	$15.	cost_center = department
6	DIRECTOR	$25.	cost_center = department

The panels used with PROC DB2EXT do not have the capability to use a map as input. Therefore, when a map is used as input to PROC DB2EXT in Display Manager, PROC DB2EXT is coded as it would be in a batch program. The IN= and OUT= options of the PROC DB2EXT statement would be used. The IN= option specifies the input map and the OUT= option specifies the resulting SAS data set containing data extracted from the DB2 table(s). The executed PROC DB2EXT is shown here in the LOG window. In the PROGRAM window a PROC PRINT is coded to print the resulting SAS data set. Refer to the next chapter, PROC DB2EXT in Batch, for more information regarding the options and statements used with PROC DB2EXT.

```
-----------------------------------------------------------------
COMMAND ===>                                    SAS(r) Log   HH:MM

  1 tso alloc dd(mapout) dsn('tsid123.sas.db2maps') old;
  2 proc db2ext; run;
NOTE: THE DATA SET MAPOUT.MAPEX5 HAS 6 OBSERVATIONS AND 9
      VARIABLES.
  3 proc print data=mapout.mapex5; run;

  4 proc db2ext in=mapout.mapex5 out=ex5; run;
NOTE: THE DATA SET WORK.EX5 HAS 60 OBSERVATIONS AND 6 VARIABLES.
-----------------------------------------------------------------
COMMAND ===>                                     Program Editor

00001 proc print data=ex5;
00002   run;
00003
00004
00005
```

The first page of this PROC PRINT is displayed in the OUTPUT window of Display Manager, as follows:

```
OBS  LNAME     FNAME   HOMEPHON OFFEXT DEPTNAME   DIRECTOR

  1  BROWN     WALLY   8708973  9871   PERSONNEL  CHERYL MORGAN
  2  CLARK     ALMA    2802340  8921   PERSONNEL  CHERYL MORGAN
  3  CONWELL   LINDA   9234928  7823   PERSONNEL  CHERYL MORGAN
  4  COOPER    MARGIE  4298713  9073   PERSONNEL  CHERYL MORGAN
  5  DAVIS     SUSAN   2347033  2398   PERSONNEL  CHERYL MORGAN
  6  JOHNSON   HAZEL   1098702  8903   PERSONNEL  CHERYL MORGAN
  7  JONES     JOAN    9780123  9873   PERSONNEL  CHERYL MORGAN
  8  MARSHALL  MICHAEL 8342044  8334   PERSONNEL  CHERYL MORGAN
  9  MILLER    DIZ     9832022  8222   PERSONNEL  CHERYL MORGAN
 10  MITCHELL  KELLY   9823933  8933   PERSONNEL  CHERYL MORGAN
 11  MOORE     RUTH    3298703  9444   PERSONNEL  CHERYL MORGAN
 12  SHEPHERD  KANDI   9870874  9384   PERSONNEL  CHERYL MORGAN
 13  ADAMS     BILL    8293232  3939   PERSONNEL  CHERYL MORGAN
 14  SMITH     SCOTT   3482835  3923   MARKETING  GERTRUDE KEESLING
 15  PHILLIPS  SARAH   9383922  8433   MARKETING  GERTRUDE KEESLING
 16  MARK      MIRON   3290323  8733   MARKETING  GERTRUDE KEESLING
 17  MEISER    MARK    2938473  8292   MARKETING  GERTRUDE KEESLING
 18  HARRIS    JULIE   2398723  9022   MARKETING  GERTRUDE KEESLING
 19  HOLLYWOOD ALICE   2398733  9392   MARKETING  GERTRUDE KEESLING
 20  CONNOR    BRUCE   9023482  3903   MARKETING  GERTRUDE KEESLING
...
```

Example 6-6

A SAS data set is needed that will contain the average Salary_december and the average Vacation_available by Employee_type and Sex. Default SAS variable names are fine, as labels will be used for reporting purposes. The SAS variable resulting from Salary_december should be formatted using the DOLLARw.d format.

The execution instructions are to be saved in either a map or a SELECT statement, whichever is appropriate. These instructions will then be used as input every time this analysis needs to be done.

This application requires an Enhanced SELECT statement, so the SELECT statement rather than a map must be saved. Although the DOLLARw.d format is also needed, that can be accomplished in a number of ways. A FORMAT statement could be used, or PROC

DATASETS could be used. If the SELECT statement is used as input to PROC DB2EXT in Display Manager, the DOLLARw.d format can be assigned in the DATA EXTRACTION panel. If the SELECT statement is used as input to PROC DB2EXT in a batch job, the FMT statement can be used.

The SELECT statement will be saved in a member of a partitioned data set. This data set must be created prior to getting into Display Manager.

A TSO allocate statement is entered in the PROGRAM window of Display Manager and executed using the SUBMIT command (PF3/PF15). The PROC DB2EXT statement and a RUN statement are then entered in the PROGRAM window and executed.

```
-----------------------------------------------------------------
COMMAND ===>                                  SAS(r) Log   HH:MM

NOTE: COPYRIGHT(C) 1984, 1988 SAS INSTITUTE INC., CARY, NC 27512
USA
NOTE: SAS RELEASE 5.18 AT COMPANY ABC (00000000).
NOTE: CPUID   VERSION = 00   SERIAL = 000000   MODEL = 0000 .
NOTE: SAS OPTIONS SPECIFIED ARE:
      DMS NONEWS FSP FS NODATE



  1  tso alloc dd(selout) dsn('tsid123.sas.db2sels') old;
-----------------------------------------------------------------
COMMAND ===>                                      Program Editor

00001 proc db2ext;
00002   run;
00003
00004
00005
```

On the DATA ACCESS panel, enter a two-level name for the OUTPUT SQL LIBRARY. The first level corresponds to the ddname specified in the TSO allocate statement. The second level is the member in the partitioned data set in which you want the SELECT statement saved. Remember, if this member already exists, it will be written over. Also, the syntax here requires a period (.) between the first- and second-level names rather than the usual syntax of putting parentheses around the member name.

Just leave the OUTPUT SAS DATA SET blank, as we will not be creating a SAS data set of any kind. To avoid this, we will be using the EXIT command.

```
                         DB2 INTERFACE
                       DATA ACCESS PANEL

COMMAND===>
NOTE: FILL IN THE FIELDS BELOW

OUTPUT SQL LIBRARY:  selout.selex6  SAVE SELECTIONS (savesel): N

OUTPUT SAS DATA SET:                UNIQUE SAS NAMES (unique): N

DB2 SUBSYSTEM ID:    DBT

          AUTHORIZATION ID               TABLE NAME
                  tsid123.               persinfo..........
                  ........               ..................
                  ........               ..................
                  ........               ..................
                  ........               ..................
```

Hitting the enter key on the DATA ACCESS panel brings up the DATA EXTRACTION panel shown. The S FUNC is used to select the desired DB2 columns and hitting enter displays the generated SAS variable names. Since the output SAS data set was not entered on the DATA ACCESS panel, the SAS data set name, DATA1, was automatically used.

```
                DB2 INTERFACE                   TABLE NAME: PERSINFO
          DATA EXTRACTION PANEL              SAS DATA SET: WORK.DATA1


COMMAND===>


FUNC    COLUMN NAME                 SAS NAME      FORMAT
 . ***  TABLE- PERSINFO                *** COLUMNS-   30 * SELECTED-   1 *
 .        SOCIAL_SECURITY           ........      $9.
 .        LAST_NAME                 ........      $15.
 .        FIRST_NAME                ........      $10.
 .        SEX                       SEX.....      $1.
 .        BIRTH_DATE                ........      7.
 .        ADDRESS                   ........      $20.
 .        CITY                      ........      $15.
 .        STATE                     ........      $2.
 .        ZIP_CODE                  ........      $5.
 .        HOME_PHONE                ........      $7.
 .        HIRE_DATE                 ........      7.
 .        OFFICE_EXTENSION          ........      $4.
 .        COST_CENTER               ........      $3.
--------------------- WHERE CLAUSE ----------------------------
```

Scrolling once (PF8/PF20) displays the second screen where an additional DB2 column is selected, and hitting enter displays the generated SAS variable name.

```
                DB2 INTERFACE                   TABLE NAME: PERSINFO
          DATA EXTRACTION PANEL               SAS DATA SET: WORK.DATA1


COMMAND===>

FUNC    COLUMN NAME           SAS NAME      FORMAT
  .      VACATION_AVAILABLE  VACATION      4.
  .      VACATION_USED       ........      4.
  .      SICK_USED           ........      4.
  .      SALARY_JANUARY      ........      6.
  .      SALARY_FEBRUARY     ........      6.
  .      SALARY_MARCH        ........      6.
  .      SALARY_APRIL        ........      6.
  .      SALARY_MAY          ........      6.
  .      SALARY_JUNE         ........      6.
  .      SALARY_JULY         ........      6.
  .      SALARY_AUGUST       ........      6.
  .      SALARY_SEPTEMBER    ........      6.
  .      SALARY_OCTOBER      ........      6.
  .      SALARY_NOVEMBER     ........      6.
-------------------- WHERE CLAUSE ---------------------------
```

Scrolling down (PF8/PF20) again displays additional DB2 columns that are needed. The S FUNC is used to select these DB2 columns and hitting enter displays the generated SAS variable names. The EDIT command is entered in the command input.

```
              DB2 INTERFACE                      TABLE NAME: PERSINFO
          DATA EXTRACTION PANEL               SAS DATA SET: WORK.DATA1

COMMAND===> edit

FUNC    COLUMN NAME            SAS NAME      FORMAT
 .       SALARY_DECEMBER       SALARY_D      6.
 .       EMPLOYEE_TYPE         EMPLOYEE      $1.
 .       MANAGEMENT            ........      $1.

--------------------- WHERE CLAUSE ---------------------------
```

Using the EDIT command in the DATA EXTRACTION panel brings up the SQL ENTRY/EDIT panel. The SELECT statement generated by the map built in the DATA EXTRACTION panel is displayed. The NUMS ON command is entered.

```
                          SQL ENTRY/EDIT SCREEN
COMMAND===> nums on                                     TEXT EDITOR

SELECT
 TSID123.PERSINFO.SEX, TSID123.PERSINFO.VACATION_AVAILABLE,
 TSID123.PERSINFO.SALARY_DECEMBER,
 TSID123.PERSINFO.EMPLOYEE_TYPE
 FROM
 TSID123.PERSINFO, TSID123.ORGINFO
```

The NUMS ON command generates line numbers on the left of the screen. The AVG function is added with the DB2 columns, Vacation_available and Salary_december. The GROUP BY and ORDER BY clauses are added. When editing is complete, the END command (PF3/PF15) is entered.

```
                            SQL ENTRY/EDIT SCREEN
COMMAND===> end                                                  TEXT EDITOR
                                                                 Col 001 072


00001 SELECT
00002  TSID123.PERSINFO.SEX, avg(vacation_available),
00003  avg(salary_december), TSID123.PERSINFO.EMPLOYEE_TYPE
00004  FROM
00005  TSID123.PERSINFO
00006  group by employee_type, sex
00007  order by employee_type, sex
00008
```

The END command (PF3/PF15) returns the user to the DATA EXTRACTION panel and writes the SELECT statement to the output SQL file specified on the DATA ACCESS panel. Since the objective is to save a SELECT statement, there is no reason to change the SAS variable names or formats. The EXIT command is issued here to return to Display Manager. If the END command were issued, the DATA ACCESS panel would be displayed and a SAS data set would be created, which we do not want.

```
                 DB2 INTERFACE                   TABLE NAME: PERSINFO
           DATA EXTRACTION PANEL               SAS DATA SET: WORK.DATA1


COMMAND===> exit


FUNC   COLUMN NAME              SAS NAME      FORMAT
 .*** DB2 TABLE- ** FROM SQL CALL ** ** COLUMNS- 4 SELECTED- 4 *
 .       SEX                    SEX           $1.
 .                              COMPOUND      16.12
 .                              COMPOUND      16.10
 .       EMPLOYEE_TYPE          EMPLOYEE      $1.

-------------------- WHERE CLAUSE ---------------------------
```

Once you have returned to Display Manager, the INCLUDE command can be used to include the saved SELECT statement into the PROGRAM window to verify the result. In this case, the command would be:

```
INCLUDE selout(selex6)
```

To use this saved SELECT statement in Display Manager, first submit a TSO allocate for the partitioned data set containing the SELECT statement. Then execute PROC DB2EXT to bring up the DATA ACCESS panel.

On the DATA ACCESS panel, enter the name of the OUTPUT SAS DATA SET you wish to contain the data to be extracted from the DB2 table, Persinfo. Do not enter a DB2 table name because we do not want to create a map and have the map generate a SELECT statement. By not specifying a DB2 table, hitting enter on the DATA ACCESS panel will bring up the SQL ENTRY/EDIT panel so that the saved SELECT statement can be included.

```
                              DB2 INTERFACE
                            DATA ACCESS PANEL

COMMAND===>
NOTE: FILL IN THE FIELDS BELOW

OUTPUT SQL LIBRARY:                  SAVE SELECTIONS (savesel): N

OUTPUT SAS DATA SET: ex6             UNIQUE SAS NAMES (unique): N

DB2 SUBSYSTEM ID:    DBT

          AUTHORIZATION ID               TABLE NAME
                 ........              ..................
                 ........              ..................
                 ........              ..................
                 ........              ..................
                 ........              ..................
```

Hitting enter from the DATA ACCESS panel without a DB2 table specified brings up a blank SQL ENTRY/EDIT panel. Enter the IN-

CLUDE command to include the saved SELECT statement in the SQL ENTRY/EDIT panel.

```
                         SQL ENTRY/EDIT SCREEN
COMMAND===> include selout(selex6)                      TEXT EDITOR
```

The following SQL ENTRY/EDIT panel is the result of the INCLUDE command. The SELECT statement could be edited at this point, but in this case it is what we want. Notice the SELECT statement now contains a semicolon.

```
                         SQL ENTRY/EDIT SCREEN
COMMAND===>                                             TEXT EDITOR

SELECT
 TSID123.PERSINFO.SEX, avg(vacation_available),
 avg(salary_december), TSID123.PERSINFO.EMPLOYEE_TYPE
 FROM
 TSID123.PERSINFO, TSID123.ORGINFO
 group by employee_type, sex
 order by employee_type, sex
 ;
```

The END command (PF3/PF15) brings up the DATA EXTRACTION panel. SAS variable names and formats can now be assigned.

```
              DB2 INTERFACE                 TABLE NAME: PERSINFO
         DATA EXTRACTION PANEL            SAS DATA SET: WORK.EX6

COMMAND===> exit

FUNC   COLUMN NAME            SAS NAME      FORMAT
 .*** DB2 TABLE- ** FROM SQL CALL ** ** COLUMNS- 4 SELECTED- 4 *
 .       SEX                  SEX           $1.
 .                            AVGVAC        16.0
 .                            AVGSAL        DOLLAR12.2
 .       EMPLOYEE_TYPE        EMPLOYEE      $1.

-------------------- WHERE CLAUSE ----------------------------
```

The END command (PF3/PF15) is used to return to the DATA ACCESS panel and create the SAS data set. The SAS data set, Ex6, contains 6 observations and 4 variables. The B command is entered.

```
                         DB2 INTERFACE
                       DATA ACCESS PANEL

COMMAND===> b

OUTPUT SQL LIBRARY:                      SAVE SELECTIONS (savesel): N

OUTPUT SAS DATA SET: WORK.EX6            UNIQUE SAS NAMES (unique): N

DB2 SUBSYSTEM ID:    DBT

          AUTHORIZATION ID                      TABLE NAME
                  TSID123.                      PROJINFO..........
                  ........                      ..................
                  ........                      ..................
                  ........                      ..................
                  ........                      ..................

EXTRACT STATISTICS: NUMBER OF SAS OBS CREATED  =       6
                    NUMBER OF SAS VARS CREATED =       4
```

Hitting enter after the B command was entered in the DATA ACCESS panel, brings up the BROWSE panel displaying the SAS data set just created, Ex6.

```
                    SAS Data Set: WORK.EX6        Observations
COMMAND ===>                                      First       1
                                                  Last        6
        OBS     SEX        AVGVAC        AVGSAL   EMPTYPE


         1       F             91     $1,608.67      H
         2       M            132     $1,893.00      H
         3       F            108     $2,699.00      S
         4       M            130     $3,430.63      S
         5       F             56       $780.00      T
         6       M             40       $587.50      T
```

Exercise 3

Test your understanding of the creation of maps and SELECT statements by completing the exercises described here. Save the extraction instructions in either a map or a SELECT statement and use this map/SELECT statement as input to PROC DB2EXT to create the appropriate SAS data set.

A print of the map/SELECT statement is shown on the following pages, along with the BROWSE panel displaying the SAS data set created from the map/SELECT statement. The DB2 tables used as input are the same tables used in the previous examples and are shown in Appendix C. The data contained in these tables can be loaded into DB2 tables at your site by keying, or refer to Chapter 1, Introduction, for information concerning ordering copies of the tables.

Report 1

A SAS data set is needed which contains hourly and salaried employees and the city where they live for possible carpooling. Temporary employees (Employee_type ¬= 'T'; use capital T - small t is not the same) should not be included. The DB2 columns needed include Last_name, First_name, and City. Select more appropriate SAS names than the first eight positions of the DB2 column name.

Report 2

A SAS data set is needed containing every hourly employee (Employee_type = 'H'; use capital H; small h is not the same). The DB2 columns needed include Last_name, First_name, and the sum of their salary for the last quarter (October, November, and December). The sum of the salaries should be formatted with the DOLLARw.d format and the SAS variable names should be Lname, Fname, and Qtrsal. The SAS data set should be sorted in descending order by last quarter's salary.

Report 1

This exercise could be completed by saving either a map or a SELECT statement.

A PROC PRINT of the map is shown below:

OBS	TABPW	TYPE	LENGTH	SCALE	NULLS	COLUMNS
1	TSID123.PERSINFO	453	15	0	1	LAST_NAME
2		453	10	0	1	FIRST_NAME
3		453	15	0	1	CITY

OBS	SASNAME	FORMAT	WHEREA
1	LNAME	$15.	employee_type Γ= 'T'
2	FNAME	$10.	employee_type Γ= 'T'
3	CITY	$15.	employee_type Γ= 'T'

If a SELECT statement were saved, it would appear as follows:

```
SELECT
 TSID123.PERSINFO.LAST_NAME, TSID123.PERSINFO.FIRST_NAME,
 TSID123.PERSINFO.CITY
 FROM
 TSID123.PERSINFO
WHERE
employee_type Γ= 'T'
;
```

The SAS data set created from either the map or the SELECT statement contains 51 observations and 3 variables. The first 19 observations are shown below in the BROWSE panel:

```
                      SAS Data Set: WORK.RPT1       Observations
COMMAND ===>                                        First       1
                                                    Last       19
           OBS     LNAME        FNAME        CITY


             1     ADAMS        BILL         INDIANAPOLIS
             2     APPLE        RICHARD      INDIANAPOLIS
             3     ATKINS       NANCY        INDIANAPOLIS
             4     ATWOOD       CHUCK        CONNERSVILLE
             5     BAKER        MARTHA       NEW CASTLE
             6     BROOKS       EDWARD       INDIANAPOLIS
             7     BROOKS       JIM          KNIGHTSTOWN
             8     BROWN        WALLY        RICHMOND
             9     BUELL        MAX          NOBLESVILLE
            10     CAMPBELL     MARGARET     MUNCIE
            11     CLARK        ALMA         CARMEL
            12     CONNOR       BRUCE        INDIANAPOLIS
            13     CONWELL      LINDA        PENDLETON
            14     COOPER       MARGIE       YORKTOWN
            15     DOUGLAS      MILTON       ANDERSON
            16     DUDLEY       LOUISA       NEW CASTLE
            17     GOETZ        JACK         MT SUMMIT
            18     HANKS        TROY         LIBERTY
            19     HARDWICK     DONNIE       SPICELAND
```

Report 2

A SELECT statement must be used in this exercise because an Enhanced SELECT statement is required to sum the three salary columns. The SAS variable names and formats can be assigned either in the DATA EXTRACTION panel when the SAS data set is created, or assigned using a method available in Base SAS. For example, LABEL and FORMAT statements in a PROC PRINT could be used, or PROC DATASETS could be used to assign labels and formats permanently.

The following SELECT statement would be saved:

```
SELECT
 TSID123.PERSINFO.LAST_NAME, TSID123.PERSINFO.FIRST_NAME,
 SALARY_OCTOBER + SALARY_NOVEMBER +
 SALARY_DECEMBER, TSID123.PERSINFO.EMPLOYEE_TYPE
 FROM
 TSID123.PERSINFO
WHERE
employee_type = 'H'
order by employee_type, 3 desc
;
```

The SAS data set created from this SELECT statement contains 25 observations and 3 variables. The first 19 observations are shown in the BROWSE panel:

```
                    SAS Data Set: WORK.RPT2       Observations
COMMAND ===>                                      First       1

          OBS    LNAME        FNAME           QTRSAL

            1    CAMPBELL     MARGARET        $7,560
            2    ATWOOD       CHUCK           $7,260
            3    CONWELL      LINDA           $6,930
            4    PAYTON       RUTH            $6,630
            5    DUDLEY       LOUISA          $6,410
            6    CONNOR       BRUCE           $6,300
            7    PAVELEK      JOE             $6,300
            8    ADAMS        BILL            $6,200
            9    BROOKS       JIM             $6,000
           10    SMITH        SCOTT           $6,000
           11    JAMES        MARVIN          $5,900
           12    HANKS        TROY            $5,670
           13    PEARCE       EVELYN          $5,040
           14    CLARK        ALMA            $4,740
           15    HOLLYWOOD    ALICE           $4,740
           16    MARK         MIRON           $4,740
           17    PRITT        JIM             $4,740
           18    PHILLIPS     SARAH           $4,340
           19    COOPER       MARGIE          $4,110
```

Review

Questions

1. Name the panels used with PROC DB2EXT in Display Manager and describe their purpose.
2. Why and when should a TSO allocate be submitted?
3. How is the DATA ACCESS panel brought up?
4. What panels are required when using PROC DB2EXT to create a SAS data set containing data extracted from DB2 tables?
5. When is the SQL ENTRY/EDIT panel required?
6. What is an Enhanced SELECT statement?
7. What is the purpose of saving maps and SELECT statements?
8. How do you know whether to save a map or a SELECT statement?
9. What determines whether a map is created or a SAS data set containing data extracted from DB2 tables?
10. When you want to save a SELECT statement, how can you avoid creating a SAS data set at the same time?
11. How do you use a saved SELECT statement as input to PROC DB2EXT in Display Manager?

Answers

1. The three primary DB2EXT panels are the DATA ACCESS, DATA EXTRACTION, and SQL ENTRY/EDIT panels. The DATA ACCESS panel is used to specify input and output files. The DATA EXTRACTION panel is used to build the map. This includes selecting the desired DB2 columns and specifying SAS variable names and formats. The SQL ENTRY/EDIT panel is used to edit a SELECT statement generated by the map, code the SELECT statement entirely, or include SELECT statements created in a previous execution of PROC DB2EXT. There are two other panels, the KEYS panel and the HELP panel. The KEYS panel is used to display and/or change commands assigned to PF keys. The HELP panel provides documentation on the SAS/DB2 procedures.
2. A TSO allocate is required if you will be using input files saved previously. Typically, these input files would be partitioned data sets containing stored SELECT statements. However, a map could also be used as input to a subsequent execution of

PROC DB2EXT. Note that maps used as input in Display Manager are coded batch-style since the DATA ACCESS panel does not provide for maps as input.

A TSO allocate statement should be executed in Display Manager prior to executing PROC DB2EXT when you wish any output files to be saved permanently. These output files include a SAS data set containing data extracted from DB2 tables, a SAS data set containing a map, or a partitioned data set to hold SELECT statements.

3. The DATA ACCESS panel is brought up by submitting

```
PROC DB2EXT; RUN;
```

4. When creating a SAS data set containing data extracted from DB2 tables, the DATA ACCESS panel and the DATA EXTRACTION panels are required.
5. The SQL ENTRY/EDIT panel is required in order to code and execute an Enhanced SELECT statement. It is also used to include and execute a SELECT statement created in a previous execution of PROC DB2EXT.
6. An Enhanced SELECT statement cannot be generated by a map. A map generates SELECT statements that include the selected DB2 columns, the DB2 table names, and optionally a WHERE clause. Enhanced SELECT statements can include other clauses (GROUP BY, HAVING, ORDER BY) and functions, and create new columns.
7. Maps and SELECT statements can be created once and used in several executions of PROC DB2EXT. This way, the user does not have to create the map/SELECT statement each time. Also, saving maps and SELECT statements allows the user to take advantage of the ease of use of PROC DB2EXT in Display Manager, even though there may not be enough computer resources in Display Manager to create the SAS data set containing DB2 data.
8. You need to ask yourself two questions relative to your application. First, is an Enhanced SELECT statement required? If so, save the SELECT statement. Second, are user-defined SAS variable names and formats required? Only maps can save user-defined SAS variable names and formats. If the answer to both is yes, save the SELECT statement. SAS variable names and formats can be assigned in the DATA EXTRACTION panel if the SELECT statement is used as input to PROC DB2EXT in Display Manager, or can be assigned in the RENAME and

FMT statements if the SELECT statement is used as input to PROC DB2EXT in a batch program.

9. If the SAVESEL field on the DATA ACCESS panel is set to Y (yes), the OUTPUT SAS DATA SET is a map. If the SAVESEL field is set to N (no), the OUTPUT SAS DATA SET is a SAS data set containing data extracted from DB2 tables.
10. No matter whether an Enhanced SELECT statement is needed or not, bring up the SQL ENTRY/EDIT panel. When the END command is issued from the SQL ENTRY/EDIT panel, the DATA EXTRACTION panel is brought up and the SELECT statement is written to the partitioned data set named on the DATA ACCESS panel. Issue the EXIT command in the DATA EXTRACTION panel and you will return to Display Manager without creating a SAS data set. It is when the END command is issued from the DATA EXTRACTION panel to return to the DATA ACCESS panel that a SAS data set is created.
11. First, submit a TSO allocate statement and then execute PROC DB2EXT. On the DATA ACCESS panel, enter the name of the OUTPUT SAS DATA SET, but do not enter a DB2 table name. Hitting enter without a DB2 table name brings up a blank SQL ENTRY/EDIT panel. The INCLUDE command is used to bring the SELECT statement into the SQL ENTRY/EDIT panel.

Chapter

7

PROC DB2EXT in Batch

PROC DB2EXT is used to create a SAS data set containing data extracted from DB2 table(s). This SAS data set can then be manipulated as needed to produce the desired result.

When a SAS data set is created, one of the following is used as input: a SAS data set, a map, or the SQL SELECT statement. Both a map and a SELECT statement can be used as input as long as they are compatible, but this is typically not done. When only a SAS data set is used as input, a map is generated, and the map generates the appropriate SELECT statement. When a map is used as input, the map generates the appropriate SELECT statement. Whether a SAS data set, a map, or a SELECT statement is used as input, it is ultimately the SQL SELECT statement that extracts the required data from the DB2 table(s).

If a map or SQL statements are used as input to PROC DB2EXT, they were usually created in a previous execution of PROC DB2EXT in Display Manager to take advantage of the ease of use. These maps and SQL statements are typically used as input to PROC DB2EXT in a batch program to create a SAS data set, due to computer resource limitations in Display Manager.

This chapter will present the use of PROC DB2EXT in batch programs to create a SAS data set containing data extracted from a DB2 table(s) by coding a SELECT statement, by using a map created in a previous execution as input, and by using a SELECT statement created in a previous execution as input. Also shown are saving a map and saving a SELECT statement in the batch execution of PROC DB2EXT. Typically, maps and SELECT statements will be created and saved through the execution of PROC DB2EXT in Display Manager.

The user should have JCL appropriate to his company to execute SAS with SAS/DB2. Just like using PROC DB2EXT in Display Manager, you will also need to know the value(s) of the DB2 SUBSYSTEM ID. Contact the SAS Consultant at your company for this information. An introduction to PROC DB2EXT was given in Chapter 5, Introduction to SAS/DB2, and this material should be fresh in your mind before beginning this chapter.

Examples given in this section are based on the DB2 tables shown in Appendix C: Sample Tables. Refer to this appendix to familiarize yourself with the sample DB2 tables before proceeding in this chapter. You may choose to follow along in these examples by performing the same operations on the mainframe at your company. These DB2 tables can be entered on your mainframe, or refer to Chapter 1, Introduction, for ordering a copy of these tables.

If permanent input or output files are needed for the execution of PROC DB2EXT, they should be coded in the JCL. These input/output files include SAS data libraries for SAS data sets that are either maps or data extracted from DB2 table(s) and partitioned data sets for SELECT statements. Other input/output files may be required in other steps in the batch program, and they would also be allocated in the JCL.

Options and Statements

In the previous chapter, PROC DB2EXT in Display Manager, only the PROC DB2EXT statement itself was coded and a series of panels with "fill-in-the-blanks" were used to define the application. In this chapter, PROC DB2EXT will be executed in the batch environment through the use of options of the PROC DB2EXT statement and other statements used in the PROC DB2EXT step. These PROC DB2EXT options and statements can also be executed in Display Manager if the user prefers this style of coding and wants to execute interactively. Also, for users who prefer the line mode execution of SAS, these options and statements must be used to execute PROC DB2EXT.

The following statements can be used with PROC DB2EXT in batch programs:

```
PROC DB2EXT option(s);
   SELECT statement;
   LIST ALL; or LIST tablename;
   FMT number = 'format' number = 'format' ...;
   RENAME number = SASname number = SASname ...;
```

The above statements can be used in batch programs, but are also used in line mode execution of PROC DB2EXT. The following statements are used exclusively in line mode execution. These statements will be defined, but will not be illustrated in examples in this chapter.

```
EXIT;
RESET;
LIST TABLE;
TABLE = tablename; or TABLE = authorization.tablename;
```

There are several options that can be used in the PROC DB2EXT statement. Of these options and the above statements, only the OUT option is required. However, one of the following must also be used: the IN option, the SELECT statement, or the LIST tablename statement. If the SELECT statement is used, it must be coded immediately after the PROC DB2EXT statement. All other statements can be coded in any order.

Options

The options which can be used with the PROC DB2EXT statement are defined as follows:

OUT=SASdataset: The OUT option is not optional; it is required. The OUT option is used to specify the name of the SAS data set that will be created as a result of executing PROC DB2EXT. This SAS data set can be either a map or a SAS data set containing data extracted from DB2 table(s).

By default, the SAS data set will contain data extracted from DB2 table(s). The creation of this SAS data set is based on specifications in the SELECT statement and optionally the RENAME, and FMT statements or specifications given in a map named in the IN option of the PROC DB2EXT statement.

If the SAVESEL option is coded, then the SAS data set named in the OUT option will be a map. When a map is created in a batch program, it is based on specifications given in the SELECT statement and optionally, the RENAME and FMT statements. Because the map is created using a SELECT statement, only a Basic SELECT statement should be used. Although an Enhanced SELECT statement can create a map, the map in turn cannot generate this Enhanced SELECT statement. When a map created in a batch program is used as sole input in subsequent executions of PROC DB2EXT, an SQL error will be generated and the resulting SAS data set will have 0 observations. A map created in a batch program will have to be edited through the SAS/FSP procedure FSEDIT or a DATA step before it can be used as the sole input to PROC DB2EXT in subsequent executions. This is because the variable, TABPW, contains missing values for all observations. This variable is supposed to contain the name of the DB2 table(s). Therefore, it is not recommended to create and save a map in a batch execution of PROC DB2EXT.

The SAS data set created by the OUT option can be temporary for the duration of the batch job or it can be saved permanently in a SAS data library. If it is to be saved permanently, a two-level SAS data set name will be specified, where the first level refers to the DD statement in the JCL and the second level is the SAS data set name.

The Base SAS data options KEEP and DROP can be used with the OUT option.

SAVESEL: When the SAVESEL option is used in the PROC DB2EXT statement, the SAS data set named in the OUT option (a required option) is a map rather than a SAS data set containing data extracted from DB2 table(s). Refer to the definition of the OUT option for more information.

IN = SASdataset: The IN option is used to specify a map to be used as input to PROC DB2EXT in Display Manager and in batch. The map will create a Basic SELECT statement, which will perform the data extraction from the DB2 table(s). The map was created in a previous execution of PROC DB2EXT, probably in Display Manager, and stored permanently as a SAS data set in a SAS data library.

SQLLIB = ddname or SQLLIB = ddname.membername:

The SQLLIB option causes either the map named in the IN option of the PROC DB2EXT statement or the SELECT statement coded in the PROC DB2EXT step to be saved to a file, usually as a member of a partitioned data set. This partitioned data set is specified in the JCL. If the JCL specification includes the member name, then the SQLLIB option includes only the ddname used in the JCL. If the JCL specification does not include the member name, then the SQLLIB option includes the ddname used in the JCL followed by a period (.) and the member name.

It is not practical to save a SELECT statement in a batch execution of PROC DB2EXT because either a map must be created first for input or the SELECT statement itself has to be coded as input. You could just as easily perform a TSO copy to copy the SELECT statement to a member of a partitioned data set or into other programs requiring the same SELECT statement.

SSID = subsystem name: The SSID is the DB2 SUBSYSTEM ID option. This option is set when SAS/DB2 is installed. If the value assigned at installation is appropriate for your application, the SSID option need not be specified. However, most companies will have two values for SSID, one for a test DB2 environment and one for a production environment. Contact the SAS Consultant at your company for the proper values of this field.

If you are running SAS/DB2 in Release 5.18 or later, a system option can also be used to change the value of the SSID parameter. For example, the DB2SSID system option could be set in the following OPTIONS statement:

```
OPTIONS DB2SSID=DBP;
```

Any SAS/DB2 procedure coded after this system option would use DBP as the value of SSID, and the SSID option would not have to be coded in the SAS/DB2 procedure. Like any other system option, the value is in effect until the batch program ends or another system option is coded which changes this value.

UNIQUE: PROC DB2EXT automatically generates SAS variable names as the first eight positions of the eighteen-position DB2 column name. Sometimes more than one DB2 column will have the same first eight positions. When this happens, duplicate SAS variable names will be generated. This results in an error and PROC DB2EXT will produce 0 observations.

If the UNIQUE option is used, all SAS variable names will be unique. When duplicate SAS variable names are generated, a numeric value from 00 to 999 is appended to the end of variable names starting with the second variable having the duplicate name. If necessary, the end of the variable name will be truncated in order to append this number.

The SAS variable names generated by the UNIQUE option are not very descriptive and you must refer to the order in which the DB2 columns were specified in the SELECT statement to be able to distinguish one SAS variable from another. The RENAME statement, whose definition follows, allows the user to assign more appropriate SAS variable names.

Statements

The following statements are used with the PROC DB2EXT procedure in the batch environment:

SELECT statement;

The SELECT statement, covered in Chapter 4, Structured Query Language, can be used as input to PROC DB2EXT in order to create the SAS data set specified in the OUT option. The SELECT statement can create a SAS data set containing data extracted from DB2 table(s) or a SAS data set that is a map. Usually the SAS data set created will be a SAS data set containing data extracted from DB2 table(s). A map is not often created in this manner because a SELECT statement, and optionally the RENAME and FMT statements, must be coded in order to create the map. You could just as easily use the SELECT, RENAME, and FMT statements in subsequent executions of PROC DB2EXT rather than creating a map for this purpose.

When a SELECT statement is used in a PROC DB2EXT step, it must be the first statement after the PROC DB2EXT statement. Other statements can be in any order.

Sometimes a SELECT statement is stored as a member of a partitioned data set, especially if it was created and saved through the execution of PROC DB2EXT in Display Manager. Many users perform a TSO copy to copy the SELECT statement into their batch program. The Base SAS %INCLUDE statement can also be used to bring the code into a batch program at execution without actually copying the code into the batch program. This alternative can be convenient when the same SELECT statement is needed in multiple programs. The two forms of the %INCLUDE statement are:

```
%INCLUDE ddname(member);
%INCLUDE ddname;
```

The file containing the SELECT statement is coded in the JCL. If the member name is coded in the JCL, then only the ddname associated with that file is coded in the %INCLUDE statement. If the member name is not coded in the JCL, then the ddname is coded followed by the member name in parentheses.

RENAME number = SASname number = SASname ...;

The RENAME statement is used to assign SAS variable names to the variables in the SAS data set created by PROC DB2EXT. This SAS data set usually contains data extracted from DB2 table(s), but can also be a map. The number is the number of the DB2 column as determined from the order specified by the user in the SELECT statement. The SASname is any valid SAS variable name, which is a maximum of eight positions beginning with a letter or underscore. One or more SAS variables can be renamed in a single RENAME statement.

If the RENAME statement is not used, SAS variable names are automatically created as the first eight positions of the eighteen-position DB2 column name.

FMT number = 'format' number = 'format' ...;

The FMT statement is used to assign formats to SAS variables in the SAS data set created by PROC DB2EXT. This SAS data set usually is a SAS data set containing data extracted from DB2 table(s), but can also be a map. The number is the number of the DB2 column as determined from the order specified by the user in the SELECT statement. The format can be any valid SAS format and must be coded in quotes. One or more formats can be assigned in a single FMT statement.

If the FMT statement is not used, standard character formats are used for DB2 character data types, standard numeric formats for DB2 numeric data types, and a SAS date/time format for DB2 date/time data types.

SAS date/time formats can be assigned to DB2 date/time columns, whether they are a numeric or a date/time DB2 data type. When a SAS date format is assigned, two operations take place. First, the date is converted to a SAS date for storage on the SAS data set. Recall that a SAS date is the number of days since 1/1/60. Second, the SAS date will be formatted when the value is written to reports or output file. If the date is a DB2 numeric data type, this conversion is performed based on the assumption that the DB2 date is stored in the form, YYMMDD, where YY is either a two or four position representation of the year. If the DB2 date is not stored in this form, code the desired format followed by a slash and the proper form. For example,

```
FMT 3 = 'DATE7./MMDDYY';
```

A DB2 value of 061752 would be stored as a SAS date value of -2754 and printed as 17JUN52.

If the date is a DB2 date data type, the SAS date format, DATE7., is automatically assigned without coding the FMT statement. The FMT statement can be used to assign SAS date formats other than DATE7. to DB2 date data types. For example, a DB2 date value of 1952-06-17 would be stored as a SAS date value of - 2754 and automatically printed as 17JUN52. If the FMT statement,

```
FMT 3='MMDDYY8.';
```

is used, the date would be printed as 06/17/52.

LIST ALL;

The LIST ALL statement produces a report on the SAS log which shows the mapping information completed during the execution of PROC DB2EXT. The LIST ALL statement produces this report only when a SELECT statement is used as input to PROC DB2EXT to create a SAS data set containing data extracted from a DB2 table(s). Included on the report are (1) the number of the DB2 column as determined from the order specified by the user in the SELECT statement or map, (2) the SAS variable name, either automatically generated or named by the RENAME statement or map, and (3) FORMATS for the SAS variables, either automatically generated or specified in the FMT statement or the map.

LIST tablename tablename ... ;

The LIST tablename statement can be used to list the DB2 columns in the table(s) specified, on the SAS log. Unlike the LIST ALL statement, it does not provide additional information such as the SAS variable names and formats. For this reason, the LIST ALL statement is preferred.

However, the LIST tablename statement can be used without a map or SELECT statement being specified as input, and without creating an output SAS data set, while the LIST ALL cannot. The OUT option must still be coded in the PROC DB2EXT statement, but 0 observations will be created. The purpose of using the LIST tablename statement in this situation is merely to provide the user with a list of the columns on a DB2 table(s). Unfortunately, the user will often need to know the data type or SAS format in order to know whether quotes should be used around values code in the selection criteria in a WHERE clause, and this information is not provided. Therefore, the user will probably obtain this data dictionary type of information from another source. You may choose to use the DB2 System Tables, do screen prints of the DATA EXTRACTION panel, or create a map and use PROC PRINT to display it. Contact the DB2 Administrator at your company for other alternatives for acquiring this information.

Line Mode

The above statements are used in batch programs and also line mode execution of SAS. The following statements are used exclusively in line mode execution:

EXIT;

The EXIT statement performs the same function as the EXIT command used when PROC DB2EXT is executed in Display Manager. The EXIT statement ends execution of PROC DB2EXT without creating output files.

RESET;

The RESET statement performs the same function as the RESET command used in the DATA EXTRACTION panel when PROC DB2EXT is executed in Display Manager. The RESET statement clears all previously selected DB2 columns, along with any user- defined SAS variable names and formats and the WHERE clause if coded.

TABLE = Tablename1 ... Tablename5;

TABLE = Authorization.tablename1 ... Authorization.tablename5;

The TABLE statement is used to specify up to 5 tables from which information is desired. The Authorization ID does not have to be specified on this statement. The TABLE statement can be compared to entering the desired table names on the DATA ACCESS panel in Display Manager. This statement is used with the LIST Table statement.

LIST Table;

The LIST Table statement is used to display DB2 columns from tables specified in the TABLE statement. The user selects the desired DB2 columns from this list. This list of DB2 column names is similar to the list displayed on the DATA EXTRACTION panel.

Application Use

Figure 7-1 outlines which PROC DB2EXT options and statements should be used depending on the input and output files needed. It also shows the output files that can be produced by a specific input file.

In addition to the options and statements shown on this chart, are the UNIQUE option, and the RENAME and FMT statements. These statements allow the user to name SAS variables and specify output formats. When a SELECT statement is used as input, these statements are used to define the map, which will result in creating a map or creating a SAS data set containing data extracted from DB2 table(s). Although these statements can be used when a map is used as input, it is unlikely because their purpose is the same as the map.

INPUT	OUTPUT	Required Options	
Map	SELECT Statement	OUT SSID IN SQLLIB	(SAS data set created too) (if other than default)
	SAS Data Set	OUT SSID IN	 (if other than default)
SELECT Statement	Map	OUT SSID SAVESEL	 (if other than default)
	SELECT Statement	OUT SSID SQLLIB	(SAS data set created too) (if other than default)
	SAS Data Set	OUT SSID	 (if other than default)

Figure 7-1 Required options of PROC DB2EXT.

Also, the LIST statement is often used in applications of PROC DB2EXT to display mapping information.

Comparison to Display Manager

Figure 7-2 shows the PROC DB2EXT panel and the field on that panel that performs the same function as the PROC DB2EXT batch options and statements.

PROC DB2EXT Panel	Field on the Panel	Batch Option/Statement
DATA ACCESS	OUTPUT SQL LIBRARY	SQLLIB Option
	OUTPUT SAS DATA SET	OUT Option
	DB2 SUBSYSTEM ID	SSID Option
	SAVE SELECTIONS	SAVESEL Option
	UNIQUE SAS NAMES	UNIQUE Option
	AUTHORIZATION ID	SELECT Statement (FROM Clause)
		Map
	TABLE NAME	SELECT Statement (FROM Clause)
		or Map
DATA EXTRACTION	FUNC	SELECT Statement (column list)
		Map
	SAS NAME	RENAME Statement
		Map
	FORMAT	FMT Statement or
		Map
	WHERE Clause	SELECT Statement (WHERE Clause)
		Map
SQL ENTRY/EDIT	INCLUDE Command	%INCLUDE Statement

Figure 7-2 PROC DB2EXT Display Manager and batch comparison.

Creating a SAS Data Set

This section illustrates the use of PROC DB2EXT in batch to create a SAS data set containing data extracted from DB2 table(s).

The examples in this section will show the creation of a SAS data set containing data extracted from DB2 tables through coding the SELECT statement in the PROC DB2EXT step. This is probably the method you will use most often. The RENAME and FMT statements are often used with the SELECT statement to define SAS variable names and formats, respectively. The use of maps and saved SELECT statements as input to PROC DB2EXT will be covered in the section, Saving Maps and SELECT Statements, later in this chapter.

The following examples show the SAS log and the reports that are produced from the SAS data sets created by extracting data from DB2 tables.

Example 7-1

When a map or SELECT statement is created using PROC DB2EXT in Display Manager, the DATA EXTRACTION panel provides the necessary information on DB2 column names and SAS formats for each column. If this map or SELECT statement is used as input to PROC DB2EXT in a batch program, the user does not have to know the DB2 column names and SAS formats, as they are already provided. Often, the user will want to code the SELECT statement in the PROC DB2EXT step in the batch program. In order to do this, the DB2 column names and SAS formats must be known. There are a number of alternatives for obtaining this information. The LIST tablename provides the DB2 column names, but SAS formats are not given and these are often needed when a WHERE clause is coded in order to know when to use quotes around column values. The DB2 System Tables could be used as input to PROC DB2EXT or screen prints of the DATA EXTRACTION panel could be used. Your company may also have a Data Dictionary product which provides this information.

This example shows creating and printing a map for the purpose of providing DB2 column names and the generated SAS variable names and formats.

The SAS log for this batch program follows:

```
1
2    PROC DB2EXT OUT=MAPEX1 SAVESEL;
3      SELECT * FROM TSID123.PROJINFO;
4
NOTE: THE DATA SET WORK.MAP HAS 6 OBSERVATIONS AND 8 VARIABLES.

5     PROC PRINT DATA=MAPEX1;
6       TITLE 'MAP FOR PROJINFO';
NOTE: THE PROCEDURE PRINT PRINTED PAGE 1.
```

The PROC PRINT shown on the SAS log results in the following report of the map:

MAP OF PROJINFO

OBS	TABPW	TYPE	LENGTH	SCALE	NULLS	COLUMN	SASNAME	FORMAT
1		453	15	0	1	LAST_NAME	LAST_NAM	$15.
2		453	10	0	1	FIRST_NAME	FIRST_NA	$10.
3		485	6	0	1	BEGIN_DATE	BEGIN_DA	7.
4		485	6	0	1	PLAN_END_DATE	PLAN_END	7.
5		485	6	0	1	ACTUAL_END	ACTUAL_E	7.
6		453	20	0	1	PROJECT	PROJECT	$20.

Example 7-2

A report is needed which shows each management employee's Hire_date and Salary_december. New variables should be created to produce the number of years of service and conditionally calculate a new salary based on Salary_december. SAS variables names should be user-defined to some descriptive name. Hire_date should be formatted using the MMDDYY8. SAS date format. Hire_date is a DB2 numeric data type stored in the format, YYMMDD, which is the form expected by SAS/DB2. Salary_december and the new salary should be formatted using the DOLLARw.d format. Last_name and First_name should be combined, separated by a comma. The report should be sorted by Hire_date.

The SAS log for this batch program follows:

```
1
2    PROC DB2EXT OUT=EX2;
3      SELECT LAST_NAME, FIRST_NAME, HIRE_DATE, SALARY_DECEMBER
4        FROM TSID123.PERSINFO
5        WHERE MANAGEMENT = 'Y'
6        ORDER BY HIRE_DATE;
7      RENAME 1=LNAME 2=FNAME 3=HIREDTE 4=CURSAL;
8      FMT 3='MMDDYY8.' 4='DOLLAR10.2';
9
--------- TABLE ITEMS -----------
***********PROJINFO***********
----------DB2COLUMN----------
.......LAST_NAME...............
.......FIRST_NAME..............
.......BEGIN_DATE..............
.......PLAN_END_DATE...........
.......ACTUAL_END_DATE.........
.......PROJECT.................
--------- TABLE ITEMS -----------
***********ORGINFO***********
----------DB2COLUMN----------
.......DEPARTMENT..............
.......DEPARTMENT_NAME.........
.......DIRECTOR................
.......VICE_PRESIDENT..........
.......PRESIDENT...............
10     LIST PROJINFO ORGINFO;
11
NOTE: THE DATA SET WORK.EX2 HAS 8 OBSERVATIONS AND 4 VARIABLES.

12    DATA EX2;
13      SET EX2;
14      YRSERV = ROUND((TODAY() - HIREDTE) / 365,1);
15      IF CURSAL < 4000
16         THEN NEWSAL = ROUND(CURSAL * 1.09 + 200,.01);
17      ELSE IF 4000 <= CURSAL < 5000
18         THEN NEWSAL = ROUND(CURSAL * 1.08 + 200,.01);
```

```
19       ELSE NEWSAL = ROUND(CURSAL * 1.07 + 200,.01);
20       NAME = TRIM(LNAME)||', '||FNAME;
21       DROP LNAME FNAME;
22

NOTE: DATA SET WORK.EX2 HAS 8 OBSERVATIONS AND 5 VARIABLES.
23     PROC PRINT DATA=EX2 SPLIT='*';
24       ID NAME;
25       VAR HIREDTE YRSERV CURSAL NEWSAL;
26       FORMAT NEWSAL DOLLAR10.2;
27       LABEL HIREDTE = 'HIRE * DATE'
28             YRSERV  = 'YEARS * SERVICE'
29             CURSAL  = 'CURRENT * SALARY'
30             NEWSAL  = 'NEW * SALARY';
31       TITLE 'NEW SALARIES FOR MANAGEMENT';
32
NOTE: THE PROCEDURE PRINT PRINTED PAGE 1.
```

The necessary DB2 columns are specified in the SELECT statement, and only those rows representing management staff are selected in the WHERE clause. The ORDER BY clause is used so that PROC SORT will not be required. The RENAME statement is used to rename the generated SAS variable names to more descriptive names. The FMT statement is used to format the DB2 columns, Hire_date and Salary_december.

The optional LIST tablename statement is used for illustration purposes. Two DB2 tables, Projinfo and Orginfo, are named in the LIST tablename statement. A list of the DB2 columns in those tables is shown on the SAS log. Table(s) named in the LIST tablename statement do not have to be used in the SELECT statement. The LIST tablename statement functions independently, whereas the LIST ALL statement is based on the table(s) named in the SELECT statement or the input map. The LIST tablename statement would be more valuable if data types or SAS formats were also displayed.

Since conditional processing is required to calculate the value of the new variable representing a new salary, a DATA step reading the SAS data set created by PROC DB2EXT will be required. To accomplish this sort of processing with SELECT statements, a SELECT statement based on a WHERE clause would have to be coded for every condition and the appropriate calculation coded as a new column in the SELECT list. The result tables from each SELECT statement would then be combined with the UNION operation. Not only does it require more effort on the part of the user, but usually it will require more computer resources, especially if a tablespace scan is required for each SELECT statement. Recall that a tablespace scan is a sequential read of a DB2 table; indexes are not used.

Since a DATA step is required for the conditional processing, you may wish to perform other functions in that DATA step rather than in the PROC DB2EXT step. A new variable, Name, is created by combining the SAS variables, lname and fname, created by PROC DB2EXT. This could have been performed in the SELECT statement. However, SQL does not have the equivalent of the TRIM function so the last name would contain trailing blanks. The number of years of service is created using the SAS function, TODAY(), for today's date as a SAS date value and the SAS variable, Hiredte, created from the DB2 column, Hire_date. Hiredte is also a SAS date value because a SAS date format was assigned in the FMT statement in the PROC DB2EXT step. It is much easier to use the FMT statement to create SAS date values, but it could be created in a DATA step using the following statement:

```
Hiredte2 = INPUT(PUT(Hiredte,6.),YYMMDD6.);
```

With DB2 Release 1.3 or later, the number of years of service can be created in the SELECT statement, using the following expression:

```
YEAR(CURRENT DATE - Hire_date)
```

The PROC PRINT shown on the SAS log results in the following report:

NEW SALARIES FOR MANAGEMENT

NAME	HIRE DATE	YEARS SERVICE	CURRENT SALARY	NEW SALARY
KAWAN, JOE	10/30/64	24	$4,280.00	$4,822.40
MICHAEL, PAT	09/01/65	24	$4,280.00	$4,822.40
DOUGLAS, MILTON	11/09/67	21	$4,490.00	$5,049.20
PEYTON, JOHN	03/25/69	20	$4,390.00	$4,941.20
BROOKS, EDWARD	08/13/75	14	$5,560.00	$6,149.20
KEESLING, GERTRUDE	08/08/76	13	$3,750.00	$4,287.50
ATKINS, NANCY	09/15/81	7	$3,750.00	$4,287.50
MORGAN, CHERYL	03/14/87	2	$4,070.00	$4,595.60

A LABEL statement was used to produce labels other than the DB2 column names. A FORMAT statement is used to format the variable, Newsal, created conditionally in the DATA step.

Example 7-3

A report is needed which shows the average and the sum of the DB2 column, Salary_december, by Employee_type and Sex. The SAS variable names should be user- defined with descriptive names. The report should be sorted by Employee_type and Sex.

The SAS log for this batch program follows:

```
   PROC DB2EXT OUT=EX3 UNIQUE;
     SELECT SEX, EMPLOYEE_TYPE, AVG(SALARY_DECEMBER),
            SUM(SALARY_DECEMBER)
       FROM TSID123.PERSINFO
       GROUP BY EMPLOYEE_TYPE, SEX
       ORDER BY EMPLOYEE_TYPE, SEX;
     RENAME 2=EMPTYP 3=AVGSAL 4=SUMSAL;

------------ USER SELECTIONS ------------
ITEM NUMBER---COLUMN NAME-------SAS NAME----FORMAT-----------
....1.......SEX.................SEX........$1.
....2.......EMPLOYEE_TYPE.......EMPTYP.....$1.
....3...........................AVGSAL.....16.10
....4...........................SUMSAL.....16.
WHERE CLAUSE ----->
     LIST ALL;

NOTE: THE DATA SET WORK.EX3 HAS 6 OBSERVATIONS AND 4 VARIABLES.
    PROC PRINT DATA=EX3 NOOBS;
      VAR EMPTYP SEX SUMSAL AVGSAL;
      FORMAT AVGSAL SUMSAL DOLLAR12.2;
      TITLE 'EXAMPLE 3';

NOTE: THE PROCEDURE PRINT PRINTED PAGE 1.
```

The GROUP BY clause is used to create a result table which is summarized by the DB2 columns, Employee_type and Sex. The ORDER BY clause is used to sort the result table by these same DB2 columns. The SELECT list also includes these columns, along with expressions for calculating the average and the sum of the DB2 column, Salary_december.

Both of these two new columns will have the SAS variable name, COMPOUND. The UNIQUE option of the PROC DB2EXT statement and the RENAME statement are used to produce unique SAS variable names for these variables. Notice the report produced by the LIST ALL statement shows the SAS variable names generated by the RENAME statement, but the DB2 column names for these new columns are blank. It is recommended that you use both the UNIQUE option and the RENAME statement when duplicate SAS names are generated in a batch execution of PROC DB2EXT. The use of only one and neither of these will be discussed after the report generated by the PROC PRINT shown here is displayed.

The PROC PRINT shown on the SAS log results in the following report:

```
                EXAMPLE 3


 EMPTYP      SEX        SUMSAL          AVGSAL


   H          F      $24,130.00      $1,608.67
   H          M      $18,930.00      $1,893.00
   S          F      $26,990.00      $2,699.00
   S          M      $54,890.00      $3,430.63
   T          F       $3,900.00        $780.00
   T          M       $2,350.00        $587.50
```

If the RENAME statement is used and the UNIQUE option is not used, the SAS log for PROC DB2EXT would be:

```

    PROC DB2EXT OUT=EX3B;
      SELECT SEX, EMPLOYEE_TYPE, AVG(SALARY_DECEMBER),
             SUM(SALARY_DECEMBER)
        FROM TSID123.PERSINFO
        GROUP BY EMPLOYEE_TYPE, SEX
 ERROR: COMPOUND IN POSITION 3 IS A DUPLICATE
+ERROR: COMPOUND IN POSITION 3 IS A DUPLICATE
+ERROR: COMPOUND IN POSITION 3 IS A DUPLICATE
 ERROR: COMPOUND IN POSITION 4 IS A DUPLICATE
+ERROR: COMPOUND IN POSITION 4 IS A DUPLICATE
+ERROR: COMPOUND IN POSITION 4 IS A DUPLICATE
```

```
              ORDER BY EMPLOYEE_TYPE, SEX;
            RENAME 2=EMPTYP 3=AVGSAL 4=SUMSAL;

NOTE: THE DATA SET WORK.EX3B HAS 6 OBSERVATIONS AND 4 VARIABLES.
```

An error is generated because the SELECT statement generates duplicate SAS variable names without the UNIQUE option. The RENAME statement which follows changes these duplicate names, so execution continues and the correct SAS data set is produced. Even though the results are the same, the UNIQUE option is recommended so that these errors will not be shown on the SAS log.

If the UNIQUE option is used and the RENAME statement is not used, the SAS log for PROC DB2EXT would be:

```

PROC DB2EXT OUT=EX3C UNIQUE;
  SELECT SEX, EMPLOYEE_TYPE, AVG(SALARY_DECEMBER),
        SUM(SALARY_DECEMBER)
    FROM TSID123.PERSINFO
    GROUP BY EMPLOYEE_TYPE, SEX
    ORDER BY EMPLOYEE_TYPE, SEX;
  RENAME 2=EMPTYP;

NOTE: THE DATA SET WORK.EX3C HAS 6 OBSERVATIONS AND 4 VARIABLES.
```

The PROC PRINT that would result from this PROC DB2EXT step follows:

EXAMPLE 3C

EMPTYP	SEX	COMPOUND	COMPOU00
H	F	$1,608.67	$24,130.00
H	M	$1,893.00	$18,930.00
S	F	$2,699.00	$26,990.00
S	M	$3,430.63	$54,890.00
T	F	$780.00	$3,900.00
T	M	$587.50	$2,350.00

The first DB2 column created, which was the average of Salary_december, is named COMPOUND. The second DB2 column created, which was the sum of Salary_december, is named COMPOU00. The

SAS variable name is truncated to 6 positions and 00 is appended to produce a unique variable name. The UNIQUE option without the RENAME statement is not recommended because the SAS variable names are not descriptive and you have to refer to the order specified in the SELECT statement to distinguish one from another.

If neither the UNIQUE option nor the RENAME statement is used, the SAS log for PROC DB2EXT would be:

```
 1
 2    PROC DB2EXT OUT=EX3D;
 3      SELECT SEX, EMPLOYEE_TYPE, AVG(SALARY_DECEMBER),
 4             SUM(SALARY_DECEMBER)
 5        FROM TSID123.PERSINFO
 6        GROUP BY EMPLOYEE_TYPE, SEX
ERROR: COMPOUND IN POSITION 3 IS A DUPLICATE
+ERROR: COMPOUND IN POSITION 3 IS A DUPLICATE
+ERROR: COMPOUND IN POSITION 3 IS A DUPLICATE
ERROR: COMPOUND IN POSITION 4 IS A DUPLICATE
+ERROR: COMPOUND IN POSITION 4 IS A DUPLICATE
+ERROR: COMPOUND IN POSITION 4 IS A DUPLICATE
 7        ORDER BY EMPLOYEE_TYPE, SEX;
 8
 ERROR: COMPOUND IN POSITION 3 IS A DUPLICATE
+ERROR: COMPOUND IN POSITION 3 IS A DUPLICATE
+ERROR: COMPOUND IN POSITION 3 IS A DUPLICATE
 ERROR: COMPOUND IN POSITION 4 IS A DUPLICATE
+ERROR: COMPOUND IN POSITION 4 IS A DUPLICATE
+ERROR: COMPOUND IN POSITION 4 IS A DUPLICATE
 9            RENAME 2=EMPTYP;
10
 ERROR: PREVIOUS ERRORS WERE NOT CORRECTED EXECUTION TERMINATED
+ERROR: PREVIOUS ERRORS WERE NOT CORRECTED EXECUTION TERMINATED
+ERROR: PREVIOUS ERRORS WERE NOT CORRECTED EXECUTION TERMINATED
 NOTE: THE DATA SET WORK.EX3D HAS 0 OBSERVATIONS AND 0 VARIABLES.
```

IF duplicate SAS names are generated and are not changed by either the UNIQUE option, the RENAME statement, or preferably both, execution terminates and the resulting SAS data set contains 0 observations.

Example 7-4

A list of all the employees in Cost_center 130 who have worked on projects is needed. The DB2 columns required are Last_name, First_name, and Project.

The SAS log for this batch program follows:

```
1
2    PROC DB2EXT OUT=EX4;
3      SELECT PE.LAST_NAME, PE.FIRST_NAME, PROJECT
4        FROM TSID123.PERSINFO PE, TSID123.PROJINFO PJ
5        WHERE PE.LAST_NAME = PJ.LAST_NAME AND
6              PE.FIRST_NAME = PJ.FIRST_NAME AND
7              COST_CENTER = '130';
8      RENAME 1=LNAME 2=FNAME;
9
------------ USER SELECTIONS ------------
ITEM NUMBER---COLUMN NAME-------SAS NAME----FORMAT-----------
....1.......LAST_NAME...........LNAME......$15.
....2.......FIRST_NAME..........FNAME......$10.
....3.......PROJECT.............PROJECT....$20.
WHERE CLAUSE ----->
PE.LAST_NAME = PJ.LAST_NAME AND PE.FIRST_NAME = PJ.FIRST_NAME
AND COST_CENTER = '130'
10           LIST ALL;
11
NOTE: THE DATA SET WORK.EX4 HAS 4 OBSERVATIONS AND 3 VARIABLES.

12    PROC PRINT DATA=EX4 NOOBS;
13      TITLE 'EXAMPLE 4';
14
NOTE: THE PROCEDURE PRINT PRINTED PAGE 1.
```

Two DB2 tables are required to obtain the desired information. The DB2 table, Persinfo, is needed to select only those employees with a Cost_center of 130. The DB2 table, Projinfo, is needed to extract the name of the project.

The WHERE clause is used to select only those rows from the CARTESIAN PRODUCT where the First_name and Last_name are the same on the two DB2 tables. The WHERE clause is also used to select only those employees in Cost_center 130. Since the DB2 columns, Last_name and First_name, have the same name in both DB2 tables, they must be prefixed with either the full DB2 table name or a qualifier representing the DB2 table name. Qualifiers for the DB2 table names are set up in the FROM clause. These qualifiers are in the WHERE clause and the SELECT list to specify which DB2 table the DB2 columns, Last_name and First_name, come from.

The RENAME statement is used to assign SAS variables names to the columns, Last_name and First_name. The LIST ALL statement, which is optional, is used to display the mapping results of the JOIN.

The PROC PRINT shown on the SAS log results in the following report:

```
           EXAMPLE 4

LNAME      FNAME       PROJECT


BAKER      MARTHA      BROKERS
GOETZ      JACK        COMMISSIONS
HUFFORD    STEPHEN     COMMISSIONS
KISLING    MARY LEA    BROKERS
```

Example 7-5

A list of all the employees in Cost_center 130 is needed. If they have worked on any projects, the name of the project is needed. The DB2 columns required are Last_name, First_name, and Project. The difference between this example and the previous one is that all employees in Cost_center 130 are desired, not just those who have worked on projects.

The SAS log for this batch program follows:

```

PROC DB2EXT OUT=EX5A;
  SELECT LAST_NAME, FIRST_NAME
    FROM TSID123.PERSINFO
    WHERE COST_CENTER = '130';
  RENAME 1=LNAME 2=FNAME;

NOTE: THE DATA SET WORK.EX5A HAS 14 OBSERVATIONS AND 2 VARIABLES.
```

```
8    PROC DB2EXT OUT=EX5B;
9      SELECT LAST_NAME, FIRST_NAME, PROJECT
10       FROM TSID123.PROJINFO;
11     RENAME 1=LNAME 2=FNAME;
12
NOTE: THE DATA SET WORK.EX5B HAS 19 OBSERVATIONS AND 3 VARIABLES.

13    DATA EX5;
14      MERGE EX5A (IN=ONE)
15            EX5B (IN=TWO);
16      BY LNAME FNAME;
17      IF ONE;
18

NOTE: DATA SET WORK.EX5 HAS 14 OBSERVATIONS AND 3 VARIABLES.

19    PROC PRINT DATA=EX5 NOOBS;
20      TITLE 'EXAMPLE 5';
21
NOTE: THE PROCEDURE PRINT PRINTED PAGE 1.
```

If the DB2 tables, Projinfo and Persinfo, are joined as they were in the previous example, only those employees in Cost_center 130 who have worked on projects would be selected. Since the CARTESIAN PRODUCT is the basis of a JOIN, a single SELECT statement cannot produce the desired results. Two PROC DB2EXT steps are used and two SAS data sets are created, one from each DB2 table is needed. The SAS data set, Ex5a, contains the Last_name and First_name of all employees in Cost_center 130. The SAS data set, Ex5b, contains the Last_name and First_name of all employees who worked on projects. These two SAS data sets are merged in a DATA step and only those observations on the SAS data set, Ex5a, are written to the SAS data set, Ex5. This will produce all employees in Cost_center 130. This example illustrates that the SAS MERGE is far more flexible than a DB2 JOIN.

The two SAS data sets must be sorted in order of the BY variables, Lname and Fname, in order to perform the MERGE. Since the DB2 tables are sorted in this order, it was not necessary to sort. If a sort was required, the ORDER BY clause could be used in the SELECT statement or PROC SORT could be used on the two SAS data sets prior to the MERGE DATA step.

The PROC PRINT shown on the SAS log results in the following report:

```
            EXAMPLE 5

  LNAME        FNAME        PROJECT


  BAKER        MARTHA       BROKERS
  CAMPBELL     MARGARET
  DUDLEY       LOUISA
  GOETZ        JACK         COMMISSIONS
  HANKS        TROY
  HARDWICK     DONNIE
  HUFFORD      STEPHEN      COMMISSIONS
  KAWAN        JOE
  KISLING      MARY LEA     BROKERS
  LAUREN       KELLY
  MICHAEL      GARTH
  OWENS        GREG
  PEARCE       EVELYN
  REEVES       JEREMY
```

It is hoped that the design of a DB2 application system will take into consideration the data analysis and reporting that will be needed, and the design will be such that a program like this one is not necessary. The space required for the SAS data sets using the approach shown here can be prohibitive when the DB2 tables are large.

Exercise 1

Test your understanding of creating SAS data sets containing data extracted from DB2 table(s) by completing the exercises described here. The reports are shown on the following pages, along with the SAS log of the program used to produce the report. Format the reports as shown, with titles, labels, formats, and the variables displayed in the order listed.

The DB2 tables used as input are the same tables used in the previous examples and are shown in Appendix C. The data contained in these tables can be loaded into DB2 tables at your site by keying, or refer to Chapter 1, Introduction, for information concerning ordering copies of the tables.

Report 1

A list of the employees aged 50 and over is needed. The DB2 columns needed include Last_name, First_name, Birth_date, and Hire_date. Based on this information, calculate and include on the list each person's age and number of years of service. The age should be age at last birthday as of 4/1/89 and the years of service should be whole years as of 4/1/89. Birth_date and Hire_date are stored as numeric values; they are not DB2 Release 1.3 dates. The list should be sorted with the oldest employee first.

Report 2

Statistics are needed on the average Vacation_available, the average Vacation_used, and the average vacation remaining (must be created) by Cost_center and Management. The report should include the Department_name, along with the Cost_center. It should be sorted by Cost_center and Management.

Report 1

```
                  EMPLOYEES 50 AND OVER

LAST       FIRST       BIRTH      AGE   HIRE       YEARS
 NAME       NAME        DATE             DATE       SERVICE

APPLE      RICHARD    03/14/24    65   11/23/47      41
ADAMS      BILL       12/22/24    64   11/14/55      33
BAKER      MARTHA     08/20/27    61   04/01/74      15
HUTSON     EVERETT    09/12/32    56   03/23/74      15
DUDLEY     LOUISA     01/04/35    54   12/04/66      22
ATWOOD     CHUCK      04/05/36    53   03/24/65      24
PAVELEK    JOE        10/04/36    52   01/01/59      30
JOHNSON    HAZEL      04/11/38    51   09/28/60      28
PAYTON     RUTH       07/17/38    50   03/26/77      12
DOUGLAS    MILTON     09/05/38    50   11/09/67      21
JAMES      MARVIN     10/09/38    50   11/10/69      19
KAWAN      JOE        03/05/39    50   10/30/64      24
```

The following SAS code can be used to generate the above report.

```

PROC DB2EXT OUT=RPT1;
  SELECT LAST_NAME, FIRST_NAME, BIRTH_DATE, HIRE_DATE
    FROM TSID123.PERSINFO
    ORDER BY BIRTH_DATE;
  RENAME 1=LNAME 2=FNAME 3=BIRTHDTE 4=HIREDTE;
  FMT 3='MMDDYY8.' 4='MMDDYY8.';

NOTE: THE DATA SET WORK.RPT1 HAS 60 OBSERVATIONS AND 4 VARIABLES.

DATA RPT1;
  SET RPT1;
  NOW = MDY(04,01,89);
  AGE = FLOOR((NOW-BIRTHDTE)/365);
  IF AGE = 50;
  YRSERV = FLOOR((NOW-HIREDTE)/365);
  DROP NOW;

NOTE: DATA SET WORK.RPT1 HAS 12 OBSERVATIONS AND 6 VARIABLES.

PROC PRINT DATA=RPT1 NOOBS SPLIT='*';
  VAR LNAME FNAME BIRTHDTE AGE HIREDTE YRSERV;
  LABEL LNAME    = 'LAST * NAME'
        FNAME    = 'FIRST * NAME'
        BIRTHDTE = 'BIRTH * DATE'
        HIREDTE  = 'HIRE * DATE'
        YRSERV   = 'YEARS * SERVICE';
   TITLE 'REPORT 1';

NOTE: THE PROCEDURE PRINT PRINTED PAGE 1.
```

Report 2

AVERAGE VACATION STATISTICS

COSTCTR	DEPTNAME	MGT	VACAVAIL	VACUSED	VACLEFT
100	PERSONNEL	N	83.08	38.77	44.31
110	MARKETING	N	94.55	51.64	42.91
120	FINANCE	N	116.67	53.33	63.33

120	FINANCE	Y	120.00	56.00	64.00
130	SALES	N	98.46	52.31	46.15
130	SALES	Y	160.00	40.00	120.00
140	DEVELOPMENT	N	133.33	50.67	82.67
140	DEVELOPMENT	Y	133.33	50.67	82.67

The following SAS code can be used to generate the above report.

```

  PROC DB2EXT OUT=RPT2 UNIQUE;
    SELECT COST_CENTER, DEPARTMENT_NAME, MANAGEMENT,
           AVG(VACATION_AVAILABLE), AVG(VACATION_USED),
           AVG(VACATION_AVAILABLE - VACATION_USED)
      FROM TSID123.PERSINFO, TSID123.ORGINFO
      WHERE COST_CENTER = DEPARTMENT
      GROUP BY COST_CENTER, DEPARTMENT_NAME, MANAGEMENT
      ORDER BY COST_CENTER, DEPARTMENT_NAME, MANAGEMENT;
    RENAME 1=COSTCTR 2=DEPTNAME 3=MGT 4=VACAVAIL
           5=VACUSED 6=VACLEFT;
          FMT 4='6.2' 5='6.2' 6='6.2';

NOTE: THE DATA SET WORK.RPT2 HAS 8 OBSERVATIONS AND 6 VARIABLES.

   PROC PRINT DATA=RPT2 NOOBS;
     VAR COSTCTR DEPTNAME MGT VACAVAIL VACUSED VACLEFT;
     TITLE 'REPORT 2';

NOTE: THE PROCEDURE PRINT PRINTED PAGE 1.
```

Maps and SELECT Statements

When PROC DB2EXT is used to create a SAS data set containing data extracted from DB2 table(s) in the batch environment, a map or a SELECT statement is used as input. The equivalent of the DATA ACCESS and DATA EXTRACTION panels does not exist, where the user can define a map and the map generates a SELECT statement which performs the extraction.

If a map is used as input, it was created from a previous execution of PROC DB2EXT, probably in Display Manager, and saved as a SAS data set in a SAS data library. To use the map as input, it is specified in the IN option of the PROC DB2EXT statement. The map will have a two-level SAS data set name, where the first level refers to a dd in the JCL pointing to the SAS data library, and the second level is the name of the map.

If a SELECT statement is used as input, it was either coded by the user or created in a previous execution of PROC DB2EXT, probably in Display Manager. If it was created in Display Manager, it is stored in an external file, usually as a member of a partitioned data set. This member can be copied into a batch program using TSO copy operations or the Base SAS statement, %INCLUDE, can be used to bring the member into the batch program without copying it. Refer to the previous section, Options and Statements, for the definition of the %INCLUDE statement. When a SELECT statement is used as input to PROC DB2EXT in a batch program, the RENAME and FMT statements are often used to define SAS variable names and formats, respectively.

There are several advantages of saving maps and SELECT statements for use in subsequent executions of PROC DB2EXT. The most obvious advantage is that it reduces the amount of effort required by the user because either the map or the SELECT statement does not have to be created for each execution. Also, since creating and saving maps and SELECT statements requires fewer computer resources than creating a SAS data set containing data extracted from DB2 table(s), Display Manager can be used. Creating and saving maps and SELECT statements in Display Manager is very straightforward and requires little coding. Often, due to limited interactive resources, the SAS data set containing data extracted from DB2 table(s) cannot be created in Display Manager. Therefore, the most common approach is to create and save either a map or a SELECT statement through the execution of PROC DB2EXT in Display Manager and use this map or SELECT statement as input to PROC DB2EXT in the batch environment.

Although PROC DB2EXT can be used to create and save maps and SELECT statements in a batch program, this method is not very practical. To save a map in the batch execution of PROC DB2EXT, the map is specified in the OUT option and the SAVESEL option is used to indicate that the SAS data set specified in the OUT option is a map. In order to define a map, the desired DB2 columns must be identified, user-defined SAS variable names and formats must be specified if they are needed, and, optionally, selection criteria specified in a WHERE clause must be available. This information was supplied to the map in Display Manager through the DATA ACCESS and DATA EXTRACTION panels. In order to provide this information in the batch execution of PROC DB2EXT, a SELECT statement and, optionally, the RENAME and FMT statements must be coded. If the user has to go to this extent to create and save a map, it defeats the purpose. The user might just as well use the SELECT, RENAME, and FMT statement in subsequent executions of PROC DB2EXT. Since the SELECT statement is used to build a map in batch, the user must be careful to code only a Basic SELECT statement. Although Enhanced SELECT statements can generate a map, when that map is used as the sole input to PROC DB2EXT, it cannot produce the Enhanced SELECT statement. In this situation, a SQL error will be produced and the resulting SAS data set will have 0 observations. Also, when maps are created in batch executions of PROC DB2EXT, the variable, TABPW, which is supposed to contain the DB2 table name, is missing for all observations. This means the map would have to be edited through the SAS/FSP procedure FSEDIT or a DATA step before it could be used as the sole input into subsequent executions of PROC DB2EXT. Therefore, when maps are used as input to PROC DB2EXT, those maps were typically created in Display Manager.

To save a SELECT statement in a batch execution of PROC DB2EXT, the SQLLIB option of the PROC DB2EXT statement is used to specify the external file to hold the SELECT statement. In order to save the SELECT statement, either a map or the SELECT statement itself must be used as input to PROC DB2EXT. If a map is used as input, a Basic SELECT statement will be generated and saved in the file named in the SQLLIB option. However, to have a map available for input, the map was probably created in Display Manager. This being the case, the straightforward approach would be to create and save the SELECT statement in Display Manager instead of a map. If a SELECT statement is used as input to save a SELECT statement, the user might as well perform a TSO copy to copy the SELECT statement to a member of a partitioned data set. Therefore, when SELECT statements are used as input to PROC DB2EXT, those SELECT statements were either coded by the user or created and saved in Display Manager.

The previous section in this chapter, Creating a SAS Data Set, covered the use of PROC DB2EXT to create a SAS data set from data extracted from DB2 table(s) using a SELECT statement as input. Basic and Enhanced SELECT statements were coded in the PROC DB2EXT step. In this section, the use of saved maps and SELECT statements as input to PROC DB2EXT in batch programs will be emphasized. Creating and saving maps and SELECT statements in batch programs will be shown in order to cover all the capabilities of PROC DB2EXT in the batch environment, but creating and saving maps and SELECT statements is easier and more practical in Display Manager. Refer to Chapter 6, PROC DB2EXT in Display Manager, section, Maps and SELECT Statements, for instructions on creating and saving maps and SELECT statements in Display Manager, the definition of a map, and guidelines for determining whether to save a map or a SELECT statement. This user will need this information before proceeding in this section.

Example 7-6

A report is needed which shows the sick time used for nonmanagement hourly employees by department name. The DB2 columns needed include Last_name, First_name, Sick_used, Cost_center, and Department_name. SAS variable names should be user-defined.

The SAS log shown below illustrates how to create and save a map which will support the reporting requirements using a batch execution of PROC DB2EXT:

```
1
2     PROC DB2EXT OUT=SASIN.MAPEX6 SAVESEL;
3       SELECT LAST_NAME, FIRST_NAME, SICK_USED, COST_CENTER,
4             DEPARTMENT_NAME
5         FROM TSID123.PERSINFO, TSID123.ORGINFO
6         WHERE MANAGEMENT = 'N' AND EMPLOYEE_TYPE = 'H'
7               AND COST_CENTER = DEPARTMENT;
8         RENAME 1=LNAME 2=FNAME 3=SICKDAYS 4=COSTCTR 5=DEPTNAME;
9
------------ USER SELECTIONS ------------
ITEM NUMBER---COLUMN NAME-------SAS NAME----FORMAT-----------
....1.......LAST_NAME...........LNAME......$15.
....2.......FIRST_NAME..........FNAME......$10.
....3.......SICK_USED...........SICKDAYS...4.
....4.......COST_CENTER.........COSTCTR....$3.
....5.......DEPARTMENT_NAME.....DEPTNAME...$15.
WHERE CLAUSE ----->
MANAGEMENT='N' AND EMPLOYEE_TYPE='H' AND COST_CENTER = DEPARTMENT
10     LIST ALL;
11
NOTE: THE DATA SET SASIN.MAPEX6 HAS 5 OBSERVATIONS AND 9 VARIABLES.

12     PROC PRINT DATA=SASIN.MAPEX6;
13       TITLE 'MAP CREATED IN EXAMPLE 6';
14
```

```
WARNING: SOME VARIABLES MAY BE TRUNCATED DUE TO THEIR EXCESSIVE
         LENGTH.
NOTE: THE PROCEDURE PRINT PRINTED PAGE 1.
```

A Basic SELECT statement is coded in the PROC DB2EXT step along with the RENAME statement to produce user-defined SAS variable names. There is no real advantage to saving this map because the SELECT and RENAME statements themselves could be used in subsequent executions of PROC DB2EXT rather than saving a map for this purpose. Also note that when saving a map using a SELECT statement as input, that the SELECT statement must be a Basic SELECT statement rather than an Enhanced SELECT statement. An Enhanced SELECT statement can generate a map, but the map could not be used as the sole input in subsequent executions of PROC DB2EXT.

The PROC PRINT shown on the SAS log shows the contents of the map:

```
                    MAP CREATED IN EXAMPLE 6

OBS TABPW TYPE LENGTH SCALE NULLS COLUMN            SASNAME   FORMAT

1         453   15     0     1    LAST_NAME         LNAME     $15.
2         453   10     0     1    FIRST_NAME        FNAME     $10.
3         485   3      0     1    SICK_USED         SICKDAYS  4.
4         453   3      0     1    COST_CENTER       COSTCTR   $3.
5         453   15     0     1    DEPARTMENT_NAME   DEPTNAME  $15.

   OBS                            WHEREA

1  MANAGEMENT = 'N' AND EMPLOYEE_TYPE = 'H' AND COST_CENTER = DEP
2  MANAGEMENT = 'N' AND EMPLOYEE_TYPE = 'H' AND COST_CENTER = DEP
3  MANAGEMENT = 'N' AND EMPLOYEE_TYPE = 'H' AND COST_CENTER = DEP
4  MANAGEMENT = 'N' AND EMPLOYEE_TYPE = 'H' AND COST_CENTER = DEP
5  MANAGEMENT = 'N' AND EMPLOYEE_TYPE = 'H' AND COST_CENTER = DEP
```

Two points should be mentioned concerning the map shown in this report. First, the variable, TABPW, contains all missing values. When a map is created and saved in Display Manager, the first observation for each table represented in the map contains the name of the DB2 table. This is required in order for the map to be used as the sole input in subsequent executions of PROC DB2EXT. Therefore, when a map is created and saved by PROC DB2EXT in batch, the user will have to edit the map using the SAS/FSP procedure FSEDIT or a DATA step before it can be used. In this example, the value of TABPW for observation 1 should be Tsid123.Persinfo. The value of TABPW for observation 5 should be Tsid123.Orginfo. This situation further supports the proposition that maps should be created and saved in Display Manager. The second situation is that the WHERE clause was truncated on the report due to its length. This is noted on the SAS log. The complete WHERE clause is actually stored in the map. This may be verified using PROC FSEDIT. A WHERE clause up to 1600 characters can be stored in the map data set, using the variables, WHEREA through WHEREH, each being 200 characters in length.

Assume that the value of the variable, TABPW, has been added to the map and it is then used as input in a subsequent execution of PROC DB2EXT, which will create the SAS data set containing data extracted from the DB2 tables. The SAS log for this batch program follows:

```
1
2    PROC DB2EXT OUT=EX6 IN=SASIN.MAPEX6;
3
NOTE: THE DATA SET WORK.EX6 HAS 25 OBSERVATIONS AND 5 VARIABLES.

4    PROC PRINT DATA=EX6;
5      TITLE 'EXAMPLE 6';
6
NOTE: THE PROCEDURE PRINT PRINTED PAGE 1.
```

When a map is used as input, the PROC DB2EXT step is very easy to code. All that is required are the IN and OUT options of the PROC DB2EXT statement.

The PROC PRINT shown on the SAS log results in the following report:

EXAMPLE 6

OBS	LNAME	FNAME	SICKDAYS	COSTCTR	DEPTNAME
1	COOPER	MARGIE	16	100	PERSONNEL
2	JOHNSON	HAZEL	8	100	PERSONNEL
3	MITCHELL	KELLY	0	100	PERSONNEL
4	MOORE	RUTH	16	100	PERSONNEL
5	ADAMS	BILL	16	100	PERSONNEL

6	CLARK	ALMA	16	100	PERSONNEL
7	CONWELL	LINDA	0	100	PERSONNEL
8	CONNOR	BRUCE	40	110	MARKETING
9	SMITH	SCOTT	16	110	MARKETING
10	BROOKS	JIM	0	110	MARKETING
11	PHILLIPS	SARAH	16	110	MARKETING
12	MARK	MIRON	24	110	MARKETING
13	HOLLYWOOD	ALICE	8	110	MARKETING
14	JAMES	MARVIN	0	120	FINANCE
15	PRITT	JIM	24	120	FINANCE
16	OLIVER	BETTY	16	120	FINANCE
17	PAVELEK	JOE	16	120	FINANCE
18	PAYTON	RUTH	0	120	FINANCE
19	STONE	JENNIFER	0	120	FINANCE
20	CAMPBELL	MARGARET	32	130	SALES
21	REEVES	JEREMY	0	130	SALES
22	PEARCE	EVELYN	0	130	SALES
23	HANKS	TROY	8	130	SALES
24	DUDLEY	LOUISA	8	130	SALES
25	ATWOOD	CHUCK	8	140	DEVELOPMENT

Example 7-7

A report is needed which lists all employees who worked on projects. The DB2 columns required include Last_name, First_name, Project, and Department_name. The report should be sorted by Department_name and Last_name.

The SAS log shown below illustrates how to create and save a SELECT statement that will support the reporting requirements using a batch execution of PROC DB2EXT:

```
PROC DB2EXT OUT=EX7 SQLLIB=CODOUT.SELEX7;
  SELECT PE.LAST_NAME, PE.FIRST_NAME, PROJECT, DEPARTMENT_NAME
    FROM TSID123.PERSINFO PE, TSID123.PROJINFO PJ,
         TSID123.ORGINFO
    WHERE PE.LAST_NAME = PJ.LAST_NAME AND
          PE.FIRST_NAME = PJ.FIRST_NAME AND
          COST_CENTER = DEPARTMENT
    ORDER BY DEPARTMENT_NAME, PE.LAST_NAME;
  RENAME 1=LNAME 2=FNAME 4=DEPTNAME;
```

```
------------ USER SELECTIONS ------------
ITEM NUMBER---COLUMN NAME-------SAS NAME----FORMAT-----------
....1.......LAST_NAME..........LNAME......$15.
....2.......FIRST_NAME.........FNAME......$10.
....3.......PROJECT............PROJECT....$20.
....4.......DEPARTMENT_NAME.....DEPTNAME...$15.
WHERE CLAUSE ----->
PE.LAST_NAME = PJ.LAST_NAME AND PE.FIRST_NAME = PJ.FIRST_NAME AND
COST_CENTER = DEPARTMENT ORDER BY DEPARTMENT_NAME, PE.LAST_NAME
12     LIST ALL;
13
NOTE: THE DATA SET WORK.EX7 HAS 19 OBSERVATIONS AND 4 VARIABLES.
```

The SQLLIB option of the PROC DB2EXT statement is used to create a member, SELEX7, in a partitioned data set referenced to the JCL dd, CODOUT. In order to save a SELECT statement, the SELECT statement itself or a map must be used as input to PROC DB2EXT. In this case, the SELECT statement itself is used as input. This could just as well have been accomplished by a TSO copy. Also, notice that since the OUT option is required, a SAS data set is created at the same time.

The following PROC DB2EXT step can be used to bring this SELECT statement in from a member of a partitioned data set:

```
PROC DB2EXT OUT=EX7;
  %INCLUDE CODOUT(SELEX7);
  LIST ALL;
```

This PROC DB2EXT step is executed along with a PROC PRINT step and the following SAS log is produced:

```
1
2   PROC DB2EXT OUT=EX7;
3     %INCLUDE CODOUT(SELEX7);
4     +SELECT PE.LAST_NAME , PE.FIRST_NAME, PROJECT, DEPARTMENT_NAME
       FROM TSID1
5     +23.PERSINFO PE, TSID123.PROJINFO PJ, TSID123.ORGINFO WHERE
       PE.LAST_NAME
6     += PJ.LAST_NAME AND PE.FIRST_NAME = PJ.FIRST_NAME AND
        COST_CENTER = DEPAR
7     +TMENT ORDER BY DEPARTMENT_NAME, PE.LAST_NAME ;
8           RENAME 1=LNAME 2=FNAME 4=DEPTNAME;
9
```

```
------------ USER SELECTIONS ------------
ITEM NUMBER---COLUMN NAME-------SAS NAME----FORMAT----------
....1.......LAST_NAME...........LNAME......$15.
....2.......FIRST_NAME..........FNAME......$10.
....3.......PROJECT.............PROJECT....$20.
....4.......DEPARTMENT_NAME.....DEPTNAME...$15.
WHERE CLAUSE ----->
PE.LAST_NAME = PJ.LAST_NAME AND PE.FIRST_NAME = PJ.FIRST_NAME AND
COST_CENTER = DEPARTMENT ORDER BY DEPARTMENT_NAME, PE.LAST_NAME
10     LIST ALL;
11
NOTE: THE DATA SET WORK.EX7 HAS 19 OBSERVATIONS AND 4 VARIABLES.
12    PROC PRINT DATA=EX7 NOOBS LABEL;
13      BY DEPTNAME;
14      VAR LNAME FNAME PROJECT;
15      TITLE 'EXAMPLE 7';
16
NOTE: THE PROCEDURE PRINT PRINTED PAGE 1.
```

The Base SAS statement, %INCLUDE, is used to bring in the SELECT statement from a member of a partitioned data set. The SELECT statement displayed on the SAS log does not actually appear in the batch program. The advantage to bringing in a SELECT statement in this fashion is that it can be shared by multiple batch programs, and if a change needs to be made, the change can be made once rather than in each batch program. Many users will still prefer to perform a TSO copy to copy the SELECT statement into each batch program rather than using the %INCLUDE statement. This gives the user the ability to see the SELECT statement and refer to it when coding other statements such as the RENAME and FMT statements and subsequent DATA and PROC steps in the batch program.

The PROC PRINT shown on the SAS log results in the following report:

```
                           EXAMPLE 7

-------------- DEPARTMENT_NAME=DEVELOPMENT ---------------
          LAST_NAME     FIRST_NAME         PROJECT


           HUTSON        EVERETT       QUALITY CONTROL
           MILLER        EMMALYNE      QUALITY CONTROL
```

```
---------------- DEPARTMENT_NAME=FINANCE -----------------
     LAST_NAME      FIRST_NAME     PROJECT

     APPLE          RICHARD        COMPENSATION PLAN
     APPLE          RICHARD        FINANCIAL STATEMENT
     HARRINGTON     MARLIN         BUDGET
     HARRINGTON     MARLIN         BROKERS
     KELLUM         ELLEN JANE     BUDGET
     KELLUM         ELLEN JANE     FINANCIAL STATEMENT
     MEEKS          EDWARD         COMMISSIONS
     MEEKS          EDWARD         BUDGET
     PALMER         NANCY          BUDGET

--------------- DEPARTMENT_NAME=MARKETING ---------------
        LAST_NAME     FIRST_NAME     PROJECT

         BUELL          MAX          SALES REPORT
         HARRIS         JULIE        PROJECT GROWTH
         MEISER         MARK         SALES REPORT


--------------- DEPARTMENT_NAME=PERSONNEL ---------------
       LAST_NAME     FIRST_NAME          PROJECT

         BROWN         WALLY        CONPEMSATION PLAN

----------------- DEPARTMENT_NAME=SALES -----------------
          LAST_NAME     FIRST_NAME     PROJECT

           BAKER         MARTHA        BROKERS
           GOETZ         JACK          COMMISSIONS
           HUFFORD       STEPHEN       COMMISSIONS
           KISLING       MARY LEA      BROKERS
```

Exercise 2

Test your understanding of using maps and SELECT statements as input to PROC DB2EXT in batch programs by completing the exercises described here. Use Display Manager to create and save either the map or SELECT statement. The reports are shown on the following pages, along with the SAS log of the batch program and a print of either the map or SELECT statement. Format the reports as shown, with titles, labels, formats, and the variables displayed in the order listed.

The DB2 tables used as input are the same tables used in the previous examples and are shown in Appendix C. The data contained in these tables can be loaded into DB2 tables at your site by keying, or refer to Chapter 1, Introduction, for information concerning ordering copies of the tables.

Report 1

A list of the employees (Last_name, First_name) who worked on the projects, 'Budget' and 'Brokers', is needed, along with the Begin_date and Actual_end_date for these projects. Note that selection criteria should capitalize the Project values, 'BUDGET' and 'BROKERS'. Begin_date and Actual_end_date should be formatted using the SAS date format, MMDDYY8.

Report 2

The sum of Vacation_available, Sick_used, and the 12 Salary columns (added to produce the annual salary) are needed for each Cost_center and a grand total for the entire company. The report should be sorted by Cost_center.

Report 1

BUDGET AND BROKER PROJECTS

OBS	LNAME	FNAME	BEGDTE	ENDDTE	PROJECT
1	BAKER	MARTHA	07/15/89	09/15/89	BROKERS
2	HARRINGTON	MARLIN	08/15/88	12/15/88	BUDGE*t
3	HARRINGTON	MARLIN	07/15/89	09/15/89	BROKERS
4	KELLUM	ELLEN JANE	08/15/88	12/15/88	BUDGET
5	KISLING	MARY LEA	07/15/89	09/15/89	BROKERS
6	MEEKS	EDWARD	08/15/88	12/15/88	BUDGET
7	PALMER	NANCY	08/15/88	12/15/88	BUDGET

A map or a SELECT statement can be used as input to PROC DB2EXT to produce the required information. If a map was created and saved in Display Manager for use in subsequent batch programs, that map would appear as follows. Note that the variable, WHEREA, has been truncated on this report, even though the complete WHERE clause is stored on the SAS data set. Refer to the SELECT statement alternative (also shown) for the complete WHERE clause.

```
                         MAP FOR REPORT 1

OBS        TABPW            TYPE  LENGTH  SCALE  NULLS  COLUMN

1   TSID123.PERSINFO        453     15      0      1    LAST_NAME
2                           453     10      0      1    FIRST_NAME
3   TSID123.PROJINFO        485      6      0      1    BEGIN_DATE
4                           485      6      0      1    ACTUAL_END_DATE
5                           453     20      0      1    PROJECT

OBS     SASNAME    FORMAT

1       LNAME      $15.
2       FNAME      $10.
3       BEGDTE     MMDDYY8.
4       ENDDTE     MMDDYY8.
5       PROJECT    $20.


OBS                          WHEREA

1  tsid123.persinfo.last_name=tsid123.projinfo.last_name and
2  tsid123.persinfo.last_name=tsid123.projinfo.last_name and
3  tsid123.persinfo.last_name=tsid123.projinfo.last_name and
4  tsid123.persinfo.last_name=tsid123.projinfo.last_name and
5  tsid123.persinfo.last_name=tsid123.projinfo.last_name and
```

If a SELECT statement was created and saved in Display Manager for use in subsequent batch programs, that SELECT statement would appear as follows:

```
SELECT
 TSID123.PERSINFO.LAST_NAME, TSID123.PERSINFO.FIRST_NAME,
 TSID123.PROJINFO.BEGIN_DATE, TSID123.PROJINFO.ACTUAL_END_DATE,
```

```
 TSID123.PROJINFO.PROJECT
 FROM
 TSID123.PERSINFO, TSID123.PROJINFO
WHERE
tsid123.persinfo.last_name=tsid123.projinfo.last_name and
tsid123.persinfo.first_name=tsid123.projinfo.first_name and
(project='BUDGET' or project='BROKERS')
```

The following SAS log is based on using a map as input. The methodology for using a SELECT statement as input is covered in Report 2, which follows.

```
1
2    PROC DB2EXT OUT=RPT1 IN=SASIN.MAPEX1;
3
NOTE: THE DATA SET WORK.RPT1 HAS 7 OBSERVATIONS AND 5 VARIABLES.

4            PROC PRINT DATA=RPT1;
5              TITLE 'BUDGET AND BROKER PROJECTS';
NOTE: THE PROCEDURE PRINT PRINTED PAGE 1.
```

Report 2

```
        ANNUAL COST CENTER STATISTICS

COSTCTR     VACAVAIL     SICKUSED           SALARY

  100         1,080         144       $190,160.00
  110         1,040         192       $219,930.00
  120         1,520         120       $350,350.00
  130         1,440          80       $371,250.00
  140         1,200          80       $404,050.00
              =====         ===     =============
              6,280         616     $1,535,740.00
```

A SELECT statement must be used as input to PROC DB2EXT rather than a map because an Enhanced SELECT statement is required. This SELECT statement was created in Display Manager and saved in a member of a partitioned data set. This partitioned data set was brought into the batch program using the %INCLUDE statement. Users may wish to copy the saved SELECT statement into their batch program rather than using the %INCLUDE.

The following SAS code shows how the above report was generated:

```
PROC DB2EXT OUT=RPT2 UNIQUE;
  %INCLUDE CODIN(SEL2);
  +SELECT
  + TSID123.PERSINFO.COST_CENTER,
  + sum(VACATION_AVAILABLE), sum(SICK_USED),
  + sum(SALARY_JANUARY + SALARY_FEBRUARY +
  +     SALARY_MARCH + SALARY_APRIL +
  +     SALARY_MAY + SALARY_JUNE +
  +     SALARY_JULY + SALARY_AUGUST +
  +     SALARY_SEPTEMBER + SALARY_OCTOBER +
  +     SALARY_NOVEMBER + SALARY_DECEMBER)
  + FROM
  + TSID123.PERSINFO
  + group by Cost_center
  + order by Cost_center
  +   ;
   RENAME 1=COSTCTR 2=VACAVAIL 3=SICKUSED 4=SALARY;
   FMT 2='COMMA7.' 3='COMMA7.' 4='DOLLAR15.2';

NOTE: THE DATA SET WORK.RPT2 HAS 5 OBSERVATIONS AND 4 VARIABLES.

       PROC PRINT DATA=RPT2 NOOBS;
         VAR COSTCTR VACAVAIL SICKUSED SALARY;
         SUM VACAVAIL SICKUSED SALARY;
         TITLE 'ANNUAL COST CENTER STATISTICS';

NOTE: THE PROCEDURE PRINT PRINTED PAGE 1.
```

Review

Questions

1. What options and/or statements are required to execute PROC DB2EXT in batch? Does the order they are specified make a difference?
2. What is used as input to PROC DB2EXT in batch in order to create a SAS data set containing data extracted from DB2 table(s)?

3. Why are maps not usually created and saved in a batch execution of PROC DB2EXT?
4. Why are SELECT statements not usually created and saved in a batch execution of PROC DB2EXT?
5. If a map is used as input to PROC DB2EXT, how is it identified as input?
6. If a SELECT statement is used as input to PROC DB2EXT, how is it identified as input?
7. How does the user specify the DB2 subsystem?
8. What is the best approach to create unique SAS variable names when more than one DB2 column has the same first eight positions?
9. What is the purpose of the LIST ALL statement?

Answers

1. The OUT option of the PROC DB2EXT statement is required; an output SAS data set will always be created. Along with the OUT option one of the following is required: a SELECT statement, the IN option, or the LIST tablename statement. If the SELECT statement is used, it must be coded (or a %INCLUDE statement representing the SELECT statement) immediately after the PROC DB2EXT statement. All other options and statements can be coded in any order.
2. A map or a SELECT statement is used as input to PROC DB2EXT in batch in order to create a SAS data set containing data extracted from DB2 table(s). If a map is used as input, it is usually created and saved in Display Manager. If a SELECT statement is used as input, it is either coded by the user or created and saved in Display Manager.
3. In order to create and save a map in a batch execution of PROC DB2EXT, a SELECT statement and optionally a RENAME and FMT statement must be coded to define the map. The user might as well use these SELECT, RENAME, and FMT statements in subsequent executions of PROC DB2EXT rather than creating and saving a map for this purpose. Also maps created in a batch execution of PROC DB2EXT contain missing values for the variable, TABPW. TABPW is supposed to contain the name of the DB2 table. Without the DB2 table name, a SELECT statement cannot be generated from the map. This produces an SQL error and 0 observations when the map is used as the sole input to PROC DB2EXT.

4. In order to create and save a SELECT statement in a batch execution of PROC DB2EXT, a map or the SELECT statement itself must be used as input to PROC DB2EXT. If a map is used as input, it was probably created in Display Manager. A more straightforward approach would be to create and save a SELECT statement in Display Manager. If the SELECT statement itself is used as input, the user might just as well use a TSO copy to copy the SELECT statement to a member of a partitioned data set or into other programs requiring the same SELECT statement.
5. If a map is used as input to PROC DB2EXT, either in Display Manager or in batch, it is specified in the IN option of the PROC DB2EXT statement.
6. If a SELECT statement is used as input to PROC DB2EXT, it can either be coded in the PROC DB2EXT step or brought in from a member of a partitioned data set using the Base SAS %INCLUDE statement. Often, even though it was created and saved in a member of a partitioned data set through execution in Display Manager, it will be copied into batch programs using a TSO copy rather than the %INCLUDE statement.
7. The DB2 subsystem is specified in the SSID option of the PROC DB2EXT statement or if you are using SAS Release 5.18 or later the DB2SSID system option can be used. If the required subsystem is the same as the default set when SAS/DB2 was installed, it need not be coded.
8. The best approach to creating SAS variable names that are not only unique, but descriptive, is to use the UNIQUE option of the PROC DB2EXT statement and the RENAME statement. The RENAME statement is used to create unique and descriptive SAS variable names. If the UNIQUE option is not also coded, an error will be produced on the SAS log concerning duplicate SAS names. This error is then rectified when the RENAME statement is encountered. Thus, the UNIQUE option is used with the RENAME statement merely to suppress the error messages on the SAS log.
9. The LIST ALL statement produces a report on the SAS log which includes the column number as determined from the order specified by the user on the SELECT statement or contained in the map, the DB2 column name, the SAS variable named either automatically generated or user-defined, and the SAS format either automatically generated or user-defined. This statement is optional, but is a good source for diagnosing problems, so it is recommended.

Chapter

8

PROC DB2LOAD in Display Manager

PROC DB2LOAD is used to create and load DB2 tables using data stored in a SAS data set. PROC DB2LOAD can also be used to execute utility-type SQL statements such as those used for creating an index or dropping a DB2 table.

When a DB2 table is loaded, one of the following is used as input: a SAS data set, a map and a SAS data set, or the SQL statements, CREATE, INSERT, and COMMIT. When only a SAS data set is used as input, a map is generated, and the map and the SAS data set generate the appropriate SQL statements. When a map created in a previous execution of PROC DB2LOAD is used as input, a SAS data set is also used as input to supply the data values for the INSERT statements. When SQL statements created in a previous execution of PROC DB2LOAD are used as input, they are the sole input to PROC DB2LOAD because they contain the specifications for creating the DB2 table and the values for loading the table. Whatever method of input is used, it is ultimately the SQL statements, CREATE, INSERT, and COMMIT that create and load the DB2 table. Because the CREATE statement is used, the DB2 table must not already exist.

If a map or SQL statements are used as input to PROC DB2LOAD, they were usually created in a previous execution of PROC DB2LOAD in Display Manager to take advantage of the ease of use. These maps and SQL statements are typically used as input to PROC DB2LOAD in a batch program to create and load a DB2 table, due to computer resource limitations in Display Manager.

PROC DB2LOAD can also be used to execute SQL statements other than the CREATE, INSERT, and COMMIT statements which are generated by the procedure. For example, PROC DB2LOAD could be used to create a tablespace, create an index, or drop a table. Although these statements can be executed in a variety of other ways, including using JCL tailored to your company, it is often convenient to execute them in the SAS environment to save you from exiting Display Manager, or from including multiple job steps in a batch program. Refer to Chapter 4, Structured Query Language, for documentation on the most commonly used SQL statements.

This chapter will present the use of PROC DB2LOAD in Display Manager to create and load a DB2 table using data stored in a SAS data set, to create and save a map, and to create and save SQL statements. Also presented is the use of PROC DB2LOAD to execute a SQL statement other than those which can be generated by PROC DB2LOAD. It is assumed that the user is already familiar with the operation of Display Manager and knows how to access it in his company. You will also need to know the value(s) of the DB2 SUBSYSTEM ID. Contact the SAS Consultant at your company for this information. An introduction to PROC DB2LOAD was given in Chapter 5, Introduction to SAS/DB2, and this material should be fresh in your mind before beginning this chapter.

Panels and commands used with PROC DB2LOAD that have already been discussed in Chapter 6, PROC DB2EXT in Display Manager, will be listed, and the user should refer to Chapter 6 for a complete definition. All other panels and commands will be defined and illustrated.

SAS data set versions of the DB2 tables shown in Appendix C: Sample Tables are used in examples in this chapter. Refer to this Appendix to familiarize yourself with the sample DB2 tables. You may choose to follow along in these examples by performing the same operations on the mainframe at your company. These DB2 tables can be entered on your mainframe, or refer to Chapter 1, Introduction, for ordering a copy of these tables.

Before executing PROC DB2LOAD in Display Manager, any input or output files needed should be allocated using the TSO allocate statement. Refer to Chapter 6, PROC DB2EXT in Display Manager, for information concerning the TSO allocate statement.

Input files used with PROC DB2LOAD include SAS data sets containing data which will be used to create and load a DB2 table and

SAS data sets containing mapping instructions. SQL statements stored in an external file, usually a partitioned data set, can also be used as input to PROC DB2LOAD. These SQL statements could be the CREATE, INSERT, and COMMIT statements used to create and load a DB2 table or they could be SQL statements which perform specific operations such as dropping a table or creating a tablespace.

Output files used with PROC DB2LOAD include SAS data sets containing mapping instructions, the SQL statements (CREATE, INSERT, and COMMIT) which will be used to create and load a DB2 table, an error file to store SQL errors, or the DB2 table itself.

After coding the appropriate TSO allocate statements in the PROGRAM window of Display Manager and submitting them, you are ready to access PROC DB2LOAD. To access the panel system of PROC DB2LOAD, submit the following statements from the PROGRAM window of Display Manager:

```
PROC DB2LOAD; RUN;
```

In Release 5.16 of SAS/DB2, missing values in SAS variables cannot be loaded into a DB2 column that was created as NOT NULL. In Release 5.18 of SAS/DB2, missing numeric values are loaded as zero and missing character values are loaded as blanks when the DB2 column is defined as NOT NULL. In either Release 5.16 or 5.18, missing values in SAS variables are loaded as NULL if the DB2 column is defined as NULL.

The panels in PROC DB2LOAD and their relationship are shown in Figure 8-1.

This diagram shows six DB2LOAD panels: DATA ACCESS, TABLE CREATE/LOAD, SQL ENTRY/EDIT, BROWSE, KEYS, and HELP. The arrows depict the flow going into these panels. The commands or actions to move to these panels is also shown.

The first panel accessed when PROC DB2LOAD is executed is normally the DATA ACCESS panel. Hitting enter takes you from the DATA ACCESS panel to the TABLE CREATE/LOAD panel. The EDIT command issued from the DATA ACCESS or TABLE CREATE/LOAD panels takes you to a blank SQL ENTRY/EDIT panel. The SQL ENTRY/EDIT panel is used to execute utility-type SQL statements such as dropping a table or creating a tablespace. These SQL statements are often coded in the SQL ENTRY/EDIT panel, but can also be included from an external file. The EDIT command should be issued without entering any information on either the DATA ACCESS or TABLE CREATE/LOAD panel because any entries will not be saved. The SQL statements, CREATE, INSERT, and

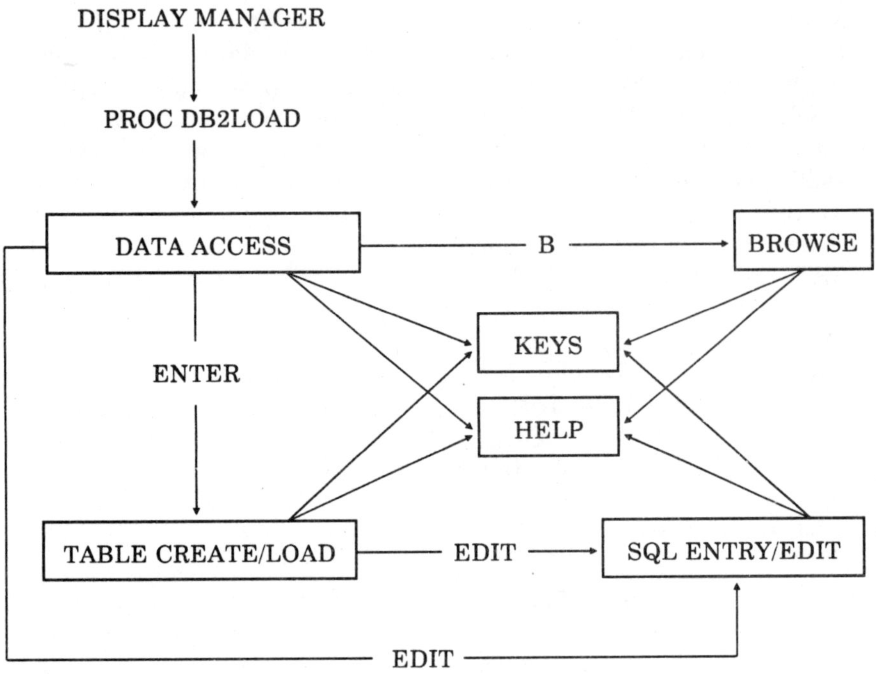

Figure 8-1 Relationship of panels in PROC DB2LOAD.

COMMIT used to create and load a DB2 table, are typically not edited, and therefore are not displayed in the SQL ENTRY/EDIT panel. Although not shown, the KEYS command or the HELP command can be specified in any of the four other panels in order to bring up the KEYS or HELP panels.

The panels are exited by the END command and will return you to the previous panel. When the END command is issued from the TABLE CREATE/LOAD panel, the following message is displayed under the command line:

```
NOTE: XXXX SQL CALL(S) WILL BE EXECUTED, ENTER (LOAD) TO
      CONTINUE OR ENTER (END) AGAIN TO ONLY PROCESS SQLOUT
      AND/OR MAP OUTPUTS.
```

XXXX is a number representing the number of SQL statements that will be executed. If the END command is issued again, only a map or SQL statements will be saved to an output file. If an output map or

SQL file was not specified on the DATA ACCESS panel, issuing the END command returns the user to the DATA ACCESS panel without creating an output file. If the LOAD command is issued instead of the END command, the user will be returned to the DATA ACCESS panel and a DB2 table will be created and loaded. When the END command is issued from the SQL ENTRY/EDIT panel, the SQL statements which were entered or included from an external file are executed immediately and you are returned to the DATA ACCESS or TABLE CREATE/LOAD panel, whichever the SQL ENTRY/EDIT panel was invoked from. When you have returned to the DATA ACCESS panel, the B or BROWSE command can be used to browse the mapping SAS data set just created, if one was created. The END command used from the DATA ACCESS panel will return you to Display Manager.

The DB2LOAD panels are described briefly below:

• DATA ACCESS:	specify input/output files
• TABLE CREATE/LOAD:	select SAS variables, name DB2 columns, specify DB2 data types, specify if NULLS are allowed (this is a map)
• BROWSE:	browse mapping SAS data set created
• SQL ENTRY/EDIT:	coded or included SQL statements
• HELP:	displays help information
• KEYS:	display/change commands assigned to function keys

The primary panels of PROC DB2LOAD are the DATA ACCESS, TABLE CREATE/LOAD, and the SQL ENTRY/EDIT. The BROWSE, HELP, and KEYS panels serve support functions. The DATA ACCESS and the TABLE CREATE/LOAD panels are described below. The other panels are the same as those used with PROC DB2EXT. Refer to Chapter 6, PROC DB2EXT in Display Manager, for information concerning these panels.

DATA ACCESS Panel

The DATA ACCESS panel is the first panel to be displayed when PROC DB2LOAD is executed from Display Manager. This panel can be skipped if the DATA and TABLE options (and SSID option if other than default) of the PROC DB2LOAD statement are coded when PROC DB2LOAD is submitted from the PROGRAM window.

The DATA ACCESS panel is used to specify input and output files. Input files specified on the DATA ACCESS panel include a SAS data set containing data and a SAS data set containing mapping instructions. When SQL statements are used as input, they are included in the SQL ENTRY/EDIT panel just as they are with PROC DB2EXT. The output files specified on the DATA ACCESS panel include a DB2 table, a mapping SAS data set, an external file containing SQL statements, and an external file to store SQL errors.

The END command is used to exit the DATA ACCESS panel and return to Display Manager.

The DATA ACCESS panel is shown in Figure 8-2.

```
                              DB2 INTERFACE
                            DATA ACCESS PANEL


COMMAND===>
FILL IN THE FIELDS BELOW

INPUT SAS DATA SET:                                  COMMIT:    3
TABLE NAME:                                          LIMIT:     5000
SUBSYSTEM ID:




MAP DATA SET:                           I=INPUT;O=OUTPUT:
OUTPUT SQL LIBRARY:                     ERROR LOG FILE:
```

Figure 8-2 PROC DB2LOAD DATA ACCESS Panel.

The following describes each of the fields on the DATA ACCESS panel. Each description is labeled optional or required to indicate whether a value is required.

INPUT SAS DATA SET (required): The input SAS data set is the name of the SAS data set to be used to create and load the DB2 table. A SAS data set is required no matter which of the possible output files are being created: a map, an external file containing SQL statements, or a DB2 table.

TABLE NAME (required); The table name is the name of the output DB2 table to be created and loaded from data stored in a

SAS data set. The DB2 table name is required no matter which of the possible output files are being created; a map, a partitioned data set containing SQL statements, or a DB2 table.

COMMIT (required): A DB2 table is loaded using the SQL INSERT statement. The number specified in the COMMIT field is the number of INSERT statements to be executed before the rows are saved or committed to the DB2 table and made available to other applications. The default value is 3. This means that the 3 INSERT statements will be generated followed by a COMMIT statement followed by 3 more INSERT statements, etc.

LIMIT (required): This is the maximum number of SQL INSERT statements to be executed by PROC DB2LOAD. The default value is 5000. If the number of observations on the input SAS data set is greater than the limit set, a warning message will be issued and you are given the option of continuing. If LIMIT is set to 0, no limit is imposed.

SUBSYSTEM ID (required): This field is the same as used with PROC DB2EXT. Refer to Chapter 6, PROC DB2EXT in Display Manager, for the definition of the field.

MAP DATA SET (optional): If a mapping SAS data set is to be used as input or output to PROC DB2LOAD, enter the name of the map in this field.

I=INPUT;O=OUTPUT (optional): If a mapping SAS data set is to be used as input or output to PROC DB2LOAD, this option is used to specify whether the map is to be used as input (I) or output (O). Maps used as input typically create and load a DB2 table. However, a map can be specified as input in order to make changes to the map. If the END command is used to exit the TABLE CREATE/LOAD panel, the map will be updated, but the DB2 table will not be created. The LOAD command is required to create and load a DB2 table.

OUTPUT SQL LIBRARY (optional); The output SQL library is used when you want to save the SQL statements CREATE, INSERT, and COMMIT, used to create and load a DB2 table to an external file. The external file is often a partitioned data set. The data set must have been allocated using a TSO allocate in Display Manager prior to bringing up the DATA ACCESS panel. If the TSO allocate statement included the member name, then only the ddname needs to be specified. If the TSO allocate did not include the member name, specify ddname.member, where ddname is the ddname used in the TSO allocate statement and member is a new member to be created. If a member that already exists is specified, that member will be replaced.

ERROR LOG FILE (optional): PROC DB2LOAD uses the SQL CREATE, INSERT, and COMMIT statements to create and load a DB2 table. If these statements contain SQL errors, the error messages are written to the SAS log. Since an INSERT statement exists for every observation on the SAS data set used as input, the number of INSERT statements executed may be quite large, and thus the number of SQL errors generated can also be quite large. The ERROR LOG FILE can be used to route any SQL errors, along with the SQL statement that produced the error to an external file rather than the SAS log. If errors are written to the SAS log, the SQL statements that generated the errors are not shown on the SAS log. Therefore, it will probably be easier to diagnose errors when the ERROR LOG FILE is used. This file is usually a partitioned data set.

The ERROR LOG FILE must be allocated using a TSO allocate in Display Manager prior to bringing up the DATA ACCESS panel. If the TSO allocate statement included the member name, then only the ddname needs to be specified. If the TSO allocate did not include the member name, specify ddname.member, where ddname is the ddname used in the TSO allocate statement and member is a new member to be created. If a member that already exists is specified, that member will be replaced.

TABLE CREATE/LOAD Panel

When the appropriate information is completed on the DATA ACCESS panel, hitting enter will bring up the TABLE CREATE/LOAD panel.

The user defines the map using the TABLE CREATE/LOAD panel. The definition of the map includes several specifications. By default all SAS variables will be loaded into DB2 columns. If there are any SAS variables that you do not want to be loaded, these must be deleted from the TABLE CREATE/LOAD panel. Generated DB2 column names are the same as the SAS variable names. Generated DB2 data types are CHAR for SAS character variables and FLOAT for SAS numeric variables. By default, NULL values are allowed for all DB2 columns. The user can specify DB2 column names and data types other than those automatically generated, and can disallow NULLS if desired.

When the TABLE CREATE/LOAD panel is complete, the user will return to the DATA ACCESS panel and the desired output file will be created. If the END command is issued from the TABLE CREATE/LOAD panel, the user returns to the DATA ACCESS panel and either a map or SQL statements are saved. If the LOAD command is issued from the TABLE CREATE/LOAD panel, the user returns to the DATA ACCESS panel and a DB2 table is created and loaded.

The TABLE CREATE/LOAD panel is shown in Figure 8-3.

```
                              DB2 INTERFACE
                         TABLE CREATE/LOAD PANEL

COMMAND===>

     CREATE TABLE TSID123.PROJINFO                IN .................

ACTION    COLUMN NAME                 FORMAT        SAS NAME       NULLS?
   .      LNAME                       CHAR(15)      LNAME            Y
   .      FNAME                       CHAR(10)      FNAME            Y
   .      BEGDTE                      FLOAT         BEGDTE           Y
   .      PLNEND                      FLOAT         PLNEND           Y
   .      ACTEND                      FLOAT         ACTEND           Y
   .      PROJECT                     CHAR(20)      PROJECT          Y
```

Figure 8-3 PROC DB2LOAD TABLE CREATE/LOAD Panel.

The input SAS data set shown above is the SAS data set version of the DB2 table, Tsid123.Projinfo, used in previous examples. The SAS variables shown here are specifically for that SAS data set and this panel will vary depending on the input SAS data set.

CREATE TABLE: The value shown in this field is the name of the DB2 table to be created and is carried from the DATA ACCESS panel.

IN (optional): Enter the name of the tablespace to store the DB2 table. This value is typically specified as authorizationid.tablespace. If a value is not specified in the IN field, the default is DSNDB04. The user probably does not have the authority required to maintain tables in DSNDB04 and will need to create his or her own tablespaces.

ACTION: When the TABLE CREATE/LOAD panel is displayed, the generated DB2 column names and data types are also displayed. By default, all SAS variables will be loaded into DB2 columns. If any of the SAS variables are not to be loaded into the DB2 table, an ACTION value of D is entered to delete the appropriate line from the screen. The line can also be deleted by entering blanks for the DB2 column name. Refer to the definition of the RESHOW and RESET commands to recall deleted lines.

COLUMN NAME: By default the generated DB2 column name is the same as the SAS variable name. These generated DB2 column names appear when the TABLE CREATE/LOAD panel is displayed. The user can change the DB2 column names, specifying a name up to 18 positions long, by typing over these generated names.

FORMAT: The format column represents the data type of the DB2 column being created. By default SAS character variables are assigned the CHAR DB2 data type and SAS numeric variables are assigned the FLOAT DB2 data type. The user can change these data types by typing over those displayed. The numeric data types will frequently need to be changed to DECIMAL or INTEGER. If you wish to assign a DB2 date/time data type, the SAS variable used to load values into this column must be stored as a SAS date/time value. Refer to Chapter 3, IBM'S Database 2, the section, Data Types, for more information about DB2 data types.

SAS NAME: This is a display of the SAS variables on the input SAS data set.

NULLS?: This value is set to Y, which means that NULL values are acceptable for the corresponding DB2 column. If NULLS should not be allowed, change this value to N.

Function Key Definitions

Table 8-1 summarizes the function key definitions for each of the PROC DB2LOAD panels. A definition of these commands is given in the next section, Commands.

The function key definitions for the DATA ACCESS and TABLE CREATE/LOAD panels are the same. However, not all commands are valid on both panels. The commands shown for the DATA

Table 8-1 Function Key Definitions by Panel.

Function Key	Data Access	Table Create/Load	Browse	SQL Entry/Edit	Keys	Help
1,13	HELP	HELP	HELP	HELP		
2,14		RESHOW	HI			
3,15	END	END	END	END	END	END
4,16	EXIT	EXIT	PREVCMD	PREVCMD		
5,17	BROWSE			RFIND		
6,18	KEYS	KEYS		RCHANGE		
7,19		BACKWARD	BACKWARD	BACKWARD	BACK	BACK
8,20		FORWARD	FORWARD	FORWARD	FORW	FORW
9,21		RESET				
10,22			LEFT	LEFT		
11,23		EDIT	RIGHT	RIGHT		
12,24			CURSOR	CURSOR		

ACCESS and TABLE CREATE/LOAD panels are commands that are actually valid in these panels.

Commands

Table 8-2 outlines the commands which are valid in the PROC DB2LOAD panels. Following this chart a definition of each command is given. If the definition of this command is the same as it is with PROC DB2EXT, it is so noted and you should refer to Chapter 6, PROC DB2EXT in Display Manager, for the definition.

Some of these commands are defined as function keys. Refer to the previous section, Function Key Definitions, for the definition of function keys.

BACKWARD (TABLE CREATE/LOAD, BROWSE, SQL ENTRY/EDIT, HELP, KEYS): Refer to Chapter 6, PROC DB2EXT in Display Manager.

BROWSE (DATA ACCESS): The BROWSE command can be issued from the DATA ACCESS panel when the user returns to this panel after excuting PROC DB2LOAD to create an output

Table 8-2 Valid command by PROC DB2LOAD Panel.

	DATA ACCESS	TABLE CREATE/ LOAD	BROWSE	SQL ENTRY/EDIT	HELP	KEYS
BACKWARD		X	X	X	X	X
BROWSE	X					
CANCEL				X		X
CAPS OFF/ON				X		
CHANGE				X		
EDIT	X	X				
END	X	X*	X	X*	X	X*
EXIT	X	X				
FIND				X		
FORWARD		X	X	X	X	X
HELP	X	X	X	X		
HI			X			
INCLUDE				X		
KEYS	X	X	X	X		
LEFT				X		
LOAD		X				
NUMS ON|OFF				X		
PREVCMD			X	X		
RCHANGE				X		
RESET		X				
RESHOW		X				
RFIND				X		
RIGHT				X		

* The END command issued from these panels may cause an action in addition to exiting to occur. Refer to the definition of the END command which follows, for more information.

map, which is stored as a SAS data set. If you need to browse a SAS data set other than the most recently created map, issue the BROWSE command followed by the name of the desired SAS data set.

CANCEL (SQL ENTRY/EDIT, KEYS): Refer to Chapter 6, PROC DB2EXT in Display Manager.

CAPS OFF/ON (SQL ENTRY/EDIT): Refer to Chapter 6, PROC DB2EXT in Display Manager.

CHANGE (SQL ENTRY/EDIT): Refer to Chapter 6, PROC DB2EXT in Display Manager.

EDIT (DATA ACCESS, TABLE CREATE/LOAD): The EDIT command can be issued from the DATA ACCESS or the TABLE CREATE/LOAD panels to display a blank SQL ENTRY/EDIT panel. SQL commands can be entered here or included from an external file, usually a partitioned data set. Included SQL statements can be edited as desired. The END command returns the user to the previous panel and executes the SQL statements.

END (DATA ACCESS, TABLE CREATE/LOAD, BROWSE, SQL ENTRY/EDIT, HELP, KEYS): The END command is used to exit the panels listed above. The function keys, PF3/PF15 are usually used instead of the END command. The END command will return you to the previous panel. If you are in the SQL ENTRY/EDIT panel, the SQL statements will be executed at this time. If you are in the TABLE CREATE/LOAD panel, issuing the END command produces a message stating that if the END command is issued again, an output map or SQL statements will be saved. The LOAD command must be used from the TABLE CREATE/LOAD panel to create and load a DB2 table; the END command will not cause a DB2 table to be created or loaded.

When the END command is issued in the TABLE CREATE/LOAD panel or the SQL ENTRY/EDIT panel, they are checked for errors. If an error is present, an error message will be displayed under the command line. The error must be corrected before the END command will return the user to the previous panel.

EXIT (DATA ACCESS, TABLE CREATE/LOAD): The EXIT command or the PF4/PF16 function keys used in the DATA ACCESS or TABLE CREATE/LOAD panels, returns the user to Display Manager without executing PROC DB2LOAD.

FIND (SQL ENTRY/EDIT): Refer to Chapter 6, PROC DB2EXT in Display Manager.

FORWARD (TABLE CREATE/LOAD, BROWSE, SQL ENTRY/EDIT, HELP, KEYS): Refer to Chapter 6, PROC DB2EXT in Display Manager.

HELP (DATA ACCESS, TABLE CREATE/LOAD, BROWSE, SQL ENTRY/EDIT): This command is used to bring up the HELP panel. The corresponding function key, PF1/PF13, can be used rather than the HELP command. The HELP information displayed depends on the panel the command was issued from. Help for PROC DB2LOAD can be accessed by issuing the HELP command from the DATA ACCESS or TABLE CREATE/LOAD panels.

HI (BROWSE): Refer to Chapter 6, PROC DB2EXT in Display Manager.

INCLUDE ddname (SQL ENTRY/EDIT): Refer to Chapter 6, PROC DB2EXT in Display Manager.

KEYS (DATA ACCESS, TABLE CREATE/LOAD, SQL ENTRY/EDIT, BROWSE): Refer to Chapter 6, PROC DB2EXT in Display Manager.

LEFT (SQL ENTRY/EDIT): Refer to Chapter 6, PROC DB2EXT in Display Manager.

LOAD (TABLE CREATE/LOAD): When the LOAD command is issued from the TABLE CREATE/LOAD panel, the DB2 table specified on the DATA ACCESS panel is created and loaded from data stored in a SAS data set.

NUMS ON | OFF (SQL ENTRY/EDIT): Refer to Chapter 6, PROC DB2EXT in Display Manager.

PREVCMD (SQL ENTRY/EDIT, BROWSE): Refer to Chapter 6, PROC DB2EXT in Display Manager.

RCHANGE (SQL ENTRY/EDIT): Refer to Chapter 6, PROC DB2EXT in Display Manager.

RESET (TABLE CREATE/LOAD): The RESET command clears all changes which have been made on the TABLE CREATE/LOAD panel. PF9/PF21 function keys can be used to issue this command.

RESHOW (TABLE CREATE/LOAD): The RESHOW command can be issued to bring back lines on the TABLE CREATE/LOAD panel that were deleted using the D ACTION code. The DB2 column names and data types will be blank.

RFIND (SQL ENTRY/EDIT): Refer to Chapter 6, PROC DB2EXT in Display Manager.

RIGHT (SQL ENTRY/EDIT): Refer to Chapter 6, PROC DB2EXT in Display Manager.

Creating and Loading a DB2 Table

This section illustrates the use of PROC DB2LOAD in Display Manager to create a DB2 table from data stored in a SAS data set. Figure 8-4 shows the panels which will be used for this purpose.

PROC DB2LOAD is executed in Display Manager to bring up the DATA ACCESS panel. The input SAS data set, the output DB2 table, and the subsystem id (if the default is not appropriate) are entered on the DATA ACCESS panel. Hitting enter on the DATA ACCESS panel displays the TABLE CREATE/LOAD panel. The map is defined on the TABLE CREATE/LOAD panel. The user can delete any SAS variables that are not to be loaded into DB2 columns, assign DB2 column names and data types, and specify whether NULL values will be allowed. When the TABLE CREATE/LOAD panel is complete, the LOAD command is used to return to the DATA AC-

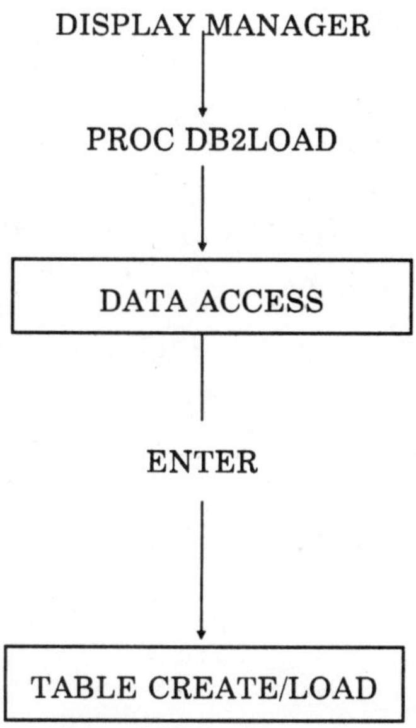

Figure 8-4 PROC DB2LOAD Panels for creating and loading a DB2 table.

CESS panel and create and load the DB2 table. If the END command is used, only output maps or SQL statements will be saved.

Example 8-1

A SAS data set version of the DB2 table, Projinfo, that was used in previous examples, is used as input to create and load a DB2 table of the same name.

Before the table can be created and loaded, a SQL CREATE statement is executed to create a tablespace to be used to store the DB2 table if one does not already exist. Tablespaces can be created in a batch program using JCL tailored to your company, in a batch program using the SQL statement in a PROC DB2LOAD or PROC DB2UTIL step, or in the SQL ENTRY/EDIT panel with PROC DB2LOAD or PROC DB2UTIL in Display Manager. Creating a tablespace will be illustrated in Chapter 9, PROC DB2LOAD in Batch.

The parameters used in the CREATE statement are also specific to your company. Consult your DB2 Database Administrator for this information. The following is an example of a CREATE statement:

```
CREATE TABLESPACE sample
  IN tsid123
  USING
    STOGROUP freegp02
    PRIQTY 1000
    SECQTY 1000
    ERASE no
  FREEPAGE 000
  PCTFREE 00
  BUFFERPOOL bp0
  LOCKSIZE tablespace
  CLOSE no;
```

The SAS data set, Projinfo, to be used as input to PROC DB2LOAD is stored permanently in a SAS data library. A TSO allocate statement is entered in the PROGRAM window and submitted using the SUBMIT command (PF3/PF15). Next, the PROC DB2LOAD and RUN statements are entered in the PROGRAM window. These are also submitted using the SUBMIT command.

```
-------------------------------------------------------------------
COMMAND ===>                                    SAS(r) Log   HH:MM

NOTE: COPYRIGHT(C) 1984, 1988 SAS INSTITUTE INC., CARY, NC 27512
USA
NOTE: SAS RELEASE 5.18 AT COMPANY ABC (00000000).
NOTE: CPUID   VERSION = 00   SERIAL = 000000   MODEL = 0000 .
NOTE: SAS OPTIONS SPECIFIED ARE:
      DMS NONEWS FSP FS NODATE



  1  tso alloc dd(sasin) dsn('tsid123.sas.data') shr;
-------------------------------------------------------------------
COMMAND ===>                                        Program Editor

00001 proc db2load;
00002   run;
00003
00004
00005
```

The execution of PROC DB2LOAD brings up the DATA ACCESS panel shown below. Enter the name of the input SAS data set and the table name for the output DB2 table. Also the SUBSYSTEM ID should be entered if the default is not appropriate.

```
                              DB2 INTERFACE
                           DATA ACCESS PANEL


COMMAND===>
FILL IN THE FIELDS BELOW

INPUT SAS DATA SET: sasin.projinfo                COMMIT:    3
TABLE NAME:         tsid123.projinfo              LIMIT:     5000
SUBSYSTEM ID:       DBT



MAP DATA SET:                             I=INPUT;O=OUTPUT:
OUTPUT SQL LIBRARY:                       ERROR LOG FILE:
```

Hitting enter on the DATA ACCESS panel brings up the TABLE CREATE/LOAD panel shown below.

```
                              DB2 INTERFACE
                        TABLE CREATE/LOAD PANEL


COMMAND===>

     CREATE TABLE TSID123.PROJINFO          IN ................

ACTION   COLUMN NAME           FORMAT        SAS NAME      NULLS?
  .      LNAME                 CHAR(15)      LNAME           Y
  .      FNAME                 CHAR(10)      FNAME           Y
  .      BEGDTE                FLOAT         BEGDTE          Y
  .      PLNEND                FLOAT         PLNEND          Y
  .      ACTEND                FLOAT         ACTEND          Y
  .      PROJECT               CHAR(20)      PROJECT         Y
```

On the TABLE CREATE/LOAD panel enter the name of the tablespace previously created in the IN field.

Suppose that the SAS variable, Plnend, is not needed on the DB2 table so a D ACTION code is entered. Hitting enter after typing the D ACTION code deletes that line from the TABLE CREATE/LOAD screen, but it is still stored on the SAS data set.

New DB2 column names are entered and the numeric data types are changed to DECIMAL. The SAS variables, Lname and Fname, are defined so that NULLS are not allowed by changing the value to N.

When this panel is completed, enter the LOAD command.

```
                         DB2 INTERFACE
                   TABLE CREATE/LOAD PANEL

COMMAND===> load

    CREATE TABLE TSID123.PROJINFO          IN tsid123.sample...

ACTION   COLUMN NAME            FORMAT          SAS NAME     NULLS?
  .      LAST_NAME              CHAR(15)        LNAME           N
  .      FIRST_NAME             CHAR(10)        FNAME           N
  .      BEGIN_DATE             DECIMAL(6,0)    BEGDTE          Y
  .      ACTUAL_END_DATE        DECIMAL(6,0)    ACTEND          Y
  .      PROJECT                CHAR(20)        PROJECT         Y
```

The LOAD command is used to return to the DATA ACCESS panel and create and load the DB2 table. The DATA ACCESS panel shows the load statistics at the bottom of the screen.

```
                          DB2 INTERFACE
                        DATA ACCESS PANEL

COMMAND===>


INPUT SAS DATA SET: SASIN.PROJINFO                      COMMIT:    3
TABLE NAME:         TSID123.PROJINFO                    LIMIT:     5000
SUBSYSTEM ID:       DBT


MAP DATA SET:                               I=INPUT;O=OUTPUT:
OUTPUT SQL LIBRARY:                         ERROR LOG FILE:

LOAD STATISTICS:   NUMBER OF ROWS INSERTED     = 19
                   NUMBER OF SAS OBS READ      = 19
                   NUMBER OF INSERTS REJECTED  = 0
```

Maps and SQL Statements

This section illustrates the use of PROC DB2LOAD in Display Manager to create and save maps and SQL statments to be used as input in subsequent executions of PROC DB2LOAD. These maps and SQL statements can be used as input to PROC DB2LOAD in Display Manager, but are more often used in batch programs due to computer resource requirements.

SQL Statements

SQL statements generated by PROC DB2LOAD include CREATE, INSERT, and COMMIT. INSERT statements make up the majority of the SQL statements. An INSERT statement exists for every observation on the SAS data set and contains the values of the SAS variables. If an output SQL file is saved, it can be quite large, depending on the size of the input SAS data set. Because the INSERT statement contains data values, SQL statements are typically saved through Display Manager, used as input in a batch program, and then deleted. Subsequent executions of PROC DB2LOAD to create and load a DB2 table would typically need to contain different data values and be based on different observations. In this case, different SQL statements would be required.

Because the INSERT statements exist for every SAS observation in the input SAS data set and because they contain actual data values, it is unlikely that the user would need to edit such SQL statements. Changes would be made to the SAS data set and new SQL statements would be generated. For this reason, the SQL statements generated by the map cannot be displayed on the SQL ENTRY/EDIT panel. If the SQL statements are saved to an external file they could be included in the SQL ENTRY/EDIT panel, but typically they would be used as input to a batch program.

Therefore, the SQL ENTRY/EDIT panel is normally used only to execute SQL statements in addition to the CREATE, INSERT, and COMMIT statements generated by the map. Typically, these are utility-type SQL statements such as creating a tablespace or dropping DB2 objects. These statements must end in a semicolon; semicolons are generated only for SQL statements that are generated by a map. Also, the COMMIT and LIMIT fields on the DATA ACCESS panel do not apply to these SQL statements. The only statement which cannot be executed by PROC DB2LOAD is the SELECT statement. The SELECT statement can only be executed by PROC DB2EXT. Other SQL statements can be entered into the SQL ENTRY/EDIT panel or included in the SQL ENTRY/EDIT panel using the INCLUDE command. SQL statements can also be executed in a batch program using DB2 utilities with JCL tailored to your company or in a batch program using the SQL statement in a PROC DB2LOAD or PROC DB2UTIL step.

The SQL ENTRY/EDIT panel is brought up by issuing the EDIT command from the DATA ACCESS panel or TABLE CREATE/LOAD panel. The user should not enter anything on either of these panels, because when you return from the SQL ENTRY/EDIT panel, any changes will not appear. When the END command is issued from the SQL ENTRY/EDIT panel, SQL statements in the panel will be executed and the user will be returned to the previous panel. Figure 8-5 shows the panels which can be used to access the SQL ENTRY/EDIT panel.

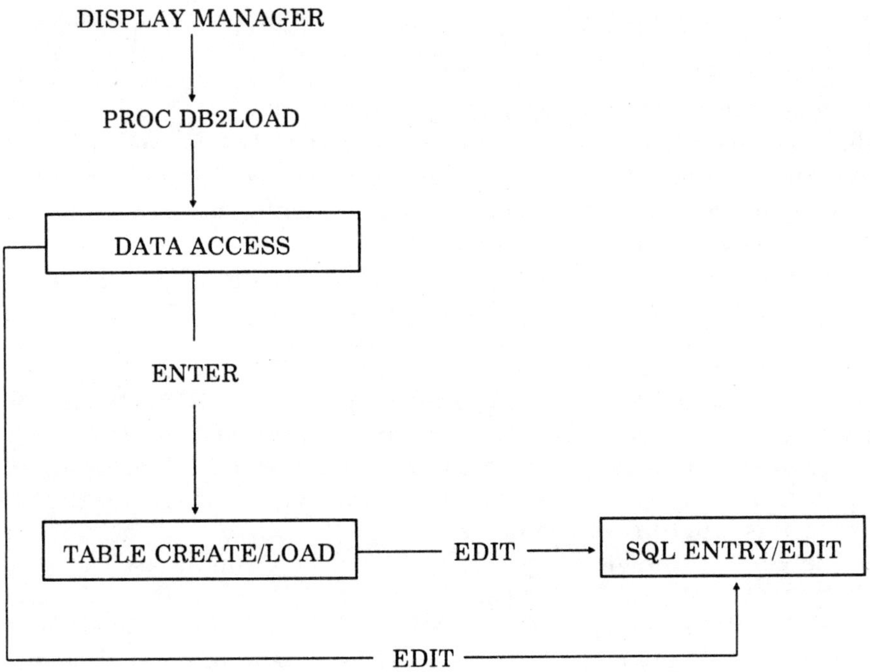

Figure 8-5 PROC DB2LOAD access to SQL ENTRY/EDIT Panel.

Example 8-2

A DB2 table created in a previous execution of PROC DB2LOAD needs to be deleted.

The SQL DROP statement is used to drop a DB2 object. The DROP statement is not generated by any of the SAS/DB2 procedures so it must be coded by the user. The DROP statement can be entered or included in the SQL ENTRY/EDIT panel and submitted for execution by issuing the END command.

PROC DB2LOAD is executed to bring up the DATA ACCESS panel, where the EDIT command (PF11/PF23) is entered.

```
                              DB2 INTERFACE
                            DATA ACCESS PANEL

COMMAND===> edit
FILL IN THE FIELDS BELOW

INPUT SAS DATA SET:                                    COMMIT:    3
TABLE NAME:                                            LIMIT:     5000
SUBSYSTEM ID:         DBT



MAP DATA SET:                           I=INPUT;O=OUTPUT:
OUTPUT SQL LIBRARY:                     ERROR LOG FILE:
```

The EDIT command brings up a blank SQL ENTRY/EDIT panel. The NUMS ON command is issued to produce line numbers on the left so that line commands can be used if needed. The DROP statement is entered, along with the COMMIT statement. The COMMIT statement must be used with the DROP in order for the table name to be used again. Since these are not generated SQL statements, a semicolon must be coded at the end of each statement.

```
                         SQL ENTRY/EDIT SCREEN
COMMAND===>                                            TEXT EDITOR
                                                       Col 001 072
00001 drop table tsid123.projinfo;
00002 commit;
00003
```

The END command issued from the SQL ENTRY/EDIT panel returns the user to the DATA ACCESS panel and executes the SQL DROP and COMMIT statements. A message appears under the command line saying that SQL processing is complete.

```
                         DB2 INTERFACE
                       DATA ACCESS PANEL

COMMAND===>
NOTE: SQL PROCESSING COMPLETE

INPUT SAS DATA SET:                                    COMMIT:    3
TABLE NAME:                                            LIMIT:     5000
SUBSYSTEM ID:         DBT



MAP DATA SET:                           I=INPUT;O=OUTPUT:
OUTPUT SQL LIBRARY:                     ERROR LOG FILE:
```

Example 8-3

A SQL output file is needed to store SQL statements which will be used to create and load a DB2 table, Tsid123.projinfo from a SAS data set, Projinfo.

An SQL output file contains the SQL statements, CREATE, INSERT, and COMMIT, used to create and load a DB2 table. These SQL statements will usually be used as input to PROC DB2LOAD in a batch program rather than in Display Manager.

A TSO allocate statement for the SAS data library containing the input SAS data set and a TSO allocate statement for the external file to be used to store the saved SQL statements must be submitted in Display Manager prior to executing PROC DB2LOAD. PROC DB2LOAD is executed to bring up the DATA ACCESS panel. The input SAS data set, the output DB2 table, and the output SQL library fields are completed on the DATA ACCESS panel.

```
                         DB2 INTERFACE
                       DATA ACCESS PANEL

COMMAND===> edit
FILL IN THE FIELDS BELOW

INPUT SAS DATA SET: sasin.projinfo                COMMIT:    3
TABLE NAME:         tsid123.projinfo              LIMIT:     5000
SUBSYSTEM ID:       DBT



MAP DATA SET:                          I=INPUT;O=OUTPUT:
OUTPUT SQL LIBRARY: code.sqll          ERROR LOG FILE:
```

Hitting enter on the DATA ACCESS panel brings up the TABLE CREATE/LOAD panel shown below.

```
                          DB2 INTERFACE
                    TABLE CREATE/LOAD PANEL

COMMAND===>

    CREATE TABLE TSID123.PROJINFO            IN ................

ACTION   COLUMN NAME           FORMAT        SAS NAME      NULLS?
  .      LNAME                 CHAR(15)      LNAME           Y
  .      FNAME                 CHAR(10)      FNAME           Y
  .      BEGDTE                FLOAT         BEGDTE          Y
  .      PLNEND                FLOAT         PLNEND          Y
  .      ACTEND                FLOAT         ACTEND          Y
  .      PROJECT               CHAR(20)      PROJECT         Y
```

On the TABLE CREATE/LOAD panel enter the name of a tablespace previously created to store the DB2 table. Enter new DB2 column names and change the numeric data types to DECIMAL. The SAS variables, Lname and Fname, are defined to disallow NULL values by changing the NULLS option to N. When the TABLE CREATE/LOAD panel is complete issue the END command (PF3/PF15) to save the output SQL file.

```
                         DB2 INTERFACE
                    TABLE CREATE/LOAD PANEL


COMMAND===> end


    CREATE TABLE TSID123.PROJINFO           IN tsid123.sample...

ACTION   COLUMN NAME           FORMAT         SAS NAME     NULLS?
  .      LAST_NAME             CHAR(15)       LNAME          N
  .      FIRST_NAME            CHAR(10)       FNAME          N
  .      BEGIN_DATE            DECIMAL(6,0)   BEGDTE         Y
  .      PLAN_END_DATE         DECIMAL(6,0)   PLNEND         Y
  .      ACTUAL_END_DATE       DECIMAL(6,0)   ACTEND         Y
  .      PROJECT               CHAR(20)       PROJECT        Y
```

The END command issued from the TABLE CREATE/LOAD panel returns the user to the DATA ACCESS panel and creates the output SQL file. A message appears under the command line saying that SQL processing is complete.

```
                              DB2 INTERFACE
                            DATA ACCESS PANEL

COMMAND===>
NOTE: SQL PROCESSING COMPLETE

INPUT SAS DATA SET:                                  COMMIT:   3
TABLE NAME:                                          LIMIT:    5000
SUBSYSTEM ID:        DBT



MAP DATA SET:                           I=INPUT;O=OUTPUT:
OUTPUT SQL LIBRARY:                     ERROR LOG FILE:
```

The SQL statements saved in the output SQL library can be viewed in TSO or included in the PROGRAM window of Display Manager. The following shows the beginning of this SQL output file. The INSERT statements are wrapped onto multiple lines due to their length.

The CREATE statement creates the DB2 table and the INSERT statements load the DB2 table. There is an INSERT statement for every observation on the SAS data set and the INSERT statements contain the SAS variable values. For every 3 INSERT statements there is a COMMIT statement. This is based on the default value of 3 on the COMMIT field in the DATA ACCESS panel.

```
CREATE TABLE TSID123.PROJINFO (
LNAME CHAR(15) , FNAME CHAR(10) , BEGDTE DECIMAL(6,0) , PLNEND
DECIMAL(6,0) , ACTEND DECIMAL(6,0) , PROJECT CHAR(20)  ) IN
TSID123.SAMPLE
;
COMMIT WORK;
INSERT INTO TSID123.PROJINFO VALUES (
'APPLE          ', 'RICHARD   ', 881001., 881201., 881201.,
'COMPENSATION PLAN   ')
;
```

```
INSERT INTO TSID123.PROJINFO VALUES (
'APPLE          ', 'RICHARD    ', 890115., 890301., 890301.,
'FINANCIAL STATEMENT ')
;
INSERT INTO TSID123.PROJINFO VALUES (
'BAKER          ', 'MARTHA     ', 890715., 890915., 890915.,
'BROKERS        ')
;
COMMIT WORK;
INSERT INTO TSID123.PROJINFO VALUES (
'BROWN          ', 'WALLY      ', 881001., 881201., 881201.,
'CONPENSATION PLAN   ')
;
INSERT INTO TSID123.PROJINFO VALUES (
'BUELL          ', 'MAX        ', 890315., 890401., 890415.,
'SALES REPORT        ')
;
INSERT INTO TSID123.PROJINFO VALUES (
'GOETZ          ', 'JACK       ', 890601., 890801., 890715.,
'COMMISSIONS         ')
;
COMMIT WORK;
 ...
```

Maps

Maps are defined by the user on the TABLE CREATE/LOAD panel. A map includes the SAS variable name, the DB2 column names, the DB2 data types, and whether NULLS are allowed. If the same map is needed frequently, users may want to save maps for subsequent executions of PROC DB2LOAD. Maps are saved as SAS data sets in SAS data libraries.

When SQL statements are saved as output from PROC DB2LOAD, they are typically used only once because they contain actual data values, which are subject to change. When maps are saved from executing PROC DB2LOAD, they can be used in many subsequent executions of PROC DB2LOAD. Even though the input SAS data sets may contain and probably do contain different variable values, the same map can be used. As long as the definition of the input SAS data sets are the same, including the same SAS variable names, data types, and lengths, then the same map can be used.

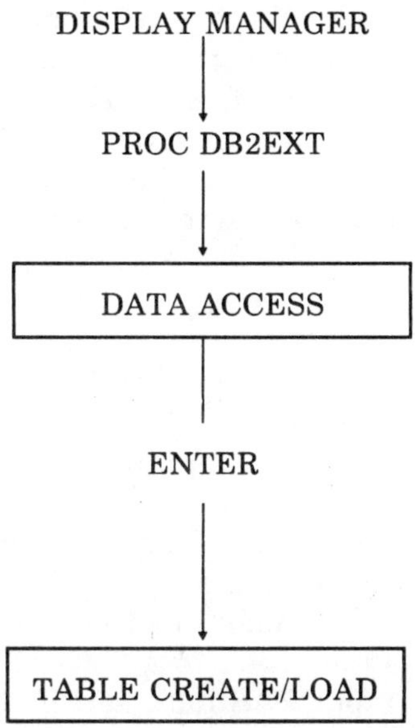

Figure 8-6 PROC DB2LOAD Panels used for saving Maps.

Maps are most often created in Display Manager to take advantage of the panels and ease of use offered in that environment. Often, the DB2 table itself cannot be created and loaded in Display Manager due to limited computer resources, so the map is used as input to PROC DB2LOAD in a batch program.

Figure 8-6 shows the panels used to save a map with PROC DB2LOAD or to use a saved map as input to PROC DB2LOAD.

To specify a map as input or output, the MAP DATA SET field is specified on the DATA ACCESS panel. The field, I=INPUT;O=OUPUT, is set to I or O depending on whether the map is an input file or an output file. After completing the DATA ACCESS panel, hitting enter brings up the TABLE CREATE/LOAD panel where the map is defined. The END command is issued from the TABLE CREATE/LOAD panel and a message is displayed. The message states that if the END command is issued again, a map or SQL statements will be saved, and if the LOAD command is issued, the DB2 table will be created and loaded. The END command is issued a second time to save a map.

If you need to make changes to an existing map, specify the map in the map data set field and set the INPUT/OUTPUT value to I. Hitting enter brings up the TABLE CREATE/LOAD panel, where the map is displayed. Make the desired changes to the map. Issue the END command twice (as described above) and the modifications will be saved to the input map. If you need to create and save a map which is similar to a map that already exists, make a copy of the map using a DATA step or the Base SAS procedure, PROC COPY. This copy can then be modified using this method.

Example 8-4

An output SAS data set containing mapping instructions for creating and loading a DB2 table, Tsid123.projinfo, from a SAS data set, Projinfo, is needed.

Assume that a tablespace, tsid123.sample, already exists to hold the DB2 table. A TSO allocate statement for the SAS data library that will be used to store the map must be submitted prior to excuting PROC DB2LOAD, in addition to a TSO allocate for a SAS data library containing the input SAS data set, if the same SAS data library is not used.

PROC DB2LOAD is executed to bring up the DATA ACCESS panel. The input SAS data set, the DB2 table, and the map data set are entered on the DATA ACCESS panel. The map is specified as output by entering an O in the INPUT/OUTPUT field.

```
                              DB2 INTERFACE
                            DATA ACCESS PANEL

COMMAND===>
NOTE: SQL PROCESSING COMPLETE

INPUT SAS DATA SET: sasin.projinfo                    COMMIT:    3
TABLE NAME:         tsid123.projinfo                  LIMIT:     5000
SUBSYSTEM ID:       DBT



MAP DATA SET:       sasout.prjmap      I=INPUT;O=OUTPUT: o
OUTPUT SQL LIBRARY:                    ERROR LOG FILE:
```

Hitting enter on the DATA ACCESS panel brings up the TABLE CREATE/LOAD panel shown below.

```
                        DB2 INTERFACE
                  TABLE CREATE/LOAD PANEL

COMMAND===>

   CREATE TABLE TSID123.PROJINFO            IN ................

ACTION   COLUMN NAME          FORMAT         SAS NAME     NULLS?
  .      LNAME                CHAR(15)       LNAME          Y
  .      FNAME                CHAR(10)       FNAME          Y
  .      BEGDTE               FLOAT          BEGDTE         Y
  .      PLNEND               FLOAT          PLNEND         Y
  .      ACTEND               FLOAT          ACTEND         Y
  .      PROJECT              CHAR(20)       PROJECT        Y
```

The existing tablespace, Tsid123.sample, is entered in the IN field. DB2 column names are changed and the data types for the numeric variables are changed from FLOAT to DECIMAL.

```
                        DB2 INTERFACE
                  TABLE CREATE/LOAD PANEL

COMMAND===>

   CREATE TABLE TSID123.PROJINFO            IN TSID123.SAMPLE...

ACTION   COLUMN NAME          FORMAT         SAS NAME     NULLS?
  .      LAST_NAME            CHAR(15)       LNAME          Y
  .      FIRST_NAME           CHAR(10)       FNAME          Y
  .      BEGIN_DATE           DECIMAL(6,0)   BEGDTE         Y
  .      PLAN_END_DATE        DECIMAL(6,0)   PLNEND         Y
  .      ACTUAL_END_DATE      DECIMAL(6,0)   ACTEND         Y
  .      PROJECT              CHAR(20)       PROJECT        Y
```

The END command issued from the TABLE CREATE/LOAD panel displays message (not shown) telling you that if the END command is issued again, output maps and/or SQL statements will be saved. If the LOAD command is issued instead, a DB2 table will be created and loaded.

The END command is issued a second time and the user is returned to the DATA ACCESS panel and the output map is saved. A message appears under the command line stating that the map contains 6 observations and 9 variables. The B (BROWSE) command is entered on the DATA ACCESS panel.

```
                                 DB2 INTERFACE
                              DATA ACCESS PANEL

 COMMAND===>
NOTE: SASOUT.PRJMAP CONTAINS: 6 OBSERVATION(S) AND: 9 VARIABLE(S)

 INPUT SAS DATA SET: SASIN.PROJINFO                    COMMIT:    3
 TABLE NAME:         TSID123.PROJINFO                  LIMIT:     5000
 SUBSYSTEM ID:       DBT



 MAP DATA SET:       SASOUT.PRJMAP     I=INPUT;O=OUTPUT: O
 OUTPUT SQL LIBRARY:                   ERROR LOG FILE:
```

The BROWSE command displays the BROWSE panel showing the mapping SAS data set just created.

```
                   SAS DATA SET: SASOUT.PRJMAP        OBSERVATIONS
COMMAND===>                                           FIRST       1
                                                      LAST        6
OBS  DB2COL            DB2FMT         SASNAME    DATATYPE
  1  LAST_NAME         CHAR(15)       LNAME      C
  2  FIRST_NAME        CHAR(10)       FNAME      C
  3  BEGIN_DATE        DECIMAL(6,0)   BEGDTE     F
  4  PLAN_END_DATE     DECIMAL(6,0)   PLNEND     F
  5  ACTUAL_END_DATE   DECIMAL(6,0)   ACTEND     F
  6  PROJECT           CHAR(20)       PROJECT    C
```

Scrolling several times to the right displays additional variables in the map.

```
                    SAS DATA SET: SASOUT.PRJMAP        OBSERVATIONS
COMMAND===>                                            FIRST      1
                                                       LAST       6

OBS  DATEFMT    DATELEN    FMTLEN    NUMDEC    NULLS
  1        0         15         0         0    Y
  2        0         10         0         0    Y
  3        4          8         0         0    Y
  4        4          8         0         0    Y
  5        4          8         0         0    Y
  6        0         20         0         0    Y
```

Example 8-5

Maps are more frequently used as input to PROC DB2LOAD in batch, but if computer resources allow, maps can be used as input to PROC DB2LOAD in Display Manager to create and load a DB2 table. This example will illustrate using the map created in the previous example as input to PROC DB2LOAD in Display Manager.

PROC DB2LOAD is executed to bring up the DATA ACCESS panel, where the input SAS data set and the output DB2 table are entered. The map data set saved in the previous example is entered, along with an I specificaton for input.

```
                             DB2 INTERFACE
                           DATA ACCESS PANEL
COMMAND===>


INPUT SAS DATA SET: sasin.projinfo                  COMMIT:    3
TABLE NAME:         tsid123.projinfo                LIMIT:     5000
SUBSYSTEM ID:       DBT

MAP DATA SET:       sasout.prjmap      I=INPUT;O=OUTPUT: i
OUTPUT SQL LIBRARY:                    ERROR LOG FILE:
```

Hitting enter on the DATA ACCESS panel displays the following TABLE CREATE/LOAD panel. Notice the DB2 column names and data types are not defaults, but are those entered when the map was saved. The IN field is blank and you must enter the tablespace name, or else the default value, DSNDB04, will be used. The LOAD command is then entered.

```
                         DB2 INTERFACE
                    TABLE CREATE/LOAD PANEL

COMMAND===> load

   CREATE TABLE TSID123.PROJINFO           IN tsid123.sample...

ACTION   COLUMN NAME         FORMAT         SAS NAME    NULLS?
  .      LAST_NAME           CHAR(15)       LNAME          Y
  .      FIRST_NAME          CHAR(10)       FNAME          Y
  .      BEGIN_DATE          DECIMAL(6,0)   BEGDTE         Y
  .      PLAN_END_DATE       DECIMAL(6,0)   PLNEND         Y
  .      ACTUAL_END_DATE     DECIMAL(6,0)   ACTEND         Y
  .      PROJECT             CHAR(20)       PROJECT        Y
```

The LOAD command is issued in the TABLE CREATE/LOAD panel to return the user to the DATA ACCESS panel and create and load the DB2 table using the map as input. Statistics are shown at the bottom of the DATA ACCESS panel to reflect this.

```
                              DB2 INTERFACE
                            DATA ACCESS PANEL

COMMAND===>

INPUT SAS DATA SET: SASIN.PROJINFO                     COMMIT:    3
TABLE NAME:         TSID123.PROJINFO                   LIMIT:     5000
SUBSYSTEM ID:       DBT


MAP DATA SET:       SASOUT.PRJMAP      I=INPUT;O=OUTPUT: o
OUTPUT SQL LIBRARY:                    ERROR LOG FILE:


LOAD STATISTICS:   NUMBER OF ROWS INSERTED    = 19
                   NUMBER OF SAS OBS READ     = 19
                   NUMBER OF INSERTS REJECTED = 0
```

Chapter

9

PROC DB2LOAD in Batch

PROC DB2LOAD is used to create and load DB2 tables using data stored in a SAS data set. PROC DB2LOAD can also be used to execute utility-type SQL statements such as those used for creating an index or dropping a DB2 table.

When a DB2 table is loaded, one of the following is used as input: a SAS data set, a map and a SAS data set, or the SQL statements, CREATE, INSERT, and COMMIT. When only a SAS data set is used as input, a map is generated, and the map and the SAS data set generate the appropriate SQL statements. When a map created in a previous execution of PROC DB2LOAD is used as input, a SAS data set is also used as input to supply the data values for the INSERT statements. When SQL statements created in a previous execution of PROC DB2LOAD are used as input, they are the sole input to PROC DB2LOAD because they contain the specifications for creating the DB2 table and the values for loading the table. Whatever method of input is used, it is ultimately the SQL statements, CREATE, INSERT, and COMMIT that create and load the DB2 table. Because the CREATE statement is used, the DB2 table must not already exist.

If a map or SQL statements are used as input to PROC DB2LOAD, they were usually created in a previous execution of PROC DB2LOAD in Display Manager to take advantage of the ease of use. These maps and SQL statements are typically used as input to PROC DB2LOAD in a batch program to create and load a DB2 table, due to computer resource limitations in Display Manager.

PROC DB2LOAD can also be used to execute SQL statements other than the CREATE, INSERT, and COMMIT statements which are generated by the procedure. For example, PROC DB2LOAD could be used to create a tablespace, create an index, or drop a table. Although these statements can be executed in a variety of other ways, including using JCL tailored to your company, it is often convenient to execute them in the SAS environment to save you from exiting Display Manager, or from including multiple job steps in a batch program. Refer to Chapter 4, Structured Query Language, for documentation on the most commonly used SQL statements.

This chapter will present the use of PROC DB2LOAD in batch programs to create and load a DB2 table using data stored in a SAS data set, to use a map created in a previous execution of PROC DB2LOAD as input, and to use SQL statements created in a previous execution of PROC DB2LOAD as input. Also presented is the use of PROC DB2LOAD to execute a SQL statement other than those which can be generated by PROC DB2LOAD. The user should have JCL appropriate to his company to execute SAS with SAS/DB2. You will also need to know the value(s) of the DB2 SUBSYSTEM ID. Contact the SAS Consultant at your company for this information. An introduction to PROC DB2LOAD was given in Chapter 5, Introduction to SAS/DB2, and this material should be fresh in your mind before beginning this chapter.

In Release 5.16 of SAS/DB2, missing values in SAS variables cannot be loaded into a DB2 column that was created as NOT NULL. In Release 5.18 of SAS/DB2, missing numeric values are loaded as zero, and missing character values are loaded as blanks when the DB2 column is defined as NOT NULL. In either Release 5.16 or 5.18, missing values in SAS variables are loaded as NULL if the DB2 column is defined as NULL.

SAS data set versions of the DB2 tables shown in Appendix C: Sample Tables are used in examples in this chapter. Refer to this appendix to familiarize yourself with the sample DB2 tables. You may choose to follow along in these examples by performing the same operations on the mainframe at your company. These DB2 tables can be entered on your mainframe or refer to Chapter 1, Introduction, for ordering a copy of these tables.

If permanent input or output files are needed for the execution of PROC DB2LOAD, they should be coded in the JCL.

Input files used with PROC DB2LOAD include SAS data sets containing data which will be used to create and load a DB2 table and

SAS data sets containing mapping instructions. SQL statements stored in an external file, usually a partitioned data set, can also be used as input to PROC DB2LOAD. These SQL statements could be the CREATE, INSERT, and COMMIT statements used to create and load a DB2 table, or they could be SQL statements which perform specific operations, such as dropping a table or creating a tablespace.

Output files used with PROC DB2LOAD include SAS data sets containing mapping instructions, the SQL statements (CREATE, INSERT, and COMMIT) which will be used to create and load a DB2 table, an error log file, and the DB2 table itself.

Options and Statements

In the previous chapter, PROC DB2LOAD in Display Manager, only the PROC DB2LOAD statement itself was coded and a series of panels with "fill-in-the-blanks" was used to define the application. In this chapter, PROC DB2LOAD will be executed in the batch environment through the use of options of the PROC DB2LOAD statement and other statements used in the PROC DB2LOAD step. These PROC DB2LOAD options and statements can also be executed in Display Manager if the user prefers this style of coding and wants to execute interactively. Also, for users who prefer to utilize the line mode execution of SAS, these options and statements must be used to execute PROC DB2LOAD.

The following statements can be used with PROC DB2LOAD in batch programs:

```
PROC DB2LOAD option(s);
   DELETE SASname SASname ...;
   IN 'authorizationid.tablespace';
   LIST ALL|SASname SASname ...|SASDATA|OPTIONS;
   NULLS SASname=YES|NO SASname=YES|NO ...;
   REPLACE SASname=DB2colname SASname=DB2colname ...;
   TYPE SASname='DB2 data type' SASname='DB2 data type' ...;
   SQL statement;
```

The above statements can be used in batch programs, but are also used in line mode execution of PROC DB2LOAD. The following statements are used exclusively in line mode execution. These statements will be defined, but will not be illustrated.

```
EXIT;
LOAD;
RESET SASname;  or RESET ALL;
RESHOW;
```

There are several options that can be used in the PROC DB2LOAD statement. Knowing which options and statements to use in a given application depends on the input and output files that are needed. Guidelines for the use of the options and statements will be given after each is defined.

Options

The options which can be used with the PROC DB2LOAD statement are defined as follows:

DATA=SASdataset: The SAS data set named here is the SAS data set which will be used to create and load the DB2 table. The DATA option is used for most applications of PROC DB2LOAD. If the SAS data set is stored permanently in a SAS data library, a two-level SAS data set name will be specified. The first level corresponds to the DD specified for the SAS data library in the JCL.

TABLE=authorizationid.tablename: The TABLE option is used to specify the name of a new DB2 table to be created and loaded. The TABLE option is used for most applications of PROC DB2LOAD. A tablespace to hold the DB2 table should be created prior to creating and loading the DB2 table.

SSID = subsystem name: This option is the same as used with PROC DB2EXT. Refer to Chapter 7, PROC DB2EXT in Batch, for the definition of this option.

COMMIT=number: The number specified in the COMMIT option controls the number of INSERT statements which will be executed before a COMMIT statement is issued to save the inserts to the DB2 table and release them to other applications. If this option is not specified, a default value of 3 is used.

LIMIT=number: The number specified in the LIMIT option sets the maximum number of SAS observations or SQL INSERT statements which can be executed. If this option is not specified, a default value of 5000 is used. If the LIMIT option is set to 0, no limit will be set and all SAS observations will be loaded to the DB2 table.

ERROR=ddname or ERROR=ddname.membername:
PROC DB2LOAD uses the SQL CREATE, INSERT, and COMMIT statements to create and load a DB2 table. If these statements contain SQL errors, error messages are written to the SAS log. If the ERROR option is used to name an external file, any SQL errors encountered during the execution of PROC DB2LOAD will be written to this file, along with the SQL statements that produced the errors. If errors are written to the SAS log, the SQL statements that produced the errors are not shown on the SAS log. Therefore, it will probably be easier to diagnose errors when the ERROR option is specified.

The external file is usually a partitioned data set. It is specified in the JCL. If the member name is specified in the JCL, only the ddname needs to be specified in the ERROR option. If the member name is not specified in the JCL, the ddname followed a period (.) and the member name is specified in the ERROR option.

LOAD: The LOAD option must be used in order to create and load a DB2 table when a SAS data set containing data is used as input, or a SAS data set containing data and a map is used as input. If the LOAD option is not used, the only output files which can be created are maps and SQL statements.

MAPIN=SASdataset: The MAPIN option is used to specify a map as input to PROC DB2LOAD. This map was created in a prior execution of PROC DB2LOAD, probably in Display Manager. The LOAD option must be used with the MAPIN option in order to create and load a DB2 table. The mapping SAS data set will probably be stored permanently in a SAS data library. In this case, a two-level SAS data set name will be specified. The first level corresponds to the DD specified for the SAS data library in the JCL. The second level is the SAS data set name.

MAPOUT=SASdataset: The MAPOUT option is used to specify a map as output to PROC DB2LOAD. The map will be used in subsequent executions of PROC DB2LOAD to create and load the DB2 table. Maps are more often created in Display Manager due to the ease of use of the panels provided in that environment. Maps can be created and saved in a batch execution of PROC DB2LOAD using the SAS data set which will be used to create and load the DB2 table as input. A map will probably be stored permanently in a SAS data library. In this case, a two-level SAS data set name will be specified. The first level corresponds to the dd specified for the SAS data library in the JCL. The second level is the SAS data set name.

SQLIN = ddname or SQLIN = ddname.membername: The SQLIN option is used to specify an external file where SQL statements are stored. These SQL statements will be used as input to the creation and loading of the DB2 table. The SQL statements were created and saved in a previous execution of PROC DB2LOAD, probably in Display Manager. When SQL statements are used as input to PROC DB2LOAD, the only output file is a DB2 table.

Since the SQLIN option is used to bring in SQL statements, these statements must be stored in an external file rather than being copied or coded in the batch program itself.

If the JCL specifications for the external file containing the SQL statements include the member name of a partitioned data set, only the ddname used in the JCL is coded in the SQLIN option. If the JCL specification does not include the member name, then the SQLIN option includes the ddname used in the JCL followed by a period (.) and the member name.

SQLOUT = ddname or SQLOUT=ddname.membername: The SQLOUT option is used to specify an external file where SQL statements are to be written as a result of executing PROC DB2LOAD. These SQL statements will be used in a subsequent execution of PROC DB2LOAD and probably deleted. Typically, SQL statements used to load a DB2 table are not used multiple times because the INSERT statements contain data values from the input SAS data set. When DB2 tables are created and loaded again, these data values would usually have changed, meaning new INSERT statements need to be created.

SQL statements are more often created in Display Manager due to the ease of use of the panels provided in that environment. SQL statements can be created and saved in a batch execution of PROC DB2LOAD using the SAS data set which will be used to create and load the DB2 table as input or a map as input.

If the JCL specifications for the external file containing the SQL statements include the member name of a partitioned data set, only the ddname used in the JCL is coded in the SQLOUT option. If the JCL specification does not include the member name, then the SQLOUT option includes the ddname used in the JCL followed by a period (.) and the member name.

Statements

The following statements are used with the PROC DB2LOAD procedure in the batch environment:

DELETE SASname SASname ...;

The DELETE statement is used when the input SAS data set contains variables which are not to be loaded in the DB2 table. The variable(s) named in the DELETE statement will not be loaded to the DB2 table, but they will still exist on the input SAS data set.

IN 'authorizationid.tablename';

The IN statement is used to specify the tablespace to be used to store the resulting DB2 table. If the IN statement is not used, the DB2 table will be stored in the default tablespace, DSNDB04.

LIST ALL | SASname SASname ... | SASDATA | OPTIONS;

The LIST statement can be used with any of the specifications shown here, ALL, SASname, SASDATA, OPTIONS or a combination of more than one of these options. The LIST ALL is the most commonly used option.

The ALL option produces a report on the SAS log which shows all the mapping specifications executed by PROC DB2LOAD. The report shows the DB2 column name and data types which were either automatically generated or user-defined, the SAS variable name, and whether NULLS are allowed.

The SASname option can be used to specify as many SAS variables as desired and produces a report on the SAS log just like the LIST ALL except only the specified SAS variables are shown.

The SASDATA option produces a report on the SAS log containing SAS variable names and whether the variable is character or numeric.

The OPTIONS (or OPT) option produces a list of the options of the PROC DB2LOAD statement and the IN statement and their values. These values include those that are specified in the PROC DB2LOAD step and values which are set to default values. Options that are not specified are noted as such.

NULLS SASname=YES | NO SASname=YES | NO ...;

The NULLS statement is used to specify whether NULL values will be allowed. The SAS variable name is specified followed by an equal sign and YES or NO. The abbreviations, Y and N, can also be used. If the NULL statement is not specified for a SAS variable, the default is YES, NULL values are allowed.

REPLACE SASname=DB2colname SASname=DB2colname ...;

The REPLACE statement is used to specify DB2 column names for the SAS variables in the input SAS data set. One or more DB2 columns can be named in a single REPLACE statement. By default, DB2 column names are the same as the SAS variable names. The REPLACE statement or an input map can be used to assign other DB2 column names.

TYPE SASname='DB2 data type' SASname='DB2 data type' ...;

The TYPE statement is used to specify DB2 data types for the SAS variables on the input SAS data set. One or more DB2 columns can be named in a single TYPE statement. By default, SAS character variables are assigned the DB2 data type, CHAR, and SAS numeric variables are assigned the DB2 data type, FLOAT. The numeric data types, DECIMAL and INTEGER, are often needed. If you wish to assign a DB2 date/time data type, the SAS variable used to load values into this column must be stored as a SAS date/time value. Refer to Chapter 3, IBM'S Database 2, the section, Data Types, for more information about DB2 data types.

SQL statement;

The SQL statement is used to execute an SQL statement. SQL statements specified here are typically utility-type statements such as creating a tablespace or dropping a table. The SQL SELECT statement cannot be executed by PROC DB2LOAD, only PROC DB2EXT can execute the SELECT statement. Only one SQL statement can be coded in a single SQL statement. If more than one SQL statement needs to be executed, multiple SQL statements are coded in the PROC DB2LOAD step.

When SQL statements are executed using the SQL statement in PROC DB2LOAD, the SAS log does not display any messages saying that execution was successful. If these SQL statements were executed using JCL tailored to your company instead, a condition code would be displayed for every SQL statement.

Refer to Example 9-1 in the next section, Creating and Loading a DB2 Table, for an illustration of executing multiple SQL statements in a PROC DB2LOAD step.

Line Mode

The above statements are used in batch programs and also line mode execution of SAS. The following statements are used exclusively in line mode execution:

EXIT;
: The EXIT statement performs the same function as the EXIT command used when PROC DB2LOAD is executed in Display Manager. The EXIT statement ends execution of PROC DB2LOAD without creating output files.

RESET SASname; or RESET ALL;
: The RESET ALL statement resets all changes made to the mapping specifications such as DB2 column names and data types. The RESET SASname statement resets those values only for the SAS variable named.

RESHOW;
: The RESHOW statement displays SAS variables previously deleted by the DELETE statement. DB2 column names and data types will be blank.

Application Use

Figure 9-1 outlines which PROC DB2LOAD options and statements should be used depending on the input and output files needed. It also shows the output files that can be produced by a specific input file.

In addition to the options and statements shown on this chart are the DELETE, REPLACE, TYPE, and NULLS statements. These statements allow the user to select SAS variables to be loaded, name DB2 columns, specify DB2 data types, and specify whether NULL values are allowed, respectively. When a SAS data set is used as input, these statements are used to define the map, which will result in saving the map itself, saving SQL statements, or creating and

INPUT	OUTPUT	Required Options	
SAS Data Set	Map	DATA TABLE SSID MAPOUT	 (does not already exist) (if other than default)
	SQL Statements	DATA TABLE SSID SQLOUT IN	 (does not already exist) (if other than default) (if other than DSNDB04)
	DB2 Table	DATA TABLE SSID LOAD IN	 (does not already exist) (if other than default) (if other than DSNDB04)
Map	SQL Statements	DATA TABLE SSID MAPIN SQLOUT	 (does not already exist) (if other than default)
	DB2 Table	DATA TABLE SSID MAPIN LOAD IN	 (does not already exist) (if other than default) (if other than DSNDB04)
SQL Statements	DB2 Table	SSID SQLIN	(if other than default)

Figure 9-1 Required options of PROC DB2LOAD.

loading the DB2 table. The definitions specified in the DELETE, REPLACE, TYPE, and NULLS statements or the saved map resulting from these statements (or the equivalent definition on the TABLE CREATE/LOAD panel) will be used in the generated SQL statements and the resulting DB2 table. Although these statements can be used when a map is used as input, this is unlikely because their purpose is the same as the map's.

When SQL statements are used as input, the DATA, TABLE, and MAPIN options cannot be specified, nor can any of the statements, DELETE, REPLACE, TYPE, and NULLS. The SQL statements,

CREATE, INSERT, and COMMIT, contain all the neccessary information to create and load the DB2 table.

The LIST statement is often used in applications of PROC DB2LOAD to display information concerning the execution of PROC DB2LOAD and to display mapping information.

Comparison to Display Manager

Figure 9-2 shows the PROC DB2LOAD panel and the field on that panel that performs the same function as the PROC DB2LOAD batch options and statements.

PROC DB2LOAD Panel	Field on the Panel	Batch Option/Statement
DATA ACCESS	INPUT SAS DATA SET	DATA Option
	TABLE NAME	TABLE Option
	DB2 SUBSYSTEM ID	SSID Option
	COMMIT	COMMIT Option
	LIMIT	LIMIT Option
	ERROR LOG FILE	ERROR Option
	MAP DATA SET I=INPUT;O=OUTPUT: I	MAPIN Option
	MAP DATA SET I=INPUT;O=OUTPUT: O	MAPOUT Option
	OUTPUT SQL LIBRARY	SQLOUT Option
TABLE CREATE/LOAD	IN	IN Statement
	ACTION D	DELETE Statement
	COLUMN NAME	REPLACE Statement
	FORMAT	TYPE Statement
	NULLS?	NULLS Statement
	LOAD Command	LOAD Option
SQL ENTRY/EDIT	INCLUDE Command	SQLIN Option
	User entered	SQL Statement

Figure 9-2 PROC DB2LOAD Display Manager and batch comparison.

Creating and Loading a DB2 Table

This section illustrates the use of PROC DB2LOAD in batch to create and load a DB2 table from data stored in a SAS data set. The SAS log is shown for each example.

Example 9-1

A SAS data set, Projinfo, needs to be loaded to a DB2 table. Before this can be done, a tablespace needs to be created. A tablespace is created with a SQL CREATE statement. The CREATE statement can be executed in a batch program using JCL tailored to your company, in the SQL ENTRY/EDIT panel of PROC DB2LOAD or PROC DB2UTIL in Display Manager, or in a batch program using the SQL statement of PROC DB2LOAD or PROC DB2UTIL. You should consult the DB2 Database Administrator at your company for the correct specifications of the CREATE statement.

Prior to the CREATE statement, a DROP and COMMIT statement for this tablespace is executed. If the create and load of the DB2 table needs to be run more than once, the table would have to be dropped before it could be created and loaded a second time. This is accomplished by the DROP TABLESPACE statement.

The following SAS log shows the use of the SQL statements DROP, COMMIT, and CREATE to produce a series of SQL statements that can be executed multiple times.

```
PROC DB2LOAD ;
  SQL DROP TABLESPACE TSID123.SAMPLE;
  IN 'TSID123.SAMPLE';
  SQL COMMIT;
  SQL CREATE TABLESPACE SAMPLE
      IN TSID123
      USING
      STOGROUP FREEGP01
      PRIQTY 1000
      SECQTY 1000
      ERASE NO
      FREEPAGE 000
      PCTFREE 00
      LOCKSIZE TABLESPACE
```

```
          BUFFERPOOL BP0
          CLOSE NO  ;
NOTE: FIELDS REQUIRED FOR LOAD WERE NOT ENTERED OR IN ERROR
NOTE: TABLE= OPTION REQUIRED FOR PROCESSING WAS NOT ENTERED
```

An SQL statement is coded for each SQL statement, DROP, COMMIT, and CREATE. There are no notes on the SAS log which indicate that these SQL statements executed correctly, but if there was a problem, a SQL error would appear on the SAS log. The notes shown are relative to PROC DB2LOAD not being used to create and load a DB2 table or create and save maps or SQL statements, and do not apply when the SQL statement is used.

Example 9-2

A tablespace was created in the previous example. This tablespace will be used to store the DB2 table created in this example using data stored in the SAS data set, Projinfo.

The following SAS log shows the PROC DB2LOAD step used to create and load the DB2 table, Tsid123.Projinfo, in the tablespace, Tsid123.sample:

```

     PROC DB2LOAD DATA=SASIN.PROJINFO TABLE=TSID123.PROJINFO
                    LOAD;
       IN 'TSID123.SAMPLE';
       REPLACE LNAME   = LAST_NAME
               FNAME   = FIRST_NAME
               BEGDTE  = BEGIN_DATE
               PLNEND  = PLAN_END_DATE
               ACTEND  = ACTUAL_END
               PROJECT = PROJECT;
       TYPE BEGDTE = 'DECIMAL(6,0)'
            PLNEND = 'DECIMAL(6,0)'
            ACTEND = 'DECIMAL(6,0)';
       NULLS LNAME=N FNAME=N;
-------- MAP FOR CREATE AND LOAD --------------------------
 COLUMN NAME          DB2 FORMAT           SAS NAME    NULLS?
  LAST_NAME            CHAR(15)             LNAME         N
  FIRST_NAME           CHAR(10)             FNAME         N
  BEGIN_DATE           DECIMAL(6,0)         BEGDTE        Y
```

```
  PLAN_END_DATE       DECIMAL(6,0)          PLNEND         Y
  ACTUAL_END          DECIMAL(6,0)          ACTEND         Y
  PROJECT             CHAR(20)              PROJECT        Y
.............................................................
           ** REQUIRED FIELDS **
 OPTION                    VALUE/DEFAULT
 DATA=                     SASIN.PROJINFO
 TABLE=                    TSID123.PROJINFO
 SSID=                     DBT
.............................................................
           ** OPTIONAL FIELDS **
 OPTION                    VALUE/DEFAULT
 IN=                       TSID123.SAMPLE
 SQLIN=                    *** NOT ENTERED ***
 SQLOUT=                   *** NOT ENTERED ***
 MAPIN=                    *** NOT ENTERED ***
 MAPOUT=                   *** NOT ENTERED ***
 ERROR=                    SAS LOG
 COMMIT=                   000003
 LIMIT=                    005000
 LOAD=                     LOAD ENTERED
.............................................................
15          LIST ALL OPTIONS;
.............................................................
     LOAD STATISTICS:
NUMBER OF ROWS INSERTED    =              19
NUMBER OF SAS OBS READ     =              19
NUMBER OF INSERTS REJECTED =               0
.............................................................
```

The REPLACE, TYPE, and NULLS statements were used to define the map rather than letting the DB2 column names be the SAS variable names, the DB2 data types be FLOAT for the numeric variables, and to disallow NULL values for the name variables. If a map had been used as input, these statements would not have to be coded. The LIST statement is used with the ALL option to display the mapping information. The OPTIONS option is also used to display the values of the PROC DB2LOAD options used.

The PROC DB2LOAD step in this example and the previous example could be executed in a single batch program with two PROC DB2LOAD steps.

Maps and SQL Statements

When PROC DB2LOAD is used to create and load a DB2 table from data stored in a SAS data set, it is based on a SAS data set containing data, a SAS data set containing mapping specifications, and the SQL statements, CREATE, INSERT, and COMMIT. The previous section illustrated the use of only a SAS data set containing data as input to PROC DB2LOAD.

If a map is used as input, it was created from a previous execution of PROC DB2LOAD, probably in Display Manager, and saved as a SAS data set in a SAS data library. To use the map as input, it is specified in the MAPIN option of the PROC DB2LOAD statement. The map will have a two-level SAS data set name, where the first level refers to a DD in the JCL pointing to the SAS data library, and the second level is the name of the map. When a map is used as input, the SAS data set containing data must also be used as input because the map does not contain data values. The map contains SAS variable names and their corresponding DB2 information: column names, data types, and whether NULLS are allowed. The map and the SAS data set containing data can be used to create and load a DB2 table, but can also be used to create and save SQL statements.

Maps can be used in several subsequent executions of PROC DB2LOAD even though the input SAS data set may contain and probably does contain different variable values. As long as the definition of the SAS data set is the same, including the same SAS variable names, data types, and lengths, then a map created from the SAS data set will be the same.

Maps are most often created in Display Manager to take advantage of the panels and ease of use offered in that environment. Often, the DB2 table cannot be created and loaded in Display Manager due to limited computer resources, but a map can always be created and saved in Display Manager. If the map turns out not to be quite what you wanted, you can also modify it in Display Manager. Although PROC DB2LOAD can be used to create and save maps in a batch program, it is not very practical. To save a map in the batch execution of PROC DB2LOAD, the DELETE, REPLACE, TYPE, and NULLS statements are used. If these have to be coded, you could just as easily use them in subsequent executions of PROC DB2LOAD. Therefore, the illustration shown in this section will use a map created in PROC DB2LOAD in Display Manager as input to

PROC DB2LOAD in batch. Creating and saving a map as output from PROC DB2LOAD in batch will not be shown.

If SQL statements are used as input, the SQL statements, CREATE, INSERT, and COMMIT are used. The CREATE statement creates the DB2 table. INSERT statements exist for every observation on the SAS data set used to create the saved SQL statements. These INSERT statements contain the variable values from this SAS data set. By default, a COMMIT statement exists for every 3 INSERT statements and causes those inserts to be saved to the output DB2 table. The COMMIT option can be used to control the number of INSERT statements for every COMMIT statement. Because an INSERT statement exists for every SAS observation and because they contain variable values, the size of the external file used to store the saved SQL statements can be quite large.

SQL statements were created and saved in a previous execution of PROC DB2LOAD, probably in Display Manager. These SQL statements are stored in an external file, usually as a member of a partitioned data set. To use the SQL statements as input, the external file is specified in the SQLIN option of the PROC DB2LOAD statement. If the JCL specifications for the external file containing the SQL statements include the member name of a partitioned data set, only the ddname used in the JCL is coded in the SQLIN option. If the JCL specification does not include the member name, then the SQLIN option includes the ddname used in the JCL followed by a period (.) and the member name.

When SQL statements are used as input, they are the sole input to PROC DB2LOAD. The INSERT statements contain the data values, so the SAS data set containing those data values is not required. The SQL statements also contain the name of the DB2 table to be created. Therefore, the DATA and TABLE options of the PROC DB2LOAD statement are not used when the SQLIN option is used. When SQL statements are used as input to PROC DB2LOAD, the only output file which can result is a DB2 table.

SQL statements will probably be used in only one subsequent execution of PROC DB2LOAD because the INSERT statements contain data values which will most likely change. Since the SAS data set containing the data used to create and save these SQL statements is available, it is normally used as input along with a map or the REPLACE, TYPE, and NULL statements rather than creating and saving SQL statements. The illustration shown in this section will use SQL statements created in PROC DB2LOAD in Display Manager as input to PROC DB2LOAD in batch. Creating and saving SQL statements as output from PROC DB2LOAD in batch will not be shown.

Example 9-3

The map saved in Example 8-4, in Chapter 8, PROC DB2LOAD in Display Manager, section, Maps and SQL Statements, is used as input to PROC DB2LOAD in a batch program to create and load a DB2 table.

The following SAS log shows the PROC DB2LOAD step used for this purpose:

```
1
2     PROC DB2LOAD DATA=SASIN1.PROJINFO TABLE=TSID123.PROJINFO
3                  MAPIN = SASIN2.PRJMAP LOAD;
4       IN 'TSID123.SAMPLE';
-------- MAP FOR CREATE AND LOAD --------------------------
  COLUMN NAME        DB2 FORMAT            SAS NAME    NULLS?
  LAST_NAME          CHAR(15)              LNAME         Y
  FIRST_NAME         CHAR(10)              FNAME         Y
  BEGIN_DATE         DECIMAL(6,0)          BEGDTE        Y
  PLAN_END_DATE      DECIMAL(6,0)          PLNEND        Y
  ACTUAL_END         DECIMAL(6,0)          ACTEND        Y
  PROJECT            CHAR(20)              PROJECT       Y
.............................................................
           ** REQUIRED FIELDS **
 OPTION                   VALUE/DEFAULT
 DATA=                    SASIN1.PROJINFO
 TABLE=                   TSID123.PROJINFO
 SSID=                    DBT
.............................................................
           ** OPTIONAL FIELDS **
 OPTION                   VALUE/DEFAULT
 IN=                      TSID123.SAMPLE
 SQLIN=                   *** NOT ENTERED ***
 SQLOUT=                  *** NOT ENTERED ***
 MAPIN=                   SASIN2.PRJMAP
 MAPOUT=                  *** NOT ENTERED ***
 ERROR=                   SAS LOG
 COMMIT=                  000003
 LIMIT=                   005000
 LOAD=                    LOAD ENTERED
.............................................................
 5          LIST ALL OPTIONS;
 6
.............................................................
```

```
      LOAD STATISTICS:
NUMBER OF ROWS INSERTED    =             19
NUMBER OF SAS OBS READ     =             19
NUMBER OF INSERTS REJECTED =              0
...........................................................
```

The required options, DATA, TABLE, MAPIN, and LOAD are used. The SSID option would also have to be coded if the default value in your company is not appropriate. The IN statement is also used to specify the tablespace to be used to store the resulting DB2 table. This tablespace must have been created prior to executing this PROC DB2LOAD step. This can be accomplished through a batch program using JCL tailored for your company, the SQL ENTRY/EDIT panels of PROC DB2LOAD or PROC DB2UTIL in Display Manager, or using the SQL statement in PROC DB2LOAD or PROC DB2TUTIL in a batch program. The LIST ALL statement displays mapping information and the OPTIONS option displays values of the PROC DB2LOAD options. The load statistics show that 19 SAS observations were loaded as 19 rows in the DB2 table.

Example 9-4

The SQL statements saved in Example 8-3, in Chapter 8, PROC DB2LOAD in Display Manager, section, Maps and SQL Statements, are used as input to PROC DB2LOAD in a batch program to create and load a DB2 table.

The following SAS log shows the PROC DB2LOAD step used for this purpose:

```
1
2    PROC DB2LOAD SQLIN=CODE.SQL1;
NOTE: FIELDS REQUIRED FOR LOAD WERE NOT ENTERED OR IN ERROR
...........................................................
      SQL STATISTICS:
NUMBER OF SQL STATEMENTS =               28
NUMBER REJECTED =                         0
...........................................................
```

The PROC DB2LOAD step specifies only the SQLIN option because the CREATE, INSERT, and COMMIT statements contain all the information neccessary to create and load the DB2 table. The load statistics show 28 SQL statements were executed. The 28 SQL statements consist of a CREATE statement, a COMMIT statement after the CREATE, 19 INSERT statements, a COMMIT for every 3 INSERT statements is 6 COMMITS, and a COMMIT after the last INSERT.

Chapter

10

PROC DB2UTIL in Display Manager

PROC DB2UTIL is used to update DB2 tables; new rows can be inserted, existing rows can be deleted, data values in existing rows can be changed, and new columns can be added. PROC DB2UTIL can also be used to execute utility-type SQL statements such as those used for creating an index or dropping a DB2 table.

When a DB2 table is updated, one of the following is used as input; a SAS data set, a map and a SAS data set, or one the SQL statements, INSERT, DELETE, UPDATE, or ALTER and UPDATE, along with the COMMIT statement. When new rows are inserted in a DB2 table, the INSERT and COMMIT statements are used. When existing rows are to be deleted, the DELETE and COMMIT statements are used. When existing data values are to be changed, the UPDATE and COMMIT statements are used. When new columns are added, a single ALTER statement is used with the UPDATE and COMMIT statements.

When only a SAS data set is used as input, a map is generated, and the map and the SAS data set generate the appropriate SQL statements. When a map created in a previous execution of PROC DB2UTIL is used as input, a SAS data set is usually also used as input to supply the data values for the INSERT or UPDATE statements or to specify criteria used in the DELETE statement. When SQL statements created in a previous execution of PROC DB2UTIL are used as input, they are the sole input to PROC DB2UTIL because they contain the specifications for updating the DB2 table and the values to be used. Whatever method of input is used, it is ultimately the SQL statements, INSERT, DELETE, UPDATE, or ALTER and UPDATE that update the DB2 table.

If a map or SQL statements are used as input to PROC DB2UTIL, they were usually created in a previous execution of PROC DB2UTIL in Display Manager to take advantage of the ease of use. These maps and SQL statements are typically used as input to PROC DB2UTIL in a batch program to update a DB2 table, due to computer resource limitations in Display Manager.

PROC DB2UTIL can also be used to execute SQL statements other than the INSERT, DELETE, UPDATE, ALTER, and COMMIT statements which are generated by the procedure. For example, PROC DB2TUIL could be used to create a tablespace, create an index, or drop a table. Although these statements can be executed in a variety of other ways, including using JCL tailored to your company, it is often convenient to execute them in the SAS environment to save you from exiting Display Manager, or from including multiple job steps in a batch program. Refer to Chapter 4, Structured Query Language, for documentation on the most commonly used SQL statements.

This chapter will present the use of PROC DB2UTIL in Display Manager to insert new rows in a DB2 table, delete existing rows from a DB2 table, update existing column values in a DB2 table, and add a new column to a DB2 table, in most cases using data stored in a SAS data set. Also shown are creating and saving SQL statements, and creating and saving a map. It is assumed that the user is already familiar with the operation of Display Manager and knows how to access it in his company. You will also need to know the value(s) of the DB2 SUBSYSTEM ID. Contact the SAS Consultant at your company for this information. An introduction to PROC DB2UTIL was given in Chapter 5, Introduction to SAS/DB2, and this material should be fresh in your mind before beginning this chapter.

PROC DB2UTIL is the most complicated of the three SAS/DB2 procedures. Not only is it complicated to use, but care should be taken when updating values in a table to insure the integrity of the data, including not only the data values but maintaining REFERENTIAL INTEGRITY in the DB2 system. Updating DB2 tables is usually handled by the DB2 Database Administrator, who is experienced in database management. SAS users will typically not perform this function.

Panels and commands used with PROC DB2UTIL that have already been discussed in Chapter 6, PROC DB2EXT in Display Manager, or in Chapter 8, PROC DB2LOAD in Display Manager will be listed and the user should refer to those chapters for a complete definition. All other panels and commands will be defined and illustrated.

Examples given in this section are based on the DB2 tables shown in Appendix C: Sample Tables. Refer to this appendix to familiarize yourself with the sample DB2 tables. You may choose to follow along in these examples by performing the same operations on the mainframe at your company. These DB2 tables can be entered on your mainframe, or refer to Chapter 1, Introduction, for ordering a copy of these tables.

Before executing PROC DB2UTIL in Display Manager, any input or output files needed should be allocated using the TSO allocate statement. Refer to Chapter 6, PROC DB2EXT in Display Manager, for information concerning the TSO allocate statement.

Input files used with PROC DB2UTIL include SAS data sets containing data which will be used to update a DB2 table or SAS data sets containing mapping instructions. SQL statements stored in an external file, usually a partitioned data set, can also be used as input to PROC DB2UTIL. These SQL statements could be the INSERT, DELETE, UPDATE, or ALTER and UPDATE statements used to update a DB2 table or they could be SQL statements which perform specific operations such as dropping a table or creating a tablespace.

Output files used with PROC DB2UTIL include SAS data sets containing mapping instructions, the SQL statements (INSERT, DELETE, UPDATE, or ALTER and UPDATE) which will be used to update a DB2 table, an error file to store SQL errors, or the updated DB2 table.

After coding the appropriate TSO allocate statements in the PROGRAM window of Display Manager and submitting them, you are ready to access PROC DB2UTIL. To access the panel system of PROC DB2UTIL, submit the following statements from the PROGRAM window of Display Manager:

```
PROC DB2UTIL; RUN;
```

In Release 5.16 of SAS/DB2, missing values in SAS variables cannot be inserted into a DB2 column that was created as NOT NULL. In Release 5.18 of SAS/DB2, missing numeric values are inserted as zero and missing character values are inserted as blanks when the

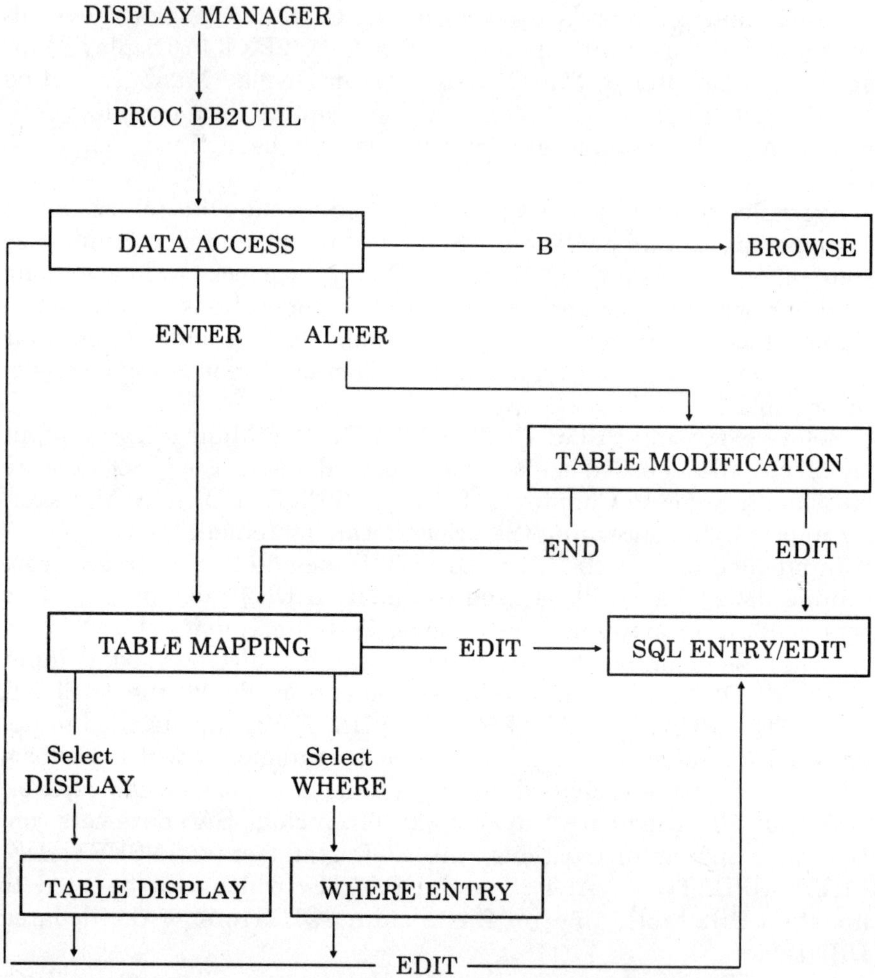

Figure 10-1 Relationship of panels in PROC DB2UTIL.

DB2 column is defined as NOT NULL. In either Release 5.16 or 5.18, missing values in SAS variables are inserted as NULL if the DB2 column is defined as NULL.

The panels in PROC DB2UTIL and their relationship are shown in Figure 10-1.

PROC DB2UTIL has nine panels. The KEYS and HELP panels are not shown on this diagram, but are the same as PROC DB2EXT and can be accessed from any of the panels shown here. The arrows depict the flow going into these panels. The commands or actions to move to these panels are also shown.

The first panel accessed when PROC DB2UTIL is executed is normally the DATA ACCESS panel. Hitting enter on the DATA ACCESS panel brings up the TABLE MAPPING panel. The TABLE MAPPING, TABLE DISPLAY, and WHERE ENTRY panels are jointly referred to as the TABLE MAPPING panels. The DISPLAY and WHERE values can be entered in the Select field on the TABLE MAPPING panel to bring up the TABLE DISPLAY and the WHERE ENTRY panels, respectively. If DELETE was entered in the Function field on the DATA ACCESS panel, hitting enter will bring up the WHERE ENTRY panel rather than the TABLE MAPPING panel. The MAP and DISPLAY values can be entered in the Select field on the WHERE ENTRY panel to bring up the TABLE MAPPING panel and the TABLE DISPLAY panel, respectively.

The ALTER command takes you from the DATA ACCESS panel to the TABLE MODIFICATION panel. The END command is used from the TABLE MODIFICATION panel to access the TABLE MAPPING panel.

The EDIT command can be issued from the DATA ACCESS, TABLE MODIFICATION, TABLE MAPPING, TABLE DISPLAY, and WHERE ENTRY to bring up a blank SQL ENTRY/EDIT panel. The SQL ENTRY/EDIT panel is used to execute utility-type SQL statements such as dropping a table or creating a tablespace. These SQL statements are often coded in the SQL ENTRY/EDIT panel, but can also be included from an external file. The EDIT command should be issued without entering any information on any of the prior panels because any entries will not be saved. The SQL statements, INSERT, DELETE, UPDATE, or ALTER and UPDATE used to update a DB2 table are typically not edited, and therefore are not displayed in the SQL ENTRY/EDIT panel.

Although not shown, the KEYS command or the HELP command can be specified in any of the six other panels in order to bring up the KEYS or HELP panels.

The panels are exited by the END command and will return you to the previous panel. When the END command is issued from the TABLE MAPPING panel, the following message is displayed under the command line:

```
NOTE: XXXX SQL CALL(S) WILL BE EXECUTED, ENTER UPDATE TO
      CONTINUE OR ENTER (END) AGAIN TO ONLY PROCESS SQLOUT
      AND/OR MAP OUTPUTS.
```

XXXX is a number representing the number of SQL statements that will be executed. If the END command is issued again, only a map or SQL statements will be saved to an output file. If an output map or SQL file was not specified on the DATA ACCESS panel, issuing the END command returns the user to the DATA ACCESS panel, without creating an output file. If the UPDATE command is issued instead of the END command, the user will be returned to the DATA ACCESS panel and the DB2 table will be updated. When the END command is issued from the SQL ENTRY/EDIT panel, the SQL statements which were entered or included from an external file are executed immediately, and you are returned to the previous panel. When you have returned to the DATA ACCESS panel, the B or BROWSE command can be used to browse the mapping SAS data set just created, if one was created. The END command used from the DATA ACCESS panel will return you to Display Manager.

The DB2TUIL panels are described briefly below:

• DATA ACCESS:	specify input/output files
• TABLE MODIFICATION:	add new column to DB2 table
• TABLE MAPPING:	map SAS variables to DB2 columns
• TABLE DISPLAY:	list DB2 columns on table
• WHERE ENTRY:	map SAS observations to DB2 rows and specifies update criteria
• BROWSE:	browse mapping SAS data set created
• SQL ENTRY/EDIT:	coded or included SQL statements
• HELP:	display help information
• KEYS:	display/change commands assigned to function keys

The primary panels of PROC DB2UTIL are the DATA ACCESS, TABLE MODIFICATION, TABLE MAPPING, TABLE DISPLAY, WHERE ENTRY, and the SQL ENTRY/EDIT. The BROWSE, HELP, and KEYS panels serve support functions. The DATA ACCESS, TABLE MODIFICATION, TABLE MAPPING, TABLE DISPLAY, and WHERE ENTRY panels are described below. The other panels are the same as those used with PROC DB2EXT. Refer to Chapter 6, PROC DB2EXT in Display Manager, for information concerning these panels.

When new rows are inserted in a table, the DATA ACCESS, the TABLE MAPPING, and optionally, the TABLE DISPLAY panel is used. When rows are deleted from a table, the DATA ACCESS, the WHERE ENTRY, and optionally, the TABLE MAPPING and TABLE DISPLAY panels are used. When data values are to be changed in a

DB2 table, the DATA ACCESS, the TABLE MAPPING, the WHERE ENTRY, and optionally, the TABLE DISPLAY panel is used. When a new column is added to a table, the DATA ACCESS, the TABLE MODIFICATION, the TABLE MAPPING, the WHERE ENTRY, and optionally, the TABLE DISPLAY panel is used.

DATA ACCESS Panel

The DATA ACCESS panel is the first panel to be displayed when PROC DB2UTIL is executed from Display Manager. This panel can be skipped if the DATA, TABLE, and FUNCTION options (and SSID option if other than default) of the PROC DB2UTIL statement are coded when PROC DB2UTIL is submitted from the PROGRAM window.

The DATA ACCESS panel is used to specify input and output files. Input files specified on the DATA ACCESS panel include a SAS data set containing data and a SAS data set containing mapping instructions. When SQL statements are used as input they are included in the SQL ENTRY/EDIT panel. The output files specified on the DATA ACCESS panel include a DB2 table, a mapping SAS data set, and a external file containing SQL statements, and an external file to store SQL errors.

The END command is used to exit the DATA ACCESS panel and return to Display Manager.

The DATA ACCESS panel is shown in Figure 10-2.

```
                          DB2 INTERFACE
                        DATA ACCESS PANEL


COMMAND===>
FILL IN THE FIELDS BELOW

INPUT SAS DATA SET:                                   COMMIT:    3
TABLE NAME:                                           LIMIT:     5000
FUNCTION:                                   CORRELATION NAME:
SUBSYSTEM ID:

MAP DATA SET:                             I=INPUT;O=OUTPUT:
OUTPUT SQL LIBRARY:                       ERROR LOG FILE:
```

Figure 10-2 PROC DB2UTIL DATA ACCESS Panel.

The following describes each of the fields on the DATA ACCESS panel. Each description is labeled optional or required to indicate whether a value is required.

INPUT SAS DATA SET (required): The input SAS data set is the name of the SAS data set which will be used to update the DB2 table. A SAS data set is required no matter which of the possible output files are being created: a map, an external file containing SQL statements, or a DB2 table.

TABLE NAME (required); The table name is the name of the DB2 table which will be updated using data stored in a SAS data set. The DB2 table name is required no matter which of the possible output files are being created: a map, a partitioned data set containing SQL statements, or a DB2 table.

COMMIT (required): A DB2 table is updated using one of the SQL statements, INSERT, DELETE, UPDATE, or ALTER and UPDATE. The number specified in the COMMIT field specifies the number of rows changed by the INSERT, DELETE, or UPDATE statements before they are saved to the DB2 table and the changes made available to other applications. The default value is 3.

LIMIT (required): This is the maximum number of SQL INSERT, DELETE, or UPDATE statements that are to be executed by PROC DB2UTIL. The default value is 5000. If the number of observations on the input SAS data set is greater than the limit set, a warning message will be issued and you are given the option of continuing. If LIMIT is set to 0, no limit is set.

FUNCTION (required): When a DB2 table is updated, only one function can be performed in a single execution of PROC DB2UTIL. Rows can be added using the SQL INSERT statement, rows can be deleted using the SQL DELETE statement, values of existing columns can be changed using the SQL UPDATE statement, or new columns can be added using the SQL ALTER and UPDATE statments. Enter the appropriate SQL statement, INSERT, DELETE, or UPDATE in the FUNCTION field. If a new column is added, the UPDATE function is used.

CORRELATION NAME (optional); The value entered here can be used with the name of the DB2 column in the WHERE clause to indicate the current value of that column. This option is rarely used.

SUBSYSTEM ID (required): This field is the same as used with PROC DB2EXT or PROC DB2LOAD. Refer to Chapter 6,

PROC DB2EXT in Display Manager, for the definition of this field.

MAP DATA SET (optional): If a mapping SAS data set is to be used as input or output to PROC DB2UTIL, enter the name of the map in this field.

I=INPUT;O=OUTPUT (optional): If a mapping SAS data set is to be used as input or output to PROC DB2UTIL, this option is used to specify whether the map is to be used as input (I) or output (O). This field can also be set to I to update the map and update the DB2 table. Make changes to the map in the TABLE MAPPING panels and issue the END command to exit the TABLE MAPPING panel rather than the UPDATE command. If the UPDATE command is used, any changes made to the map will be saved and the DB2 table will be updated.

OUTPUT SQL LIBRARY (optional); The output SQL library is used when you want to save the SQL statements, INSERT, DELETE, UPDATE, or ALTER and UPDATE, used to update a DB2 table, to an external file. The external file is often a partitioned data set. The data set must have been allocated using a TSO allocate in Display Manager prior to bringing up the DATA ACCESS panel. If the TSO allocate statement included the member name, then only the ddname needs to be specified. If the TSO allocate did not include the member name, specify ddname.member, where ddname is the ddname used in the TSO allocate statement and member is a new member to be created. If a member that already exists is specified, that member will be replaced.

ERROR LOG FILE (optional): PROC DB2UTIL uses the SQL INSERT, DELETE, UPDATE, or ALTER and UPDATE statements to update a DB2 table. If these statements contain SQL errors, the error messages are written to the SAS log. Since an SQL statement often exists for every observation on the SAS data set used as input, the number of SQL statements executed may be quite large, and thus the number of SQL errors generated can also be quite large. The ERROR LOG FILE can be used to route any SQL errors, along with the SQL statement that produced the error, to an external file rather than the SAS log. If errors are written to the SAS log, the SQL statements that generated the errors are not shown on the SAS log. Therefore, it will probably be easier to diagnose errors when the ERROR LOG FILE is used. This file is usually a partitioned data set.

The ERROR LOG FILE must be allocated using a TSO allocate in Display Manager prior to bringing up the DATA ACCESS panel. If the TSO allocate statement included the member name, then only the ddname needs to be specified. If the TSO allocate did not include the member name, specify ddname.member, where ddname is the ddname used in the TSO allocate statement and member is a new member to be created. If a member that already exists is specified, that member will be replaced.

TABLE MODIFICATION Panel

After the input SAS data set, the table name, the UPDATE function, and the subsystem ID (if default is not appropriate) are completed on the DATA ACCESS panel, the ALTER command will bring up the TABLE MODIFICATION panel.

The TABLE MODIFICATION panel is used to add a new column(s) to a DB2 table. The name(s) of the new DB2 columns are entered along with their data type. When the TABLE MODIFICATION panel is complete, the END command is issued and the TABLE MAPPING panel is displayed. This panel is used to indicate the SAS variable(s) whose values will be used to load the new DB2 column(s). The WHERE entry panel is used when the input SAS data set contains more than one observation to match SAS observations with the appropriate DB2 row. When the TABLE MAPPING and WHERE entry panels are complete, the UPDATE command (rather than the END command) is issued to update the DB2 table.

The TABLE MODIFICATION panel is shown in Figure 10-3.

ALTER TABLE: The value shown in this field is the name of the DB2 table to be updated and is carried from the DATA ACCESS panel.

DISPLAY: When the TABLE MODIFICATION panel is displayed, the DISPLAY field is set to N. The columns, COLUMN NAME and DATA TYPE are blank, to be used to enter new DB2 columns and their data types. When DISPLAY is set to Y, the existing DB2 columns in the table specified on the DATA ACCESS panel are displayed along with their data types. They are denoted as existing columns to the right of the data type.

```
                         DB2 INTERFACE
                   TABLE MODIFICATION PANEL


COMMAND===>


    ALTER TABLE: TSID123.PROJINFO        DISPLAY:  N
COLUMN NAME                        DATA TYPE
..................                 ...............
..................                 ...............
..................                 ...............
..................                 ...............
..................                 ...............
..................                 ...............
..................                 ...............
..................                 ...............
..................                 ...............
..................                 ...............
..................                 ...............
..................                 ...............
..................                 ...............
..................                 ...............
```

Figure 10-3 PROC DB2UTIL TABLE MODIFICATION Panel.

COLUMN NAME: This field is used to enter new DB2 column names. If DISPLAY is set to Y, existing DB2 column names for the table specified on the DATA ACCESS panel will also be displayed.

DATA TYPE: This field is used to enter the data types for new DB2 columns added in the COLUMN NAME field. If you wish to assign a DB2 date/time data type, the SAS variable used to insert values into this column must be stored as a SAS date/time value. Refer to Chapter 3, IBM'S Database 2, the section, Data Types, for more information about DB2 data types. If DISPLAY is set to Y, existing DB2 columns for the table specified on the DATA ACCESS panel will be displayed, along with their data types.

TABLE MAPPING Panels

The TABLE MAPPING panels consist of three panels, the TABLE MAPPING panel, the TABLE DISPLAY panel, and the WHERE ENTRY panel. When the DATA ACCESS panel is complete, hitting enter will bring up the TABLE MAPPING panel, unless the DELETE function was entered on the DATA ACCESS panel. In that case the WHERE ENTRY panel is displayed.

The TABLE DISPLAY panel is used to "map" SAS variables to DB2 columns. The SAS variables on the input SAS data set are displayed on the TABLE MAPPING panel and the user must specify the corresponding DB2 columns that are needed depending on the function entered on the DATA ACCESS panel and the requirements of the application. If the INSERT function is specified on the DATA ACCESS panel, new row(s) are to be added to the DB2 table. In order to add new rows, each DB2 column must be mapped to a SAS variable in the SAS data set containing the new rows. If the UPDATE function is specified on the DATA ACCESS panel, value(s) in DB2 column(s) can be changed using values in a SAS data set. In order to make these changes, the DB2 column(s) being changed must be mapped to a SAS variable in the input SAS data set. Also, if the UPDATE function is specified on the DATA ACCESS panel, new column(s) can be added to the table. The name of the new DB2 column(s) must be specified for the corresponding SAS variable(s) on the input SAS data set. If the DELETE function is specified on the DATA ACCESS panel, existing row(s) in the DB2 table are to be deleted. In order to delete these rows, the delete condition specified in the WHERE clause may require some mapping of DB2 columns to variables in the input SAS data set.

To specify the DB2 columns to be mapped to SAS variables on the input SAS data set, the user must know the DB2 column name or the number representing the position of the column in the table. This information is provided on the TABLE DISPLAY panel. The DB2 column name or number shown on this panel can be entered on the TABLE MAPPING panel for the corresponding SAS variable. The TABLE DISPLAY panel is just for displaying this information, no entries are made on this panel.

When the functions UPDATE or DELETE are specified on the DATA ACCESS panel, a WHERE clause is usually needed to specify a condition to update or delete. This condition is entered in the WHERE ENTRY panel. The word, WHERE, is not entered.

The SELECT field on the three TABLE MAPPING panels is used to bring up another TABLE MAPPING panel. Often, the user will prefer to display two or three of the TABLE MAPPING panels simultaneously. If this is the case, enter the appropriate SELECT value and place the cursor the desired location on the screen and hit enter.

When the TABLE MAPPING panels are complete, the END command issued from the TABLE MAPPING panel will create and save an output map or SQL statements. The UPDATE command issued from the TABLE MAPPING panel will alter the DB2 table.

TABLE MAPPING Panel

The TABLE MAPPING panel is shown in Figure 10-4.

```
                DB2 INTERFACE                   DB2 TABLE- TSID123.PROJINFO
            TABLE MAPPING PANEL                 SAS DATA SET- SASIN.PROJIN
  COMMAND===>                                          SELECT: MAP

              MAPTO COLUMN                 SAS NAME      FORMAT
              ..................            LNAME        $15.
              ..................            FNAME        $10.
              ..................            BEGDTE       8.
              ..................            PLNEND       8.
              ..................            ACTEND       8.
              ..................            PROJECT      $20.
```

Figure 10-4 PROC DB2UTIL TABLE MAPPING Panel.

The SAS data set shown is Projinfo. The SAS variables shown here are specifically for that SAS data set and this panel will vary depending on the input SAS data set.

DB2 TABLE: This is the name of the DB2 table to be updated and was specified on the DATA ACCESS panel.

SAS DATA SET: This is the name of the SAS data set containing data which will be used to alter the DB2 table. This SAS data set was specified on the DATA ACCESS panel.

SELECT: The SELECT field is used to bring up the type of TABLE MAPPING panel named, MAP (shown here), DISPLAY, or WHERE. If the cursor is on the SELECT field when enter is hit, the TABLE MAPPING panel specified in the SELECT option will be displayed as a full screen. If the cursor is somewhere else on the screen when enter is hit, the screen will be split at that location, displaying more than one TABLE MAPPING panel. All three TABLE MAPPING panels can be displayed simultaneously.

MAPTO COLUMN: The MAPTO COLUMN is used to enter the name of the DB2 column which is to be updated using the SAS variable shown in the SAS NAME column. If the DB2 column name is not known, the TABLE DISPLAY panel can be used to list the columns on the DB2 table specified on the DATA ACCESS panel. The number corresponding to the DB2 column, shown on the TABLE DISPLAY panel, can be entered rather than the full DB2 column name. If the same DB2 column name or number is entered for different SAS NAMES, the SAS variable values will be concatenated in the order they are displayed and the result used to update the DB2 table.

SAS NAME: This column lists the SAS variables stored on the SAS data set specified on the DATA ACCESS panel. This column cannot be changed by the user.

FORMAT: This is the SAS format for the SAS variables listed in the SAS NAME column. This column cannot be changed by the user.

TABLE DISPLAY Panel

The TABLE DISPLAY panel is shown in Figure 10-5.

```
          DB2 INTERFACE                    DB2 TABLE- TSID123.PROJINFO
       TABLE DISPLAY PANEL                 SAS DATA SET- SASIN.PROJIN
COMMAND===>                                       SELECT: DISPLAY

         NUM    COLUMN                   TYPE
         001    LAST_NAME                CHAR(15)
         002    FIRST_NAME               CHAR(10)
         003    BEGIN_DATE               DECIMAL(6,0)
         004    PLAN_END_DATE            DECIMAL(6,0)
         005    ACTUAL_END_DATE          DECIMAL(6,0)
         006    PROJECT                  CHAR(20)
```

Figure 10-5 PROC DB2UTIL TABLE DISPLAY Panel.

The DB2 table shown above is Tsid123.Projinfo, used in previous examples. The DB2 columns shown here are specifically for that DB2 table and this panel will vary depending on the DB2 table.

DB2 TABLE: Same as defined for Table Mapping Panel.
SAS DATA SET: Same as defined for Table Mapping Panel.
SELECT: Same as defined for the Table Mapping Panel.
NUM: This number represents the order the DB2 columns are stored on the DB2 table. This number can be entered on the TABLE MAPPING panel to map the corresponding DB2 column to the desired SAS variable rather than entering the complete DB2 column name.
COLUMN: The DB2 columns stored on the DB2 table specified on the DATA ACCESS panel are listed here.
TYPE: This is the data type for the DB2 column shown in the COLUMN list.

WHERE ENTRY Panel

The WHERE ENTRY panel is shown in Figure 10-6.

```
          DB2 INTERFACE                  DB2 TABLE- TSID123.PROJINFO
      DB2 WHERE ENTRY PANEL              SAS DATA SET- SASIN.PROJIN
COMMAND===>                                        SELECT: WHERE

 DB2 WHERE STATEMENT:
```

Figure 10-6 PROC DB2UTIL WHERE ENTRY Panel.

DB2 TABLE: Same as defined for Table Mapping Panel.
SAS DATA SET: Same as defined for Table Mapping Panel.
SELECT: Same as defined for the Table Mapping Panel.

DB2 WHERE STATEMENT: When the UPDATE or DELETE function is specified on the DATA ACCESS panel, a WHERE condition will usually be needed to specify when a DB2 column is to be updated or when a DB2 row is to be deleted. The WHERE statement can contain DB2 column names, constants, arithmetic expressions, and SAS variable names. SAS variables are denoted by a preceding % sign and are resolved to their value before the WHERE condition is executed.

Function Key Definitions

Table 10-1 summarizes the function key definitions for each of the PROC DB2UTIL panels. A definition of these commands is given in the next section, Commands.

The function key definitions for the DATA ACCESS, TABLE MODIFICATION, and the three TABLE MAPPING panels are the same. However, not all commands are valid in all panels. The commands shown above for the DATA ACCESS, TABLE MODIFICATION, TABLE MAPPING, TABLE DISPLAY, and WHERE ENTRY panels are commands that are actually valid in these panels. The BROWSE, SQL ENTRY/EDIT, HELP, and KEYS function key defini-

Table 10-1 Function Key Definitions by Panel.

Function Key	Data Access	Table Modification	Table Mapping	Table Display	Where Entry
1,13	HELP	HELP	HELP	HELP	HELP
2,14	ALTER				
3,15	END	END (MAP)	END	END (MAP)	END (MAP)
4,16	EXIT	EXIT	EXIT	EXIT	EXIT
5,17	BROWSE				
6,18	KEYS	KEYS	KEYS	KEYS	KEYS
7,19		BACKWARD	BACKWARD	BACKWARD	BACKWARD
8,20		FORWARD	FORWARD	FORWARD	FORWARD
9,21		RESET	RESET		RESET
10,22		QUIT (DA)	QUIT (DA)	QUIT (DA)	QUIT (DA)
11,23	EDIT	EDIT	EDIT	EDIT	EDIT
12,24					

tions are not shown, but are the same as PROC DB2EXT and PROC DB2LOAD.

Commands shown followed by parentheses indicate the panel that is displayed when the command is issued. MAP refers to the TABLE MAPPING panel and DA to the DATA ACCESS panel.

Commands

Table 10-2 outlines the commands which are valid in the PROC DB2UTIL panels. Following this chart, a definition of each command is given. If the definition of this command is the same as it is with PROC DB2EXT or PROC DB2LOAD, it is so noted and you should refer to Chapter 6, PROC DB2EXT in Display Manager, or Chapter 8, PROC DB2LOAD in Display Manager for the definition. Commands for the BROWSE, SQL ENTRY/EDIT, HELP, and KEYS pan-

Table 10-2 Valid command by PROC DB2UTIL Panel.

	DATA ACCESS	TABLE MODIFICATION	TABLE MAPPING	TABLE DISPLAY	WHERE ENTRY
ALTER	X				
BACKWARD		X	X	X	X
BROWSE	X				
COMPRESS			X	X	
EDIT	X	X	X	X	X
END	X	X	X*	X	X
EXIT	X	X	X	X	X
FORWARD		X	X	X	X
HELP	X	X	X	X	X
KEYS	X	X	X	X	X
RESET		X	X		X
UPDATE			X		

* The END command issued from this panel may cause an action in addition to exiting to occur. Refer to the definition of the END command which follows for more information.

els are not shown, but are the same as those used with PROC DB2EXT and PROC DB2LOAD.

Some of these commands are defined as function keys. Refer to the previous section, Function Key Definitions, for the definition of function keys.

ALTER (DATA ACCESS): This command can be issued from the DATA ACCESS panel to bring up the TABLE MODIFICATION panel, which is used to add new column(s) to a DB2 table.

BACKWARD (TABLE MODIFICATION, TABLE MAPPING, TABLE DISPLAY, WHERE ENTRY, BROWSE, SQL ENTRY/EDIT, HELP, KEYS): Refer to Chapter 6, PROC DB2EXT in Display Manager.

BROWSE (DATA ACCESS): Refer to Chapter 8, PROC DB2LOAD in Display Manager.

COMPRESS (TABLE MAPPING, TABLE DISPLAY) When this command is issued, two displays of columns are shown on one screen, providing the user with more fields that can be entered (MAPPING) or more fields displayed (DISPLAY). This command is issued a second time to return the screen display to its original form.

EDIT (DATA ACCESS, TABLE MODIFICATION, TABLE MAPPING, TABLE DISPLAY, WHERE ENTRY): The EDIT command issued from one of these panels displays a blank SQL ENTRY/EDIT panel. SQL commands can be entered here or included from an external file, usually a partitioned data set. Included SQL statements can be edited as desired. The END command returns the user to the previous panel and executes the SQL statements.

END (DATA ACCESS, TABLE MODIFICATION, TABLE DISPLAY, WHERE ENTRY, SQL ENTRY/EDIT, BROWSE, HELP, KEYS): The END command is used to exit the panels listed above. The function keys, PF3/PF15, are usually used instead of the END command. The END command will return you to the previous panel. If you are in the SQL ENTRY/EDIT panel, the SQL statements will be executed at this time. If the END command is issued from the TABLE MAPPING panel, maps or SQL statements are saved. The UPDATE command must be used from the TABLE MAPPING panel to alter a DB2 table.

When the END command is issued, the panels are checked for errors. If an error is present, an error message will be displayed. The error must be corrected before the END command will return the user to the previous panel.

EXIT (DATA ACCESS, TABLE MODIFICATION, TABLE MAPPING, TABLE DISPLAY, WHERE ENTRY): The EXIT command or the PF4/PF16 function keys used in the DATA ACCESS or any of the TABLE MAPPING panels returns the user to Display Manager without executing PROC DB2UTIL.

FORWARD (TABLE MODIFICATION, TABLE MAPPING, TABLE DISPLAY, WHERE ENTRY, SQL ENTRY/EDIT, BROWSE, HELP, KEYS): Refer to Chapter 6, PROC DB2EXT in Display Manager.

HELP (DATA ACCESS, TABLE MODIFICATION, TABLE MAPPING, TABLE DISPLAY, WHERE ENTRY, SQL ENTRY/EDIT, BROWSE): This command is used to bring up the HELP panel. The corresponding function key, PF1/PF13, can be used rather than the HELP command. The HELP information displayed depends on the panel the command was issued from. Help for PROC DB2UTIL can be accessed by issuing the HELP command from the DATA ACCESS, TABLE MODIFICATION, or any of the TABLE MAPPING panels.

KEYS (DATA ACCESS, TABLE MODIFICATION, TABLE MAPPING, TABLE DISPLAY, WHERE ENTRY, SQL ENTRY/EDIT, BROWSE): Refer to Chapter 6, PROC DB2EXT in Display Manager.

RESET (TABLE MODIFICATION, TABLE MAPPING, WHERE ENTRY): The RESET command clears all changes which have been made on these panels. PF9/PF21 function keys can be used to issue this command.

UPDATE (TABLE MAPPING): This command is used to execute the updates to the DB2 table. If the END command is used, only maps or SQL statements are saved.

Updating a DB2 Table

This section illustrates the use of PROC DB2UTIL in Display Manager to update a DB2 table using data stored in a SAS data set. Four examples are given to illustrate the four ways PROC DB2UTIL can be used to update a DB2 table: add rows, delete rows, change column values, and add a new column. The panels used with these illustrations include DATA ACCESS, TABLE MODIFICATION, TABLE MAPPING, TABLE DISPLAY, and WHERE ENTRY.

Example 10-1

A SAS data set, Projadd, contains observations representing a new project. These observations need to be added as new rows to the DB2 table, Tsid123.projinfo. The following shows the SAS data set, Projadd:

```
                              PROJADD

OBS  LNAME      FNAME        PROJECT          BEGDTE  PLNEND  ACTEND

 1   KEESLING   GERTRUDE  ACTUARIAL RATING  890101  900101    .
 2   CAMPBELL   MARGARET  ACTUARIAL RATING  890101  900101    .
 3   DUDLEY     LOUISA    ACTUARIAL RATING  890101  900101    .
 4   HOLLYWOOD  ALICE     ACTUARIAL RATING  890101  900101    .
 5   KAWAN      JOE       ACTUARIAL RATING  890101  900101    .
```

The SAS data set, Projadd, is stored permanently in a SAS data library. A TSO allocate statement is submitted for this SAS data library. Next, the PROC DB2UTIL and RUN statements are entered in the PROGRAM window for submission.

```
-------------------------------------------------------------------
COMMAND ===>                                    SAS(r) Log   HH:MM

NOTE: COPYRIGHT(C) 1984, 1988 SAS INSTITUTE INC., CARY, NC 27512
USA
NOTE: SAS RELEASE 5.18 AT COMPANY ABC (00000000).
NOTE: CPUID   VERSION = 00   SERIAL = 000000   MODEL = 0000 .
NOTE: SAS OPTIONS SPECIFIED ARE:
      DMS NONEWS FSP FS NODATE


  1  tso alloc dd(sasin) dsn('tsid123.sas.data') shr;
-------------------------------------------------------------------
COMMAND ===>                                       Program Editor

00001 proc db2util;
00002   run;
00003
00004
00005
```

The execution of PROC DB2UTIL brings up the DATA ACCESS panel shown below. The input SAS data set and the DB2 table to be updated are entered along with the function, INSERT. The SUBSYSTEM ID should be entered if the default is not appropriate.

```
                          DB2 INTERFACE
                        DATA ACCESS PANEL

COMMAND===>
FILL IN THE FIELDS BELOW

INPUT SAS DATA SET:   sasin.projadd                  COMMIT:    3
TABLE NAME:          tsid123.projinfo                LIMIT:     5000
FUNCTION:            insert               CORRELATION NAME:
SUBSYSTEM ID:        DBT

MAP DATA SET:                            I=INPUT;O=OUTPUT:
OUTPUT SQL LIBRARY:                      ERROR LOG FILE:
```

Hitting enter on the DATA ACCESS panel brings up the TABLE MAPPING panel. In order to add these SAS observations to the DB2 table, we need to specify which DB2 columns the values of the SAS variables should be placed in. To do this, the DB2 columns are specified in the MAPTO COLUMN. Most likely, the user will not know the DB2 column names or their position in the DB2 table. To obtain this information, the TABLE DISPLAY panel can be used. The SELECT field is changed to display and the cursor can be placed in the middle of the screen before hitting enter to display both the TABLE MAPPING panel and the TABLE DISPLAY panel simultaneously.

```
          DB2 INTERFACE                  DB2 TABLE- TSID123.PROJINFO
       TABLE MAPPING PANEL               SAS DATA SET- SASIN.PROJADD
COMMAND===>                                     SELECT: display

            MAPTO COLUMN           SAS NAME     FORMAT
            ..................      LNAME       $15.
            ..................      FNAME       $10.
            ..................      PROJECT     $20.
            ..................      BEGDTE      8.
            ..................      PLNEND      8.
            ..................      ACTEND      8.
```

The TABLE MAPPING and TABLE DISPLAY panels are now shown in split screen mode. Rather than entering the complete DB2 column name, the numbers (NUM) from the TABLE DISPLAY panel are entered on the appropriate line of the TABLE MAPPING panel.

```
          DB2 INTERFACE                  DB2 TABLE- TSID123.PROJINFO
       TABLE MAPPING PANEL               SAS DATA SET- SASIN.PROJADD
COMMAND===>                                     SELECT: MAP

            MAPTO COLUMN           SAS NAME     FORMAT
            1.................      LNAME       $15.
            2.................      FNAME       $10.
            6.................      PROJECT     $20.
            3.................      BEGDTE      8.
            4.................      PLNEND      8.
            5.................      ACTEND      8.

COMMAND===>                                     SELECT: DISPLAY

            NUM   COLUMN                TYPE


            001   LAST_NAME             CHAR(15)
            002   FIRST_NAME            CHAR(10)
            003   BEGIN_DATE            DECIMAL(6,0)
            004   PLAN_END_DATE         DECIMAL(6,0)
            005   ACTUAL_END_DATE       DECIMAL(6,0)
            006   PROJECT               CHAR(20)
```

Although not required, hitting enter on the TABLE MAPPING panel will display the DB2 column names in the MAPTO COLUMN rather than the numbers entered. If the END command were issued from the TABLE MAPPING panel, a message would be produced stating that the UPDATE command must be issued in order to update the DB2 table. The END command will result only in saving a map or SQL statements, if they were specified on the DATA ACCESS panel. The UPDATE command is entered to update the DB2 table.

```
          DB2 INTERFACE                DB2 TABLE- TSID123.PROJINFO
       TABLE MAPPING PANEL             SAS DATA SET- SASIN.PROJADD
COMMAND===> update                           SELECT: MAP

          MAPTO COLUMN          SAS NAME     FORMAT
          LAST_NAME.........     LNAME        $15.
          FIRST_NAME........     FNAME        $10.
          PROJECT...........     PROJECT      $20.
          BEGIN_DATE........     BEGDTE       8.
          PLAN_END_DATE.....     PLNEND       8.
          ACTUAL_END_DATE...     ACTEND       8.

COMMAND===>                                  SELECT: DISPLAY

          NUM    COLUMN                 TYPE
          001    LAST_NAME              CHAR(15)
          002    FIRST_NAME             CHAR(10)
          003    BEGIN_DATE             DECIMAL(6,0)
          004    PLAN_END_DATE          DECIMAL(6,0)
          005    ACTUAL_END_DATE        DECIMAL(6,0)
          006    PROJECT                CHAR(20)
```

The UPDATE command adds the new rows to the DB2 table and returns the user to the DATA ACCESS panel. The insert statistics show that 5 rows were added.

```
                          DB2 INTERFACE
                        DATA ACCESS PANEL

COMMAND===>

INPUT SAS DATA SET:    SASIN.PROJADD                COMMIT:    3
TABLE NAME:           TSID123.PROJINFO              LIMIT:     5000
FUNCTION:             INSERT              CORRELATION NAME:
SUBSYSTEM ID:         DBT


MAP DATA SET:                            I=INPUT;O=OUTPUT:
OUTPUT SQL LIBRARY:                      ERROR LOG FILE:

UTILITY STATISTICS: SQL INSERTS ISSUED =           5
                    NUMBER OF SAS OBS READ =       5
                    SQL STATEMENTS REJECTED =      0
```

PROC DB2EXT is used to create a SAS data set from the updated DB2 table, Tsid123.projinfo. This table had 19 observations and 5 were added. The BROWSE panel shows the 5 new rows. The column Actual_end_date contains missing values. If you scrolled to the right, you would see the value of the column, Project, is 'Actuarial Rating'.

```
                    SAS DATA SET: PROJINFO                OBSERVATIONS
COMMAND===>                                               FIRST      19
                                                          LAST       24
OBS  LAST_NAM      FIRST_NA         BEGIN_DA    PLAN_END     ACTUAL_E
 19  PALMER        NANCY              880815      881201       881215
 20  KEESLING      GERTRUDE           891001      900101            .
 21  CAMPBELL      MARGARET           891001      900101            .
 22  DUDLEY        LOUISA             891001      900101            .
 23  HOLLYWOOD     ALICE              891001      900101            .
 24  KAWAN         JOE                891001      900101            .
```

Example 10-2

All projects which have an Actual_end_date prior to 890101 are to be deleted from the DB2 table, Tsid123.projinfo.

An input SAS data set is not actually needed to delete these rows, an SQL DELETE statement could be coded in the SQL ENTRY/EDIT panel and executed. The WHERE condition can also be entered in the WHERE ENTRY panel. However, to bring up the TABLE MAPPING panels, an input SAS data set must be entered on the DATA ACCESS panel, even though it will not be used. The WHERE ENTRY panel will be used in this example.

PROC DB2UTIL is executed to display the DATA ACCESS panel, where any existing SAS data set can be specified as input. The table name and the DELETE function are also entered.

```
                          DB2 INTERFACE
                        DATA ACCESS PANEL


COMMAND===>
FILL IN THE FIELDS BELOW

INPUT SAS DATA SET:   dummy                         COMMIT:    3
TABLE NAME:         tsid123.projinfo                LIMIT:     5000
FUNCTION:           delete               CORRELATION NAME:
SUBSYSTEM ID:       DBT


MAP DATA SET:                          I=INPUT;O=OUTPUT:
OUTPUT SQL LIBRARY:                    ERROR LOG FILE:
```

When the DELETE function is entered on the DATA ACCESS panel, hitting enter brings up the WHERE ENTRY panel. The delete condition is specified here.

```
        DB2 INTERFACE                 DB2 TABLE- TSID123.PROJINFO
     DB2 WHERE ENTRY PANEL            SAS DATA SET- DUMMY
COMMAND===>                                  SELECT: WHERE

 DB2 WHERE STATEMENT:    actual_end_date < 890101
```

The UPDATE command is issued from the WHERE ENTRY panel to update the DB2 table. The DATA ACCESS panel shows that 1 SQL DELETE statement was executed, but does not state how many rows were deleted.

```
                           DB2 INTERFACE
                         DATA ACCESS PANEL

COMMAND===>

INPUT SAS DATA SET:   DUMMY                       COMMIT:    3
TABLE NAME:          TSID123.PROJINFO             LIMIT:     5000
FUNCTION:            DELETE               CORRELATION NAME:
SUBSYSTEM ID:        DBT


MAP DATA SET:                         I=INPUT;O=OUTPUT:
OUTPUT SQL LIBRARY:                   ERROR LOG FILE:

UTILITY STATISTICS: SQL DELETES ISSUED =         1
                    NUMBER OF SAS OBS READ =     1
                    SQL STATEMENTS REJECTED =    0
```

PROC DB2EXT is used to create a SAS data set from the updated DB2 table, Tsid123.projinfo. This table had 24 observations including the 5 that were added in Example 10-1. The following BROWSE panel shows 18 rows, which means 6 rows were deleted. Viewing the original 19 rows in Projinfo in Appendix C shows that the projects, 'Compensation Plan' and 'Budget', have Actual_end_dates prior to 890101. Two people worked on 'Compensation Plan' and four people worked on 'Budget', making the six rows that were eliminated. Scrolling to the right will display the value of the column, Project.

```
                    SAS DATA SET: PROJINFO                  OBSERVATIONS
COMMAND===>                                                 FIRST      1
                                                            LAST      18
OBS  LAST_NAM     FIRST_NA       BEGIN_DA     PLAN_END     ACTUAL_E
  1  APPLE        RICHARD          890115       890301       890301
  2  BAKER        MARTHA           890715       890915       890915
  3  BUELL        MAX              890315       890401       890415
  4  GOETZ        JACK             890601       890801       890715
  5  HARRINGTON   MARLIN           890715       890915       890915
  6  HARRIS       JULIE            890101       890201       890201
  7  HUFFORD      STEPHEN          890601       890801       890715
  8  HUTSON       EVERETT          890101       890301       890315
  9  KELLUM       ELLEN JANE       890115       890301       890301
 10  KISLING      MARY LEA         890715       890915       890915
 11  MEEKS        EDWARD           890601       890801       890715
 12  MEISER       MARK             890315       890401       890415
 13  MILLER       EMMALYNE         890101       890301       890315
 14  KEESLING     GERTRUDE         891001       900101            .
 15  CAMPBELL     MARGARET         891001       900101            .
 16  DUDLEY       LOUISA           891001       900101            .
 17  HOLLYWOOD    ALICE            891001       900101            .
 18  KAWAN        JOE              891001       900101            .
```

Example 10-3

The Actual_end_date for the Project, 'Brokers', needs to be changed from 890915 to 891031. A SAS data set, Projupdt, containing this change is shown below:

```
          PROJUPDT


OBS     ACTEND     PROJECT


 1      891031     BROKERS
```

A TSO allocate statement is submitted for the SAS data library containing the SAS data set, Projupdt, and PROC DB2UTIL is executed to bring up the DATA ACCESS panel. The input SAS data set, the table name, and the UPDATE function are entered.

```
                              DB2 INTERFACE
                            DATA ACCESS PANEL

COMMAND===>
FILL IN THE FIELDS BELOW

INPUT SAS DATA SET:   sasin.projupdt                COMMIT:   3
TABLE NAME:          tsid123.projinfo               LIMIT:    5000
FUNCTION:            update                 CORRELATION NAME:
SUBSYSTEM ID:        DBT


MAP DATA SET:                             I=INPUT;O=OUTPUT:
OUTPUT SQL LIBRARY:                       ERROR LOG FILE:
```

Hitting enter displays the TABLE MAPPING panel. DISPLAY is entered in the SELECT field and the cursor is moved halfway down the screen before hitting enter. This displays the TABLE DISPLAY panel on the bottom half of the screen. The only DB2 column which is going to be updated is Actual_end_date, so it is the only column which needs to be mapped to a SAS variable. The number 5 is entered on the TABLE MAPPING panel for this purpose.

```
          DB2 INTERFACE                    DB2 TABLE- TSID123.PROJINFO
       TABLE MAPPING PANEL              SAS DATA SET- SASIN.PROJUPDT
COMMAND===>                                        SELECT: MAP

          MAPTO COLUMN           SAS NAME     FORMAT
          ..................      LNAME        $15.
          ..................      FNAME        $10.
          ..................      PROJECT      $20.
          ..................      BEGDTE       8.
          ..................      PLNEND       8.
          5.................      ACTEND       8.

COMMAND===>                                        SELECT: DISPLAY

          NUM    COLUMN                  TYPE
          001    LAST_NAME               CHAR(15)
          002    FIRST_NAME              CHAR(10)
          003    BEGIN_DATE              DECIMAL(6,0)
          004    PLAN_END_DATE           DECIMAL(6,0)
          005    ACTUAL_END_DATE         DECIMAL(6,0)
          006    PROJECT                 CHAR(20)
```

WHERE is entered in the SELECT field of the TABLE MAPPING panel and the cursor is taken to the middle of the screen before hitting enter. This displays the WHERE ENTRY panel on the bottom half of the screen. The WHERE condition specifies that the only rows to be updated are those where the DB2 column, Project, is equal to the SAS variable, Project. SAS variables are named in a WHERE condition by preceding the variable name with a % sign. The WHERE clause that is executed contains the value of the SAS variable, which is 'Brokers' in this example.

```
            DB2 INTERFACE                DB2 TABLE- TSID123.PROJINFO
        TABLE MAPPING PANEL            SAS DATA SET- SASIN.PROJUPDT
COMMAND===>                                   SELECT: MAP

          MAPTO COLUMN             SAS NAME     FORMAT
          ..................        LNAME       $15.
          ..................        FNAME       $10.
          ..................        PROJECT     $20.
          ..................        BEGDTE      8.
          ..................        PLNEND      8.
          ACTUAL_END_DATE           ACTEND      8.

COMMAND===>                                   SELECT: WHERE

 DB2 WHERE STATEMENT:   project = %project
```

The UPDATE command is issued from the TABLE MAPPING panel to update the DB2 table. The DATA ACCESS panel shows that 1 SQL UPDATE statement was executed, but does not state how many rows were updated.

```
DB2 INTERFACE
                              DATA ACCESS PANEL

COMMAND===>

INPUT SAS DATA SET:   SASIN.PROJUPDT                COMMIT:   3
TABLE NAME:          TSID123.PROJINFO               LIMIT:    5000
FUNCTION:            UPDATE               CORRELATION NAME:
SUBSYSTEM ID:        DBT


MAP DATA SET:                            I=INPUT;O=OUTPUT:
OUTPUT SQL LIBRARY:                      ERROR LOG FILE:

UTILITY STATISTICS: SQL UPDATES ISSUED =          1
                    NUMBER OF SAS OBS READ =      1
                    SQL STATEMENTS REJECTED =     0
```

PROC DB2EXT is used to create a SAS data set from the updated DB2 table, Tsid123.projinfo. This table now has 18 observations after being updated in Example 10-1 and Example 10-2. Scrolling to the right on the BROWSE panel shows the Actual_end_date for the Project, 'Brokers' has been changed from 890915 to 891031.

```
                       SAS DATA SET: PROJINFO          OBSERVATIONS
COMMAND===>                                            FIRST       1
                                                       LAST       18
OBS  FIRST_NA    BEGIN_DA  PLAN_END  ACTUAL_E  PROJECT
 1   RICHARD      890115    890301    890301   FINANCIAL STATEMENT
 2   MARTHA       890715    890915    890915   BROKERS
 3   MAX          890315    890401    890415   SALES REPORT
 4   JACK         890601    890801    890715   COMMISSIONS
 5   MARLIN       890715    890915    890915   BROKERS
 6   JULIE        890101    890201    890201   PROJECT GROWTH
 7   STEPHEN      890601    890801    890715   COMMISSIONS
 8   EVERETT      890101    890301    890315   QUALITY CONTROL
 9   ELLEN JANE   890115    890301    890301   FINANCIAL STATEMENT
10   MARY LEA     890715    890915    890915   BROKERS
11   EDWARD       890601    890801    899715   COMMISSIONS
12   MARK         890315    890401    890415   SALES REPORT
13   EMMALYNE     890101    890301    890315   QUALITY CONTROL
14   GERTRUDE     891001    900101         .   ACTUARIAL RATING
15   MARGARET     891001    900101         .   ACTUARIAL RATING
16   LOUISA       891001    900101         .   ACTUARIAL RATING
17   ALICE        891001    900101         .   ACTUARIAL RATING
18   JOE          891001    900101         .   ACTUARIAL RATING
```

Example 10-4

A new column, Dept_responsible, needs to be added to the DB2 table, Tsid123.projinfo. The SAS data set, Projnew, shown below, is to be used to add this column, with the value stored in the SAS variable, Dept.

```
                PROJNEW

 OBS      PROJECT                DEPT

  1       ACTUARIAL RATING       ACTUARIAL
  2       BUDGET                 FINANCE
  3       PROJECT GROWTH         FINANCE
  4       FINANCIAL STATEMENT    FINANCE
  5       QUALITY CONTROL        PRODUCT DEVELP
  6       SALES REPORT           MARKETING
  7       COMMISSIONS            MARKETING
  8       BROKERS                MARKETING
```

A TSO allocate statement is submitted for the SAS data library containing the SAS data set, Projnew, and PROC DB2UTIL is executed to bring up the DATA ACCESS panel. The input SAS data set, the table name, and the UPDATE function are entered. The ALTER command is entered.

```
                              DB2 INTERFACE
                            DATA ACCESS PANEL

COMMAND===> alter
FILL IN THE FIELDS BELOW

INPUT SAS DATA SET:   sasin.projnew                COMMIT:    3
TABLE NAME:         tsid123.projinfo               LIMIT:     5000
FUNCTION:           update                CORRELATION NAME:
SUBSYSTEM ID:       DBT


MAP DATA SET:                            I=INPUT;O=OUTPUT:
OUTPUT SQL LIBRARY:                      ERROR LOG FILE:
```

The ALTER command brings up the TABLE MODIFICATION panel shown below:

```
                          DB2 INTERFACE
                    TABLE MODIFICATION PANEL

COMMAND===>

     ALTER TABLE: TSID123.PROJINFO        DISPLAY:  N
COLUMN NAME                      DATA TYPE
..................               ...............
..................               ...............
..................               ...............
..................               ...............
..................               ...............
..................               ...............
..................               ...............
..................               ...............
..................               ...............
..................               ...............
..................               ...............
..................               ...............
..................               ...............
..................               ...............
```

The DISPLAY is changed to Y and hitting enter displays the existing columns on the table. The new column, Dept_responsible, is entered with a data type of CHAR(15).

```
                          DB2 INTERFACE
                    TABLE MODIFICATION PANEL

COMMAND===>

     ALTER TABLE: TSID123.PROJINFO        DISPLAY:  Y
COLUMN NAME                DATA TYPE
LAST_NAME                  CHAR(15)          * EXISTING COLUMN *
FIRST_NAME                 CHAR(10)          * EXISTING COLUMN *
BEGIN_DATE                 FLOAT             * EXISTING COLUMN *
PLAN_END_DATE              FLOAT             * EXISTING COLUMN *
ACTUAL_END_DATE            FLOAT             * EXISTING COLUMN *
PROJECT                    CHAR(20)          * EXISTING COLUMN *
dept_responsible..         char(15).......
..................         ...............
..................         ...............
..................         ...............
..................         ...............
..................         ...............
..................         ...............
..................         ...............
```

The END command is issued from the TABLE MODIFICATION panel and this brings up the TABLE MAPPING panel, which displays the variables on the input SAS data set. The new column, Dept_responsible, is mapped to the SAS variable, Dept.

WHERE is entered in the SELECT field of the TABLE MAPPING panel and the cursor is taken to the middle of the screen before hitting enter. This displays the WHERE ENTRY panel on the bottom half of the screen. The WHERE condition specifies that the only rows to be updated are those where the DB2 column, Project, is equal to the SAS variable, Project. SAS variables are named in a WHERE condition by preceding the variable name with a % sign. The WHERE clause that is executed contains the value of the SAS variable, Project.

```
          DB2 INTERFACE                   DB2 TABLE- TSID123.PROJINFO
      TABLE MAPPING PANEL                 SAS DATA SET- SASIN.PROJNEW
COMMAND===>                                         SELECT: MAP

         MAPTO COLUMN             SAS NAME     FORMAT
         ..................        PLNEND      $20.
         dept_responsible..        DEPT        $15.

COMMAND===>                                         SELECT: WHERE

 DB2 WHERE STATEMENT:   project = %project
```

The UPDATE command is issued from the TABLE MAPPING panel to update the DB2 table. The DATA ACCESS panel shows that 8 SQL UPDATE statements were executed.

```
DB2 INTERFACE
                               DATA ACCESS PANEL

COMMAND===>


INPUT SAS DATA SET:   SASIN.PROJNEW                       COMMIT:    3
TABLE NAME:         TSID123.PROJINFO                      LIMIT:     5000
FUNCTION:           UPDATE                       CORRELATION NAME:
SUBSYSTEM ID:       DBT


MAP DATA SET:                                  I=INPUT;O=OUTPUT:
OUTPUT SQL LIBRARY:                            ERROR LOG FILE:

UTILITY STATISTICS: SQL UPDATES ISSUED =              8
                    NUMBER OF SAS OBS READ =          8
                    SQL STATEMENTS REJECTED =         0
```

PROC DB2EXT is used to create a SAS data set from the updated DB2 table, Tsid123.projinfo. This table now has 18 observations after being updated in Example 10-1 and Example 10-2. Scrolling to the right on the BROWSE panel shows the new column, Dept_responsible.

```
                     SAS DATA SET: PROJINFO                OBSERVATIONS
COMMAND===>                                                FIRST      1
                                                           LAST      18
OBS BEGIN_DA PLAN_END ACTUAL_E  PROJECT                  DEPT_RES
  1  890115   890301   890301  FINANCIAL STATEMENT      FINANCE
  2  890715   890915   890915  BROKERS                  MARKETING
  3  890315   890401   890415  SALES REPORT             MARKETING
  4  890601   890801   890715  COMMISSIONS              MARKETING
  5  890715   890915   890915  BROKERS                  MARKETING
  6  890101   890201   890201  PROJECT GROWTH           FINANCE
  7  890601   890801   890715  COMMISSIONS              MARKETING
  8  890101   890301   890315  QUALITY CONTROL          PRODUCT DEVELP
  9  890115   890301   890301  FINANCIAL STATEMENT      FINANCE
 10  890715   890915   890915  BROKERS                  MARKETING
 11  890601   890801   899715  COMMISSIONS              MARKETING
 12  890315   890401   890415  SALES REPORT             MARKETING
 13  890101   890301   890315  QUALITY CONTROL          PRODUCT DEVELP
 14  891001   900101        .  ACTUARIAL RATING         ACTUARIAL
 15  891001   900101        .  ACTUARIAL RATING         ACTUARIAL
 16  891001   900101        .  ACTUARIAL RATING         ACTUARIAL
 17  891001   900101        .  ACTUARIAL RATING         ACTUARIAL
 18  891001   900101        .  ACTUARIAL RATING         ACTUARIAL
```

Maps and SQL Statements

This section illustrates the use of PROC DB2UTIL in Display Manager to create and save maps and SQL statments to be used as input in subsequent executions of PROC DB2UTIL. These maps and SQL statements can be used as input to PROC DB2UTIL in Display Manager, but are more often used in batch programs due to computer resource requirements.

SQL Statements

SQL statements generated by PROC DB2UTIL include INSERT, DELETE, UPDATE, or ALTER and UPDATE, used to insert new rows, delete existing rows, update existing data value, and add new columns, respectively. Only one of these functions can be performed in a single execution of PROC DB2UTIL. If an output SQL file is saved, it can be quite large, depending on the size of the input SAS data set and the requirements of the application. Since the INSERT and UPDATE statements contain data values, SQL statements are typically saved through Display Manager, used as input in a batch program, and then deleted. Subsequent executions of PROC DB2UTIL to update a DB2 table would typically need to contain different data values and be based on different observations. In this case, different SQL statements would be required. If the SQL DELETE is used, the same DELETE statement would probably not be used multiple times because once the rows are deleted, the same DELETE statement would not accomplish anything.

Because INSERT and UPDATE statements contain actual data values, it is unlikely that the user would need to edit such SQL statements. Changes would be made to the SAS data set and new SQL statements would be generated. If the DELETE statement is used, the user specifies the complete delete condition on the WHERE ENTRY panel. For these reasons, the SQL statements generated by the map cannot be displayed on the SQL ENTRY/EDIT panel. If the SQL statements are saved to an external file they could be included in the SQL ENTRY/EDIT panel, but typically they would be used as input to a batch program.

Therefore, the SQL ENTRY/EDIT panel is normally used only to execute SQL statements other than the INSERT, DELETE, UPDATE, or ALTER and UPDATE statements generated by the map. Typically, these are utility-type SQL statements such as creating a tablespace or dropping DB2 objects. These statements must end in a semicolon; semicolons are generated only for SQL statements that are generated by a map. Also, the COMMIT and LIMIT fields on the DATA ACCESS panel do not apply to these SQL statements. The only statement which cannot be executed by PROC DB2UTIL is the SELECT statement. The SELECT statement can only be executed by PROC DB2EXT. Other SQL statements can be entered into the SQL ENTRY/EDIT panel or included in the SQL ENTRY/EDIT panel using the INCLUDE command. SQL statements can also be executed in a batch program using DB2 utilities with JCL tailored to your company, or in a batch program using the SQL statement in a PROC DB2LOAD or PROC DB2UTIL step.

The SQL ENTRY/EDIT panel is brought up by issuing the EDIT command from the DATA ACCESS panel, TABLE MODIFICATION panel, or any of the three TABLE MAPPING panels. The user should not enter anything on either of these panels, because when you return from the SQL ENTRY/EDIT panel, any changes will not appear. When the END command is issued from the SQL ENTRY/EDIT panel, SQL statements in the panel will be executed and the user will be returned to the previous panel.

This section will illustrate how to use PROC DB2UTIL in Display Manager to save SQL statements. Since these SQL statements are typically input to PROC DB2UTIL in batch; using SQL statements as input to PROC DB2UTIL will not be illustrated here. The procedure for doing so is just like PROC DB2EXT, the EDIT command is issued from the DATA ACCESS panel to bring up the SQL ENTRY/EDIT panel. The INCLUDE command brings in the SQL statements and they are executed using the END command.

PROC DB2UTIL, like PROC DB2LOAD, is often used to execute utility-type SQL statements such as dropping a table or creating an index. The procedure is exactly the same and the result is exactly the same so it will not be illustrated here. Refer to Example 8-2, section Maps and SQL Statements, in Chapter 8, PROC DB2LOAD in Display Manager. Substitute PROC DB2UTIL in this example and there is no difference.

Example 10-5

Example 10-3 in the previous section, Updating a DB2 Table, will be used in this example, except that an output SQL file is to be created and saved.

The Actual_end_date for the Project, 'Brokers', needs to be changed from 890915 to 891031. A SAS data set, Projupdt, containing this change is shown below:

```
              PROJUPDT

OBS       ACTEND       PROJECT

  1       891031       BROKERS
```

A TSO allocate statement is submitted for the SAS data library containing the SAS data set, Projupdt, and a TSO allocate statement is submitted for a partitioned data set to store the SQL statements. PROC DB2UTIL is executed to bring up the DATA ACCESS panel. The input SAS data set, the table name, the UPDATE function, and the output SQL library are entered.

```
                              DB2 INTERFACE
                            DATA ACCESS PANEL


COMMAND===>
FILL IN THE FIELDS BELOW

INPUT SAS DATA SET:    sasin.projupdt                COMMIT:    3
TABLE NAME:          tsid123.projinfo                LIMIT:     5000
FUNCTION:            update               CORRELATION NAME:
SUBSYSTEM ID:        DBT


MAP DATA SET:                           I=INPUT;O=OUTPUT:
OUTPUT SQL LIBRARY:  codin.sqlupdt      ERROR LOG FILE:
```

Hitting enter displays the TABLE MAPPING panel. DISPLAY is entered in the SELECT field and the cursor is moved halfway down the screen before hitting enter. This displays the TABLE DISPLAY panel on the bottom half of the screen. The only DB2 column which is going to be updated is Actual_end_date, so it is the only column which needs to be mapped to a SAS variable. The number 5 is entered on the TABLE MAPPING panel and hitting enter displays the column name. The END command is entered.

```
             DB2 INTERFACE                 DB2 TABLE- TSID123.PROJINFO
          TABLE MAPPING PANEL            SAS DATA SET- SASIN.PROJUPDT
COMMAND===> end                                 SELECT: MAP

          MAPTO COLUMN          SAS NAME    FORMAT
          ..................     LNAME       $15.
          ..................     FNAME       $10.
          ..................     PROJECT     $20.
          ..................     BEGDTE      8.
          ..................     PLNEND      8.
          ACTUAL_END_DATE...     ACTEND      8.

COMMAND===>                                     SELECT: DISPLAY

          NUM   COLUMN                TYPE
          001   LAST_NAME             CHAR(15)
          002   FIRST_NAME            CHAR(10)
          003   BEGIN_DATE            DECIMAL(6,0)
          004   PLAN_END_DATE         DECIMAL(6,0)
          005   ACTUAL_END_DATE       DECIMAL(6,0)
          006   PROJECT               CHAR(20)
```

WHERE is entered in the SELECT field of the TABLE MAPPING panel and the cursor is taken to the middle of the screen before hitting enter. This displays the WHERE ENTRY panel on the bottom half of the screen. The WHERE condition specifies that the only rows to be updated are those where the DB2 column, Project, is equal to the SAS variable, Project. SAS variables are named in a WHERE condition by preceding the variable name with a % sign. The WHERE clause that is executed contains the value of the SAS variable, which is 'Brokers' in this example.

```
          DB2 INTERFACE                  DB2 TABLE- TSID123.PROJINFO
       TABLE MAPPING PANEL             SAS DATA SET- SASIN.PROJUPDT
COMMAND===>                                     SELECT: MAP

         MAPTO COLUMN              SAS NAME     FORMAT
         ..................         LNAME       $15.
         ..................         FNAME       $10.
         ..................         PROJECT     $20.
         ..................         BEGDTE      8.
         ..................         PLNEND      8.
         ACTUAL_END_DATE            ACTEND      8.

COMMAND===>                                     SELECT: WHERE

 DB2 WHERE STATEMENT:    project = %project
```

The END command is issued from the TABLE MAPPING panel to return to the DATA ACCESS panel and save the SQL statements as a member of a partitioned data set. Since the UPDATE command was not used, the DB2 table is not updated. A note indicates that 2 SQL statements were executed.

```
                         DB2 INTERFACE
                       DATA ACCESS PANEL


COMMAND===>
NOTE: CODIN.SQLUPDT CONTAINS: 2 SQL STATEMENT(S)

INPUT SAS DATA SET:    SASIN.PROJUPDT              COMMIT:    3
TABLE NAME:          TSID123.PROJINFO              LIMIT:     5000
FUNCTION:            UPDATE              CORRELATION NAME:
SUBSYSTEM ID:        DBT


MAP DATA SET:                          I=INPUT;O=OUTPUT:
OUTPUT SQL LIBRARY:  codin.sqlupdt     ERROR LOG FILE:
```

The SQL statements created and saved are shown below. Actual_end_date is set to the value, 891031, are stored in the SAS variable, Actend. The value, BROKERS, is substituted for the %project coded in the WHERE ENTRY panel. When testing for a character string, SQL executes more efficiently if the value is padded with blanks to its full length, which is 20 positions for Project.

```
UPDATE TSID123.PROJINFO SET
ACTUAL_END_DATE = 891031.
WHERE project = 'BROKERS
COMMIT WORK;
```

Maps

Maps are defined by the user using the TABLE MAPPING panels. A map includes the SAS variable name, the DB2 column names, the DB2 data types, and what function is to be performed (INSERT, DELETE, UPDATE). If the same map is needed frequently, users may want to save maps for subsequent executions of PROC DB2UTIL. Maps are saved as SAS data sets in SAS data libraries.

When the SQL statements INSERT and UPDATE are saved as output from PROC DB2UTIL, they are typically used only once because they contain actual data values, which are subject to change. The SQL DELETE function is typically used once because the rows are deleted. When maps are saved from executing PROC DB2UTIL, they can be used in many subsequent executions of PROC DB2UTIL. Even though the input SAS data sets may contain and probably do contain different variable values, the same map can be used. As long as the definition of the input SAS data sets are the same, including the same SAS variable names, data types, and lengths, then the same map can be used.

Maps are most often created in Display Manager to take advantage of the panels and ease of use offered in that environment. Often, the DB2 table can not be created and loaded in Display Manager due to limited computer resources, so the map is used as input to PROC DB2UTIL in a batch program.

To specify a map as input or output the MAP DATA SET field is specified on the DATA ACCESS panel. The field, I=INPUT;O=OUPUT, is set to I or O depending on whether the map is an input file or an output file. After completing the DATA ACCESS panel, hitting enter brings up the TABLE MAPPING panel where the map is defined. When the END command is issued from the TABLE MAPPING panel, a message is displayed. This message states that if the END command is issued again, a map or SQL statements will be saved and if the UPDATE command is issued, the DB2 table will be updated. The END command is issued a second time to save a map.

If you need to make changes to an existing map, specify the map in the map data set field and set the INPUT/OUTPUT value to I. Hitting enter brings up the TABLE MAPPING panel, where the map is displayed. Make the desired changes to the map. Issue the END command twice (as described above) and the modifications will be saved to the input map. If you need to create and save a map which is similar to a map that already exists, make a copy of the map using a DATA step or the Base SAS procedure, PROC COPY. This copy can then be modified using this method.

Example 10-6

Example 10-1 in the previous section, Updating a DB2 Table, will be used in this example, except that an output map is to be created and saved rather than updating the DB2 table.

A SAS data set, Projadd, contains observations representing a new project. These observations need to be added as new rows to the DB2 table, Tsid123.projinfo. The following shows the SAS data set, Projadd:

```
                                PROJADD

OBS  LNAME        FNAME        PROJECT            BEGDTE  PLNEND  ACTEND


 1   KEESLING    GERTRUDE ACTUARIAL RATING   890101  900101     .
 2   CAMPBELL    MARGARET ACTUARIAL RATING   890101  900101     .
 3   DUDLEY      LOUISA   ACTUARIAL RATING   890101  900101     .
 4   HOLLYWOOD   ALICE    ACTUARIAL RATING   890101  900101     .
 5   KAWAN       JOE      ACTUARIAL RATING   890101  900101     .
```

TSO allocate statements were submitted for the SAS data library containing the SAS data set, Projadd, and for the SAS data library to be used to store the map. The execution of PROC DB2UTIL brings up the DATA ACCESS panel shown. The input SAS data set, the DB2 table, the INSERT function, the map data set, and an input/output of O are entered. The SUBSYSTEM ID should be entered if the default is not appropriate.

```
                             DB2 INTERFACE
                          DATA ACCESS PANEL


COMMAND===>
FILL IN THE FIELDS BELOW

INPUT SAS DATA SET:    sasin.projadd              COMMIT:    3
TABLE NAME:          tsid123.projinfo             LIMIT:     5000
FUNCTION:            insert            CORRELATION NAME:
SUBSYSTEM ID:        DBT



MAP DATA SET:        sasout.mapadd      I=INPUT;O=OUTPUT: o
OUTPUT SQL LIBRARY:                     ERROR LOG FILE:
```

Hitting enter on the DATA ACCESS panel brings up the TABLE MAPPING panel. The SELECT field is changed to display and the cursor is placed in the middle of the screen before hitting enter. This displays the TABLE MAPPING and TABLE DISPLAY panels in split screen mode. Rather than entering the complete DB2 column name, the numbers (NUM) from the TABLE DISPLAY panel are entered on the appropriate line of the TABLE MAPPING panel.

```
              DB2 INTERFACE                     DB2 TABLE- TSID123.PROJINFO
           TABLE MAPPING PANEL                  SAS DATA SET- SASIN.PROJADD
COMMAND===>                                            SELECT: MAP

            MAPTO COLUMN              SAS NAME     FORMAT
            1.................         LNAME        $15.
            2.................         FNAME        $10.
            6.................         PROJECT      $20.
            3.................         BEGDTE       8.
            4.................         PLNEND       8.
            5.................         ACTEND       8.

COMMAND===>                                            SELECT: DISPLAY

            NUM    COLUMN                   TYPE
            001    LAST_NAME                CHAR(15)
            002    FIRST_NAME               CHAR(10)
            003    BEGIN_DATE               DECIMAL(6,0)
            004    PLAN_END_DATE            DECIMAL(6,0)
            005    ACTUAL_END_DATE          DECIMAL(6,0)
            006    PROJECT                  CHAR(20)
```

Although not required, hitting enter on the TABLE MAPPING panel will display the DB2 column names in the MAPTO COLUMN rather than the numbers entered. The END command is issued from the TABLE MAPPING panel. A message is displayed stating that if the END command is issued again, a map or SQL statements will be saved and if the UPDATE command is issued, the DB2 table will be altered. The END command is issued a second time to save a map.

```
            DB2 INTERFACE                    DB2 TABLE- TSID123.PROJINFO
          TABLE MAPPING PANEL                SAS DATA SET- SASIN.PROJADD
COMMAND===> end                                    SELECT: MAP

              MAPTO COLUMN            SAS NAME      FORMAT
              LAST_NAME.........       LNAME        $15.
              FIRST_NAME........       FNAME        $10.
              PROJECT...........       PROJECT      $20.
              BEGIN_DATE........       BEGDTE       8.
              PLAN_END_DATE.....       PLNEND       8.
              ACTUAL_END_DATE...       ACTEND       8.

COMMAND===>                                        SELECT: DISPLAY

              NUM    COLUMN                 TYPE
              001    LAST_NAME              CHAR(15)
              002    FIRST_NAME             CHAR(10)
              003    BEGIN_DATE             DECIMAL(6,0)
              004    PLAN_END_DATE          DECIMAL(6,0)
              005    ACTUAL_END_DATE        DECIMAL(6,0)
              006    PROJECT                CHAR(20)
```

The END command is issued twice to create and save the map and return to the DATA ACCESS panel. A note indicates that a map was created containing 6 observations and 5 variables.

```
                        DB2 INTERFACE
                      DATA ACCESS PANEL

COMMAND===>
NOTE: SASIN.MAPADD CONTAINS: 6 OBSERVATION(S) AND: 5 VARIABLE(S)

INPUT SAS DATA SET:   SASIN.PROJADD               COMMIT:   3
TABLE NAME:         TSID123.PROJINFO              LIMIT:    5000
FUNCTION:           INSERT               CORRELATION NAME:
SUBSYSTEM ID:       DBT


MAP DATA SET:       SASOUT.MAPADD      I=INPUT;O=OUTPUT: O
OUTPUT SQL LIBRARY:                    ERROR LOG FILE:
```

The BROWSE command displays the BROWSE panel showing the mapping SAS data set just created.

```
                   SAS DATA SET: SASOUT.MAPADD       OBSERVATIONS
COMMAND===>                                          FIRST       1
                                                     LAST        6
OBS FUNCTION  DB2COL           SASNAME DB2FMT              DATEFMT
  1  INSERT   LAST_NAME        LNAME   ....................      7
  2  INSERT   FIRST_NAME       FNAME   ....................      7
  3  INSERT   BEGIN_DATE       BEGDTE  ....................      7
  4  INSERT   PLAN_END_DATE    PLNEND  ....................      4
  5  INSERT   ACTUAL_END_DATE  ACTEND  ....................      4
  6  INSERT   PROJECT          PROJECT ....................      4
```

Chapter

11

PROC DB2UTIL in Batch

PROC DB2UTIL is used to update DB2 tables; new rows can be inserted, existing rows can be deleted, data values in existing rows can be changed, and new columns can be added. PROC DB2UTIL can also be used to execute utility-type SQL statements such as those used for creating an index or dropping a DB2 table.

When a DB2 table is updated, one of the following is used as input: a SAS data set, a map and a SAS data set, or one of the SQL statements, INSERT, DELETE, UPDATE, or ALTER and UPDATE, along with the COMMIT statement. When new rows are inserted in a DB2 table, the INSERT and COMMIT statements are used. When existing rows are to be deleted, the DELETE and COMMIT statements are used. When existing data values are to be changed, the UPDATE and COMMIT statements are used. When new columns are added, a single ALTER statement is used with the UPDATE and COMMIT statements.

When only a SAS data set is used as input, a map is generated, and the map and the SAS data set generate the appropriate SQL statements. When a map created in a previous execution of PROC DB2UTIL is used as input, a SAS data set is also used as input to supply the data values for the INSERT or UPDATE statements or to specify criteria used in the DELETE statement. When SQL statements created in a previous execution of PROC DB2UTIL are used as input, they are the sole input to PROC DB2UTIL because they contain the specifications for updating the DB2 table and the values to be used. Whatever method of input is used, it is ultimately the SQL statements, INSERT, DELETE, UPDATE, or ALTER and UPDATE that update the DB2 table.

If a map or SQL statements are used as input to PROC DB2UTIL, they were usually created in a previous execution of PROC DB2UTIL in Display Manager to take advantage of the ease of use. These maps and SQL statements are typically used as input to PROC DB2UTIL in a batch program to update a DB2 table, due to computer resource limitations in Display Manager.

PROC DB2UTIL can also be used to execute SQL statements other than the INSERT, DELETE, UPDATE, ALTER, and COMMIT statements generated by the procedure. For example, PROC DB2UTIL could be used to create a tablespace, create an index, or drop a table. Although these statements can be executed in a variety of other ways, including using JCL tailored to your company, it is often convenient to execute them in the SAS environment to save you from exiting Display Manager, or from including multiple job steps in a batch program. Refer to Chapter 4, Structured Query Language, for documentation on the most commonly used SQL statements.

This chapter will present the use of PROC DB2UTIL in batch programs to insert new rows in a DB2 table, delete existing rows from a DB2 table, update existing column values in a DB2 table, and add a new column to a DB2 table, in most cases using data stored in a SAS data set. Also shown, using SQL statements created in a previous execution of PROC DB2UTIL as input to PROC DB2UTIL and using a map created in a previous execution of PROC DB2UTIL as input to PROC DB2UTIL. The user should have JCL appropriate in his company to execute SAS with SAS/DB2. You will also need to know the value(s) of the DB2 SUBSYSTEM ID. Contact the SAS Consultant at your company for this information.

PROC DB2UTIL is the most complicated of the three SAS/DB2 procedures. Not only is it complicated to use, but care should be taken when updating values in a table to insure the integrity of the data, including not only the data values but maintaining REFERENTIAL INTEGRITY in the DB2 system. Updating DB2 tables is usually handled by the DB2 Database Administrator, who is experienced in database management. SAS users will typically not perform this function.

In Release 5.16 of SAS/DB2, missing values in SAS variables cannot be inserted into a DB2 column that was created as NOT NULL. In Release 5.18 of SAS/DB2, missing numeric values are inserted as zero and missing character values are inserted as blanks when the

DB2 column is defined as NOT NULL. In either Release 5.16 or 5.18, missing values in SAS variables are inserted as NULL if the DB2 column is defined as NULL.

Examples given in this section are based on the DB2 tables shown in Appendix C: Sample Tables. Refer to this appendix to familiarize yourself with the sample DB2 tables. You may choose to follow along in these examples by performing the same operations on the mainframe at your company. These DB2 tables can be entered on your mainframe, or refer to Chapter 1, Introduction, to order a copy of these tables.

If permanent input or output files are needed for the execution of PROC DB2UTIL, they should be coded in the JCL.

Input files used with PROC DB2UTIL include SAS data sets containing data which will be used to update a DB2 table and SAS data sets containing mapping instructions. SQL statements stored in an external file, usually a partitioned data set, can also be used as input to PROC DB2UTIL. These SQL statements could be INSERT, DELETE, UPDATE, or ALTER and UPDATE statements used to update a DB2 table or they could be SQL statements which perform specific operations such as dropping a table or creating a tablespace.

Output files used with PROC DB2UTIL include SAS data sets containing mapping instructions, the SQL statements (INSERT, DELETE, UPDATE, or ALTER and UPDATE) which will be used to update a DB2 table, an error log file, or the updated DB2 table itself.

Options and Statements

In the previous chapter, PROC DB2UTIL in Display Manager, only the PROC DB2UTIL statement itself was coded and a series of panels with "fill-in-the-blanks" were used to define the application. In this chapter, PROC DB2UTIL will be executed in the batch environment through the use of options of the PROC DB2UTIL statement and other statements used in the PROC DB2UTIL step. These PROC DB2UTIL options and statements can also be executed in Display Manager if the user prefers this style of coding and wants to execute interactively. Also, for users to utilize the line mode execution of SAS, these options and statements must be used to execute PROC DB2UTIL.

The following statements can be used with PROC DB2UTIL in batch programs:

```
PROC DB2UTIL option(s);
   ADDCOL DB2colname = 'data type' DB2colname = 'data type' ...;
   LIST ALL|SASname SASname ...|SASDATA|TABLE|OPTIONS;
   MAPTO SASname=DB2colname SASname=DB2colname ...;
   SQL statement;
   WHERE clause;
```

The above statements can be used in batch programs, but are also used in line mode execution of PROC DB2UTIL. The following statements are used exclusively in line mode execution. These statements will be defined, but will not be illustrated.

```
DELCOL DB2colname DB2colname ...;
DELETE SASname SASname ...;
EXIT;
RESET SASname;  or RESET ALL;  or RESET SASname SASname ...;
UPDATE;
```

There are several options that can be used in the PROC DB2UTIL statement. Knowing which options and statements to use in a given application depends on the input and output files that are needed. Guidelines for the use of the options and statements will be given after each is defined.

Options

The options which can be used with the PROC DB2UTIL statement are defined as follows:

DATA=SASdataset: The SAS data set named here is the SAS data set which will be used to update the DB2 table. The DATA option is used for most applications of PROC DB2UTIL. If the SAS data set is stored permanently in a SAS data library, a two-level SAS data set name will be specified. The first level corresponds to the DD specified for the SAS data library in the JCL.

TABLE=authorizationid.tablename: The TABLE option is used to specify the name of the DB2 table to be updated. The TABLE option is used for most applications of PROC DB2UTIL.

FUNCTION = INSERT|DELETE|UPDATE: The FUNCTION option is used to specify the action to be taken against the DB2 table using data stored in a SAS data set. INSERT, DELETE, or UPDATE can be specified or I, D, and U respectively. The FUNCTION option is used for most applications of PROC DB2UTIL. The INSERT function is used to insert new rows, the DELETE function is used to delete existing rows, the UPDATE function is used to change existing data values, and the UPDATE function is used to add new columns. Only one function can be specified in a single execution of PROC DB2UTIL.

SSID = subsystem name: This option is the same as used with PROC DB2EXT and PROC DB2LOAD. Refer to Chapter 6, PROC DB2EXT in Display Manager, for the definition of this option.

COMMIT=number: The number specified in the COMMIT option controls the number of rows updated by the INSERT, DELETE, or UPDATE statements before the changes are saved and made available to other applications. If this option is not specified, a default value of 3 is used.

LIMIT=number: The number specified in the LIMIT option sets the maximum number of SQL statements which can be executed. If this option is not specified, a default value of 5000 is used. If the LIMIT option is set to 0, no limit will be set and all updates will be executed.

CORREL=DB2 correlation name: The value specified here can be used with the name of the DB2 column in the WHERE clause to indicate the current value of that column. This option is rarely used.

ERROR=ddname or ERROR=ddname.membername:
PROC DB2UTIL uses the SQL INSERT, DELETE, UPDATE, or ALTER and UPDATE statements to update a DB2 table. If these statements contain SQL errors, the error messages are written to the SAS log. Since a SQL statement often exists for every observation on the SAS data set used as input, the number of SQL statements executed may be quite large, and thus the number of SQL errors generated can also be quite large. If the ERROR option is used to name an external file, any SQL errors encountered during the execution of PROC DB2UTIL will be written to this file, along with the SQL statements that produced the errors. If errors are written to the SAS log, the SQL statements that produced the errors are not shown on the SAS log. Therefore, it will probably be easier to diagnose errors when the ERROR option is specified.

The external file is usually a partitioned data set. It is specified in the JCL. If the member name is specified in the JCL, only the ddname needs to be specified in the ERROR option. If the member name is not specified in the JCL, the ddname followed a period (.) and the member name is specified in the ERROR option.

MAPIN=SASdataset: The MAPIN option is used to specify a map as input to PROC DB2UTIL. This map was created in a prior execution of PROC DB2UTIL, probably in Display Manager. The UPDATE option must be used with the MAPIN option in order to update a DB2 table. If the UPDATE option is not used, any changes to the map in this PROC DB2UTIL step will be saved to the map. The mapping SAS data set will probably be stored permanently in a SAS data library. In this case, a two-level SAS data set name will be specified. The first level corresponds to the dd specified for the SAS data library in the JCL. The second level is the SAS data set name.

MAPOUT=SASdataset: The MAPOUT option is used to specify a map as output to PROC DB2UTIL. The map will be used in subsequent executions of PROC DB2UTIL to update the DB2 table. Maps are more often created in Display Manager due to the ease of use of the panels provided in that environment. Maps can be created and saved in a batch execution of PROC DB2UTIL using the SAS data set which will be used to update the DB2 table as input. A map will probably be stored permanently in a SAS data library. In this case, a two-level SAS data set name will be specified. The first level corresponds to the DD specified for the SAS data library in the JCL. The second level is the SAS data set name.

SQLIN = ddname or SQLIN = ddname.membername: The SQLIN option is used to specify an external file where SQL statements are stored. These SQL statements will be used as input to PROC DB2UTIL to update the DB2 table. The SQL statements were created and saved in a previous execution of PROC DB2UTIL, probably in Display Manager. When SQL statements are used as input to PROC DB2UTIL, the only output file is a DB2 table, and the TABLE, DATA, FUNCTION, and MAPIN options are not used.

Since the SQLIN option is used to bring in SQL statements, they must be stored in an external file rather than being copied or coded in the batch program itself.

If the JCL specifications for the external file containing the SQL statements include the member name of a partitioned data set, only the ddname used in the JCL is coded in the SQLIN option. If the JCL specification does not include the member name, then the SQLIN option includes the ddname used in the JCL followed by a period (.) and the member name.

SQLOUT = ddname or SQLOUT=ddname.membername: The SQLOUT option is used to specify an external file where SQL statements are to be written as a result of executing PROC DB2UTIL. These SQL statements will be used in a subsequent execution of PROC DB2UTIL and probably deleted. Typically, SQL statements used to update a DB2 table are not used multiple times. INSERT, DELETE, and UPDATE statements typically contain data values from the input SAS data set. When DB2 tables are updated again, these data values would usually have changed and new SQL statements would be created.

SQL statements are more often created in Display Manager due to the ease of use of the panels provided in that environment. SQL statements can be created and saved in a batch execution of PROC DB2UTIL using the SAS data set which will be used to update the DB2 table as input or a map as input.

If the JCL specifications for the external file containing the SQL statements include the member name of a partitioned data set, only the ddname used in the JCL is coded in the SQLOUT option. If the JCL specification does not include the member name, then the SQLOUT option includes the ddname used in the JCL followed by a period (.) and the member name.

UPDATE: The UPDATE option must be used in order to update a DB2 table when a SAS data set containing data or a map is used as input. If the UPDATE option is not used, the only output files which can be created are maps and SQL statements.

Statements

The following statements are used with the PROC DB2UTIL procedure in the batch environment:

ADDCOL DB2colname = 'data type' DB2colname = 'data type' ...;
The ADDCOL statement is used when a new column is to be added to the DB2 table. The column name is specified followed by an equal sign and the data type for that column in quotes. If you wish to assign a DB2 date/time data type, the SAS variable used to insert values into this column must be stored as a SAS date/time value. Refer to Chapter 3, IBM'S Database 2,

the section Data Types, for more information about DB2 data types. One or more new columns can be added in a single ADDCOL statement. The UPDATE function is specified in the FUNCTION option of the PROC DB2UTIL statement when the ADDCOL statement is used.

MAPTO SASname=DB2colname SASname=DB2colname ...;

The MAPTO statement maps the SAS variable names in the input SAS data set to the DB2 columns in the DB2 table to be updated. If the INSERT function is used, a SAS variable is usually mapped to every column in the DB2 table. If the UPDATE function is used, a SAS variable is mapped to every column in the DB2 table which will be updated. If the DELETE function is used, the MAPTO statement is not used.

WHERE clause;

The WHERE statement is used to specify a WHERE clause which contains conditions to be used when updating the DB2 table. The WHERE clause is frequently used with the UPDATE and DELETE functions and rarely used with the INSERT function. The WHERE clause can contain DB2 column names, constants, arithmetic expressions, and SAS variable names. SAS variables are denoted by a preceding % sign and are resolved to their value before the WHERE condition is executed.

LIST ALL | SASname SASname ... | SASDATA | TABLE | OPTIONS;

The LIST statement can be used with any of the specifications shown here, ALL, SASname, SASDATA, TABLES, OPTIONS or a combination of more than one of these options. The LIST ALL is the most commonly used option.

The ALL option produces a report on the SAS log which shows all the mapping specifications executed by PROC DB2UTIL. The report shows the DB2 column name, data types, and generated or user-defined, the SAS variable name.

The SASname option can be used to specify as many SAS variables as desired and produces a report on the SAS log just like the LIST ALL except only the specified SAS variables are shown.

The SASDATA option produces a report on the SAS log containing SAS variable names and whether the variable is character or numeric.

The TABLE option produces a report on the SAS log showing the columns and data types on the table specified in the TABLE option of the PROC DB2UTIL statement.

The OPTIONS (or OPT) option produces a list of the options of the PROC DB2UTIL statement and the IN statement and their values. These values include those that are specified in the PROC DB2UTIL step and values which are set to default values. Options that are not specified are noted as such.

SQL statement;

The SQL statement is used to execute a SQL statement. SQL statements specified here are typically utility-type statements such as creating a tablespace or dropping a table. The SQL SELECT statement cannot be executed by PROC DB2UTIL; only PROC DB2EXT can execute the SELECT statement. Only one SQL statement can be executed in a single SQL statement. If more than one SQL statement needs to be executed, multiple SQL statements are coded in the PROC DB2UTIL step.

When SQL statements are executed using the SQL statement in PROC DB2UTIL, the SAS log does not display any messages saying that execution was successful. If these SQL statements were executed using JCL tailored to your company, a condition code would be displayed for every SQL statement.

Refer to Example 9-1 in the section, Creating and Loading a DB2 Table, of Chapter 9, PROC DB2LOAD in Batch, for an illustration of executing multiple SQL statements in a PROC DB2LOAD step. PROC DB2UTIL could have been used instead of PROC DB2LOAD to obtain the same results.

Line Mode

The above statements are used in batch programs and also line mode execution of SAS. The following statements are used exclusively in lne mode execution:

DELCOL DB2colname DB2colname ...;

If an ADDCOL statement was used to add a new column to the DB2 table, the DELCOL statement can be used to delete one or more new columns. The DELCOL statement cannot delete existing columns on the DB2 table.

DELETE SASname SASname ...;

In line mode, all SAS variables on the input SAS data set will be used to update the DB2 table. The DELETE statement can be used to specify one or more of these SAS variables which are not to be used to update the DB2 table.

EXIT;

The EXIT statement performs the same function as the EXIT command used when PROC DB2UTIL is executed in Display Manager. The EXIT statement ends execution of PROC DB2UTIL without creating output files.

RESET SASname; or RESET ALL; or RESET COLS;

The RESET ALL statement resets all changes made to the mapping specifications. The RESET SASname statement resets values only for the SAS variable named. The COLS option is used to reset changes made to column values.

UPDATE;

The UPDATE statement is used to update the DB2 table based on mapping specifications provided.

Application Use

Figure 11-1 outlines which PROC DB2UTIL options and statements should be used depending on the input and output files needed. It also shows the output files that can be produced by a specific input file.

In addition to the options and statements shown on this chart are the ADDCOL, MAPTO, and WHERE statements. These statements allow the user to select SAS variables, specify new columns, map SAS variables to DB2 columns, and specify a condition for update. When a SAS data set is used as input, these statements are used to define the map, which will result in saving the map itself, saving SQL statements, or updating the DB2 table. The definitions specified in the ADDCOL, MAPTO, and WHERE statements or the saved map resulting from these statements (or the equivalent definition on the TABLE MODIFICATION and/or TABLE MAPPING panel) will be used in the generated SQL statements and the resulting DB2 table. Although these statements can be used when a map is used as input, it is unlikely this will occur because their purpose is the same as the map's.

When SQL statements are used as input, the DATA, TABLE, FUNCTION, and MAPIN options cannot be specified, nor can any of the statements, ADDCOL, MAPTO, or WHERE. The SQL statements, INSERT, DELETE, and UPDATE, contain all the neccessary information to create and load the DB2 table.

INPUT	OUTPUT	Required Options
SAS Data Set	Map	DATA TABLE (does not already exist) FUNCTION (INSERT, DELETE, UPDATE) SSID (if other than default) MAPOUT
	SQL Statements	DATA TABLE (does not already exist) FUNCTION (INSERT, DELETE, UPDATE) SSID (if other than default) SQLOUT IN (if other than DSNDB04)
	DB2 Table	DATA TABLE (does not already exist) FUNCTION (INSERT, DELETE, UPDATE) SSID (if other than default) UPDATE IN (if other than DSNDB04)
Map	SQL Statements	DATA TABLE (does not already exist) FUNCTION (INSERT, DELETE, UPDATE) SSID (required) MAPIN SQLOUT
	DB2 Table	DATA TABLE (does not already exist) FUNCTION (INSERT, DELETE, UPDATE) SSID (required) MAPIN UPDATE
SQL Statements	DB2 Table	SSID (if other than default) SQLIN

Figure 11-1 Required options of PROC DB2UTIL.

The LIST statement is often used in applications of PROC DB2TUIL to display information concerning the execution of PROC DB2UTIL and to display mapping information.

Comparison to Display Manager

Figure 11-2 shows the PROC DB2UTIL panel and the field on that panel that performs the same function as the PROC DB2UTIL batch options and statements.

PROC DB2LOAD Panel	Field on the Panel	Batch Option/Statement
DATA ACCESS	INPUT SAS DATA SET	DATA Option
	TABLE NAME	TABLE Option
	FUNCTION	FUNCTION Option
	DB2 SUBSYSTEM ID	SSID Option
	COMMIT	COMMIT Option
	LIMIT	LIMIT Option
	CORRELATION NAME	CORREL Option
	ERROR LOG FILE	ERROR Option
	MAP DATA SET I=INPUT;O=OUTPUT: I	MAPIN Option
	MAP DATA SET I=INPUT;O=OUTPUT: O	MAPOUT Option
	OUTPUT SQL LIBRARY	SQLOUT Option
TABLE MODIFICATION	COLUMN NAME	ADDCOL Statement
	DATA TYPE	ADDCOL Statement
TABLE MAPPING	MAPTO COLUMN	MAPTO Statement
	UPDATE Command	UPDATE Option
WHERE ENTRY	DB2 WHERE Statement	WHERE Statement
SQL ENTRY/EDIT	INCLUDE Command	SQLIN Option
	User entered	SQL Statement

Figure 11-2 PROC DB2UTIL Display Manager and batch comparison.

Updating a DB2 Table

This section illustrates the use of PROC DB2UTIL in batch to update a DB2 table using data stored in a SAS data set. The examples shown here are the same as the examples showed in Chapter 10, PROC DB2UTIL in Display Manager, except they are executed in batch. Four examples are given to illustrate the four ways PROC DB2UTIL can be used to update a DB2 table; add rows, delete rows, change column values, and add a new column. The SAS log is shown for each example. Each example contains a PROC DB2EXT step following the PROC DB2UTIL step to verify the changes made to the table. Refer to the corresponding examples in Chapter 10 to view the updated DB2 table resulting from each update.

Example 11-1

A SAS data set, Projadd, contains observations representing a new project. These observations need to be added as new rows to the DB2 table, Tsid123.projinfo. The following shows the SAS data set, Projadd:

PROJADD

OBS	LNAME	FNAME	PROJECT	BEGDTE	PLNEND	ACTEND
1	KEESLING	GERTRUDE	ACTUARIAL RATING	890101	900101	.
2	CAMPBELL	MARGARET	ACTUARIAL RATING	890101	900101	.
3	DUDLEY	LOUISA	ACTUARIAL RATING	890101	900101	.
4	HOLLYWOOD	ALICE	ACTUARIAL RATING	890101	900101	.
5	KAWAN	JOE	ACTUARIAL RATING	890101	900101	.

The following SAS log produces the desired result:

```

PROC DB2UTIL DATA=SASIN.PROJADD TABLE=TSID123.PROJINFO
             FUNCTION=I UPDATE;
  MAPTO LNAME    = LAST_NAME
        FNAME    = FIRST_NAME
        BEGDTE   = BEGIN_DATE
```

```
7             PLNEND  = PLAN_END_DATE
8             ACTEND  = ACTUAL_END_DATE
9             PROJECT = PROJECT;
10
...............................................................
...............................................................
-------------- MAP FOR TABLE UPDATE --------FUNCTION:INSERT
  COLUMN NAME         DB2 FORMAT            SAS NAME
  LAST_NAME           CHAR(15)              LNAME
  FIRST_NAME          CHAR(10)              FNAME
  PROJECT             CHAR(20)              PROJECT
  BEGIN_DATE          DECIMAL(6,0)          BEGDTE
  PLAN_END_DATE       DECIMAL(6,0)          PLNEND
  ACTUAL_END_DATE     DECIMAL(6,0)          ACTEND
---------------- WHERE STATEMENT ----------------
...............................................................
           ** REQUIRED FIELDS **
 OPTION                    VALUE/DEFAULT
 DATA=                     SASIN.PROJADD
 TABLE=                    TSID123.PROJINFO
 SSID=                     DBT
 FUNCTION=                 INSERT
...............................................................
           ** OPTIONAL FIELDS **
 OPTION                    VALUE/DEFAULT
 SQLIN=                    *** NOT ENTERED ***
 SQLOUT=                   *** NOT ENTERED ***
 MAPIN=                    *** NOT ENTERED ***
 MAPOUT=                   *** NOT ENTERED ***
 ERROR=                    SAS LOG
 COMMIT=                   000003
 LIMIT=                    005000
 UPDATE=                   UPDATE ENTERED
...............................................................
11     LIST ALL OPTIONS;
12
.....................................................
UTILITY STATISTICS:
SQL INSERTS ISSUED =                5
NUMBER OF SAS OBS READ =            5
SQL STATEMENTS REJECTED =           0
.....................................................
```

```
PROC DB2EXT OUT=EX1;
  SELECT * FROM TSID123.PROJINFO;

NOTE: THE DATA SET WORK.EX1 HAS 24 OBSERVATIONS AND 6 VARIABLES.
```

The SAS data set containing the new rows is specified in the DATA option. The table to be updated is specified in the TABLE option. The FUNCTION required to add rows is INSERT or I. The UPDATE option must be specified to update a DB2 table. Without the UPDATE option, only output maps and SQL statements can be saved. All columns on the DB2 table are specified in the MAPTO statement along with the corresponding SAS variables. The DB2 table had 19 observations prior to executing this PROC DB2UTIL step. The PROC DB2EXT step shows that the table now has 24 observations.

Example 11-2

All projects which have an Actual_end_date prior to 890101 are to be deleted from the DB2 table, Tsid123.projinfo.

The following SAS log produces the desired result:

```

PROC DB2UTIL TABLE=TSID123.PROJINFO
             FUNCTION=D UPDATE;
  SQL DELETE FROM TSID123.PROJINFO
      WHERE ACTUAL_END_DATE < 890101 ;
  SQL COMMIT WORK;

NOTE: FIELDS REQUIRED FOR UPDATE WERE NOT ENTERED OR IN ERROR
...........................................................
          ** REQUIRED FIELDS **
 OPTION                       VALUE/DEFAULT
 DATA=                        *** NOT ENTERED ***
 TABLE=                       TSID123.PROJINFO
 SSID=                        DBT
 FUNCTION=                    DELETE
...........................................................
          ** OPTIONAL FIELDS **
 OPTION                       VALUE/DEFAULT
 SQLIN=                       *** NOT ENTERED ***
```

```
SQLOUT=                    *** NOT ENTERED ***
MAPIN=                     *** NOT ENTERED ***
MAPOUT=                    *** NOT ENTERED ***
ERROR=                     SAS LOG
COMMIT=                    000003
LIMIT=                     005000
UPDATE=                    UPDATE ENTERED
.............................................................
8      LIST ALL OPTIONS;
9
NOTE: FIELDS REQUIRED FOR UPDATE WERE NOT ENTERED OR IN ERROR
NOTE: DATA= OPTION REQUIRED FOR UPDATE PROCESSING WAS NOT ENTERED

10     PROC DB2EXT OUT=EX2;
11       SELECT * FROM TSID123.PROJINFO;
12
NOTE: THE DATA SET WORK.EX2 HAS 18 OBSERVATIONS AND 6 VARIABLES.
```

The TABLE option specified the DB2 table to be updated and the FUNCTION is specified as DELETE or D. The UPDATE option is required to update a DB2 table. An input SAS data set is not required to delete these rows because the criteria are based solely on values in the DB2 column, Actual_end_date. The DATA option is not coded in the PROC DB2UTIL statement and this is what produces the message, FIELDS REQUIRED FOR UPDATE WERE NOT ENTERED OR IN ERROR. In this case, this message can be ignored because a SAS data set was not needed to execute the SQL statements. Refer to Chapter 4, Structured Query Language, for information concerning the SQL DELETE statement. The SQL COMMIT statement is used to save or "commit" the deletions to the table.

The DB2 table, Tsid123.projinfo, had 24 observations as a result of the previous Example 11-1 and PROC DB2EXT shows there are now 18 observations. Viewing the original 19 rows as shown in Appendix C shows that the projects, 'Compensation Plan' and 'Budget', have Actual_end_dates prior to 890101. Two people worked on the 'Compensation Plan' and four people worked on the 'Budget', making a total of 6 rows deleted.

Example 11-3

The Actual_end_date for the Project, 'Brokers', needs to be changed from 890915 to 891031. A SAS data set, Projupdt, contains this change and is shown below:

```
            PROJUPDT

 OBS      ACTEND      PROJECT

  1       891031      BROKERS
```

The following SAS log produces the desired results:

```
 1
 2    PROC DB2UTIL DATA=SASIN.PROJUPDT TABLE=TSID123.PROJINFO
 3                 FUNCTION=U UPDATE;
 4      MAPTO ACTEND  = ACTUAL_END_DATE;
 5      WHERE PROJECT = %PROJECT;
+                       ________
                         1353
+                        1353
+                        1353
 6
 ............................................................
 -------------- MAP FOR TABLE UPDATE --------FUNCTION:UPDATE
   COLUMN NAME         DB2 FORMAT           SAS NAME
   ACTUAL_END_DATE     DECIMAL(6,0)         ACTEND
 ---------------- WHERE STATEMENT  ----------------
 PROJECT = %PROJECT
 ............................................................
 ............................................................
           ** REQUIRED FIELDS **
  OPTION                    VALUE/DEFAULT
  DATA=                     SASIN.PROJUPDT
  TABLE=                    TSID123.PROJINFO
  SSID=                     DBT
  FUNCTION=                 UPDATE
 ............................................................
```

```
             ** OPTIONAL FIELDS **
 OPTION                      VALUE/DEFAULT
 SQLIN=                      *** NOT ENTERED ***
 SQLOUT=                     *** NOT ENTERED ***
 MAPIN=                      *** NOT ENTERED ***
 MAPOUT=                     *** NOT ENTERED ***
 ERROR=                      SAS LOG
 COMMIT=                     000003
 LIMIT=                      005000
 UPDATE=                     UPDATE ENTERED
............................................................
7     LIST ALL OPTIONS;
8
..................................................
UTILITY STATISTICS:
SQL UPDATES ISSUED =                  1
NUMBER OF SAS OBS READ =              1
SQL STATEMENTS REJECTED =             0
..................................................
WARNING 1353: APPARENT MACRO INVOCATION NOT RESOLVED.

9     PROC DB2EXT OUT=EX3;
10      SELECT * FROM TSID123.PROJINFO;
11
NOTE: THE DATA SET WORK.EX3 HAS 18 OBSERVATIONS AND 6 VARIABLES.
```

The input SAS data set is specified in the DATA option and the DB2 table to be updated is named in the TABLE option. The FUNCTION required is UPDATE or U. The UPDATE option is required to alter a DB2 table. The MAPTO statement specifies only the DB2 table which is to be updated.

The WHERE clause designates how to match the rows in the DB2 table with the SAS observation containing the update. In this case the DB2 column, Project, should be equal to the SAS variable, Project. The SAS variable is specified by preceding it with a % sign. When the WHERE statement is executed, the value of the SAS variable is substituted for %project. In this case that value is 'Brokers'. The % sign is first interpreted as a MACRO if SAS was invoked with MACRO on. This MACRO error can be ignored; the updates are applied correctly. MACRO can be turned off at the inital invocation of SAS with the appropriate specification in the JCL.

Example 11-4

A new column, Dept_responsible, needs to be added to the DB2 table, Tsid123.projinfo. The SAS data set, Projnew, shown below is to be used to add this column, with the value stored in the SAS variable, Dept.

PROJNEW

OBS	PROJECT	DEPT
1	ACTUARIAL RATING	ACTUARIAL
2	BUDGET	FINANCE
3	PROJECT GROWTH	FINANCE
4	FINANCIAL STATEMENT	FINANCE
5	QUALITY CONTROL	PRODUCT DEVELP
6	SALES REPORT	MARKETING
7	COMMISSIONS	MARKETING
8	BROKERS	MARKETING

The SAS log shown below produces the desired result:

```
 1
 2      PROC DB2UTIL DATA=SASIN.PROJNEW TABLE=TSID123.PROJINFO
 3                   FUNCTION=U UPDATE;
 4        ADDCOL DEPT_RESPONSIBLE = 'CHAR(15)';
 5        MAPTO DEPT = DEPT_RESPONSIBLE;
 6        WHERE PROJECT = %PROJECT;
+                               _______
                                 1353
+                                1353
+                                1353
 7
 ............................................................
 -------------- MAP FOR TABLE UPDATE --------FUNCTION:UPDATE
   COLUMN NAME        DB2 FORMAT            SAS NAME
   DEPT_RESPONSIBLE   CHAR(15)              DEPT
 ---------------- WHERE STATEMENT  ----------------
 PROJECT = %PROJECT
 ............................................................
 ............................................................
```

```
            ** REQUIRED FIELDS **
 OPTION                       VALUE/DEFAULT
 DATA=                        SASIN.PROJNEW
 TABLE=                       TSID123.PROJINFO
 SSID=                        DBT
 FUNCTION=                    UPDATE
.............................................................
            ** OPTIONAL FIELDS **
 OPTION                       VALUE/DEFAULT
 SQLIN=                       *** NOT ENTERED ***
 SQLOUT=                      *** NOT ENTERED ***
 MAPIN=                       *** NOT ENTERED ***
 MAPOUT=                      *** NOT ENTERED ***
 ERROR=                       SAS LOG
 COMMIT=                      000003
 LIMIT=                       005000
 UPDATE=                      UPDATE ENTERED
.............................................................
8    LIST ALL OPTIONS;
9
...................................................
UTILITY STATISTICS:
SQL UPDATES ISSUED =                8
NUMBER OF SAS OBS READ =            8
SQL STATEMENTS REJECTED =           0
...................................................
WARNING 1353: APPARENT MACRO INVOCATION NOT RESOLVED.

10   PROC DB2EXT OUT=EX4;
11     SELECT * FROM TSID123.PROJINFO;
12
NOTE: THE DATA SET WORK.EX4 HAS 18 OBSERVATIONS AND 7 VARIABLES.
```

The input SAS data set is specified in the DATA option and the DB2 table to be updated is named in the TABLE option. The FUNCTION required is UPDATE or U. The UPDATE option is required to update a DB2 table. The ADDCOL statement is used to name the new column and its data type. The MAPTO statement to used to map this new column to the appropriate SAS variable. PROC DB2EXT shows that the table now has 7 variables rather than 6.

The WHERE clause designates how to match the rows in the DB2 table with the SAS observation containing the update. In this case the DB2 column, Project, should be equal to the SAS variable,

Project. The SAS variable is specified by preceding it with a % sign. When the WHERE statement is executed, the value of the SAS variable is substituted for %project. The % sign is first interpreted as a MACRO if SAS was invoked with MACRO on. This MACRO error can be ignored; the updates are applied correctly. MACRO can be turned off at the inital execution of SAS with a specification in the JCL.

Maps and SQL Statements

When PROC DB2UTIL is used to update a DB2 table using data stored in a SAS data set, it is based on a SAS data set containing data, a SAS data set containing mapping specifications, and the SQL statements, INSERT, DELETE, UPDATE, or ALTER and UPDATE.

If a map is used as input, it was created from a previous execution of PROC DB2UTIL, probably in Display Manager, and saved as a SAS data set in a SAS data library. To use the map as input, it is specified in the MAPIN option of the PROC DB2UTIL statement. The map will have a two-level SAS data set name, where the first level refers to a dd in the JCL pointing to the SAS data library, and the second level is the name of the map. The SAS data set containing data is named in the DATA option and the DB2 table to be updated is specified in the TABLE option. The UPDATE option must be specified to update a DB2 table, otherwise only the SQL statements or a map are saved. An input map takes the place of the MAPTO statement since each observation in the map contains a SAS variable and its corresponding DB2 column. Even though the map contains a variable, Function, which specifies the operation to be performed (INSERT, DELETE, or UPDATE), the FUNCTION option must be specified in the PROC DB2UTIL statement. Also, the SSID option must always be specified because the default subsystem id is not used when the MAPIN option is used.

Maps can be used in several subsequent executions of PROC DB2UTIL even though the input SAS data set may contain and probably does contain different variable values. As long as the definition of the SAS data set is the same, including the same SAS variable names, data types, and lengths, then a map created from the SAS data set will be the same.

Maps are most often created in Display Manager to take advantage of the panels and ease of use offered in that environment. Often, the DB2 table cannot be created and loaded in Display Manager due to limited computer resources, but a map can always be defined in Display Manager. If the map turns out to be not quite what you wanted, you can also modify it in Display Manager. Although PROC DB2UTIL can be used to create and save maps in a batch program, it is not very practical. To save a map in the batch execution of PROC DB2UTIL, the MAPTO statement and optionally the ADDCOL statement are used. If they have to be coded, you could just as easily use them in subsequent executions of PROC DB2UTIL. Therefore, the illustration shown in this section will use a map created in PROC DB2UTIL in Display Manager as input to PROC DB2UTIL in batch. Creating and saving a map as output from PROC DB2UTIL in batch will not be shown.

If SQL statements are used as input, the SQL statements, INSERT, DELETE, UPDATE, or ALTER and UPDATE are used. INSERT and UPDATE statements usually contain the variable values from the input SAS data set. By default, a COMMIT statement exists for every 3 rows updated and causes the changes to be saved to the output DB2 table and frees the data for access by other applications. The COMMIT option can be used to control the number of rows updated before a COMMIT statement is executed.

SQL statements were created and saved in a previous execution of PROC DB2UTIL, probably in Display Manager. These SQL statements are stored in an external file, usually as a member of a partitioned data set. To use the SQL statements as input, the external file is specified in the SQLIN option of the PROC DB2UTIL statement. If the JCL specifications for the external file containing the SQL statements include the member name of a partitioned data set, only the ddname used in the JCL is coded in the SQLIN option. If the JCL specification does not include the member name, then the SQLIN option includes the ddname used in the JCL followed by a period (.) and the member name.

When SQL statements are used as input, they are the sole input to PROC DB2UTIL. The INSERT, DELETE, UPDATE, or ALTER and UPDATE statements contain the data values so the SAS data set containing those data values is not required. The SQL statements also contain the name of the DB2 table to be updated and the function to be used (INSERT, DELETE, or UPDATE). Therefore, the DATA, TABLE, and FUNCTION options of the PROC DB2UTIL statement are not used when the SQLIN option is used. When SQL statements are used as input to PROC DB2UTIL, the only output file which can result is a DB2 table.

SQL statements will probably be used in only one subsequent execution of PROC DB2UTIL. The INSERT and UPDATE statements contain data values which will most likely change. Since the SAS data set containing the data used to create and save these SQL statements is available, it is normally used as input along with a map or the ADDCOL, MAPTO, and WHERE statements rather than creating and saving SQL statements. The illustration shown in this section will use SQL statements created in PROC DB2UTIL in Display Manager as input to PROC DB2UTIL in batch. Creating and saving SQL statements as output from PROC DB2UTIL in batch will not be shown.

Example 11-5

The SQL statement saved in Example 10-5, in Chapter 10, PROC D2BUTIL in Display Manager, section, Maps and SQL Statements, is used as input to PROC DB2UTIL in a batch program to update data values.

The following SAS log shows the PROC DB2UTIL step used for this purpose:

```
1
2    PROC DB2UTIL SQLIN=CODIN.SQLUPDT;
3
NOTE: FIELDS REQUIRED FOR UPDATE WERE NOT ENTERED OR IN ERROR
..............................................................
          ** REQUIRED FIELDS **
 OPTION                   VALUE/DEFAULT
 DATA=                    *** NOT ENTERED ***
 TABLE=                   *** NOT ENTERED ***
 SSID=                    DBT
 FUNCTION=                INSERT
..............................................................
          ** OPTIONAL FIELDS **
 OPTION                   VALUE/DEFAULT
 SQLIN=                   CODIN.SQLUPDT
 SQLOUT=                  *** NOT ENTERED ***
 MAPIN=                   *** NOT ENTERED ***
 MAPOUT=                  *** NOT ENTERED ***
 ERROR=                   SAS LOG
 COMMIT=                  000003
 LIMIT=                   005000
 UPDATE=                  *** NOT ENTERED ***
..............................................................
4      LIST ALL OPTIONS;
```

```
.................................................
SQL STATISTICS
TOTAL PROCESSED =                     2
SQL STATEMENTS REJECTED =             0
.................................................

    PROC DB2EXT OUT=EX5;
     SELECT * FROM TSID123.PROJINFO;

NOTE: THE DATA SET WORK.EX5 HAS 19 OBSERVATIONS AND 6 VARIABLES.
```

The PROC DB2UTIL step specifies only the SQLIN option because the UPDATE and COMMIT statements contain all the information necessary to update the DB2 table. Refer to Example 10-5, in Chapter 10, PROC DBUTIL in Display Manager, section, Maps and SQL Statements, to view the SQL UPDATE statement executed in this PROC DB2UTIL step.

Example 11-6

The map saved in Example 10-6, in Chapter 10, PROC DB2UTIL in Display Manager, section, Maps and SQL Statements, is used as input to PROC DB2UTIL in a batch program to add rows to a DB2 table.

The following SAS log shows the PROC DB2UTIL step used for this purpose:

```
  PROC DB2UTIL DATA=SASIN.PROJADD TABLE=TSID123.PROJINFO
               MAPIN=SASIN.MAPADD UPDATE
               SSID=DBT FUNCTION=INSERT;

......................................................
------------- MAP FOR TABLE UPDATE --------FUNCTION:INSERT
 COLUMN NAME        DB2 FORMAT           SAS NAME
 LAST_NAME          CHAR(15)             LNAME
 FIRST_NAME         CHAR(10)             FNAME
 PROJECT            CHAR(20)             PROJECT
 BEGIN_DATE         DECIMAL(6,0)         BEGDTE
 PLAN_END_DATE      DECIMAL(6,0)         PLNEND
 ACTUAL_END_DATE    DECIMAL(6,0)         ACTEND
```

```
---------------- WHERE STATEMENT ----------------
.................................................................
.................................................................
           ** REQUIRED FIELDS **
 OPTION                    VALUE/DEFAULT
 DATA=                     SASIN.PROJADD
 TABLE=                    TSID123.PROJINFO
 SSID=                     DBT
 FUNCTION=                 INSERT
.................................................................
           ** OPTIONAL FIELDS **
 OPTION                    VALUE/DEFAULT
 SQLIN=                    *** NOT ENTERED ***
 SQLOUT=                   *** NOT ENTERED ***
 MAPIN=                    SASIN.MAPADD
 MAPOUT=                   *** NOT ENTERED ***
 ERROR=                    SAS LOG
 COMMIT=                   000003
 LIMIT=                    005000
 UPDATE=                   UPDATE ENTERED
.................................................................
6            LIST ALL OPTIONS;
7

....................................................
UTILITY STATISTICS:
SQL INSERTS ISSUED =                  5
NUMBER OF SAS OBS READ =              5
SQL STATEMENTS REJECTED =             0
....................................................

8      PROC DB2EXT OUT=EX6;
9         SELECT * FROM TSID123.PROJINFO;
10
NOTE: THE DATA SET WORK.EX6 HAS 24 OBSERVATIONS AND 6 VARIABLES.
```

When a map is used as input to PROC DB2UTIL, the map is specified in the MAPIN option. The other options that are required include DATA, TABLE, UPDATE, SSID, and FUNCTION. The DATA option names the SAS data set containing the observations to be added as rows in the DB2 table named in the TABLE option. The UPDATE option must be used to update the DB2 table. The SSID option must always be specified because the default subsystem id is not used when the MAPIN option is used. Also, even though the map contains a variable, Function, which specifies the operation to be performed (INSERT, DELETE, or UPDATE), the FUNCTION option must be specified in the PROC DB2UTIL statement.

The PROC DB2EXT step shows that 5 observations were added to the original 19 observations.

Chapter

12

Advanced Applications

This chapter contains examples which use all of the SAS/DB2 procedures and a variety of SQL statements, bringing together the topics covered in the earlier chapters of this book.

A tablespace is created to store a PLAN TABLE and a PLAN TABLE is created to store the results of the EXPLAIN statement. EXPLAIN statements are executed based on a SELECT statement and the access method which would be used by this SELECT statement is placed in a PLAN TABLE. The PLAN TABLE can then be examined to insure that the access method is appropriate prior to submitting the program using this SELECT statement. The contents of the PLAN TABLE are displayed to verify the efficiency of the access method selected by the DB2 Optimizer. The PLAN TABLE can also be used to abend a program if the access method selected is not appropriate.

Two examples illustrate applications where a DB2 table must be created by the user in order to extract the desired information from a DB2 table. The DB2 utility, RUNSTATS, is used in these examples to inform the DB2 System Catalog Tables of the existence of these new DB2 tables and provide statistics on them. If RUNSTATS is not executed, the DB2 System Catalog Tables will not recognize the tables and they will be accessed last when the DB2 Optimizer determines the data access method. Typically, it is more efficient if user-created tables are accessed first because they are usually the smallest.

Examples given in this section are based on the DB2 tables shown in Appendix C: Sample Tables. Refer to this appendix to familiarize yourself with the sample DB2 tables. You may choose to follow along in these examples by performing the same operations on the mainframe at your company. These DB2 tables can be entered on your mainframe, or refer to Chapter 1, Introduction, for ordering a copy of these tables.

Example 12-1

The following SAS log shows creation of a tablespace and a PLAN TABLE in this tablespace. The PLAN TABLE will be used to hold the results of the SQL EXPLAIN statement. These results show how the DB2 Optimizer will execute a SELECT statement. This is particularly valuable when a JOIN is performed or large DB2 tables are read.

The SQL CREATE statement is used to create the tablespace and the table. This statement is not automatically generated by any of the SAS/DB2 procedures, so they are coded in the SQL statement used with PROC DB2UTIL. PROC DB2LOAD could also have been used.

```

PROC DB2UTIL;
  SQL
  CREATE TABLESPACE PLNTBL
    IN TSID123
    USING
    STOGROUP FREEGP01
    PRIQTY 1000
    SECQTY 1000
    ERASE NO
    FREEPAGE 000
    PCTFREE 00
    LOCKSIZE TABLESPACE
    BUFFERPOOL BP0
    CLOSE NO  ;

```

```
NOTE: FIELDS REQUIRED FOR UPDATE WERE NOT ENTERED OR IN ERROR
NOTE: TABLE= OPTION REQUIRED FOR UPDATE PROCESSING WAS NOT ENTERED
17    PROC DB2UTIL;
18      SQL
19      CREATE TABLE TSID123.PLAN_TABLE
20             (QUERYNO           INTEGER        NOT NULL,
21              QBLOCKNO          SMALLINT       NOT NULL,
22              APPLNAME          CHAR(8)        NOT NULL,
23              PROGNAME          CHAR(8)        NOT NULL,
24              PLANNO            SMALLINT       NOT NULL,
25              METHOD            SMALLINT       NOT NULL,
26              CREATOR           CHAR(8)        NOT NULL,
27              TNAME             CHAR(18)       NOT NULL,
28              TABNO             SMALLINT       NOT NULL,
29              ACCESSTYPE        CHAR(2)        NOT NULL,
30              MATCHCOLS         SMALLINT       NOT NULL,
31              ACCESSCREATOR     CHAR(8)        NOT NULL,
32              ACCESSNAME        CHAR(18)       NOT NULL,
33              INDEXONLY         CHAR(1)        NOT NULL,
34              SORTN_UNIQ        CHAR(1)        NOT NULL,
35              SORTN_JOIN        CHAR(1)        NOT NULL,
36              SORTN_ORDERBY     CHAR(1)        NOT NULL,
37              SORTN_GROUPBY     CHAR(1)        NOT NULL,
38              SORTC_UNIQ        CHAR(1)        NOT NULL,
39              SORTC_JOIN        CHAR(1)        NOT NULL,
40              SORTC_ORDERBY     CHAR(1)        NOT NULL,
41              SORTC_GROUPBY     CHAR(1)        NOT NULL,
42              TSLOCKMODE        CHAR(3)        NOT NULL,
43              TIMESTAMP         CHAR(16)       NOT NULL,
44              REMARKS           VARCHAR(254)   NOT NULL)
45              IN TSID123.PLNTBL;
NOTE: FIELDS REQUIRED FOR UPDATE WERE NOT ENTERED OR IN ERROR
NOTE: TABLE= OPTION REQUIRED FOR UPDATE PROCESSING WAS NOT ENTERED
```

A tablespace, PLNTBL, is created to hold the PLAN TABLE, TSID123.Plan_table. Since DB2UTIL was not used to update a DB2 table or create and save a map or SQL statements, notes appear on the SAS log stating that fields required were not entered or are in error. When executing an SQL statement, these messages can be ignored.

Example 12-2

A SQL EXPLAIN statement is executed for a SELECT statement which joins the three DB2 tables, Tsid123.projinfo, Tsid123.persinfo, and Tsid123.orginfo. Since the EXPLAIN statement is not generated by any of the SAS/DB2 procedures, the SQL statement with PROC DB2UTIL is used. The results of the EXPLAIN are stored in the PLAN TABLE created in Example 12-1, Tsid123.plan_table. Since the PLAN TABLE is a DB2 table, PROC DB2EXT can be used to extract information from this table and place it in a SAS data set. PROC PRINT is then used to print this SAS data set.

The SAS log of this program is shown below:

```
.

       PROC DB2UTIL;
         SQL
         EXPLAIN PLAN SET QUERYNO=1
           FOR
           SELECT PE.LAST_NAME, PE.FIRST_NAME, PROJECT,
                  DEPARTMENT_NAME
              FROM TSID123.PERSINFO PE, TSID123.PROJINFO PJ,
                   TSID123.ORGINFO
              WHERE PE.LAST_NAME = PJ.LAST_NAME AND
                    PE.FIRST_NAME = PJ.FIRST_NAME AND
                    COST_CENTER = DEPARTMENT
              ORDER BY DEPARTMENT_NAME, PE.LAST_NAME;

NOTE: FIELDS REQUIRED FOR UPDATE WERE NOT ENTERED OR IN ERROR
NOTE: TABLE= OPTION REQUIRED FOR UPDATE PROCESSING WAS NOT ENTERED

       PROC DB2EXT OUT=PLAN UNIQUE;
         SELECT * FROM TSID123.PLAN_TABLE;

NOTE: THE DATA SET WORK.PLAN HAS 3 OBSERVATIONS AND 25 VARIABLES.

       PROC PRINT DATA=PLAN;
         TITLE1 'PLAN TABLE RESULTS OF EXPLAIN';
NOTE: THE PROCEDURE PRINT PRINTED PAGE 1.
```

PROC PRINT produces the following report:

PLAN TABLE RESULTS OF EXPLAIN

OBS	QUERYNO	QBLOCKNO	APPLNAME	PROGNAME	PLANNO	METHOD	CREATOR	TNAME	TABNO	ACCESSTY	MATCHCOL
1	1	1		DB2UTILI	1	0	TSID123	PROJINFO	2	R	0
2	1	1		DB2UTILI	2	2	TSID123	PERSINFO	1	R	0
3	1	1		DB2UTILI	3	2	TSID123	ORGINFO	3	R	0

OBS	ACCESSCR	ACCESSNA	INDEXONL	SORTN_UN	SORTN_JO	SORTN_OR	SORTN_GR	SORTC_UN	SORTC_JO	SORTC_OR	SORTC_GR	TSLOCKMO	TIMESTAM	REMARKS
1			N	N	N	N	N	N	N	N	N	S	1989031412145074	
2			N	N	Y	N	N	N	Y	N	N	S	1989031412145074	
3			N	N	Y	N	N	N	Y	N	N	S	1989031412145074	

The PLAN TABLE contains a row for every DB2 table specified in the FROM clause. The column, Queryno, is set by the user in the SET QUERYNO option of the EXPLAIN statement. Two columns of particular interest are Planno and Accessty. The column, Planno, indicates the order that the DB2 table shown in the column, Tname, is accessed. Projinfo is accessed first, followed by Persinfo, and then Orginfo. The value of Accessty can be I or R. I indicates that an index will be used by the DB2 Optimizer. R indicates that an index will not be used and the table will be read sequentially (tablespace scan). In this example, all DB2 tables will be read sequentially. Indexes were not created for these tables. For large DB2 tables, the user should try to get the DB2 Optimizer to use an index if it is appropriate for the application. The DB2 Optimizer often uses an index if the user uses it in the WHERE clause for row selection. For more information on the EXPLAIN statement and the PLAN TABLE, refer to Chapter 3, IBM'S Database 2, section, Data Access.

Example 12-3

Another EXPLAIN statement is executed, with a different SELECT statement. The SET QUERYNO option of the EXPLAIN statement is set to 2, where a value of 1 was used in the previous example.

The SAS log is shown below:

```

     PROC DB2UTIL SSID=DSP;
       SQL
       EXPLAIN PLAN SET QUERYNO=2
         FOR
         SELECT PE.LAST_NAME, PE.FIRST_NAME, PROJECT,
                DEPARTMENT_NAME
            FROM TSID123.PERSINFO PE, TSID123.PROJINFO PJ,
                 TSID123.ORGINFO
            WHERE PE.LAST_NAME = PJ.LAST_NAME AND
                  PE.FIRST_NAME = PJ.FIRST_NAME AND
                  COST_CENTER = DEPARTMENT AND
                  DEPARTMENT = '130'
            ORDER BY DEPARTMENT_NAME, PE.LAST_NAME;

NOTE: FIELDS REQUIRED FOR UPDATE WERE NOT ENTERED OR IN ERROR
NOTE: TABLE= OPTION REQUIRED FOR UPDATE PROCESSING WAS NOT ENTERED

     PROC DB2EXT OUT=PLAN UNIQUE;
       SELECT * FROM TSID123.PLAN_TABLE;

NOTE: THE DATA SET WORK.PLAN HAS 6 OBSERVATIONS AND 25 VARIABLES.

     PROC PRINT DATA=PLAN;
       TITLE1 'PLAN TABLE RESULTS OF EXPLAIN';
NOTE: THE PROCEDURE PRINT PRINTED PAGE 1.
```

PROC PRINT produces the following report:

PLAN TABLE RESULTS OF EXPLAIN

OBS	QUERYNO	QBLOCKNO	APPLNAME	PROGNAME	PLANNO	METHOD	CREATOR	TNAME	TABNO	ACCESSTY	MATCHCOL
1	1	1		DB2UTILI	1	0	TSID123	PROJINFO	2	R	0
2	1	1		DB2UTILI	2	2	TSID123	PERSINFO	1	R	0
3	1	1		DB2UTILI	3	2	TSID123	ORGINFO	3	R	0
4	2	1		DB2UTILI	1	0	TSID123	PROJINFO	2	R	0
5	2	1		DB2UTILI	2	2	TSID123	PERSINFO	1	R	0
6	2	1		DB2UTILI	3	2	TSID123	ORGINFO	3	R	0

OBS	ACCESSCR	ACCESSNA	INDEXONL	SORTN_UN	SORTN_JO	SORTN_OR	SORTN_GR	SORTC_UN	SORTC_JO	SORTC_OR	SORTC_GR	TSLOCKMO	TIMESTAM	REMARKS
1			N	N	N	N	N	N	N	N	N	S	1989031412145074	
2			N	N	Y	N	N	N	Y	N	N	S	1989031412145074	
3			N	N	Y	N	N	N	Y	N	N	S	1989031412145074	
4			N	N	N	N	N	N	N	N	N	S	1989031412295870	
5			N	N	Y	N	N	N	Y	N	N	S	1989031412295870	
6			N	N	Y	N	N	N	Y	N	N	S	1989031412295870	

When PROC DB2EXT was executed, 6 observations were produced. The value of the column, Queryno, is 1 for the first three observations and 2 for the last three observations. The PLAN TABLE is not replaced when the EXPLAIN statement is executed; instead, results of subsequent EXPLAIN statements are added to the end of the existing PLAN TABLE. By setting the value of the SET QUERYNO option of the EXPLAIN statement, you will be able to distinguish one result from another. The next example shows how to delete the contents of the PLAN TABLE.

Example 12-4

Frequently, the results of previous executions of an EXPLAIN should be deleted. This example shows the SQL DELETE statement used in the SQL statement of PROC DB2UTIL to delete the contents of the PLAN TABLE, Tsid123.plan_table. The table will still exist, but will be empty. The next PROC DB2UTIL step executes an EXPLAIN and the results stored in the PLAN TABLE, Tsid123.plan_table.

A DATA step is used to read the SAS data set created by PROC DB2EXT and containing the results of the EXPLAIN. The purpose of this DATA step is to abend the SAS program if the DB2 table, Tsid123.orginfo, is not accessed first by the DB2 Optimizer. The Optimizer does not always select the most efficient access path. If you know that it is more efficient for a specific table to be accessed first (because it is the smallest, or it contains an index that is used in the selection criteria of the WHERE clause), the SAS program shown below can be used to front end your actual program. In other words, the SAS code shown below would be followed by a PROC DB2EXT that executes the SELECT statement shown in the EXPLAIN statement and performs any other DATA and PROC steps required by the application. In this example, the ABEND statement is executed so the remainder of the program will not execute.

The DB2 Optimizer determines the access path when the SELECT statement is executed. The access path can change for the same SELECT statement if changes have been made to any of the DB2 tables and the DB2 utility, RUNSTATS, has been executed to inform the DB2 System Catalog Tables of these changes. Therefore, this program can be used as a frontend to the actual application to insure that the program does not execute if the access path is not appropriate.

```

      PROC DB2UTIL SSID=DSP;
        SQL DELETE FROM TSID123.PLAN_TABLE ;

NOTE: FIELDS REQUIRED FOR UPDATE WERE NOT ENTERED OR IN ERROR
NOTE: TABLE= OPTION REQUIRED FOR UPDATE PROCESSING WAS NOT ENTERED
```

```
      PROC DB2UTIL SSID=DSP;
        SQL
        EXPLAIN PLAN SET QUERYNO=2
        FOR
        SELECT PE.LAST_NAME, PE.FIRST_NAME, PROJECT,
               DEPARTMENT
          FROM TSID123.PERSINFO PE, TSID123.PROJINFO PJ,
               TSID123.ORGINFO
          WHERE PE.LAST_NAME = PJ.LAST_NAME AND
                PE.FIRST_NAME = PJ.FIRST_NAME AND
                COST_CENTER = DEPARTMENT AND
                DEPARTMENT = '130'
          ORDER BY DEPARTMENT_NAME, PE.LAST_NAME;

NOTE: FIELDS REQUIRED FOR UPDATE WERE NOT ENTERED OR IN ERROR
NOTE: TABLE= OPTION REQUIRED FOR UPDATE PROCESSING WAS NOT ENTERED

      PROC DB2EXT OUT=PLAN UNIQUE;
        SELECT * FROM TSID123.PLAN_TABLE;

NOTE: THE DATA SET WORK.PLAN HAS 3 OBSERVATIONS AND 25 VARIABLES.

      PROC PRINT DATA=PLAN;
        TITLE1 'PLAN TABLE RESULTS OF EXPLAIN';

NOTE: THE PROCEDURE PRINT PRINTED PAGE 1.

      DATA _NULL_;
        SET PLAN;
        IF CREATOR = 'TSID123' AND TNAME='ORGINFO'
           AND PLANNO G= 1 THEN ABORT 777;

ERROR: ABORT STATEMENT EXECUTED.
+ERROR: ABORT STATEMENT EXECUTED.
+ERROR: ABORT STATEMENT EXECUTED.
QUERYNO=2 QBLOCKNO=1 APPLNAME=  PROGNAME=DB2UTILI PLANNO=3
METHOD=2 CREATOR=TSID123 TNAME=ORGINFO TABNO=3 ACCESSTY=R
MATCHCOL=0 ACCESSCR=  ACCESSNA=  INDEXONL=N SORTN_UN=N SORTN_JO=Y
SORTN_OR=N SORTN_GR=N SORTC_UN=N SORTC_JO=Y SORTC_OR=N SORTC_GR=N
TSLOCKMO=S TIMESTAM=1989031412374686 REMARKS=  _ERROR_=1 _N_=2
NOTE: SAS SET OPTION OBS=0 AND WILL CONTINUE TO CHECK STATEMENTS.
      THIS MAY CAUSE NOTE: NO OBSERVATIONS IN DATA SET.
```

Example 12-5

A list of employees who worked on the 'Budget' project is needed, along with all other projects they have worked on.

There are several approaches which can be taken to produce this information. If the DB2 table is small, as it is in this case, you might create a SAS data set containing all employees using PROC DB2EXT. This SAS data set could be processed using the capabilities of Base SAS to reduce it to the desired information. The methodolgy shown here is a good alternative when computer resource utilization is a concern. Often, the size of the DB2 table makes it prohibitive to read sequentially (tablespace scan) and the amount of storage required by the resulting SAS data set can also be a problem.

The approach shown here includes extracting employees who worked on the 'Budget' project, loading those into a DB2 table, and joining this DB2 table with the original, Tsid123.projinfo. Typically in this situation, the most efficient access path would be to access the newly created DB2 table first and match those values with values in the DB2 table, Tsid123.projinfo. The DB2 Optimizer selects the access path based on information stored in the DB2 System Tables. A DB2 utility, RUNSTATS, must be executed in order to update the DB2 System Tables with information on newly created DB2 tables. If RUNSTATS is not executed and the DB2 System Tables do not contain any information on a table specified in a SELECT statement, that table will be accessed last. RUNSTATS cannot be executed in SAS, so the approach to this application includes three program steps; SAS is executed first to extract employees who worked on the 'Budget' project, RUNSTATS is executed, and SAS is executed again to produce the final result. Consult your DB2 Database Administrator for the appropriate JCL in your company to execute RUNSTATS.

The SAS log for the first program step is:

```
PROC DB2EXT OUT=BUDSTAFF;
  SELECT LAST_NAME, FIRST_NAME
    FROM TSID123.PROJINFO
    WHERE PROJECT = 'BUDGET                    ';
  RENAME 1=LNAME 2=FNAME;
```

```
NOTE: THE DATA SET WORK.BUDSTAFF HAS 4 OBSERVATIONS AND 2
      VARIABLES.

8   PROC DB2LOAD DATA=BUDSTAFF
9                TABLE=TSID123.BUDSTAFF LOAD;
10    IN 'TSID123.SAMPLE';
11
-------- MAP FOR CREATE AND LOAD ---------------------------
  COLUMN NAME        DB2 FORMAT           SAS NAME    NULLS?
  LNAME              CHAR(15)             LNAME         Y
  FNAME              CHAR(10)             FNAME         Y
12     LIST ALL;
13
............................................................
    LOAD STATISTICS:
NUMBER OF ROWS INSERTED    =              4
NUMBER OF SAS OBS READ     =              4
NUMBER OF INSERTS REJECTED =              0
............................................................
```

Thus, data has been extracted from a DB2 table and placed in a SAS data set, which in turn has been loaded into a new DB2 table. Next, the system will be informed of the existence and properties of this new table through the RUNSTATS utility. This statement is coded as follows:

```
RUNSTATS TABLESPACE TSID123.SAMPLE INDEX (ALL)
```

When the RUNSTATS utility is executed using JCL tailored to your company, the following messages will be generated:

```
DSNU050I   DSNUGUTC - RUNSTATS TABLESPACE TSID123.SAMPLE INDEX
                      (ALL)
DSNU610I # DSNUSCAT - SYSTABLESPACE CATALOG UPDATE FOR
                      TSID123.SAMPLE SUCCESSFUL
DSNU610I # DSNUSCAT - SYSTABLES CATALOG UPDATE FOR TSID123.BUDSTAFF
                      SUCCESSFUL
DSNU610I # DSNUSCAT - SYSTABLEPART CATALOG UPDATE FOR
                      TSID123.SAMPLE SUCCESSFUL
DSNU010I # DSNUSCAT - UTILITY EXECUTION COMPLETE, HIGHEST RETURN
                      CODE=0
```

Now the new table can be joined with the original table to produce the required data. The SAS log for this process, which is the third step in the program, is shown below:

```
   PROC DB2EXT OUT=STAFF;
     SELECT LAST_NAME, FIRST_NAME, PROJECT
       FROM TSID123.PROJINFO, TSID123.BUDSTAFF
       WHERE LAST_NAME = LNAME AND
             FIRST_NAME = FNAME;

NOTE: THE DATA SET WORK.STAFF HAS 7 OBSERVATIONS AND 3 VARIABLES.

    PROC PRINT DATA=STAFF LABEL;
      TITLE 'ALL PROJECTS WORKED BY STAFF';
      TITLE2 'WHO ALSO WORKED ON BUDGET PROJECT';
NOTE: THE PROCEDURE PRINT PRINTED PAGE 1.
```

PROC PRINT executed in this step produces the following results:

```
                ALL PROJECTS WORKED BY STAFF
             WHO ALSO WORKED ON BUDGET PROJECT

OBS    LAST_NAME      FIRST_NAME     PROJECT

 1     HARRINGTON     MARLIN         BUDGET
 2     HARRINGTON     MARLIN         BROKERS
 3     KELLUM         ELLEN JANE     BUDGET
 4     KELLUM         ELLEN JANE     FINANCIAL STATEMENT
 5     MEEKS          EDWARD         BUDGET
 6     MEEKS          EDWARD         COMMISSIONS
 7     PALMER         NANCY          BUDGET
```

PROC DB2EXT is used to extract those employees who worked on the 'Budget' project. Notice that the value, 'Budget', is padded with blanks to the full length of the column because this will execute more efficiently. The SAS data set created is then loaded into a DB2 table using PROC DB2LOAD. This completes the first step in your program. The next step uses JCL tailored to your company to execute RUNSTATS, which updates the DB2 System Tables. The third program step executes SAS again. PROC DB2EXT is used to join Tsid123.Projinfo and the user-created table, Tsid123.budstaff.

Since the DB2 tables used in this example are small, the access method does not have a great impact on the computer resources required to extract the desired data. However, if the DB2 table, Tsid123.Projinfo, were large, it would be critical to access the DB2 table, Tsid123.budstaff, first and join only these rows with the appropriate rows in Tsid123.projinfo. If Tsid123.projinfo were accessed first, all rows would be read sequentially (tablespace scan), only to end up eliminating those rows that did not match rows in Tsid123.budstaff.

Example 12-6

This example illustrates creation of a DB2 table for the purpose of selecting rows from a DB2 table. This method may be used in at least two situations. First, you may need to extract data from a DB2 table based on values contained in file which is not a DB2 table. Base SAS can be used to read the file and create a SAS data set. The SAS/DB2 procedure, PROC DB2LOAD, can then be used to create and load a DB2 table from this SAS data set. PROC DB2EXT can then be used to join the two DB2 tables to extract the desired data. Another alternative can be used if the DB2 table containing the desired data is small. All the rows in the DB2 table can be extracted and stored in a SAS data set using PROC DB2EXT. Base SAS can then be used to merge this SAS data set with a SAS data set created from the other file structure.

A second situation in which this approach can be used is when selection criteria needed in the WHERE clause of the SELECT statement exceeds the maximum 32,000 characters. This situation is unlikely, but can be handled. In this case, these values could be loaded into a DB2 table and joined with the DB2 table containing the desired data in order to select specific rows. The DB2 table which needs to be created to support these applications can be loaded in a number of ways. The values could be entered into a file using TSO, Base SAS used to read this file and create a SAS data set, and PROC DB2LOAD used to create and load a DB2 table from the SAS data set. The values could be entered into a SAS data set using the SAS/FSP procedure, PROC FSEDIT, and PROC DB2LOAD could then create and load the DB2 table from this SAS data set. Another alternative would be to enter the values directly into a DB2 table using the SAS/FSP procedure, PROC FSEDIT. This capability is covered in the next chapter, The SAS/FSP Interface.

In either of these situations, it will probably be more efficient if the user-created DB2 table is accessed first, because it is typically smaller than the DB2 table containing the desired data. The DB2 Optimizer will make this determination. The DB2 utility, RUNSTATS, must be executed to update the DB2 System Tables with information on the user-created DB2 table in order for it to be available to the Optimizer. As the user-created DB2 table increases, you may find that the DB2 Optimizer no longer selects it as the first DB2 table accessed, even though it may still be more efficient to do so. The methodology shown in the previous example, where the program is forced to abend if Planno in the PLAN TABLE is not equal to 1, could be utilized. A second approach is used in this example. A single observation is loaded in the user-created DB2 table, RUNSTATS is executed to update the DB2 System Tables, and then the remainder of the observations are inserted in the DB2 table. The DB2 Optimizer will use the information in the DB2 System Tables, which is based on a DB2 table with only one row, to determine the access path. Because RUNSTATS is not run after the remainder of the observations are inserted in the DB2 table, the system is fooled into thinking the DB2 table has only one row. A table with one row is usually selected by the Optimizer as the first table to access.

The selection criteria for this application are based on social security numbers stored in a flat file. Data for these social security numbers are needed from the DB2 table, Tsid123.persinfo.

The approach shown here includes three program steps. SAS is executed in the first step to create a tablespace, read the flat file, and create and load the DB2 table. The second program step is the DB2 utility, RUNSTATS, which must be executed to update the DB2 system table with information on the newly created DB2 table. RUNSTATS can not be executed in SAS. SAS is executed again in the third program step to join the user created DB2 table with the existing DB2 table, Tsid123.persinfo.

The SAS log for the first program step is:

```
1
2     PROC DB2UTIL;
3       SQL DROP TABLESPACE TSID123.SOCSEC;
4       SQL COMMIT;
5
NOTE: FIELDS REQUIRED FOR UPDATE WERE NOT ENTERED OR IN ERROR
NOTE: TABLE= OPTION REQUIRED FOR UPDATE PROCESSING WAS NOT ENTERED


6     PROC DB2UTIL;
```

```
7       SQL
8       CREATE TABLESPACE SOCSEC
9         IN TSID123
10        USING
11        STOGROUP FREEGP01
12          PRIQTY 1000
13          SECQTY 1000
14          ERASE NO
15        FREEPAGE 000
16        PCTFREE 00
17        LOCKSIZE TABLESPACE
18        BUFFERPOOL BP0
19        CLOSE NO  ;
20
NOTE: FIELDS REQUIRED FOR UPDATE WERE NOT ENTERED OR IN ERROR
NOTE: TABLE= OPTION REQUIRED FOR UPDATE PROCESSING WAS NOT ENTERED

21      DATA SELSSN1 SAVE.SELSSN2;
22        INFILE SASIN;
23        INPUT @3 SSN $9.;
24        IF _N_ = 1 THEN OUTPUT SELSSN1;
25        ELSE OUTPUT SAVE.SELSSN2;
26

NOTE: INFILE SASIN IS:
      DSNAME=TEST.T123.SSN,
      UNIT=DISK,VOL=SER=DSKV21,DISP=SHR,
      DCB=(BLKSIZE=5600,LRECL=80,RECFM=FB)
NOTE: 38 LINES WERE READ FROM INFILE SASIN.
NOTE: DATA SET WORK.SELSSN1 HAS 1 OBSERVATIONS AND 1 VARIABLES.
NOTE: DATA SET SAVE.SELSSN2 HAS 37 OBSERVATIONS AND 1 VARIABLES.

27      PROC DB2LOAD DATA=SELSSN1
28                   TABLE=TSID123.SELSSN LOAD;
29        IN 'TSID123.SOCSEC';
30        NULLS SSN=N;
31
-------- MAP FOR CREATE AND LOAD ---------------------------
  COLUMN NAME          DB2 FORMAT            SAS NAME    NULLS?
  SSN                  CHAR(9)               SSN           N
32        LIST ALL;
33
...........................................................
```

```
     LOAD STATISTICS:
NUMBER OF ROWS INSERTED     =            1
NUMBER OF SAS OBS READ      =            1
NUMBER OF INSERTS REJECTED =             0
.............................................................
```

The RUNSTATS utility is executed to inform the system of the existence and properties of this new table. The RUNSTATS statement is coded as follows:

```
RUNSTATS TABLESPACE TSID123.SAMPLE INDEX (ALL)
```

When the RUNSTATS utility is executed using JCL tailored to your company, the following messages will be generated:

```
DSNU050I   DSNUGUTC - RUNSTATS TABLESPACE TSID123.SOCSEC INDEX
                      (ALL)
DSNU610I # DSNUSCAT - SYSTABLESPACE CATALOG UPDATE FOR
                      TSID123.SOCSEC SUCCESSFUL
DSNU610I # DSNUSCAT - SYSTABLES CATALOG UPDATE FORTSID123.SELSSN
                      SUCCESSFUL
DSNU610I # DSNUSCAT - SYSTABLEPART CATALOG UPDATE FOR
                      TSID123.SOCSEC SUCCESSFUL
DSNU010I # DSNUSCAT - UTILITY EXECUTION COMPLETE, HIGHEST RETURN
                      CODE=0
```

The SAS log for the third program step is:

```
1
2     PROC DB2UTIL DATA=SAVE.SELSSN2 TABLE=TSID123.SELSSN
3                  SSID=DSP FUNCTION=INSERT;
4       UPDATE;
5       MAPTO SSN = SSN;
6
.............................................................
-------------- MAP FOR TABLE UPDATE --------FUNCTION:INSERT
  COLUMN NAME          DB2 FORMAT           SAS NAME
  SSN                  CHAR(9)              SSN
---------------- WHERE STATEMENT ----------------
.............................................................
7       LIST ALL;
8
```

```
.............................................
UTILITY STATISTICS:
SQL INSERTS ISSUED =                  37
NUMBER OF SAS OBS READ =              37
SQL STATEMENTS REJECTED =             0
.............................................

9       PROC DB2EXT OUT=EMPINFO;
10        SELECT LAST_NAME, FIRST_NAME, COST_CENTER, SALARY_DECEMBER
11          FROM TSID123.PERSINFO, TSID123.SELSSN
12          WHERE SOCIAL_SECURITY = SSN;
13
NOTE: THE DATA SET WORK.EMPINFO HAS 38 OBSERVATIONS AND 4
      VARIABLES.

14      PROC PRINT DATA=EMPINFO LABEL;
15        TITLE 'EMPLOYEE INFORMATION';
16        TITLE2 'FOR SELECTED SALARIES';
NOTE: THE PROCEDURE PRINT PRINTED PAGE 1.
```

The report produced by PROC PRINT is shown below:

EMPLOYEE INFORMATION
FOR SELECTED SALARIES

OBS	LAST_NAME	FIRST_NAME	COST_CENTER	SALARY_DECEMBER
1	ADAMS	BILL	100	2100
2	APPLE	RICHARD	120	3210
3	ATKINS	NANCY	120	3750
4	BROWN	WALLY	100	2570
5	BUELL	MAX	110	2890
6	BURNETT	ERIC	110	400
7	CAMPBELL	MARGARET	130	2520
8	CONNOR	BRUCE	110	2100
9	CONWELL	LINDA	100	2310
10	COOPER	MARGIE	100	1370
11	DAVIS	SUSAN	100	1000
12	DOUGLAS	MILTON	140	4490
13	DUDLEY	LOUISA	130	2210
14	GOETZ	JACK	130	3320
15	HANKS	TROY	130	1890
16	HARRINGTON	MARLIN	120	3210

17	HARRIS	JULIE	110	1820
18	HUFFORD	STEPHEN	130	2350
19	HUTSON	EVERETT	140	3530
20	JONES	JOAN	100	500
21	KEESLING	GERTRUDE	140	3750
22	KELLUM	ELLEN JANE	120	2570
23	KISLING	MARY LEA	130	2140
24	MARK	MIRON	110	1580
25	MARSHALL	MICHAEL	100	500
26	MEEKS	EDWARD	120	3000
27	MEISER	MARK	110	2030
28	MEYER	VIVIAN	100	450
29	MICHAEL	PAT	140	4280
30	MILLER	EMMALYNE	140	2140
31	MORGAN	CHERYL	140	4070
32	OLIVER	BETTY	120	1050
33	PALMER	NANCY	120	1820
34	PAYTON	RUTH	120	2210
35	PEARCE	EVELYN	130	1680
36	PHILLIPS	SARAH	110	1470
37	SMITH	SCOTT	110	2000
38	STONE	JENNIFER	120	1370

Since this program will be executed more than once, a SQL DROP statement is used to drop previous versions of the DB2 table by executing the SQL statement with PROC DB2UTIL. A SQL CREATE statement is executed to create a tablespace, Tsid123.socsec, to hold the DB2 table to be created. The flat file is read in a DATA step and two SAS data sets are created. The SAS data set, Selssn1, contains only the first input record and Selssn2 contains the remainder. Selssn1 is loaded into the DB2 table, Tsid123.selssn. This table is used to update the DB2 System Tables using the RUNSTATS utility. The SAS data set, Selssn2, is given a two-level SAS data set name because it is passed to the third program step, where it is added to the DB2 table using PROC DB2UTIL. PROC DB2EXT is used to join the user-created table with the DB2 table containing the desired data.

Chapter

13

The SAS/FSP Interface

The SAS/FSP (Full Screen Product) procedures, PROC FSEDIT and PROC FSBROWSE, used to edit and browse data stored in SAS data sets, respectively, can also be used to access data stored in DB2 tables. SAS/FSP must be installed at your company in addition to SAS/DB2 in order to use these procedures. PROC FSEDIT is used for data entry and editing. PROC FSBROWSE is used only to browse; changes cannot be made.

PROC FSEDIT and PROC FSBROWSE are used almost exclusively interactively. Each displays a full screen per SAS observation or DB2 row showing the SAS variable names/DB2 column names along with the data values. The operation of these procedures with DB2 tables is nearly identical to their operation with SAS data sets. The function key definitions and commands are the same. Custom screens can be designed and DB2 data can be used as input to letters with PROC FSLETTER.

The syntax of PROC FSEDIT and PROC FSBROWSE with DB2 tables will be covered, along with differences between processing SAS data sets versus DB2 tables. It is not the intent of this chapter to cover the entire operation of these SAS/FSP procedures.

PROC FSBROWSE

PROC FSBROWSE is used to browse SAS data sets or DB2 tables. This can be helpful in familiarizing yourself with the data or for looking up specific information. When accessing DB2 tables, the general form of the PROC FSBROWSE statement is:

```
PROC FSBROWSE TABLE = authorizationid.table;
```

or

```
PROC FSBROWSE QTABLE = 'authorizationid.table';
```

The TABLE or QTABLE option is used to specify the name of the DB2 table you wish to browse. One of these options is used rather than the DATA option, which is used to specify the name of a SAS data set you wish to browse.

TABLE Option: A DB2 table name up to 16 positions in length and adhering to SAS naming conventions can be specified in the TABLE option. SAS naming conventions include: (1) the first character must be a letter or underscore; (2) later characters can be letters, numbers, or underscores; and (3) blanks and special characters other than the underscore cannot be used anywhere in the name.

QTABLE Option: A DB2 table name up to 18 positions in length can be specified in the QTABLE (or QTAB) option. The table name can contain special characters not allowed by SAS naming conventions. The DB2 table name must be specified in quotes.

SSID Option: Same as definition with PROC DB2EXT. Refer to Chapter 7, PROC DB2EXT in Batch, for more information.

LABEL Option: When the LABEL option is used, DB2 column names are displayed. If the LABEL option is not used, the DB2 column names are truncated to the first eight positions.

Other Options

Other options available with PROC FSBROWSE when browsing SAS data sets can also be used with DB2 tables.

Differences

The only difference between browsing SAS data sets and DB2 tables is the BACKWARD command, normally issued using the function keys, PF7/PF19. When scrolling backward in a SAS data set, operationally the pointer backs up one observation. When scrolling backward in a DB2 table, operationally the pointer begins with the first row and reads sequentially until the row previous to the one displayed is reached. For example, if a DB2 table has 10,000 rows and you are displaying row 7,621 and you issue the BACKWARD command, rows 1 through 7,620 are read sequentially. This can present performance problems when accessing DB2 tables, especially when you are currently displaying a row toward the end of the table.

PROC FSEDIT

PROC FSEDIT is used to edit SAS data sets or DB2 tables. It is often used for data entry and can be useful when data values need to be edited. You must have authority to update the DB2 table specified. When accessing DB2 tables, the general form of the PROC FSEDIT statement is:

```
PROC FSEDIT TABLE = authorizationid.table;
```

or

```
PROC FSEDIT QTABLE = 'authorizationid.table';
```

The TABLE or QTABLE option is used to specify the name of the DB2 table you wish to edit. One of these options is used rather than the DATA or NEW options, which is used to specify the name of a SAS data set you wish to browse.

The TABLE, QTABLE, SSID, and LABEL options, defined for PROC FSBROWSE are also valid for PROC FSEDIT, along with other options used with PROC FSEDIT when accessing SAS data sets.

Differences

The BACKWARD command, as described with PROC FSBROWSE, also applies to PROC FSEDIT.

The DELETE command used with PROC FSEDIT works differently with DB2 tables than with SAS data sets. When the DELETE command is used with SAS data sets to delete an observation, the observation is not actually deleted, but all values are set to missing. When the DELETE command is used with DB2 tables, the row is actually deleted. The only exception to this is when the DUP command has been used to create the row and the DELETE command is issued before moving to another row. This is the same as processing with SAS data sets.

The AUTOSAVE command used with PROC FSEDIT against SAS data sets specifies the number of observations which can be entered/edited before the changes are automatically saved. The SAVE command with PROC FSEDIT against SAS data sets is issued by the user when he wishes to save changes entered since the last SAVE or AUTOSAVE was executed. When the AUTOSAVE and SAVE commands are used with PROC FSEDIT against DB2 tables, a SQL COMMIT statement is issued which saves changes to the DB2 table and frees appropriate locks on the table. If more than one user is using the same DB2 table, you should set the AUTOSAVE value low in order to free locks and thus make the data available to other users. The AUTOSAVE and SAVE commands take more time to execute with DB2 tables than with SAS data sets, and users may find this distracting.

Example 13-1

To browse the DB2 table, Tsid123.projinfo, the following statement could be submitted from the PROGRAM window of Display Manager:

```
PROC FSBROWSE QTABLE='TSID123.PROJINFO' SSID=DST LABEL; RUN;
```

The TABLE option could be used in this case instead of the QTABLE option because the table name is under 16 positions and does not contain special characters. The SSID option needs to be specified only when the default value is not appropriate. The LABEL option is used to display DB2 column names rather than SAS variable names. The syntax for PROC FSEDIT is identical, but gives the user update capabilities.

The following screen is displayed:

```
                 Browse Table: tsid123.projinfo          Screen 1
Command ===>                                             Obs    1

              LAST_NAME         APPLE
              FIRST_NAME        RICHARD
              BEGIN_DATE         881001
              PLAN_END_DATE      881201
              ACTUAL_END_DATE    881201
              PROJECT           COMPENSATION PLAN
```

Appendix

A

DB2 System Catalog Tables

This appendix contains a description of the DB2 system catalog tables most often needed by users. Not all of the columns in these tables are described. Only those columns most often needed by users are shown. Refer to IBM documentation for a complete description.

SYSCOLUMNS: Column information for every table and view.

Column Name	*Data Type*	*Description*
NAME	VARCHAR(18)	Column name
TBNAME	VARCHAR(18)	Table or view name
TBCREATOR	CHAR(8)	Creator of table or view; first level of name
COLNO	SMALLINT	Location of column in table/ view
COLTYPE	CHAR(8)	Data type
LENGTH	SMALLINT	Length of column
SCALE	SMALLINT	Scale for decimals; 0 otherwise
NULLS	CHAR(1)	Y/N; can column contain NULLS?
COLCARD	INTEGER	Number of unique values of column; -1 if no data are available or column is not the first column of index

UPDATES	CHAR(1)	Y/N; can the column be updated?
REMARKS	VARCHAR(254)	Comments
DEFAULT	CHAR(1)	Y/N; does column (NULL or NOT NULL) have a default value?
KEYSEQ	SMALLINT	Location in the primary key; 0 if not in primary key
FOREIGNKEY	CHAR(1)	Y/N; is column part of foreign key?
LABEL	VARCHAR(30)	Label of column if one exists

SYSFOREIGNKEYS: Information on foreign keys.

Column Name	*Data Type*	*Description*
CREATOR	CHAR(8)	Creator of the table/view; first level of name
TBNAME	VARCHAR(18)	Table or view name
RELNAME	CHAR(8)	Name of relationship with foreign key
COLNAME	VARCHAR(18)	Column name
COLNO	SMALLINT	Location of column in table/ view
COLSEQ	SMALLINT	Location of column in foreign key

SYSINDEXES: Information on indexes.

Column Name	*Data Type*	*Description*
NAME	VARCHAR(18)	Index name
CREATOR	CHAR(8)	Creator of index
TBNAME	VARCHAR(18)	Name of table with index
TBCREATOR	CHAR(8)	Creator of table, first level of name
UNIQUERULE	CHAR(1)	Is index unique?; D(no), U(yes)
COLCOUNT	SMALLINT	Number of columns in key
CLUSTERING	CHAR(1)	Y/N; cluster specified at index creation
CLUSTERED	CHAR(1)	Y/N; is index clustered?
DBNAME	CHAR(8)	Database name with index

INDEXSPACE	CHAR(8)	Indexspace name
FIRSTKEYCARD	INTEGER	Number of unique values of first key column; -1 if data not available
FULLKEYCARD	INTEGER	Number of unique values of key; -1 if data not available

SYSSYNONYMS: Information on synonyms.

Column Name	*Data Type*	*Description*
NAME	VARCHAR(18)	Synonym for table or view
CREATOR	CHAR(8)	Creator of synonym
TBNAME	VARCHAR(18)	Name of table or view
TBCREATOR	CHAR(8)	Creator of table, first level of name

SYSTABLES: Table information.

Column Name	*Data Type*	*Description*
NAME	VARCHAR(18)	Table or view name
CREATOR	CHAR(8)	Creator of table or view
TYPE	CHAR(1)	Table (T) or view (V)?
DBNAME	CHAR(8)	Database name
TSNAME	CHAR(8)	Tablespace
COLCOUNT	SMALLINT	Number of columns in table or view
CARD	INTEGER	Number of rows in table
REMARKS	VARCHAR(254)	Comments
KEYCOLUMNS	SMALLINT	Number of columns in primary key
LABEL	VARCHAR(30)	Label of table if one exists

SYSTABLESPACE: Tablespace information.

Column Name	*Data Type*	*Description*
NAME	VARCHAR(18)	Tablespace name
CREATOR	CHAR(8)	Creator of tablespace
DBNAME	CHAR(8)	Database name

SYSVIEWDEP: Information on views as related to tables and other views.

Column Name	*Data Type*	*Description*
BNAME	VARCHAR(18)	Table/view that view depends on
BCREATOR	CHAR(8)	Creator of BNAME
DNAME	CHAR(8)	View name
DCREATOR	CHAR(8)	Creator of view

Appendix

B

The DB2 Plan Table

Columns in the PLAN_TABLE and a brief description follow:

QUERYNO:	A number which distinguishes one plan from another. It is often assigned by the user using the SET QUERYNO option in the EXPLAIN statement. If it is not assigned by the user, DB2 will create a number.
QBLOCKNO:	Number which distinguishes levels within a subselect, with the top level being number 1.
APPLNAME:	Name of the application.
PROGNAME:	Name of the program containing the EXPLAIN. If executed inside SAS, it would be DB2UTIL.
PLANNO:	A number which indicates the order in which tables (TNAME) will be accessed, with 1 being the first.
METHOD:	One of the following values: 0 First table accessed (PLANNO=1) 1 Nested Loop Join 2 Merge Scan Join 3 Additional Sorts (ORDER BY, GROUP BY, DISTINCT)

CREATOR:	The first level of the table name represented by this row in the PLAN_TABLE, blank for METHOD 3.
TNAME:	The second level of the table name represented by this row in the PLAN_TABLE, blank for METHOD 3.
TABNO:	A number which distinguishes different references to the same table, 0 for METHOD 3.
ACCESSTYPE:	The access method used for the table: I — Index as identified by ACCESSNAME was used. R — Tablespace scan. Blank — Either by the first index on the table or by cursors (Update/Delete)
MATCHCOLS:	For ACCESSTYPE I, the number of indexes used, 0 otherwise.
ACCESSCREATOR:	The first level of the index name for ACCESSTYPE I, blank otherwise.
ACCESSNAME:	The second level of the index name for ACCESSTYPE I, blank otherwise.
INDEXONLY:	A value of Y (yes) indicates that only the index was accessed and not any data in the corresponding table, an N (no) indicates that not just the index was accessed.

The following refers to sorting information; the SORTN refers to a new table, and SORTC refers to a composite table. A composite table is a preliminary result table representing an executed join operation. A new table is a table which must now be joined with the composite table to produce the final result table. All the SORT columns have a value of Y (yes) or N (no).

SORTN_UNIQ:	Sort to delete duplicate rows.
SORTN_JOIN:	A sort performed in preparation for a METHOD 2 join.
SORTN_ORDERBY:	A sort that resulted from a SQL statement using the ORDER BY clause.
SORTN_GROUPBY:	A sort that resulted from a SQL statement using the GROUP BY clause.
SORTC_UNIQ:	Sort to delete duplicate rows.
SORTC_JOIN:	A sort performed in preparation for a METHOD 2 join.

SORTC_ORDERBY:	A sort that resulted from a SQL statement using the ORDER BY clause.
SORTC_GROUPBY:	A sort that resulted from a SQL statement using the GROUP BY clause.
TSLOCKMODE:	The type of locking on the tablespace.
TIMESTAMP:	Execution time of the EXPLAIN.
REMARKS:	Users can put remarks of up to 254 positions in length.

The following SQL CREATE statement can be used to create a PLAN_TABLE. Use JCL tailored to your company, obtained from the Database Administrator.

```
CREATE TABLE PLAN_TABLE
   (QUERYNO        INTEGER NOT NULL,
    QBLOCKNO       SMALLINT NOT NULL,
    APPLNAME       CHAR(8) NOT NULL,
    PROGNAME       CHAR(8) NOT NULL,
    PLANNO         SMALLINT NOT NULL,
    METHOD         SMALLINT NOT NULL,
    CREATOR        CHAR(8) NOT NULL,
    TNAME          CHAR(18) NOT NULL,
    TABNO          SMALLINT NOT NULL,
    ACCESSTYPE     CHAR(2) NOT NULL,
    MATCHCOLS      SMALLINT NOT NULL,
    ACCESSCREATOR CHAR(8) NOT NULL,
    ACCESSNAME     CHAR(18) NOT NULL,
    INDEXONLY      CHAR(1) NOT NULL,
    SORTN_UNIQ     CHAR(1) NOT NULL,
    SORTN-JOIN     CHAR(1) NOT NULL,
    SORTN-ORDERBY CHAR(1) NOT NULL,
    SORTN-GROUPBY CHAR(1) NOT NULL,
    SORTC-UNIQ     CHAR(1) NOT NULL,
    SORTC-JOIN     CHAR(1) NOT NULL,
    SORTC-ORDERBY CHAR(1) NOT NULL,
    SORTC-GROUPBY CHAR(1) NOT NULL,
    TSLOCKMODE     CHAR(3) NOT NULL,
    TIMESTAMP      CHAR(16) NOT NULL,
    REMARKS        VARCHAR(254) NOT NULL)
  IN database.table ;
```

For user PLAN_TABLES, database will be the TSO user id. Table is the name of the table; most often PLAN_TABLE is used.

Appendix

C

Sample Tables

This appendix contains documentation for three DB2 tables used in SAS/DB2 examples:

```
TSID123.PERSINFO
TSID123.PROJINFO
TSID123.ORGINFO
```

A list of the columns on each of these tables and their data types is provided. In addition, PROC DB2EXT was used to create a SAS data set of each table and a report generated by PROC PRINT is shown. The column headings shown on this report are the DB2 column names.

PERSINFO and ORGINFO can be joined by the columns, COST_CENTER on PERSINFO and DEPARTMENT on ORGINFO. This is a many (PERSINFO) to one (ORGINFO) join. PERSINFO and PROJINFO can be joined by the columns, LAST_NAME and FIRST_NAME on both tables. Practically, the database would have been designed to have social security numbers used for this join, as names are not too dependable. LAST_NAME and FIRST_NAME were chosen for the purpose of illustrating a JOIN that uses more than one column. This is a one (PERSINFO) to many (PROJINFO) join. These relationships are shown in Figure C-1.

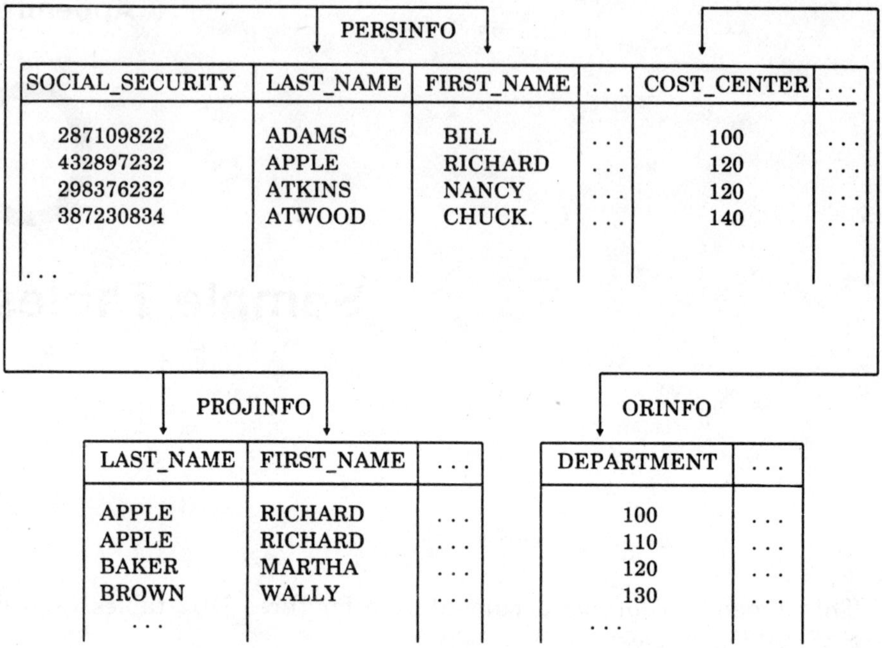

Figure C-1 DB2 sample table relationships.

Table Columns and Data Types

TABLE NAME: TSID123.PERSINFO

DB2 Column Name	*Data Type*
SOCIAL_SECURITY	CHAR(9)
LAST_NAME	CHAR(15)
FIRST_NAME	CHAR(10)
SEX	CHAR(1)
BIRTH_DATE	DECIMAL(6,0)
ADDRESS	CHAR(20)
CITY	CHAR(15)
STATE	CHAR(2)
ZIP_CODE	CHAR(5)
HOME_PHONE	CHAR(7)
HIRE_DATE	DECIMAL(6,0)

OFFICE_EXTENSION	CHAR(4)
COST_CENTER	CHAR(3)
VACATION_AVAILABLE	DECIMAL(3,0)
VACATION_USED	DECIMAL(3,0)
SICK_USED	DECIMAL(3,0)
SALARY_JANUARY	DECIMAL(5,0)
SALARY_FEBRUARY	DECIMAL(5,0)
SALARY_MARCH	DECIMAL(5,0)
SALARY_APRIL	DECIMAL(5,0)
SALARY_MAY	DECIMAL(5,0)
SALARY_JUNE	DECIMAL(5,0)
SALARY_JULY	DECIMAL(5,0)
SALARY_AUGUST	DECIMAL(5,0)
SALARY_SEPTEMBER	DECIMAL(5,0)
SALARY_OCTOBER	DECIMAL(5,0)
SALARY_NOVEMBER	DECIMAL(5,0)
SALARY_DECEMBER	DECIMAL(5,0)
EMPLOYEE_TYPE	CHAR(1)
MANAGEMENT	CHAR(1)

TABLE NAME: TSID123.PROJINFO

DB2 Column Name	*Data Type*
LAST_NAME	CHAR(15)
FIRST_NAME	CHAR(10)
BEGIN_DATE	DECIMAL(6,0)
PLAN_END_DATE	DECIMAL(6,0)
ACTUAL_END_DATE	DECIMAL(6,0)
PROJECT	CHAR(20)

TABLE NAME: TSID123.ORGINFO

DB2 Column Name	*Data Type*
DEPARTMENT	CHAR(3)
DEPARTMENT_NAME	CHAR(15)
DIRECTOR	CHAR(25)
VICE_PRESIDENT	CHAR(25)
PRESIDENT	CHAR(25)

PERSINFO Sample Table

PERSINFO (OBS 1–16)

OBS	SOCIAL_SECURITY	LAST_NAME	FIRST_NAME	SEX	BIRTH_DATE
1	287109822	ADAMS	BILL	M	241222
2	432897232	APPLE	RICHARD	M	240314
3	298376232	ATKINS	NANCY	F	530308
4	387230834	ATWOOD	CHUCK	M	360405
5	123456789	BAKER	MARTHA	F	270820
6	316989292	BROOKS	EDWARD	M	470202
7	213487293	BROOKS	JIM	M	440921
8	871027234	BROWN	WALLY	M	401123
9	778119233	BUELL	MAX	M	450304
10	319838743	BURNETT	ERIC	M	690303
11	301928392	CAMPBELL	MARGARET	F	440903
12	128719874	CLARK	ALMA	F	430805
13	987123611	CONNOR	BRUCE	M	501123
14	871837831	CONWELL	LINDA	F	431119
15	313412343	COOPER	MARGIE	F	671205
16	231231239	DAVIS	SUSAN	F	630707

OBS	ADDRESS	CITY	STATE	ZIP_CODE	HOME_PHONE
1	123 W. 62ND ST.	INDIANAPOLIS	IN	46233	8293232
2	1839 VALLEY BROOK	INDIANAPOLIS	IN	46932	9829823
3	1182 APPLEWOOD DR.	INDIANAPOLIS	IN	46921	9872342
4	221 LARK LANE	CONNERSVILLE	IN	47322	8234233
5	1102 FRANKLIN LANE	NEW CASTLE	IN	47362	8712343
6	6767 HICKORY LANE	INDIANAPOLIS	IN	46382	9078123
7	7892 HICKORY LANE	KNIGHTSTOWN	IN	47292	9078232
8	9520 ANCHOR WAY	RICHMOND	IN	47292	8708973
9	3538 MANOR CT.	NOBLESVILLE	IN	46282	9870133
10	12101 HOOSIER RD	CENTERVILLE	IN	47322	9781334
11	4292 BEECH ST	MUNCIE	IN	46205	2298422
12	1982 HANNA ROAD	CARMEL	IN	46292	2802340
13	2892 KESSLER BLVD	INDIANAPOLIS	IN	46292	9023482
14	283 OAKBROOK DRIVE	PENDLETON	IN	47282	9234928
15	8293 RAYMOND ST	YORKTOWN	IN	46289	4298713
16	282 RILEY ROAD	INDIANAPOLIS	IN	46320	2347033

OBS	HIRE_DATE	OFFICE_EXTENSION	COST_CENTER	VACATION_AVAILABLE
1	551114	3939	100	160
2	471123	9870	120	160
3	810915	9824	120	120
4	650324	9832	140	160
5	740401	9874	130	120
6	750813	9876	140	120
7	720901	8709	110	160
8	720505	9871	100	160
9	830405	8022	110	120
10	890101	9822	110	40
11	790203	9825	130	120
12	880304	8921	100	40
13	790502	3903	110	120
14	850311	7823	100	80
15	870618	9073	100	80
16	880305	2398	100	40

OBS	VACATION_USED	SICK_USED	SALARY_JANUARY	SALARY_FEBRUARY
1	40	16	2000	2000
2	80	16	3000	3000
3	56	24	3500	3500
4	72	8	2300	2300
5	40	0	2500	2500
6	80	16	5200	5200
7	120	0	1900	1900
8	80	8	2400	2400
9	48	16	2700	2700
10	8	16	400	400
11	40	32	2400	2520
12	40	16	1500	1500
13	80	40	2000	2000
14	40	0	2200	2200
15	80	16	1300	1300
16	16	8	1000	1000

OBS	SALARY_MARCH	SALARY_APRIL	SALARY_MAY	SALARY_JUNE	SALARY_JULY
1	2000	2000	2000	2000	2000
2	3000	3000	3000	3000	3000
3	3500	3500	3500	3500	3500
4	2420	2420	2420	2420	2420
5	2500	2680	2680	2680	2680
6	5200	5200	5200	5200	5200
7	1900	1900	1900	1900	1900
8	2400	2400	2570	2570	2570
9	2700	2890	2890	2890	2890
10	400	400	400	400	400
11	2520	2520	2520	2520	2520
12	1580	1580	1580	1580	1580
13	2000	2000	2100	2100	2100
14	2310	2310	2310	2310	2310
15	1300	1300	1300	1370	1370
16	1000	1000	1000	1000	1000

OBS	SALARY_AUGUST	SALARY_SEPTEMBER	SALARY_OCTOBER	SALARY_NOVEMBER
1	2000	2000	2000	2100
2	3000	3000	3000	3210
3	3500	3750	3750	3750
4	2420	2420	2420	2420
5	2680	2680	2680	2680
6	5560	5560	5560	5560
7	1900	2000	2000	2000
8	2570	2570	2570	2570
9	2890	2890	2890	2890
10	400	400	400	400
11	2520	2520	2520	2520
12	1580	1580	1580	1580
13	2100	2100	2100	2100
14	2310	2310	2310	2310
15	1370	1370	1370	1370
16	1000	1000	1000	1000

OBS	SALARY_DECEMBER	EMPLOYEE_TYPE	MANAGEMENT
1	2100	H	N
2	3210	S	N
3	3750	S	Y
4	2420	H	N
5	2680	S	N
6	5560	S	Y
7	2000	H	N
8	2570	S	N
9	2890	S	N
10	400	T	N
11	2520	H	N
12	1580	H	N
13	2100	H	N
14	2310	H	N
15	1370	H	N
16	1000	T	N

PERSINFO (OBS 17–32)

OBS	SOCIAL_SECURITY	LAST_NAME	FIRST_NAME	SEX	BIRTH_DATE
17	341234783	DODD	MARLENA	F	531123
18	321872982	DOUGLAS	MILTON	M	380905
19	312872033	DUDLEY	LOUISA	F	350104
20	341234322	GOETZ	JACK	M	440305
21	312412383	HANKS	TROY	F	480306
22	234182373	HARDWICK	DONNIE	M	600309
23	213871234	HARRINGTON	MARLIN	M	440905
24	321413287	HARRIS	JULIE	F	551123
25	324133214	HOLLYWOOD	ALICE	F	450404
26	231234334	HUFFORD	STEPHEN	M	650712
27	21341253	HUGHES	PEGGY	F	580623
28	232903983	HUTSON	EVERETT	M	320912
29	423147823	JAMES	MARVIN	M	381009
30	231487234	JOHNSON	HAZEL	F	380411
31	143328472	JONES	JOAN	F	400705
32	133248713	KAWAN	JOE	M	390305

OBS	ADDRESS	CITY	STATE	ZIP_CODE	HOME_PHONE
17	3983 ORCHARD LANE	MARKLEVILLE	IN	46282	5934020
18	833 HOOVER DRIVE	ANDERSON	IN	46282	2329842
19	1232 WALNUT ST	NEW CASTLE	IN	47362	2398234
20	192 E. MICHIGAN ST	MT SUMMIT	IN	46292	3987234
21	32 TWIN OAKS LANE	LIBERTY	IN	46282	9823492
22	833 LASALLE BLVD	SPICELAND	IN	46282	3209872
23	788 CAREFREE CT	KNIGHTSTOWN	IN	46282	3983515
24	922 CARDINAL WAY	DALEVILLE	IN	46282	2398723
25	923 BUCK CREEK RD	MILTON	IN	46292	2398733
26	829 WINDSONG WAY	KENNARD	IN	46209	2209853
27	595 TEXAS DRIVE	SULPHER SPRINGS	IN	46282	3298702
28	R. R. #1	CADIZ	IN	46290	1870435
29	920 FOX HILL RD	SHIRLEY	IN	46239	3087098
30	55 CRAIG ST	HAGERSTOWN	IN	46920	1098702
31	5537 THICKETT DR.	KNIGHTSTOWN	IN	47282	9780123
32	8146 ARAGON WOODS	MUNCIE	IN	48292	3982033

OBS	HIRE_DATE	OFFICE_EXTENSION	COST_CENTER	VACATION_AVAILABLE
17	890101	2343	110	40
18	671109	9835	140	160
19	661204	9823	130	160
20	790523	9552	130	120
21	820415	9827	130	120
22	860425	7826	130	80
23	830415	3292	120	120
24	860304	9022	110	80
25	881019	9392	110	40
26	870316	9288	130	80
27	830622	9837	120	120
28	740323	9888	140	120
29	691110	9855	120	160
30	600928	8903	100	160
31	841201	9873	100	80
32	641030	3822	130	160

OBS	VACATION_USED	SICK_USED	SALARY_JANUARY	SALARY_FEBRUARY
17	0	16	850	850
18	40	40	4200	4200
19	104	8	2100	2100
20	80	0	3100	3100
21	40	8	1800	1800
22	0	0	2700	2700
23	24	8	3000	3000
24	40	8	1700	1700
25	0	8	1500	1500
26	56	16	2200	2200
27	80	0	2100	2100
28	24	0	3300	3300
29	80	0	1900	1900
30	0	8	1000	1000
31	8	16	500	500
32	40	16	4000	4000

OBS	SALARY_MARCH	SALARY_APRIL	SALARY_MAY	SALARY_JUNE	SALARY_JULY
17	850	850	850	850	850
18	4200	4200	4200	4200	4200
19	2100	2100	2100	2100	2100
20	3100	3100	3320	3320	3320
21	1800	1890	1890	1890	1890
22	2700	2890	2890	2890	2890
23	3000	3210	3210	3210	3210
24	1820	1820	1820	1820	1820
25	1500	1500	1500	1500	1500
26	2350	2350	2350	2350	2350
27	2100	2100	2100	2250	2250
28	3530	3530	3530	3530	3530
29	1900	1900	1900	1900	1900
30	1000	1000	1000	1000	1000
31	500	500	500	500	500
32	4000	4000	4000	4000	4000

OBS	SALARY_AUGUST	SALARY_SEPTEMBER	SALARY_OCTOBER	SALARY_NOVEMBER
17	850	850	850	850
18	4200	4200	4200	4490
19	2100	2100	2100	2100
20	3320	3320	3320	3320
21	1890	1890	1890	1890
22	2890	2890	2890	2890
23	3210	3210	3210	3210
24	1820	1820	1820	1820
25	1500	1500	1580	1580
26	2350	2350	2350	2350
27	2250	2250	2250	2250
28	3530	3530	3530	3530
29	1900	1900	1900	2000
30	1000	1050	1050	1050
31	500	500	500	500
32	4000	4000	4280	4280

OBS	SALARY_DECEMBER	EMPLOYEE_TYPE	MANAGEMENT
17	850	T	N
18	4490	S	Y
19	2210	H	N
20	3320	S	N
21	1890	H	N
22	2890	S	N
23	3210	S	N
24	1820	S	N
25	1580	H	N
26	2350	S	N
27	2250	S	N
28	3530	S	N
29	2000	H	N
30	1050	H	N
31	500	T	N
32	4280	S	Y

PERSINFO (OBS 33–48)

OBS	SOCIAL_SECURITY	LAST_NAME	FIRST_NAME	SEX	BIRTH_DATE
33	123487098	KEESLING	GERTRUDE	F	510928
34	123487013	KELLUM	ELLEN JANE	F	440623
35	341431242	KISLING	MARY LEA	F	480303
36	138274102	LAUREN	KELLY	F	700905
37	187410928	MARK	MIRON	M	450315
38	348701234	MARSHALL	MICHAEL	M	710314
39	124321983	MEEKS	EDWARD	M	550429
40	123479834	MEISER	MARK	M	640707
41	124887344	MICHAEL	GARTH	M	550910
42	343214234	MICHAEL	PAT	M	400118
43	148713439	MILLER	DIZ	M	590804
44	341234134	MILLER	EMMALYNE	F	471028
45	142837414	MITCHELL	KELLY	F	660430
46	321412343	MOORE	RUTH	F	680828
47	148734123	MORGAN	CHERYL	F	560809
48	213423883	OLIVER	BETTY	F	440822

OBS	ADDRESS	CITY	STATE	ZIP_CODE	HOME_PHONE
33	6648 MAPLE LEAF RD	CADIZ	IN	46302	3498703
34	3902 CHESTERFIELD DR	KENNARD	IN	46282	4987122
35	5423 WARBLER WAY	MT SUMMIT	IN	46902	3098723
36	4393 PARKVIEW DR.	CAMBRIDE CITY	IN	46302	9329321
37	929 ALABAMA ST	HAGERSTOWN	IN	46902	3290323
38	4382 MCGALLIARD	MUNCIE	IN	47292	8342044
39	88 N IRVINGTON	GREENWOOD	IN	46282	2378622
40	3833 CEDAR RIDGE	SPEEDWAY	IN	47363	2938473
41	432 E. 14TH ST	NEW CASTLE	IN	47362	2987044
42	105 CLEARVIEW DR.	YORKTOWN	IN	47362	2929383
43	78 TIMBER LANE	SPEEDWAY	IN	46282	9832022
44	1234 WALNUT ST	NEW CASTLE	IN	47367	2078098
45	421 ROSEWAY CT	MOORELAND	IN	46282	9823933
46	322 GLENARM RD.	NOBLESVILLE	IN	46289	3298703
47	3933 WHEELER RD	ZIONSVILLE	IN	46239	3929838
48	39 GRAND AVE	MUNCIE	IN	46282	3829328

OBS	HIRE_DATE	OFFICE_EXTENSION	COST_CENTER	VACATION_AVAILABLE
33	760808	7883	140	120
34	690909	4894	120	160
35	780523	7232	130	120
36	890215	8923	130	40
37	720305	8733	110	160
38	890301	8334	100	40
39	760903	8922	120	120
40	780530	8292	110	120
41	770401	8239	130	120
42	650901	9294	140	160
43	880623	8222	100	40
44	810328	7833	140	120
45	850415	8933	100	80
46	880922	9444	100	40
47	870314	9245	140	80
48	861024	9323	120	80

OBS	VACATION_USED	SICK_USED	SALARY_JANUARY	SALARY_FEBRUARY
33	24	0	3500	3500
34	80	8	2400	2400
35	80	0	2000	2000
36	40	0	700	700
37	72	24	1500	1500
38	40	16	500	500
39	0	0	2800	2800
40	80	32	1900	1900
41	80	0	2700	2700
42	80	0	4000	4000
43	40	24	450	450
44	56	0	2000	2000
45	40	0	900	900
46	0	16	850	850
47	40	8	3800	3800
48	0	16	1000	1000

OBS	SALARY_MARCH	SALARY_APRIL	SALARY_MAY	SALARY_JUNE	SALARY_JULY
33	3500	3500	3500	3500	3500
34	2400	2400	2400	2400	2400
35	2000	2000	2140	2140	2140
36	700	700	700	700	700
37	1580	1580	1580	1580	1580
38	500	500	500	500	500
39	2800	2800	2800	2800	2800
40	1900	1900	2030	2030	2030
41	2700	2890	2890	2890	2890
42	4000	4000	4000	4000	4000
43	450	450	450	450	450
44	2140	2140	2140	2140	2140
45	900	950	950	950	950
46	850	850	850	850	850
47	4070	4070	4070	4070	4070
48	1000	1000	1000	1000	1000

OBS	SALARY_AUGUST	SALARY_SEPTEMBER	SALARY_OCTOBER	SALARY_NOVEMBER
33	3750	3750	3750	3750
34	2400	2570	2570	2570
35	2140	2140	2140	2140
36	700	700	700	700
37	1580	1580	1580	1580
38	500	500	500	500
39	2800	3000	3000	3000
40	2030	2030	2030	2030
41	2890	2890	2890	2890
42	4000	4280	4280	4280
43	450	450	450	450
44	2140	2140	2140	2140
45	950	950	950	950
46	850	890	890	890
47	4070	4070	4070	4070
48	1000	1000	1050	1050

OBS	SALARY_DECEMBER	EMPLOYEE_TYPE	MANAGEMENT
33	3750	S	Y
34	2570	S	N
35	2140	S	N
36	700	T	N
37	1580	H	N
38	500	T	N
39	3000	S	N
40	2030	S	N
41	2890	S	N
42	4280	S	Y
43	450	T	N
44	2140	S	N
45	950	H	N
46	890	H	N
47	4070	S	Y
48	1050	H	N

PERSINFO (OBS 49–60)

OBS	SOCIAL_SECURITY	LAST_NAME	FIRST_NAME	SEX	BIRTH_DATE
49	314384710	OWENS	GREG	M	690806
50	123432873	PALMER	NANCY	F	630808
51	134183783	PAVELEK	JOE	M	361004
52	341324123	PAYTON	RUTH	F	380717
53	349873412	PEARCE	EVELYN	F	480204
54	214870983	PEYTON	JOHN	M	420325
55	349872314	PHILLIPS	SARAH	F	570722
56	134138733	PRITT	JIM	M	550930
57	312498734	REEVES	JEREMY	M	671109
58	123987083	SHEPHERD	KANDI	F	581122
59	213478033	SMITH	SCOTT	M	640303
60	131870982	STONE	JENNIFER	F	690415

OBS	ADDRESS	CITY	STATE	ZIP_CODE	HOME_PHONE
49	340 HARBOR DR.	BROOKVILLE	IN	46329	3287093
50	43 FALCON RIDGE	SULPHER SPRINGS	IN	46222	3098722
51	3292 CEDAR RUN RD.	INDIANAPOLIS	IN	46233	3083293
52	2233 BEECH ST.	CONNERSVILLE	IN	46383	3939383
53	494 JESSUP RD	DUNKIRK	IN	46229	3039933
54	449 PEDIMOUNT RD	SPICELAND	IN	46393	9830783
55	3839 WINTHROP DR.	BROAD RIPPLE	IN	46383	9383922
56	1035 JEFFERSON AVE	PENDLETON	IN	46929	8493453
57	32 OAKLAND DR.	SHELBYVILLE	IN	46922	5339333
58	2332 LAWRENCE DE.	SPICELAND	IN	46383	9870874
59	343 SOMERSET	MARKLEVILLE	IN	46764	3482835
60	55 BURBANK ST.	MOORELAND	IN	46383	5439384

OBS	HIRE_DATE	OFFICE_EXTENSION	COST_CENTER	VACATION_AVAILABLE
49	890115	8937	130	40
50	880314	8932	120	40
51	590101	8484	120	160
52	770326	9393	120	120
53	820323	8393	130	120
54	690325	8939	140	160
55	851130	8433	110	80
56	800519	3944	120	120
57	880606	4390	130	40
58	860422	9384	100	80
59	870729	3923	110	80
60	880715	3847	120	40

OBS	VACATION_USED	SICK_USED	SALARY_JANUARY	SALARY_FEBRUARY
49	40	0	1000	1000
50	16	8	1700	1700
51	120	16	2100	2100
52	40	0	2100	2100
53	80	0	1600	1600
54	40	8	4100	4100
55	40	16	1400	1400
56	80	24	1500	1500
57	0	0	1000	1000
58	80	0	850	850
59	80	16	1900	1900
60	40	0	1300	1300

OBS	SALARY_MARCH	SALARY_APRIL	SALARY_MAY	SALARY_JUNE	SALARY_JULY
49	1000	1000	1000	1000	1000
50	1820	1820	1820	1820	1820
51	2100	2100	2100	2100	2100
52	2210	2210	2210	2210	2210
53	1680	1680	1680	1680	1680
54	4390	4390	4390	4390	4390
55	1400	1400	1400	1400	1400
56	1500	1500	1580	1580	1580
57	1000	1000	1000	1050	1050
58	850	850	850	850	850
59	1900	1900	1900	1900	2000
60	1300	1300	1300	1300	1370

OBS	SALARY_AUGUST	SALARY_SEPTEMBER	SALARY_OCTOBER	SALARY_NOVEMBER
49	1000	1000	1000	1000
50	1820	1820	1820	1820
51	2100	2100	2100	2100
52	2210	2210	2210	2210
53	1680	1680	1680	1680
54	4390	4390	4390	4390
55	1400	1400	1400	1470
56	1580	1580	1580	1580
57	1050	1050	1050	1050

58	850	850	850	850
59	2000	2000	2000	2000
60	1370	1370	1370	1370

OBS	SALARY_DECEMBER	EMPLOYEE_TYPE	MANAGEMENT
49	1000	T	N
50	1820	S	N
51	2100	H	N
52	2210	H	N
53	1680	H	N
54	4390	S	Y
55	1470	H	N
56	1580	H	N
57	1050	H	N
58	850	T	N
59	2000	H	N
60	1370	H	N

PROJINFO Sample Table

PROJINFO (OBS 1–6)

OBS	LAST_NAME	FIRST_NAME	BEGIN_DATE	PLAN_END_DATE
1	APPLE	RICHARD	881001	881201
2	APPLE	RICHARD	890115	890301
3	BAKER	MARTHA	890715	890915
4	BROWN	WALLY	881001	881201
5	BUELL	MAX	890315	890401
6	GOETZ	JACK	890601	890801

OBS	ACTUAL_END_DATE	PROJECT
1	881201	COMPENSATION PLAN
2	890301	FINANCIAL STATEMENT
3	890915	BROKERS
4	881201	COMPENSATION PLAN
5	890415	SALES REPORT
6	890715	COMMISSIONS

PROJINFO (OBS 7–12)

OBS	LAST_NAME	FIRST_NAME	BEGIN_DATE	PLAN_END_DATE
7	HARRINGTON	MARLIN	880815	881201
8	HARRINGTON	MARLIN	890715	890915
9	HARRIS	JULIE	890101	890201
10	HUFFORD	STEPHEN	890601	890801
11	HUTSON	EVERETT	890101	890301
12	KELLUM	ELLEN JANE	880815	881201

OBS	ACTUAL_END_DATE	PROJECT
7	881215	BUDGET
8	890915	BROKERS
9	890201	PROJECT GROWTH
10	890715	COMMISSIONS
11	890315	QUALITY CONTROL
12	881215	BUDGET

PROJINFO (OBS 13–17)

OBS	LAST_NAME	FIRST_NAME	BEGIN_DATE	PLAN_END_DATE
13	KELLUM	ELLEN JANE	890115	890301
14	KISLING	MARY LEA	890715	890915
15	MEEKS	EDWARD	880815	881201
16	MEEKS	EDWARD	890601	890801
17	MEISER	MARK	890315	890401

OBS	ACTUAL_END_DATE	PROJECT
13	890301	FINANCIAL STATEMENT
14	890915	BROKERS
15	881215	BUDGET
16	890715	COMMISSIONS
17	890415	SALES REPORT

PROJINFO (OBS 18, 19)

OBS	LAST_NAME	FIRST_NAME	BEGIN_DATE	PLAN_END_DATE
18	MILLER	EMMALYNE	890101	890301
19	PALMER	NANCY	880815	881201

OBS	ACTUAL_END_DATE	PROJECT
18	890315	QUALITY CONTROL
19	881215	BUDGET

ORIGINFO Sample Table

ORGINFO (OBS 1–5)

OBS	DEPARTMENT	DEPARTMENT_NAME	DIRECTOR
1	100	PERSONNEL	CHERYL MORGAN
2	110	MARKETING	GERTRUDE KEESLING
3	120	FINANCE	NANCY ATKINS
4	130	SALES	PAT MICHAEL
5	140	DEVELOPMENT	JOE KAWAN

OBS	VICE_PRESIDENT	PRESIDENT
1	MILTON DOUGLAS	EDWARD BROOKS
2	MILTON DOUGLAS	EDWARD BROOKS
3	MILTON DOUGLAS	EDWARD BROOKS
4	JOHN PEYTON	EDWARD BROOKS
5	JOHN PEYTON	EDWARD BROOKS

Index